MYTHS AND LEGENDS
SERIES

THE BRITISH
M. I. EBBUTT

William of Cloudeslee and his Son

[Page 245]

MYTHS AND LEGENDS SERIES

THE BRITISH

M. I. EBBUTT

WITH ILLUSTRATIONS
FROM DRAWINGS AND
FAMOUS PAINTINGS

AVENEL BOOKS
NEW YORK

Previously published by Gresham Publishing Co

This edition published 1986 by Avenel Books
distributed by Crown Publishers Inc.,
225 Park Avenue South
New York, New York 10003

Copyright © BRACKEN BOOKS 1985

ISBN 0-517-60441-8

Printed and bound by
Grafoimpex, Yugoslavia

h g f e d c b

PREFACE

IN refashioning, for the pleasure of readers of the twentieth century, these versions of ancient tales which have given pleasure to story-lovers of all centuries from the eighth onward, I feel that some explanation of my choice is necessary. Men's conceptions of the heroic change with changing years, and vary with each individual mind; hence it often happens that one person sees in a legend only the central heroism, while another sees only the inartistic details of mediæval life which tend to disguise and warp the heroic quality.

It may be that to some people the heroes I have chosen do not seem heroic, but there is no doubt that to the age and generation which wrote or sang of them they appeared real heroes, worthy of remembrance and celebration, and it has been my object to come as close as possible to the mediæval mind, with its elementary conceptions of honour, loyalty, devotion, and duty. I have therefore altered the tales as little as I could, and have tried to put them as fairly as possible before modern readers, bearing in mind the altered conditions of things and of intellects to-day.

In the work of selecting and retelling these stories I have to acknowledge with most hearty thanks the help and advice of Mr. F. E. Bumby, B.A., of the University College, Nottingham, who has been throughout a most kind and candid censor or critic. His help has been in every way invaluable. I have also to acknowledge the generous permission given me by Mr. W. B. Yeats to write in prose the story of his beautiful play, "The Countess Cathleen," and to adorn it with quotations from that play.

The poetical quotations are attributed to the authors

PREFACE

from whose works they are taken wherever it is possible. When mediæval passages occur which are not thus attributed they are my own versions from the original mediæval poems.

M. I. EBBUTT

TANGLEWOOD
BARNT GREEN
July 1910

CONTENTS

CHAP.   PAGE

I. BEOWULF 1

II. THE DREAM OF MAXEN WLEDIG 42

III. THE STORY OF CONSTANTINE AND ELENE . . . 50

IV. THE COMPASSION OF CONSTANTINE 63

V. HAVELOK THE DANE 73

VI. HOWARD THE HALT 95

VII. ROLAND, THE HERO OF EARLY FRANCE . . . 119

VIII. THE COUNTESS CATHLEEN 156

IX. CUCHULAIN, THE CHAMPION OF IRELAND . . 184

X. THE TALE OF GAMELYN 204

XI. WILLIAM OF CLOUDESLEE 225

XII. BLACK COLIN OF LOCH AWE 248

XIII. THE MARRIAGE OF SIR GAWAYNE 265

XIV. KING HORN 286

XV. ROBIN HOOD 314

XVI. HEREWARD THE WAKE 334

GLOSSARY AND INDEX 353

LIST OF ILLUSTRATIONS

William of Cloudeslee and his son (*Patten Wilson*) *Frontispiece*

To face page

" The demon of evil, with his fierce ravening, greedily grasped them " (*J. H. F. Bacon, A.R.A.*) 4

Beowulf replies haughtily to Hunferth (*J. H. F. Bacon, A.R.A.*) 5

Beowulf tears off the arm and shoulder of Grendel (*J. H. F. Bacon, A.R.A.*) 16

Beowulf finds the head of Aschere (*J. H. F. Bacon, A.R.A.*) 17

Beowulf shears off the head of Grendel (*J. H. F. Bacon, A.R.A.*) 26

" Both warriors stood behind the iron shield " (*J. H. F. Bacon, A.R.A.*) 27

The death of Beowulf (*J. H. F. Bacon, A.R.A.*) 40

" The Emperor remained in his apartments and slept " (*Byam Shaw*) 41

The dream of the Emperor (*Byam Shaw*) 46

" There came from heaven a leaping flame, which touched the surface of the ground here and there " (*Byam Shaw*) 47

The Queen's dilemma (*Byam Shaw*) 60

" What raptures of rejoicing there were ! " (*Byam Shaw*) 61

They filled the great vessel of silver with pure water (*Byam Shaw*) 70

" Havelok sat up surprised " (*J. H. F. Bacon, A.R.A.*) 71

" Havelok again overthrew the porters " (*J. H. F. Bacon, A.R.A.*) 82

" 'Welcome, dear lord ! ' " (*J. H. F. Bacon, A.R.A.*) 83

" With great joy they fell on their knees " (*J. H. F. Bacon, A.R.A.*) 88

" On a miserable jade with his face to the tail " (*J. H. F. Bacon, A.R.A.*) 89

Olaf and Sigrid (*J. H. F. Bacon, A.R.A.*) 98

Howard leaves the house of Thorbiorn (*J. H. F. Bacon, A.R.A.*) 99

" The silver rolled in all directions from his cloak " (*J. H. F. Bacon, A.R.A.*) 110

LIST OF ILLUSTRATIONS

To face page

"Thorbiorn lifted the huge stone"   111

"Here sits Charles the King"   124

"Ganelon rode away"   125

"The saintly Archbishop Turpin"   138

"Charlemagne heard it again"   139

"Turpin fell forward dying"   148

"The angels of God descended around him"   149

"Under the trees lay the body of Roland"   152

Aude the Fair falls dead at the Emperor's feet   153

"Day by day Cathleen went among them"   162

The peasant's story   163

"Thieves have broken into the treasure-chamber"   176

"Cathleen signed the bond"   177

"All three drove furiously towards Cruachan"   190

"Three monstrous cats were let into the room"   191

"The dragon sank towards him, opening its terrible jaws"   196

"The body of Uath arose"   197

"Go and do your own baking!"   206

"Lords, for Christ's sake help poor Gamelyn out of prison!"   207

"Then cheer thee, Adam"   218

"Come from the seat of justice!"   219

"William continued his wonderful archery"   232

Adam Bell writes the letter   233

The fight at the gate   238

"Wait for me seven years, dear wife"   239

"She looked earnestly into his face"   258

"The King blew a loud note on his bugle"   259

LIST OF ILLUSTRATIONS

To face page

"He hung his head and rode slowly away"   274

"Lady, I will be a true and loyal husband"   275

"Now you have released me from the spell completely"   282

Queen Godhild prays ever for her son Horn   283

Horn kills the Saracen Leader   298

"Now, in her misery, she set the dagger to her heart"   299

Horn and his followers disguised as minstrels   312

"Little John caught the horse by the bridle"   313

"I have no money worth offering"   320

"Sir Richard knelt in courteous salutation"   321

"Much shot the monk to the heart"   330

"Her pleading won relief for them"   331

Alftruda   340

Hereward and the Princess   341

Hereward and Sigtryg   348

INTRODUCTION

THE writer who would tell again for people of the twentieth century the legends and stories that delighted the folk of the thirteenth and fourteenth centuries finds himself confronted with a vast mass of material ready to his hand. Unless he exercises a wise discrimination and has some system of selection, he becomes lost in the mazes of as enchanted a land,

"Where Truth and Dream walk hand in hand," [1]

as ever bewildered knights of old in days of romance. Down all the dimly lighted pathways of mediæval literature mystical figures beckon him in every direction; fairies, goblins, witches, knights and ladies and giants entice him, and unless, like Theseus of old, he follows closely his guiding clue, he will find that he reaches no goal, attains to no clear vision, achieves no quest. He will remain spell-bound, captivated by the Middle Ages—

"The life, the delight, and the sorrow
Of troublous and chivalrous years
That knew not of night nor of morrow,
Of hopes or of fears.
The wars and the woes and the glories
That quicken, and lighten, and rain
From the clouds of its chronicled stories
The passion, the pride, and the pain." [2]

Such a golden clue to guide the modern seeker through the labyrinths of the mediæval mind is that which I have tried to suggest in the title "*Hero* Myths and Legends of the British Race"—the pursuit and representation of the ideal hero as the mind of Britain and of early and mediæval England imagined him, together with

[1] Lightfoot.   [2] Swinburne.

the study of the characteristics which made this or that particular person, mythical or legendary, a hero to the century which sang or wrote about him. The interest goes deeper when we study, not merely

> " Old heroes who could grandly do
> As they could greatly dare," [1]

but

> " Heroes of our island breed
> And men and women of our British birth." [2]

" Hero-worship endures for ever while man endures," wrote Thomas Carlyle, and this fidelity of men to their admiration for great heroes is one of the surest tokens by which we can judge of their own character. Such as the hero is, such will his worshippers be ; and the men who idolised Robin Hood will be found to have been men who were themselves in revolt against oppressive law, or who, finding law powerless to prevent tyranny, glorified the lawless punishment of wrongs and the bold denunciation of perverted justice. The warriors who listened to the saga of Beowulf looked on physical prowess as the best of all heroic qualities, and the Normans who admired Roland saw in him the ideal of feudal loyalty. To every age, and to every nation, there is a peculiar ideal of heroism, and in the popular legends of each age this ideal may be found.

Again, these legends give not only the hero as he seemed to his age ; they also show the social life, the virtues and vices, the superstitions and beliefs, of earlier ages embedded in the tradition, as fossils are found in the uplifted strata of some ancient ocean-bed. They have ceased to live ; but they remain, tokens of a life long past. So in the hero-legends of our nation we

[1] Gerald Massey.   [2] J. R. Denning.

may find traces of the thoughts and religions of our ancestors many centuries ago ; traces which lie close to one another in these romances, telling of the nations who came to these Islands of the West, settled, were conquered and driven away to make room for other races whose supremacy has been as brief, till all these superimposed races have blended into one, to form the British nation, the most widespread race of modern times.   For

> " Britain's might and Britain's right
> And the brunt of British spears " [1]

are not the boast of the English race alone.   No man in England now can boast of unmixed descent, but must perforce trace his family back through many a marriage of Frank, and Norman, and Saxon, and Dane, and Roman, and Celt, and even Iberian, back to prehistoric man—

> " Scot and Celt and Norman and Dane,
> With the Northman's sinew and heart and brain,
> And the Northman's courage for blessing or bane,
> Are England's heroes too." [2]

When Tennyson sang his greeting at the coming of Alexandra,

> " Saxon or Dane or Norman we,
> Teuton or Celt or whatever we be,"

he was only recognising a truth which no boast of pure birth can cover—the truth that the modern Englishman is a compound of many races, with many characteristics ; and if we would understand him, we must seek the clue to the riddle in early England and Scotland and Ireland and Wales, while even France adds her

---

[1] W. W. Campbell.   [2] *Ibid.*

share of enlightenment towards the solution of the
riddle.

> " The Saxon force, the Celtic fire,
> These are thy manhood's heritage." [1]

Britain, as far as we can trace men in our island,
was first inhabited by cave-men, who have left no
history at all. In the course of ages they passed away
before the Iberians or Ivernians, who came from the
east, and bore a striking resemblance to the Basques.
It may be that some Mongolian tribe, wandering west,
drawn by the instinct which has driven most race-
migrations westward, sent offshoots north and south—
one to brave the dangers of the sea and inhabit Britain
and Ireland, one to cross the Pyrenees and remain
sheltered in their deep ravines ; or it may be that
Basques from the Pyrenees, daring the storms of the
Bay of Biscay in their frail coracles, ventured to the
shores of Britain. Short and dark were these sturdy
voyagers, harsh-featured and long-headed, worshipping
the powers of Nature with mysterious and cruel rites of
human sacrifice, holding beliefs in totems and ancestor-
worship and in the superiority of high descent claimed
through the mother to that claimed through the father.
When the stronger and more civilised Celt came he drove
before him these little dark men, he enslaved their survivors or wedded their women, and in his turn fell into
slavery to the cruel Druidic religion of his subjects. To
these Iberians, and to the Celtic dread of them, we
probably owe all the stories of dwarfs, goblins, elves,
and earth-gnomes which fill our fairy-tale books ; and
if we examine carefully the descriptions of the abodes
of these beings we shall find them not inconsistent with
the earth-dwellings, caves, circle huts, or even with the
burial mounds, of the Iberian race.

[1] C. Roberts.

INTRODUCTION

The race that followed the Iberians, and drove them out or subdued them, so that they served as slaves where they had once ruled as lords, was the proud Aryan Celtic race. Of different tribes, Gaels, Brythons, and Belgæ, they were all one in spirit, and one in physical feature.

Tall, blue-eyed, with fair or red hair, they overpowered in every way the diminutive Iberians, and their tattooing, while it gave them a name which has often been mistaken for a national designation (Picts, or painted men), made them dreadful to their enemies in battle, and ferocious-looking even in time of peace. Their civilisation was of a much higher type than that of the Iberians ; their weapons, their war-chariots, their mode of life and their treatment of women, are all so closely similar to that of the Greeks of Homer that a theory has been advanced and ably defended, that the Homeric Greeks were really invading Celts—Gaelic or Gaulish tribes from the north of Europe. If it indeed be so, we owe to the Celts a debt of imperishable culture and civilisation. To them belongs more especially, in our national amalgam, the passion for the past, the ardent patriotism, the longing for spiritual beauty, which raises and relieves the Saxon materialism.

" Though fallen the state of Erin and changed the Scottish land,
  Though small the power of Mona, though unwaked Llewellyn's band,
  Though Ambrose Merlin's prophecies are held as idle tales,
  Though Iona's ruined cloisters are swept by northern gales,
          One in name and in fame
          Are the sea-divided Gaels.

" In Northern Spain and Italy our brethren also dwell,
  And brave are the traditions of their fathers that they tell ;
  The Eagle or the Crescent in the dawn of history pales
  Before the advancing banners of the great Rome-conquering Gaels :
          One in name and in fame
          Are the sea-divided Gaels." [1]

[1] T. Darcy McGee.

It is almost impossible to overestimate the value of the Celtic contribution to our national literature and character : the race that gave us Ossian, and Finn, and Cuchulain, that sang of the sorrowful love and doom of Deirdre, that told of the pursuit of Diarmit and Grania, till every dolmen and cromlech in Ireland was associated with these lovers ; the race that preserved for us

> " That grey king whose name, a ghost,
> Streams like a cloud, man-shaped, from mountain-peak
> And cleaves to cairn and cromlech still," [1]

the King Arthur whose Arthur's Seat overhangs Edinburgh, whose presence haunts the Lakes, and Wales, and Cornwall, and the forests of Brittany; the race that held up for us the image of the Holy Grail—that race can claim no small share in the moulding of the modern Briton.

The Celt, however, had his day of supremacy and passed : the Roman crushed his power of initiative and made him helpless and dependent, and the Teuton, whether as Saxon, Angle, Frisian, or Jute, dwelt in his homes and ruled as slaves the former owners of the land. These new-comers were not physically unlike the Celts whom they dispossessed. Tall and fair, grey-eyed and sinewy, the Teuton was a hardier, more sturdy warrior than the Celt : he had not spent centuries of quiet settlement and imitative civilisation under the ægis of Imperial Rome : he had not learnt to love the arts of peace and he cultivated none but those of war ; he was by choice a warrior and a sailor, a wanderer to other lands, a plougher of the desolate places of the " vasty deep," yet withal a lover of home, who trod at times, with bitter longing for his native land, the thorny paths of exile. To him physical cowardice was

---

[1] Tennyson.

the unforgivable sin, next to treachery to his lord ; for the loyalty of thane to his chieftain was a very deep and abiding reality to the Anglo-Saxon warrior, and in the early poems of our English race, love for " his dear lord, his chieftain-friend," takes the place of that love of woman which other races felt and expressed. A quiet death-bed was the worst end to a man's life, in the Anglo-Saxon's creed ; it was " a cow's death," to be shunned by every means in a man's power ; while a death in fight, victor or vanquished, was a worthy finish to a warrior's life. There was no fear of death itself in the English hero's mind, nor of Fate ; the former was the inevitable,

> " Seeing that Death, a necessary end,
> Will come when it will come," [1]

and the latter a goddess whose decrees must needs be obeyed with proud submission, but not with meek acceptance. Perhaps there was little of spiritual insight in the minds of these Angles and Saxons, little love of beauty, little care for the amenities of life ; but they had a sturdy loyalty, an uprightness, a brave disregard of death in the cause of duty, which we can still recognise in modern Englishmen. To the Saxon belong the tales where

> " The warrior kings,
> In height and prowess more than human, strive
> Again for glory, while the golden lyre
> Is ever sounding in heroic ears
> Heroic hymns." [2]

When the English (Anglo-Saxons, as we generally call them) had settled down in England, had united their warring tribes, and developed a somewhat centralised

---

[1] Shakespeare, *Julius Cæsar*.   [2] Tennyson.

government, their whole national existence was imperilled by the incursions of the Danes. Kindred folk to the Anglo-Saxons were these Danes, these Vikings from Christiania Wik, these Northmen from Norway or Iceland, whose fame went before them, and the dread of whom inspired the petition in the old Litany of the Church, "From the fury of the Northmen, good Lord, deliver us!" Their fair hair and blue or grey eyes, their tall and muscular frames, bore testimony to their kinship with the races they harried and plundered, but their spirit was different from that of the conquered Teutonic tribes. The Viking *loved* the sea; it was his summer home, his field of war and profit. To go "a-summer-harrying" was the usual employment of the true Viking, and in the winter only could he enjoy domestic life and the pleasures of the family circle. The rapturous fight with the elements, in which the Northman lived and moved and had his being, gave him a strain of ruthless cruelty unlike anything in the more peaceful Anglo-Saxon character: his disregard of death for himself led to a certain callousness with regard to human life, and to a certain enjoyment in inflicting physical anguish. There was an element of Red Indian ruthlessness in the Viking, which looms large in the story of the years of Norse ascendancy over Western Europe. Yet there was also a power of bold and daring action, of reckless valour, of rapid conception and execution, which contrasted strongly with the slower and more placid temperament of the Anglo-Saxon, and to this Danish strain modern Englishmen probably owe the power of initiative, the love of adventure, and the daring action which have made England the greatest colonising nation on the earth. The Danish, Norse, or Viking element spread far and wide in mediæval Europe—Iceland, Normandy (Northman's

Land), the Isle of Man, the Hebrides, the east of Ireland, the Danelagh of East Anglia, and the Cumberland dales all show traces of the conquering Danish race ; and raider after raider came to England and stayed, until half of our island was Danish, and even our royal family became for a time one with the royal line of Denmark. The acceptance of Christianity by the Danes in England when Guthrum was baptized rendered much more easy their amalgamation with the English ; but it was not so in Ireland, where the Round Towers still stand to show (as some authorities hold) how the terrified native Irish sheltered from the Danish fury which nearly destroyed the whole fabric of Irish Christianity. The legends of Ireland, too, are full of the terror of the men of " Lochlann," which is generally taken to mean Norway ; and the great coast cities of Ireland—Dublin, Cork, Waterford, Wexford, and others—were so entirely Danish that only the decisive battle of Clontarf, in which the saintly and victorious Brian Boru was slain, saved Ireland to Christendom and curbed the power of the heathen invaders.

A second wave of Norse invasion swept over England at the Norman Conquest, and for a time submerged the native English population. The chivalrous Norman knights who followed William of Normandy's sacred banner, whether from religious zeal or desire of plunder, were as truly Vikings by race as were the Danes who settled in the Danelagh. The days when Rolf (Rollo, or Rou), the Viking chief, won Normandy were not yet so long gone by that the fierce piratical instincts of his followers had ceased to influence their descendants : piety and learning, feudal law and custom, had made some impression upon the character of the Norman, but at heart he was still a Northman. The Norman barons fought for their independence against Duke William with all the determination of those Norse chiefs who would not acknowledge the overlordship of Harold Fairhair, but fled to colonise Iceland when he made himself King of Norway. The seafaring instincts which drove the Vikings to harry other lands in like manner drove the Normans to piratical plundering up and down the English Channel, and, when they had settled in England, led to continual sea-fights in the Channel between English and French, hardy Kentish and Norman, or Cornish and Breton, sailors, with a common strain of fighting blood, and a common love of the sea.

The Norman Conquest of England was but one instance of Norman activity : Sicily, Italy, Constantinople, even Antioch, and the Holy Land itself, showed in time Norman states, Norman laws, Norman civilisation, and all alike felt the impulse of Norman energy and inspiration. England lay ready to hand for Norman invasion—the hope of peaceable succession to the saintly Edward the Confessor had to be abandoned by William ; the gradual permeation of sluggish England with Norman earls, churchmen, courtiers, had been comprehended and checked by Earl Godwin and his sons (themselves of Danish race) ; but there still remained the way or open war and an appeal to religious zeal ; and this way William took. There was genius as well as statesmanship in the idea of combining a personal claim to the throne held by Harold the usurper with a crusading summons against the schismatic and heretical English, who refused obedience to the true successor of St. Peter. The success of the idea was its justification : the success of the expedition proved the need that England had of some new leaven to energise the sluggish temperament of her sons. The Norman Conquest not only revived and quickened, but unified and solidified the English nation. The tyranny of the Norman nobles,

held in check at first only by the tyranny of the
Norman king, was the factor in mediæval English life
that made for a national consciousness ; it also helped
the appreciation of the heroism of revolt against tyranny
which is seen in Hereward the Wake, in Robin Hood,
in William of Cloudeslee, and in many other English
hero-rebels ; but it gradually led men to a realization of
their own rights as Englishmen. When all men alike
felt themselves sons of England, the days were past
when Norman and Saxon were aliens to each other,
and Norman robber soon became as truly English as
Danish viking, Anglo-Saxon seafarer, or Celtic settler.
Then the full value of the Norman infusion was seen in
quicker intellectual apprehension, nimbler wit, a keener
sense of reverence, a more spiritual piety, a more refined
courtesy, and a more enlightened perception of the value
of law. The materialism of the original Saxon race was
successively modified by many influences, and not least
of these was the Norman Conquest.

From the Norman Conquest onward England has
welcomed men of many nations—French, Flemings,
Germans, Dutch : men brought by war, by trade, by
love of adventure, by religion ; traders, refugees, exiles,
all have found in her a hospitable shelter and a second
home, and all have come to love the "grey old
mother" that counted them among her sons and grew
to think them her own in very truth.

Geographically, also, we must recognise the admixture
of races in our islands. The farthest western borders
show most strongly the type of man whom we can
imagine the Iberian to have been : Western Ireland, the
Hebrides, Central and South Wales, and Cornwall are
still inhabited by folk of Iberian descent. The blue-
eyed Celt yet dwells in the Highlands and the greater
part of Wales and the Marches—Hereford and Shrop-

shire, and as far as Worcestershire and Cheshire ; still the Dales of Cumberland, the Fen Country, East Anglia, and the Isle of Man show traces of Danish blood, speech, manners, and customs ; still the slow, stolid Saxon inhabits the lands south of the Thames from Sussex to Hampshire and Dorset. The Angle has settled permanently over the Lowlands of Scotland, with the Celt along the western fringe, and Flemish blood shows its traces in Pembroke on the one side (" Little England beyond Wales ") and in Norfolk on the other.

With all these nations, all these natures, amalgamated in our own, it is no wonder that the literature of our isles contains many different ideals of heroism, changing according to nationality and epoch. Thus the physical valour of Beowulf is not the same quality as the valour of Havelok the Dane, though both are heroes of the strong arm ; and the chivalry of Diarmit is not the same as the chivalry of Roland. Again, religion has its share in changing the ideals of a nation, and Constantine, the warrior of the Early English poem of " Elene," is far from being the same in character as the tenderhearted Constantine of " moral Gower's " apocryphal tale. The law-abiding nature of the earliest heroes, whose obedience to their king and their priest was absolute, differs almost entirely from the lawlessness of Gamelyn and Robin Hood, both of whom set church and king at defiance, and even account it a merit to revolt from the rule of both. It follows from this that we shall find our chosen heroes of very different types and characters ; but we shall recognise that each represented to his own age an ideal of heroism, which that age loved sufficiently to put into literature, and perpetuate by the best means in its power. Of many another hero besides Arthur—of Barbarossa, of Hiawatha, even of Napoleon—has the tradition grown that he is not dead, but has passed away into the deathless land, whence he shall come again in his own time. As Tennyson has sung,

> " Great bards of him will sing
> Hereafter ; and dark sayings from of old
> Ranging and ringing through the minds of men,
> And echoed by old folk beside their fires
> For comfort after their wage-work is done,
> Speak of the King."

CHAPTER I : BEOWULF

Introduction

THE figure which meets us as we enter on the study of Heroes of the British Race is one which appeals to us in a very special way, since he is the one hero in whose legend we may see the ideals of our English forefathers before they left their Continental home to settle in this island. Opinions may differ as to the date at which the poem of "Beowulf" was written, the place in which it was localised, and the religion of the poet who combined the floating legends into one epic whole, but all must accept the poem as embodying the life and feelings of our Forefathers who dwelt in North Germany on the shores of the North Sea and of the Baltic. The life depicted, the characters portrayed, the events described, are such as a simple warrior race would cherish in tradition and legend as relics of the life lived by their ancestors in what doubtless seemed to them the Golden Age. Perhaps stories of a divine Beowa, hero and ancestor of the English, became merged in other myths of sun-hero and marsh-demon, but in any case the stories are now crystallized around one central human figure, who may even be considered an historical hero, Beowulf, the thane of Hygelac, King of the Geats. It is this grand primitive hero who embodies the ideal of English heroism. Bold to rashness for himself, prudent for his comrades, daring, resourceful, knowing no fear, loyal to his king and his kinsmen, generous in war and in peace, self-sacrificing, Beowulf stands for all that is best in manhood in an age of strife. It is fitting that our first British hero should be physically and mentally strong, brave to seek danger and brave to look on death and Fate undaunted, one whose life is a struggle against evil

I

forces, and whose death comes in a glorious victory over the powers of evil, a victory gained for the sake of others to whom Beowulf feels that he owes protection and devotion.

The Story. The Coming and Passing of Scyld

Once, long ago, the Danish land owned the sway of a mighty monarch, Scyld Scefing, the founder of a great dynasty, the Scyldings. This great king Scyld had come to Denmark in a mysterious manner, since no man knew whence he sprang. As a babe he drifted to the Danish shore in a vessel loaded with treasures ; but no man was with him, and there was no token to show his kindred and race. When Scyld grew up he increased the power of Denmark and enlarged her borders ; his fame spread far and wide among men, and his glory shone undimmed until the day when, full of years and honours, he died, leaving the throne securely established in his family. Then the sorrowing Danes restored him to the mysterious ocean from which he had come to them. Choosing their goodliest ship, they laid within it the corpse of their departed king, and heaped around him all their best and choicest treasures, until the venerable countenance of Scyld looked to heaven from a bed of gold and jewels ; then they set up, high above his head, his glorious gold-wrought banner, and left him alone in state. The vessel was loosed from the shore where the mourning Danes bewailed their departing king, and drifted slowly away to the unknown west from which Scyld had sailed to his now sorrowing people ; they watched until it was lost in the shadows of night and distance, but no man under heaven knoweth what shore now holds the vanished Scyld. The descendants of Scyld ruled and prospered till the days of his great-grandson Hrothgar,

2

one of a family of four, who can all be identified historically with various Danish kings and princes.

Hrothgar's Hall

Hrothgar was a mighty warrior and conqueror, who won glory in battle, and whose fame spread wide among men, so that nobly born warriors, his kinsmen, were glad to serve as his bodyguard and to fight for him loyally in strife. So great was Hrothgar's power that he longed for some outward sign of the magnificence of his sway ; he determined to build a great hall, in which he could hold feasts and banquets, and could entertain his warriors and thanes, and visitors from afar. The hall rose speedily, vast, gloriously adorned, a great meeting-place for men; for Hrothgar had summoned all his people to the work, and the walls towered up high and majestic, ending in pinnacles and gables resembling the antlers of a stag. At the great feast which Hrothgar gave first in his new home the minstrels chanted the glory of the hall, " Heorot," " The Hart," as the king named it ; Hrothgar's desire was well fulfilled, that he should build the most magnificent or banquet-halls. Proud were the mighty warriors who feasted within it, and proud the heart of the king, who from his high seat on the daïs saw his brave thanes carousing at the long tables below him, and the lofty rafters of the hall rising black into the darkness.

Grendel

Day by day the feasting continued, until its noise and the festal joy of its revellers aroused a mighty enemy, Grendel, the loathsome fen-monster. This monstrous being, half-man, half-fiend, dwelt in the fens near the hill on which Heorot stood. Terrible was he, dangerous to men, of extraordinary strength, human

3

in shape but gigantic of stature, covered with a green horny skin, on which the sword would not bite. His race, all sea-monsters, giants, goblins, and evil demons, were offspring of Cain, outcasts from the mercy of the Most High, hostile to the human race ; and Grendel was one of mankind's most bitter enemies ; hence his hatred of the joyous shouts from Heorot, and his determination to stop the feasting.

> " This the dire mighty fiend,   he who in darkness dwelt,
> Suffered with hatred fierce,   that every day and night
> He heard the festal shouts   loud in the lofty hall ;
> Sound of harp echoed there,   and gleeman's sweet song.
> Thus they lived joyously,   fearing no angry foe
> Until the hellish fiend   wrought them great woe.
> Grendel that ghost was called,   grisly and terrible,
> Who, hateful wanderer,   dwelt in the moorlands,
> The fens and wild fastnesses ;   the wretch for a while abode
> In homes of the giant-race,   since God had cast him out.
> When night on the earth fell,   Grendel departed
> To visit the lofty hall,   now that the warlike Danes
> After the gladsome feast   nightly slept in it.
> A fair troop of warrior-thanes   guarding it found he ;
> Heedlessly sleeping,   they recked not of sorrow.
> The demon of evil,   the grim wight unholy,
> With his fierce ravening,   greedily grasped them,
> Seized in their slumbering   thirty right manly thanes ;
> Thence he withdrew again,   proud of his lifeless prey,
> Home to his hiding-place,   bearing his booty,
> In peace to devour it."

When dawn broke, and the Danes from their dwellings around the hall entered Heorot, great was the lamentation, and dire the dismay, for thirty noble champions had vanished, and the blood-stained tracks of the monster showed but too well the fate that had overtaken them. Hrothgar's grief was profound, for he had lost thirty of his dearly loved bodyguard, and he himself was too old to wage a conflict against the foe—a foe who repeated night by night his awful deeds,

" The demon of evil, with his fierce ravening, greedily
grasped them "

Beowulf replies haughtily to Hunferth

in spite of all that valour could do to save the Danes from his terrible enmity. At last no champion would face the monster, and the Danes, in despair, deserted the glorious hall of which they had been so proud. Useless stood the best of dwellings, for none dared remain in it, but every evening the Danes left it after their feast, and slept elsewhere. This affliction endured for twelve years, and all that time the beautiful hall of Heorot stood empty when darkness was upon it. By night the dire fiend visited it in search of prey, and in the morning his footsteps showed that his deadly enmity was not yet appeased, but that any effort to use the hall at night would bring down his fatal wrath on the careless sleepers.

Far and wide spread the tidings of this terrible oppression, and many champions came from afar to offer King Hrothgar their aid, but none was heroic enough to conquer the monster, and many a mighty warrior lost his life in a vain struggle against Grendel. At length even these bold adventurers ceased to come; Grendel remained master of Heorot, and the Danes settled down in misery under the bondage of a perpetual nightly terror, while Hrothgar grew old in helpless longing for strength to rescue his people from their foe.

Beowulf

Meanwhile there had come to manhood and full strength a hero destined to make his name famous for mighty deeds of valour throughout the whole of the Teutonic North. In the realm of the Geats (Götaland, in the south of Sweden) ruled King Hygelac, a mighty ruler who was ambitious enough to aim at conquering his neighbours on the mainland of Germany. His only sister, daughter of the dead king Hrethel, had married a great noble, Ecgtheow, and they had one son, Beowulf, who from the age of seven was brought up at the Geatish court. The boy was a lad of great stature and handsome appearance, with fair locks and gallant bearing ; but he greatly disappointed his grandfather, King Hrethel, by his sluggish character. Beowulf as a youth had been despised by all for his sloth and his unwarlike disposition ; his good-nature and his rarely stirred wrath made others look upon him with scorn, and the mighty stature to which he grew brought him nothing but scoffs and sneers and insults in the banquet-hall when the royal feasts were held. Yet wise men might have seen the promise of great strength in his powerful sinews and his mighty hands, and the signs of great force of character in the glance of his clear blue eyes and the fierceness of his anger when he was once aroused. At least once already Beowulf had distinguished himself in a great feat—a swimming-match with a famous champion, Breca, who had been beaten in the contest. For this and other victories, and for the bodily strength which gave Beowulf's hand-grip the force of thirty men, the hero was already famed when the news of Grendel's ravages reached Geatland. Beowulf, eager to try his strength against the monster, and burning to add to his fame, asked and obtained permission from his uncle, King Hygelac, to seek the stricken Danish king and offer his help against Grendel ; then, choosing fourteen loyal comrades and kinsfolk, he took a cheerful farewell of the Geatish royal family and sailed for Denmark.

Thus it happened that one day the Warden of the Coast, riding on his round along the Danish shores, saw from the white cliffs a strange war-vessel running in to shore. Her banners were unknown to him, her crew were strangers and all in war-array, and as the

6

Warden watched them they ran the ship into a small creek among the mountainous cliffs, made her fast to a rock with stout cables, and then landed and put themselves in readiness for a march. Though there were fifteen of the strangers and the Warden was alone, he showed no hesitation, but, riding boldly down into their midst, loudly demanded :

" What are ye warlike men   wielding bright weapons,
  Wearing grey corslets   and boar-adorned helmets,
  Who o'er the water-paths   come with your foaming keel
  Ploughing the ocean surge ?   I was appointed
  Warden of Denmark's shores ;   watch hold I by the wave
  That on this Danish coast   no deadly enemy
  Leading troops over sea   should land to injure.
  None have here landed yet   more frankly coming
  Than this fair company :   and yet ye answer not
  The password of warriors,   and customs of kinsmen.
  Ne'er have mine eyes beheld   a mightier warrior,
  An earl more lordly, than   is he, the chief of you ;
  He is no common man ;   if looks belie him not,
  He is a hero bold,   worthily weaponed.
  Anon must I know of you   kindred and country,
  Lest ye as spies should go   free on our Danish soil.
  Now ye men from afar,   sailing the surging sea,
  Have heard my earnest thought :   best is a quick reply,
  That I may swiftly know   whence ye have hither come."

So the aged Warden sat on his horse, gazing attentively on the faces of the fifteen strangers, but watching most carefully the countenance of the leader ; for the mighty stature, the clear glance of command, the goodly armour, and the lordly air of Beowulf left no doubt as to who was the chieftain of that little band. When the questions had been asked the leader of the new-comers moved forward till his mighty figure stood beside the Warden's horse, and as he gazed up into the old man's eyes he answered : " We are warriors of the Geats, members of King Hygelac's bodyguard. My father, well known among men of wisdom, was named Ecgtheow, a wise counsellor who died full of years and famous for his wisdom, leaving a memory dear to all good men."

> " We come to seek thy king   Healfdene's glorious son,
> Thy nation's noble lord,   with friendly mind.
> Be thou a guardian good   to us strangers here !
> We have an errand grave   to the great Danish king,
> Nor will I hidden hold   what I intend !
> Thou canst tell if it is   truth (as we lately heard)
> That some dire enemy,   deadly in evil deed,
> Cometh in dark of night,   sateth his secret hate,
> Worketh through fearsome awe,   slaughter and shame.
> I can give Hrothgar bold   counsel to conquer him,
> How he with valiant mind   Grendel may vanquish,
> If he would ever lose   torment of burning care,
> If bliss shall bloom again   and woe shall vanish."

The aged Warden replied : " Every bold warrior of noble mind must recognise the distinction between words and deeds. I judge by thy speech that you are all friends to our Danish king ; therefore I bid you go forward, in warlike array, and I myself will guide you to King Hrothgar ; I will also bid my men draw your vessel up the beach, and make her fast with a barricade of oars against any high tide. Safe she shall be until again she bears you to your own land. May your expedition prove successful."

Thus speaking, he turned his horse's head and led the way up the steep cliff paths, while the Geats followed him, resplendent in shining armour, with boar-crests on their helmets, shields and spears in their hands, and mighty swords hanging in their belts : a goodly band were they, as they strode boldly after the Warden. Anon there appeared a roughly trodden path, which soon became a stone-paved road, and the way led on to where the great hall, Heorot, towered aloft, gleaming white in the sun ; very glorious it seemed,

8

with its pinnacled gables and its carved beams and rafters, and the Geats gazed at it with admiration as the Warden of the Coast said : " Yonder stands our monarch's hall, and your way lies clear before you. May the All-Father keep you safe in the conflict! Now it is time for me to return ; I go to guard our shores from every foe."

Hrothgar and Beowulf

The little band of Geats, in their shining war-gear, strode along the stone-paved street, their ring-mail sounding as they went, until they reached the door of Heorot ; and there, setting down their broad shields and their keen spears against the wall, they prepared to enter as peaceful guests the great hall of King Hrothgar. Wulfgar, one of Hrothgar's nobles, met them at the door and asked whence such a splendid band of warlike strangers, so well armed and so worthily equipped, had come. Their heroic bearing betokened some noble enterprise. Beowulf answered : " We are Hygelac's chosen friends and companions, and I am Beowulf. To King Hrothgar, thy master, will I tell mine errand, if the son of Healfdene will allow us to approach him."

Wulfgar, impressed by the words and bearing of the hero, replied : " I will announce thy coming to my lord, and bring back his answer " ; and then made his way up the hall to the high seat where Hrothgar sat on the daïs amidst his bodyguard of picked champions. Bowing respectfully, he said :

" Here are come travelling   over the sea-expanse,
  Journeying from afar,   heroes of Geatland.
  Beowulf is the name   of their chief warrior.
  This is their prayer, my lord,   that they may speak with thee ;
  Do not thou give them   a hasty refusal !

9

Do not deny them   the gladness of converse!
They in their war-gear seem   worthy of men's respect.
Noble their chieftain seems,   he who the warriors
Hither has guided."

At these words the aged king aroused himself from the sad reverie into which he had fallen and answered: "I knew him as a boy. Beowulf is the son of Ecgtheow, who wedded the daughter of the Geat King Hrethel. His fame has come hither before him ; seafarers have told me that he has the might of thirty men in his hand-grip. Great joy it is to know of his coming, for he may save us from the terror of Grendel. If he succeeds in this, great treasures will I bestow upon him. Hasten ; bring in hither Beowulf and his kindred thanes, and bid them welcome to the Danish folk ! "

Wulfgar hurried down the hall to the place where Beowulf stood with his little band ; he led them gladly to the high seat, so that they stood opposite to Hrothgar, who looked keenly at the well-equipped troop, and kindly at its leader. A striking figure was Beowulf as he stood there in his gleaming ring-mail, with the mighty sword by his side. It was, however, but a minute that Hrothgar looked in silence, for with respectful greeting Beowulf spoke :

"Hail to thee, Hrothgar King !   Beowulf am I,
Hygelac's kinsman   and loyal companion.
Great deeds of valour   wrought I in my youth.
To me in my native land   Grendel's ill-doing
Came as an oft-heard tale   told by our sailors.
They say that this bright hall,   noblest of buildings,
Standeth to every man   idle and useless
After the evening-light   fails in the heavens.
Thus, Hrothgar, ancient king,   all my friends urged me,
Warriors and prudent thanes,   that I should seek thee,
Since they themselves had known   my might in battle.

HROTHGAR AND BEOWULF

Now I will beg of thee,   lord of the glorious Danes,
Prince of the Scylding race,   Folk-lord most friendly,
Warden of warriors,   only one boon.
Do not deny it me,   since I have come from far;
I with my men alone,   this troop of heroes good,
Would without help from thee   cleanse thy great hall!
Oft have I also heard   that the fierce monster
Through his mad recklessness   scorns to use weapons;
Therefore will I forego   (so may King Hygelac,
My friendly lord and king,   find in me pleasure)
That I should bear my sword   and my broad yellow shield
Into the conflict: with my hand-grip alone
I 'gainst the foe will strive,   and struggle for my life—
He shall endure God's doom   whom death shall bear away.
I know that he thinketh   in this hall of conflict
Fearless to eat me,   if he can compass it,
As he has oft devoured   heroes of Denmark.
Then thou wilt not need   my head to hide away,
Grendel will have me   all mangled and gory;
Away will he carry,   if death then shall take me,
My body with gore stained   will he think to feast on,
On his lone track will bear it   and joyously eat it,
And mark with my life-blood   his lair in the moorland;
Nor more for my welfare   wilt thou need to care then.
Send thou to Hygelac,   if strife shall take me,
That best of byrnies   which my breast guardeth,
Brightest of war-weeds,   the work of Smith Weland,
Left me by Hrethel.   Ever Wyrd has her way."

The aged King Hrothgar, who had listened attentively while the hero spoke of his plans and of his possible fate, now greeted him saying: "Thou hast sought my court for honour and for friendship's sake, O Beowulf: thou hast remembered the ancient alliance between Ecgtheow, thy father, and myself, when I shielded him, a fugitive, from the wrath of the Wilfings, paid them the due wergild for his crime, and took his oath of loyalty to myself. Long ago that time is; Ecgtheow is dead, and I am old and in misery. It were too long now to tell of all the woe

11

that Grendel has wrought, but this I may say, that
many a hero has boasted of the great valour he would
display in strife with the monster, and has awaited his
coming in this hall ; in the morning there has been no
trace of each hero but the dark blood-stains on benches
and tables. How many times has that happened !
But sit down now to the banquet and tell thy plans, if
such be thy will."

Thereupon room was made for the Geat warriors
on the long benches, and Beowulf sat in the place of
honour opposite to the king : great respect was shown
to him, and all men looked with wonder on this mighty
hero, whose courage led him to hazard this terrible
combat. Great carved horns of ale were borne to
Beowulf and his men, savoury meat was placed before
them, and while they ate and drank the minstrels
played and sang to the harp the deeds of men of old.
The mirth of the feast was redoubled now men hoped
that a deliverer had come indeed.

The Quarrel

Among all the Danes who were rejoicing over Beowulf's coming there was one whose heart was sad and
his brow gloomy—one thane whom jealousy urged to
hate any man more distinguished than himself. Hunferth, King Hrothgar's orator and speech-maker, from
his official post at Hrothgar's feet watched Beowulf
with scornful and jealous eyes. He waited until a pause
came in the clamour of the feast, and suddenly spoke,
coldly and contemptuously : "Art thou that Beowulf
who strove against Breca, the son of Beanstan, when
ye two held a swimming contest in the ocean and
risked your lives in the deep waters ? In vain all
your friends urged you to forbear—ye would go on
the hazardous journey ; ye plunged in, buffeting the

12

wintry waves through the rising storm. Seven days and nights ye toiled, but Breca overcame thee : he had greater strength and courage. Him the ocean bore to shore, and thence he sought his native land, and the fair city where he ruled as lord and chieftain. Fully he performed his boast against thee. So I now look for a worse issue for thee, for thou wilt find Grendel fiercer in battle than was Breca, if thou darest await him this night."

Beowulf's brow flushed with anger as he replied haughtily : "Much hast thou spoken, friend Hunferth, concerning Breca and our swimming contest ; but belike thou art drunken, for wrongly hast thou told the tale. A youthful folly of ours it was, when we two boasted and challenged each other to risk our lives in the ocean ; that indeed we did. Naked swords we bore in our hands as we swam, to defend ourselves against the sea-monsters, and we floated together, neither outdistancing the other, for five days, when a storm drove us apart. Cold were the surging waves, bitter the north wind, rough was the swelling flood, under the darkening shades of night. Yet this was not the worst : the sea-monsters, excited by the raging tempest, rushed at me with their deadly tusks and bore me to the abyss. Well was it then for me that I wore my well-woven ring-mail, and had my keen sword in hand ; with point and edge I fought the deadly beasts, and killed them. Many a time the hosts of monsters bore me to the ocean-bottom, but I slew numbers among them, and thus we battled all the night, until in the morning came light from the east, and I could see the windy cliffs along the shore, and the bodies of the slain sea-beasts floating on the surge. Nine there were of them, for Wyrd is gracious to the man who is valiant and unafraid. Never have I heard of a

13

sterner conflict, nor a more unhappy warrior lost in the waters ; yet I saved my life, and landed on the shores of Finland. Breca wrought not so mightily as I, nor have I heard of such warlike deeds on thy part, even though thou, O Hunferth, didst murder thy brothers and nearest kinsmen.

> " Truly I say to thee,   O son of Ecglaf bold,
>   Grendel the grisly fiend   ne'er dared have wrought
> So many miseries,   such shame and anguish dire,
> To thy lord, Hrothgar old,   in his bright Heorot,
> Hadst thou shown valiant mood,   sturdy and battle-fierce,
> As thou now boastest."

Very wroth was Hunferth over the reminder of his former wrongdoing and the implied accusation of cowardice, but he had brought it on himself by his unwise belittling of Beowulf's feat, and the applause of both Danes and Geats showed him that he dared no further attack the champion ; he had to endure in silence Beowulf's boast that he and his Geats would that night await Grendel in the hall, and surprise him terribly, since the fiend had ceased to expect any resistance from the warlike Danes. The feast continued, with laughter and melody, with song and boast, until the door from the women's bower, in the upper end of the hall, opened suddenly, and Hrothgar's wife, the fair and gracious Queen Wealhtheow, entered. The tumult lulled for a short space, and the queen, pouring mead into a goblet, presented it to her husband ; joyfully he received and drank it. Then she poured mead or ale for each man, and in due course came to Beowulf, as to the guest of honour. Gratefully Wealhtheow greeted the lordly hero, and thanked him for the friendship which brought him to Denmark to risk his life against Grendel. Beowulf, rising respectfully and taking the cup from the queen's hand, said with dignity :

BEOWULF AND GRENDEL

> " This I considered well   when I the ocean sought,
> Sailed in the sea-vessel   with my brave warriors,
> That I alone would win   thy folk's deliverance,
> Or in the fight would fall   fast in the demon's grip.
> Needs must I now perform   knightly deeds in this hall,
> Or here must meet my doom   in darksome night."

Well pleased, Queen Wealhtheow went to sit beside her lord, where her gracious smile cheered the assembly. Then the clamour of the feast was renewed, until Hrothgar at length gave the signal for retiring. Indeed, it was necessary to leave Heorot when darkness fell, for the fiend came each night when sunlight faded. So the whole assembly arose, each man bade his comrades " Good night," and the Danes dispersed ; but Hrothgar addressed Beowulf half joyfully, half sadly, saying :

> " Never before have I   since I held spear and shield
> Given o'er to any man   this mighty Danish hall,
> Save now to thee alone.   Keep thou and well defend
> This best of banquet-halls.   Show forth thy hero-strength,
> Call up thy bravery,   watch for the enemy !
> Thou shalt not lack gifts of worth   if thou alive remain
> Winner in this dire strife."

Thus Hrothgar departed, to seek slumber in a less dangerous abode, where, greatly troubled in mind, he awaited the dawn with almost hopeless expectation, and Beowulf and his men prepared themselves for the perils of the night.

Beowulf and Grendel

The fourteen champions of the Geats now made ready for sleep; but while the others lay down in their armour, with weapons by their sides, Beowulf took off his mail, unbelted his sword, unhelmed himself, and gave his sword to a thane to bear away. For, as he

15

said to his men, " I will strive against this fiend weaponless. With no armour, since he wears none, will I wrestle
with him, and try to overcome him. I will conquer,
if I win, by my hand-grip alone ; and the All-Father
shall judge between us, and grant the victory to whom
He will."

The Geats then lay down—brave men who slept
calmly, though they knew they were risking their lives,
for none of them expected to see the light of day again,
or to revisit their native land : they had heard, too,
much during the feast of the slaughter which Grendel
had wrought. So night came, the voices of men grew
silent, and the darkness shrouded all alike—calm
sleepers, anxious watchers, and the deadly, creeping foe.

When everything was still Grendel came. From
the fen-fastnesses, by marshy tracts, through mists and
swamp-born fogs, the hideous monster made his way to
the house he hated so bitterly. Grendel strode fiercely
to the door of Heorot, and would fain have opened it
as usual, but it was locked and bolted. Then the fiend's
wrath was roused ; he grasped the door with his mighty
hands and burst it in. As he entered he seemed to
fill the hall with his monstrous shadow, and from his
eyes shone a green and uncanny light, which showed
him a troop of warriors lying asleep in their war-gear ;
it seemed that all slept, and the fiend did not notice
that one man half rose, leaning on his elbow and
peering keenly into the gloom. Grendel hastily put
forth his terrible scaly hand and seized one hapless
sleeper. Tearing him limb from limb, so swiftly that
his cry of agony was unheard, he drank the warm blood
and devoured the flesh ; then, excited by the hideous
food, he reached forth again. Great was Grendel's
amazement to find that his hand was seized in a grasp
such as he had never felt before, and to know that he

Beowulf tears off the arm and shoulder of Grendel

Beowulf finds the head of Aschere

had at last found an antagonist whom even he must fight warily. Beowulf sprang from his couch as the terrible claws of the monster fell upon him, and wrestled with Grendel in the darkness and gloom of the unlighted hall, where the flicker of the fire had died down to a dim glow in the dull embers. That was a dreadful struggle, as the combatants, in deadly conflict, swayed up and down the hall, overturning tables and benches, trampling underfoot dishes and goblets in the darkling wrestle for life. The men of the Geats felt for their weapons, but they could not see the combatants distinctly, though they heard the panting and the trampling movements, and occasionally caught a gleam from the fiend's eyes as his face was turned towards them. When they struck their weapons glanced harmlessly off Grendel's scaly hide. The struggle continued for some time, and the hall was an utter wreck within, when Grendel, worsted for once, tried to break away and rush out into the night; but Beowulf held him fast in the grip which no man on earth could equal or endure, and the monster writhed in anguish as he vainly strove to free himself—vainly, for Beowulf would not loose his grip. Suddenly, with one great cry, Grendel wrenched himself free, and staggered to the door, leaving behind a terrible blood-trail, for his arm and shoulder were torn off and left in the victor's grasp. So the monster fled wailing over the moors to his home in the gloomy mere, and Beowulf sank panting on a shattered seat, scarce believing in his victory, until his men gathered round, bringing a lighted torch, by the flaring gleam of which the green, scaly arm of Grendel looked ghastly and threatening. But the monster had fled, and after such a wound as the loss of his arm and shoulder must surely die; therefore the Geats raised a shout of

17

triumph, and then took the hateful trophy and fastened it high up on the roof of the hall, that all who entered might see the token of victory and recognise that the Geat hero had performed his boast, that he would conquer with no weapon, but by the strength of his hands alone.

In the morning many a warrior came to Heorot to learn the events of the night, and all saw the grisly trophy, praised Beowulf's might and courage, and followed with eager curiosity the bloodstained track of the fleeing demon till it came to the brink of the gloomy lake, where it disappeared, though the waters were stained with gore, and boiled and surged with endless commotion. There on the shore the Danes rejoiced over the death of their enemy, and returned to Heorot care-free and glad at heart. Meanwhile Beowulf and his Geats stayed in Heorot, for Hrothgar had not yet come to receive an account of their night-watch. Throughout the day there was feasting and rejoicing, with horse-races, and wrestling, and manly contests of skill and endurance ; or the Danes collected around the bard as he chanted the glory of Sigmund and his son Fitela. Then came King Hrothgar himself, with his queen and her maiden train, and they paused to gaze with horror on the dreadful trophy, and to turn with gratitude to the hero who had delivered them from this evil spirit. Hrothgar said : " Thanks be to the All-Father for this happy sight ! Much sorrow have I endured at the hands of Grendel, many warriors have I lost, many uncounted years of misery have I lived, but now my woe has an end ! Now a youth has performed, with his unaided strength, what all we could not compass with our craft ! Well might thy father, O Beowulf, rejoice in thy fame ! Well may thy mother, if she yet lives, praise the All-Father for

18

the noble son she bore ! A son indeed shalt thou be to me in love, and nothing thou desirest shalt thou lack, that I can give thee. Often have I rewarded less heroic deeds with great gifts, and to thee I can deny nothing."

Beowulf answered : " We have performed our boast, O King, and have driven away the enemy. I intended to force him down on one of the beds, and to deprive him of his life by mere strength of my hand-grip, but in this I did not succeed, for Grendel escaped from the hall. Yet he left here with me his hand, his arm, and shoulder as a token of his presence, and as the ransom with which he bought off the rest of his loathsome body ; yet none the longer will he live thereby, since he bears with him so deadly a wound."

Then the hall was cleared of the traces of the conflict and hasty preparation was made for a splendid banquet. There was joy in Heorot. The Danes assembled once again free from fear in their splendid hall, the walls were hung with gold-wrought embroideries and hangings of costly stuffs, while richly chased goblets shone on the long tables, and men's tongues waxed loud as they discussed and described the heroic struggle of the night before. Beowulf and King Hrothgar sat on the high seats opposite to each other, and their men, Danes and Geats, sitting side by side, shouted and cheered and drank deeply to the fame of Beowulf. The minstrels sang of the Fight in Finnsburg and the deeds of Finn and Hnæf, of Hengest and Queen Hildeburh. Long was the chant, and it roused the national pride of the Danes to hear of the victory of their Danish forefathers over Finn of the Frisians ; and merrily the banquet went forward, gladdened still more by the presence of Queen· Wealhtheow. Now Hrothgar showed his lavish generosity and his thankfulness by the gifts with which he loaded the Geat chief; and not only Beowulf, but every man of the little troop. Beowulf received a gold-embroidered banner, a magnificent sword, helmet, and corslet, a goblet of gold, and eight fleet steeds. On the back of the best was strapped a cunningly wrought saddle, Hrothgar's own, with gold ornaments. When the Geat hero had thanked the king fittingly, Queen Wealhtheow arose from her seat, and, lifting the great drinking-cup, offered it to her lord, saying:

> "Take thou this goblet, my lord and my ruler,
> O giver of treasure, O gold-friend of heroes,
> And speak to the Geats fair speeches of kindness,
> Be mirthful and joyous, for so should a man be!
> To the Geats be gracious, mindful of presents
> Now that from far and near thou hast firm peace!
> Tidings have come to me that thou for son wilt take
> This mighty warrior who has cleansed Heorot,
> Brightest of banquet-halls! Enjoy while thou mayest
> These manifold pleasures, and leave to thy kinsmen
> Thy lands and thy lordships when thou must journey forth
> To meet thy death."

Turning to Beowulf, the queen said: "Enjoy thy reward, O dear Beowulf, while thou canst, and live noble and blessed! Keep well thy widespread fame, and be a friend to my sons in time to come, should they ever need a protector." Then she gave him two golden armlets, set with jewels, costly rings, a corslet of chain-mail and a wonderful jewelled collar of exquisite ancient workmanship, and, bidding them continue their feasting, with her maidens she left the hall. The feast went on till Hrothgar also departed to his dwelling, and left the Danes, now secure and careless, to prepare their beds, place each warrior's shield at the head, and go to sleep in their armour ready for an

alarm.   Meanwhile Beowulf and the Geats were joyfully escorted to another lodging, where they slept
soundly without disturbance.

Grendel's Mother

In the darkness of the night an avenger came to
Heorot, came in silence and mystery as Grendel had
done, with thoughts of murder and hatred raging in her
heart.   Grendel had gone home to die, but his mother,
a fiend scarcely less terrible than her son, yet lived to
avenge his death.   She arose from her dwelling in the
gloomy lake, followed the fen paths and moorland
ways to Heorot, and opened the door.   There was a
horrible panic when her presence became known, and
men ran hither and thither vainly seeking to attack
her ; yet there was less terror among them than
before when they saw the figure of a horrible woman.
In spite of all, the monster seized Aschere, one of
King Hrothgar's thanes, and bore him away to the
fens, leaving a house of lamentation where men had
feasted so joyously a few hours before.   The news was
brought to King Hrothgar, who bitterly lamented the
loss of his wisest and dearest counsellor, and bade
them call Beowulf to him, since he alone could help in
this extremity.   When Beowulf stood before the king
he courteously inquired if his rest had been peaceful.
Hrothgar answered mournfully : " Ask me not of
peace, for care is renewed in Heorot.   Dead is
Aschere, my best counsellor and friend, the truest of
comrades in fight and in council.   Such as Aschere
was should a true vassal be !   A deadly fiend has
slain him in Heorot, and I know not whither she has
carried his lifeless body.   This is doubtless her vengeance for thy slaying of Grendel ; he is dead, and his
kinswoman has come to avenge him."

21

" I have heard it reported   by some of my people
That they have looked on   two such unearthly ones,
Huge-bodied march-striders   holding the moor wastes;
One of them seemed to be   shaped like a woman,
Her fellow in exile   bore semblance of manhood,
Though huger his stature   than man ever grew to :
In years that are long gone by   Grendel they named him,
But know not his father   nor aught of his kindred.
Thus these dire monsters   dwell in the secret lands,
Haunt the hills loved by wolves,   the windy nesses,
Dangerous marshy paths,   where the dark moorland stream
'Neath the o'erhanging cliffs   downwards departeth,
Sinks in the sombre earth.   Not far remote from us
Standeth the gloomy mere,   round whose shores cluster
Groves with their branches mossed,   hoary with lichens grey,
A wood firmly rooted   o'ershadows the water.
There is a wonder seen   nightly by wanderers,
Flame in the waterflood :   liveth there none of men
Ancient or wise enough   to know its bottom.
Though the poor stag may be   hard by the hounds pursued,
Though he may seek the wood,   chased by his cruel foes,
Yet will he yield his life   to hunters on the brink
Ere he will hide his head   in the dark waters.
'Tis an uncanny place.   Thence the surge swelleth up
Dark to the heavens above,   when the wind stirreth oft
Terrible driving storms,   till the air darkens,
The skies fall to weeping."

Then Hrothgar burst forth in uncontrollable emotion : "O Beowulf, help us if thou canst ! Help is only to be found in thee. But yet thou knowest not the dangerous place thou must needs explore if thou seek the fiend in her den. I will richly reward thy valour if thou returnest alive from this hazardous journey."

Beowulf was touched by the sorrow of the grey-haired king, and replied :

" Grieve not, O prudent King !   Better it is for each
That he avenge his friend,   than that he mourn him much.
Each man must undergo   death at the end of life.
Let him win while he may   warlike fame in the world !
That is best after death   for the slain warrior."

THE FIGHT WITH GRENDEL'S MOTHER

"Arise, my lord; let us scan the track left by the monster, for I promise thee I will never lose it, wheresoever it may lead me. Only have patience yet for this one day of misery, as I am sure thou wilt."

Hrothgar sprang up joyously, almost youthfully, and ordered his horse to be saddled; then, with Beowulf beside him, and a mixed throng of Geats and Danes following, he rode away towards the home of the monsters, the dread lake which all men shunned. The blood-stained tracks were easy to see, and the avengers moved on swiftly till they came to the edge of the mere, and there, with grief and horror, saw the head of Aschere lying on the bank.

"The lake boiled with blood,   with hot welling gore;
   The warriors gazed awe-struck,   and the dread horn sang
   From time to time fiercely   eager defiance.
   The warriors sat down there,   and saw on the water
   The sea-dragons swimming   to search the abysses.
   They saw on the steep nesses   sea-monsters lying,
   Snakes and weird creatures: these madly shot away
   Wrathful and venomous   when the sound smote their ears,
   The blast of the war-horn."

As Beowulf stood on the shore and watched the uncouth sea-creatures, serpents, nicors, monstrous beasts of all kinds, he suddenly drew his bow and shot one of them to the heart. The rest darted furiously away, and the thanes were able to drag the carcase of the slain beast on shore, where they surveyed it with wonder.

The Fight with Grendel's Mother

Meanwhile Beowulf had made ready for his task. He trusted to his well-woven mail, the corslet fitting closely to his body and protecting his breast, the shining helm guarding his head, bright with the boar-image on the crest, and the mighty sword Hrunting, which Hunferth, his jealousy forgotten in admiration, pressed on the adventurous hero.

> "That sword was called Hrunting,   an ancient heritage :
> Steel was the blade itself,   tempered with poison-twigs,
> Hardened with battle-blood :   never in fight it failed
> Any who wielded it,   when he would wage a strife
> In the dire battlefield,   folk-moot of enemies."

When Beowulf stood ready with naked sword in hand, he turned and looked at his loyal followers, his friendly hosts, the grey old King Hrothgar, the sun and the green earth, which he might never see again ; but it was with no trace of weakness or fear that he spoke :

> "Forget not, O noble   kinsman of Healfdene,
> Illustrious ruler,   gold-friend of warriors,
> What we two settled   when we spake together,
> If I for thy safety should   end here my life-days,
> That thou wouldst be to me,   though dead, as a father.
> Be to my kindred thanes,   my battle-comrades,
> A worthy protector   should death o'ertake me.
> Do thou, dear Hrothgar,   send all these treasures here
> Which thou hast given me,   to my king, Hygelac.
> Then may the Geat king,   brave son of Hrethel dead,
> See by the gold and gems,   know by the treasures there,
> That I found a generous lord,   whom I loved in my life.
> Give thou to Hunferth too   my wondrous old weapon,
> The sword with its graven blade;   let the right valiant man
> Have the keen war-blade :   I will win fame with his,
> With Hrunting, noble brand,   or death shall take me."

Beowulf dived downward, as it seemed to him, for the space of a day ere he could perceive the floor of that sinister lake, and all that time he had to fight the sea-beasts, for they, attacking him with tusk and horn, strove to break his ring-mail, but in vain. As Beowulf came near the bottom he felt himself seized in long, scaly arms of gigantic strength. The fierce claws of the wolfish sea-woman strove eagerly to reach his heart through his mail, but in vain ; so the she-wolf of the waters, a being awful and loathsome, bore him to her abode, rushing through thick clusters of horrible sea-beasts.

> "The hero now noticed   he was in some hostile hall,
> Where him the water-stream   no whit might injure,
> Nor for the sheltering roof   the rush of the raging flood
> Ever could touch him.   He saw the strange flickering flame,
> Weird lights in the water,   shining with livid sheen :
> He saw, too, the ocean-wolf,   the hateful sea-woman."

Terrible and almost superhuman was the contest which now followed : the awful sea-woman flung Beowulf down on his back and stabbed at him with point and edge of her broad knife, seeking some vulnerable point ; but the good corslet resisted all her efforts, and Beowulf, exerting his mighty force, overthrew her and sprang to his feet. Angered beyond measure, he brandished the flaming sword Hrunting, and flashed one great blow at her head which would have killed her had her scales and hair been vulnerable ; but alas ! the edge of the blade turned on her scaly hide, and the blow failed. Wrathfully Beowulf cast aside the useless sword, and determined to trust once again to his handgrip. Grendel's mother now felt, in her turn, the deadly power of Beowulf's grasp, and was borne to the ground ; but the struggle continued long, for Beowulf was weaponless, since the sword failed in its work. Yet some weapon he must have.

> " So he gazed at the walls,   saw there a glorious sword,
> An old brand gigantic,   trusty in point and edge,
> An heirloom of heroes ;   that was the best of blades,
> Splendid and stately,   the forging of giants ;
> But it was huger than   any of human race
> Could bear to battle-strife,   save Beowulf only."

This mighty sword, a relic of earlier and greater races, brought new hope to Beowulf. Springing up, he snatched it from the wall and swung it fiercely round his head. The blow fell with crushing force on the neck of the sea-woman, the dread wolf of the abyss, and broke the bones. Dead the monster sank to the ground, and Beowulf, standing erect, saw at his feet the lifeless carcase of his foe. The hero still grasped his sword and looked warily along the walls of the water-dwelling, lest some other foe should emerge from its recesses ; but as he gazed Beowulf saw his former foe, Grendel, lying dead on a bed in some inner hall. He strode thither, and, seizing the corpse by the hideous coiled locks, shore off the head to carry to earth again. The poisonous hot blood of the monster melted the blade of the mighty sword, and nothing remained but the hilt, wrought with curious ornaments and signs of old time. This hilt and Grendel's head were all that Beowulf carried off from the water-fiends' dwelling ; and laden with these the hero sprang up through the now clear and sparkling water.

Meanwhile the Danes and Geats had waited long for his reappearance. When the afternoon was well advanced the Danes departed sadly, lamenting the hero's death, for they concluded no man could have survived so long beneath the waters ; but his loyal Geats sat there still gazing sadly at the waves, and hoping against all hope that Beowulf would reappear. At length they saw changes in the mere—the blood boiling upwards in the lake, the quenching of the unholy light, then the flight of the sea-monsters and a gradual clearing of the waters, through which at last they could see their lord uprising. How gladly they greeted him ! What awe and wonder seized them as they surveyed his dreadful booty, the ghastly

Beowulf shears off the head of Grendel

"Both warriors stood behind the iron shield"

head of Grendel and the massive hilt of the gigantic
sword! How eagerly they listened to his story, and
how they vied with one another for the glory of bearing his armour, his spoils, and his weapons back over
the moorlands and the fens to Heorot. It was a
proud and glad troop that followed Beowulf into the
hall, and up through the startled throng until they laid
down before the feet of King Hrothgar the hideous
head of his dead foe, and Beowulf, raising his voice that
all might hear above the buzz and hum of the great
banquet-hall, thus addressed the king:

"Lo! we this sea-booty,   O wise son of Healfdene,
    Lord of the Scyldings, have   brought for thy pleasure,
    In token of triumph,   as thou here seest.
    From harm have I hardly   escaped with my life,
    The war under water   sustained I with trouble,
    The conflict was almost   decided against me,
    If God had not guarded me!   Nought could I conquer
    With Hrunting in battle,   though 'tis a doughty blade.
    But the gods granted me   that I saw suddenly
    Hanging high in the hall   a bright brand gigantic:
    So seized I and swung it   that in the strife I slew
    The lords of the dwelling.   The mighty blade melted fast
    In the hot boiling blood,   the poisonous battle-gore;
    But the hilt have I here   borne from the hostile hall.
    I have avenged the crime,   the death of the Danish folk,
    As it behovèd me.   Now can I promise thee
    That thou in Heorot   care-free mayest slumber
    With all thy warrior-troop   and all thy kindred thanes,
    The young and the aged: thou needst not fear for them
    Death from these mortal foes,   as thou of yore hast done."

King Hrothgar was now more delighted than ever at
the return of his friend and the slaughter of his foes.
He gazed in delight and wonder at the gory head of
the monster, and the gigantic hilt of the weapon which
struck it off. Then, taking the glorious hilt, and scan-
ning eagerly the runes which showed its history, as the

tumult stilled in the hall, and all men listened for his speech, he broke out : " Lo ! this may any man say, who maintains truth and right among his people, that good though he may be this hero is even better ! Thy glory is widespread, Beowulf my friend, among thine own and many other nations, for thou hast fulfilled all things by patience and prudence. I will surely perform what I promised thee, as we agreed before ; and I foretell of thee that thou wilt be long a help and protection to thy people."

King Hrothgar spoke long and eloquently while all men listened, for he reminded them of mighty warriors of old who had not won such glorious fame, and warned them against pride and lack of generosity and self-seeking ; and then, ending with thanks and fresh gifts to Beowulf, he bade the feast continue with increased jubilation. The tumultuous rejoicing lasted till darkness settled on the land, and when it ended all retired to rest free from fear, since no more fiendish monsters would break in upon their slumbers; gladly and peacefully the night passed, and with the morn came Beowulf's resolve to return to his king and his native land.

When Beowulf had come to this decision he went to Hrothgar and said :

> " Now we sea-voyagers   come hither from afar
> Must utter our intent   to seek King Hygelac.
> Here were we well received,   well hast thou treated us.
> If on this earth I can   do more to win thy love,
> O prince of warriors,   than I have wrought as yet,
> Here stand I ready now   weapons to wield for thee.
> If I shall ever hear   o'er the encircling flood
> That any neighbouring foes   threaten thy nation's fall,
> As Grendel grim before,   swift will I bring to thee
> Thousands of noble thanes,   heroes to help thee.
> I know of Hygelac,   King of the Geat folk,
> That he will strengthen me   (though he is young in years)

BEOWULF'S RETURN

In words and warlike deeds   to bear my warrior-spear
Over the ocean surge,   when arms would serve thy need,
Swift to thine aid.   If thy son Hrethric young
Comes to the Geat court,   there to gain skill in arms,
Then will he surely find   many friends waiting him :
Better in distant lands   learneth by journeying
He who is valiant."

Hrothgar was greatly moved by the words of the Geat hero and his promise of future help. He wondered to find such wisdom in so young a warrior, and felt that the Geats could never choose a better king if battle should cut off the son of Hygelac, and he renewed his assurance of continual friendship between the two countries and of enduring personal affection. Finally, with fresh gifts of treasure and with tears of regret Hrothgar embraced Beowulf and bade him go speedily to his ship, since a friend's yearning could not retain him longer from his native land. So the little troop of Geats with their gifts and treasures marched proudly to their vessel and sailed away to Geatland, their dragon-prowed ship laden with armour and jewels and steeds, tokens of remembrance and thanks from the grateful Danes.

Beowulf's Return

Blithe-hearted were the voyagers, and gaily the ship danced over the waves, as the Geats strained their eyes towards the cliffs of their home and the well-known shores of their country. When their vessel approached the land the coast-warden came hurrying to greet them, for he had watched the ocean day and night for the return of the valiant wanderers. Gladly he welcomed them, and bade his underlings help to bear their spoils up to the royal palace, where King Hygelac, himself young and valiant, awaited his victorious kinsman, with his beauteous queen, Hygd, beside him. Then came Beowulf, treading proudly the rocky paths to the royal abode, for messengers had gone in advance to announce to the king his nephew's success, and a banquet was being prepared, where Beowulf would sit beside his royal kinsman.

Once more there was a splendid feast, with tumultuous rejoicing. Again a queenly hand—that of the beauteous Hygd—poured out the first bowl in which to celebrate the safe return of the victorious hero. And now the wonderful story of the slaying of the fen-fiends must be told.

Beowulf was called upon to describe again his perils and his victories, and told in glowing language of the grisly monsters and the desperate combats, and of the boundless gratitude and splendid generosity of the Danish king, and of his prophecy of lasting friendship between the Danes and the Geats. Then he concluded :

> " Thus that great nation's king   lived in all noble deeds.
> Of guerdon I failed not,   of meed for my valour,
> But the wise son of Healfdene   gave to me treasures great,
> Gifts to my heart's desire.   These now I bring to thee,
> Offer them lovingly :   now are my loyalty
> And service due to thee,   O hero-king, alone !
> Near kinsmen have I few   but thee, O Hygelac ! "

As the hero showed the treasures with which Hrothgar had rewarded his courage, he distributed them generously among his kinsmen and friends, giving his priceless jewelled collar to Queen Hygd, and his best steed to King Hygelac, as a true vassal and kinsman should. So Beowulf resumed his place as Hygelac's chief warrior and champion, and settled down among his own people.

Fifty Years After

When half a century had passed away, great and sorrowful changes had taken place in the two kingdoms

of Denmark and Geatland. Hrothgar was dead, and had
been succeeded by his son Hrethric, and Hygelac had
been slain in a warlike expedition against the Hetware.
In this expedition Beowulf had accompanied Hygelac,
and had done all a warrior could do to save his kinsman
and his king. When he saw his master slain he had
fought his way through the encircling foes to the sea-
shore, where, though sorely wounded, he flung himself
into the sea and swam back to Geatland. There he had
told Queen Hygd of the untimely death of her husband,
and had called on her to assume the regency of the kingdom for her young son Heardred. Queen Hygd called
an assembly of the Geats, and there, with the full consent
of the nation, offered the crown to Beowulf, the wisest
counsellor and bravest hero among them ; but he
refused to accept it, and so swayed the Geats by his
eloquence and his loyalty that they unanimously raised
Heardred to the throne, with Beowulf as his guardian
and protector. When in later years Heardred also
fell before an enemy, Beowulf was again chosen king,
and as he was now the next of kin he accepted the
throne, and ruled long and gloriously over Geatland.
His fame as a warrior kept his country free from invasion, and his wisdom as a statesman increased its
prosperity and happiness ; whilst the vengeance he took
for his kinsman's death fulfilled all ideals of family and
feudal duty held by the men of his time. Beowulf, in
fact, became an ideal king, as he was an ideal warrior
and hero, and he closed his life by an ideal act of self-
sacrifice for the good of his people.

Beowulf and the Fire-Dragon

In the fiftieth year of Beowulf's reign a great terror
fell upon the land : terror of a monstrous fire-dragon,
who flew forth by night from his den in the rocks,

lighting up the blackness with his blazing breath, and burning houses and homesteads, men and cattle, with the flames from his mouth. The glare from his fiery scales was like the dawn-glow in the sky, but his passage left behind it every night a trail of black, charred desolation to confront the rising sun. Yet the dragon's wrath was in some way justified, since he had been robbed, and could not trace the thief. Centuries before Beowulf's lifetime a mighty family of heroes had gathered together, by feats of arms, and by long inheritance, an immense treasure of cups and goblets, of necklaces and rings, of swords and helmets and armour, cunningly wrought by magic spells; they had joyed in their cherished hoard for long years, until all had died but one, and he survived solitary, miserable, brooding over the fate of the dearly loved treasure. At last he caused his servants to make a strong fastness in the rocks, with cunningly devised entrances, known only to himself, and thither, with great toil and labour of aged limbs, he carried and hid the precious treasure. As he sadly regarded it, and thought of its future fate, he cried aloud :

" Hold thou now fast, O earth, now men no longer can,
 The treasure of mighty earls. From thee brave men won it
 In days that are long gone by, but slaughter seized on them,
 Death fiercely vanquished them, each of my warriors,
 Each one of my people, who closed their life-days here
 After the joy of earth. None have I sword to wield
 Or bring me the goblet, the richly wrought vessel.
 All the true heroes have elsewhere departed !
 Now must the gilded helm lose its adornments,
 For those who polished it sleep in the gloomy grave,
 Those who made ready erst war-gear of warriors.
 Likewise the battle-sark which in the fight endured
 Bites of the keen-edged blades midst the loud crash of shields
 Rusts, with its wearer dead. Nor may the woven mail
 After the chieftain's death wide with a champion rove.

BEOWULF AND THE FIRE-DRAGON

Gone is the joy of harp,   gone is the music's mirth.
Now the hawk goodly-winged   hovers not through the hall,
Nor the swift-footed mare   tramples the castle court :
Baleful death far has sent   all living tribes of men."

When this solitary survivor of the ancient race died his hoard remained alone, unknown, untouched, until at length the fiery dragon, seeking a shelter among the rocks, found the hidden way to the cave, and, creeping within, discovered the lofty inner chamber and the wondrous hoard. For three hundred winters he brooded over it unchallenged, and then one day a hunted fugitive, fleeing from the fury of an avenging chieftain, in like manner found the cave, and the dragon sleeping on his gold. Terrified almost to death, the fugitive eagerly seized a marvellously wrought chalice and bore it stealthily away, feeling sure that such an offering would appease his lord's wrath and atone for his offence. But when the dragon awoke he discovered that he had been robbed, and his keen scent assured him that some one of mankind was the thief. As he could not at once see the robber, he crept around the outside of the barrow snuffing eagerly to find traces of the spoiler, but it was in vain ; then, growing more wrathful, he flew over the inhabited country, shedding fiery death from his glowing scales and flaming breath, while no man dared to face this flying horror of the night.

The news came to Beowulf that his folk were suffering and dying, and that no warrior dared to risk his life in an effort to deliver the land from this deadly devastation ; and although he was now an aged man he decided to attack the fire-drake. Beowulf knew that he would not be able to come to hand-grips with this foe as he had done with Grendel and his mother : the fiery breath of this dragon was far too deadly, and

33

he must trust to armour for protection. He commanded men to make a shield entirely of iron, for he knew that the usual shield of linden-wood would be instantly burnt up in the dragon's flaming breath. He then chose with care eleven warriors, picked men of his own bodyguard, to accompany him in this dangerous quest. They compelled the unhappy fugitive whose theft had begun the trouble to act as their guide, and thus they marched to the lonely spot where the dragon's barrow stood close to the sea-shore. The guide went unwillingly, but was forced thereto by his lord, because he alone knew the way.

Beowulf Faces Death

When the little party reached the place they halted for a time, and Beowulf sat down meditating sadly on his past life, and on the chances of this great conflict which he was about to begin. When he had striven with Grendel, when he had fought against the Hetware, he had been confident of victory and full of joyous self-reliance, but now things were changed. Beowulf was an old man, and there hung over him a sad foreboding that this would be his last fight, and that he would rid the land of no more monsters. Wyrd seemed to threaten him, and a sense of coming woe lay heavy on his heart as he spoke to his little troop: " Many great fights I had in my youth. How well I remember them all ! I was only seven years old when King Hrethel took me to bring up, and loved me as dearly as his own sons, Herebeald, Hathcyn, or my own dear lord Hygelac. Great was our grief when Hathcyn, hunting in the forest, slew all unwittingly his elder brother : greater than ordinary sorrow, because we could not avenge him on the murderer ! It would have given no joy to Hrethel to see his second

BEOWULF AND THE FIRE-DRAGON

son killed disgracefully as a murderer! So we endured the pain till King Hrethel died, borne down by his bitter loss, and I wept for my protector, my kinsman. Then Hathcyn died also, slain by the Swedes, and my dear lord Hygelac came to the throne: he was gracious to me, a giver of weapons, a generous distributor of treasure, and I repaid him as much as I could in battle against his foes. Daghrefn, the Frankish warrior who slew my king, I sent to his doom with my deadly hand-grip: he, at least, should not show my lord's armour as trophy of his prowess. But this fight is different: here I must use both point and edge, as I was not wont in my youth: but here too will I, old though I be, work deeds of valour. I will not give way the space of one foot, but will meet him here in his own abode and make all my boasting good. Abide ye here, ye warriors, for this is not your expedition, nor the work of any man but me alone; wait till ye know which is triumphant, for I will win the gold and save my people, or death shall take me." So saying he raised his great shield, and, unaccompanied, set his face to the dark entrance, where a stream, boiling with strange heat, flowed forth from the cave; so hot was the air that he stood, unable to advance far for the suffocating steam and smoke. Angered by his impotence, Beowulf raised his voice and shouted a furious defiance to the awesome guardian of the barrow. Thus aroused, the dragon sprang up, roaring hideously and flapping his glowing wings together; out from the recesses of the barrow came his fiery breath, and then followed the terrible beast himself. Coiling and writhing he came, with head raised, and scales of burnished blue and green, glowing with inner heat; from his nostrils rushed two streams of fiery breath, and his flaming eyes shot flashes of consuming fire. He half

35

flew, half sprang at Beowulf. But the hero did not retreat one step. His bright sword flashed in the air as he wounded the beast, but not mortally, striking a mighty blow on his scaly head. The guardian of the hoard writhed and was stunned for a moment, and then sprang at Beowulf, sending forth so dense a cloud of flaming breath that the hero stood in a mist of fire. So terrible was the heat that the iron shield glowed red-hot and the ring-mail on the hero's limbs seared him as a furnace, and his breast swelled with the keen pain : so terrible was the fiery cloud that the Geats, seated some distance away, turned and fled, seeking the cool shelter of the neighbouring woods, and left their heroic lord to suffer and die alone.

Beowulf's Death

Among the cowardly Geats, however, there was one who thought it shameful to flee—Wiglaf, the son of Weohstan. He was young, but a brave warrior, to whom Beowulf had shown honour, and on whom he had showered gifts, for he was a kinsman, and had proved himself worthy. Now he showed that Beowulf's favour had been justified, for he seized his shield, of yellow linden-wood, took his ancient sword in hand, and pre-pared to rush to Beowulf's aid. With bitter words he reproached his cowardly comrades, saying : " I re-member how we boasted, as we sat in the mead hall and drank the foaming ale, as we took gladly the gold and jewels which our king lavished upon us, that we would repay him for all his gifts, if ever such need there were ! Now is the need come upon him, and we are here ! Beowulf chose us from all his bodyguard to help him in this mighty struggle, and we have betrayed and deserted him, and left him alone against a terrible foe. Now the day has come when our lord should

36

see our valour, and we flee from his side ! Up, let us go and aid him, even while the grim battle-flame flares around him. God knows that I would rather risk my body in the fiery cloud than stay here while my king fights and dies ! Not such disloyalty has Beowulf deserved through his long reign that he should stand alone in the death-struggle. He and I will die together, or side by side will we conquer." The youthful warrior tried in vain to rouse the courage of his companions : they trembled, and would not move. So Wiglaf, holding on high his shield, plunged into the fiery cloud and moved towards his king, crying aloud : " Beowulf, my dear lord, let not thy glory be dimmed. Achieve this last deed of valour, as thou didst promise in days of yore, that thy fame should not fall, and I will aid thee."

The sound of another voice roused the dragon to greater fury, and again came the fiery cloud, burning up like straw Wiglaf's linden shield, and torturing both warriors as they stood behind the iron shield with their heated armour. But they fought on manfully, and Beowulf, gathering up his strength, struck the dragon such a blow on the head that his ancient sword was shivered to fragments. The dragon, enraged, now flew at Beowulf and seized him by the neck with his poisonous fangs, so that the blood gushed out in streams, and ran down his corslet. Wiglaf was filled with grief and horror at this dreadful sight, and, leaving the protection of Beowulf's iron shield, dashed forth at the dragon, piercing the scaly body in a vital part. At once the fire began to fade away, and Beowulf, mastering his anguish, drew his broad knife, and with a last effort cut the hideous reptile asunder. Then the agony of the envenomed wound came upon him, and his limbs burnt and ached with intolerable pain. In growing distress he staggered to a rough ancient seat, carved out

37

of the rock, hard by the door of the barrow. There he sank down, and Wiglaf laved his brow with water from the little stream, which boiled and steamed no longer. Then Beowulf partially recovered himself, and said: "Now I bequeath to thee, my son, the armour which I also inherited. Fifty years have I ruled this people in peace, so that none of my neighbours durst attack us. I have endured and toiled much on this earth, have held my own justly, have pursued none with crafty hatred, nor sworn unjust oaths. At all this may I rejoice now that I lie mortally wounded. Do thou, O dear Wiglaf, bring forth quickly from the cave the treasures for which I lose my life, that I may see them and be glad in my nation's wealth ere I die."

Thereupon Wiglaf entered the barrow, and was dazed by the bewildering hoard of costly treasures. Filling his arms with such a load as he could carry, he hastened out of the barrow, fearing even then to find his lord dead. Then he flung down the treasures—magic armour, dwarf-wrought swords, carved goblets, flashing gems, and a golden standard—at Beowulf's feet, so that the ancient hero's dying gaze could fall on the hoard he had won for his people. But Beowulf was now so near death that he swooned away, till Wiglaf again flung water over him, and the dying champion roused himself to say, as he grasped his kinsman's hand and looked at the glittering heap before him :

> " I thank God eternal,   the great King of Glory,
> For the vast treasures   which I here gaze upon,
> That I ere my death-day   might for my people
> Win so great wealth.   Since I have given my life,
> Thou must now look to   the needs of the nation ;
> Here dwell I no longer,   for Destiny calleth me !
> Bid thou my warriors   after my funeral pyre
> Build me a burial-cairn   high on the sea-cliff's head ;
> It shall for memory   tower up on Hronesness,

BEOWULF'S DEATH

So that the seafarers   Beowulf's Barrow
Henceforth shall name it,   they who drive far and wide
Over the mighty flood   their foamy keels.
Thou art the last of all   the kindred of Wagmund !
Wyrd has swept all my kin,   all the brave chiefs away !
Now must I follow them ! "

These last words spoken, Beowulf fell back, and his soul passed away, to meet the joy reserved for all true and steadfast spirits. The hero was dead, but amid his grief Wiglaf yet remembered that the dire monster too lay dead, and the folk were delivered from the horrible plague, though at terrible cost ! Wiglaf, as he mourned over his dead lord, resolved that no man should joy in the treasures for which so grievous a price had been paid—the cowards who deserted their king should help to lay the treasures in his grave and bury them far from human use and profit. Accordingly, when the ten faithless dastards ventured out from the shelter of the wood, and came shamefacedly to the place where Wiglaf sat, sorrowing, at the head of dead Beowulf, he stilled their cries of grief with one wave of the hand, which had still been vainly striving to arouse his king by gentle touch, and, gazing scornfully at them, he cried : "Lo ! well may a truthful man say, seeing you here, safely in the war-gear and ornaments which our dead hero gave you, that Beowulf did but throw away his generous gifts, since all he bought with them was treachery and cowardice in the day of battle ! No need had Beowulf to boast of his warriors in time of danger ! Yet he alone avenged his people and conquered the fiend—I could help him but little in the fray, though I did what I could : all too few champions thronged round our hero when his need was sorest. Now are all the joys of love and loyalty ended ; now is all prosperity gone from our nation, when foreign princes hear of your flight and the shameless deed of this day. Better is death to every man than a life of shame ! "

The Geats stood silent, abashed before the keen and deserved reproaches of the young hero, and they lamented the livelong day. None left the shore and their lord's dead corpse ; but one man who rode over the cliff near by saw the mournful little band, with Beowulf dead in the midst. This warrior galloped away to tell the people, saying : " Now is our ruler, the lord of the Geats, stretched dead on the plain, stricken by the dragon which lies dead beside him ; and at his head sits Wiglaf, son of Weohstan, lamenting his royal kinsman. Now is the joy and prosperity of our folk vanished ! Now shall our enemies make raids upon us, for we have none to withstand them ! But let us hasten to bury our king, to bear him royally to his grave, with mourning and tears of woe." These un-happy tidings roused the Geats, and they hastened to see if it were really true, and found all as the messenger had said, and wondered at the mighty dragon and the glorious hoard of gold. They feared the monster and coveted the treasure, but all felt that the command now lay with Wiglaf. At last Wiglaf roused himself from his silent grief and said : "O men of the Geats, I am not to blame that our king lies here lifeless. He would fight the dragon and win the treasure ; and these he has done, though he lost his life therein ; yea, and I aided him all that I might, though it was but little I could do. Now our dear lord Beowulf bade me greet you from him, and bid you to make for him, after his funeral pyre, a great and mighty cairn, even as he was the most glorious of men in his lifetime. Bring ye all the treasures, bring quickly a bier, and place thereon our king's corpse, and let us bear our dear lord to Hrones-

The Death of Beowulf

"The Emperor remained in his own apartments and slept"

ness, where his funeral fire shall be kindled, and his burial cairn built."

The Geats, bitterly grieving, fulfilled Wiglaf's commands. They gathered wood for the fire, and piled it on the cliff-head ; then eight chosen ones brought thither the treasures, and threw the dragon's body over the cliff into the sea ; then a wain, hung with shields, was brought to bear the corpse of Beowulf to Hronesness, where it was solemnly laid on the funeral pile and consumed to ashes.

"There then the Weder Geats   wrought for their ruler dead
A cairn on the ocean cliff   widespread and lofty,
Visible far and near   by vessels' wandering crews.
They built in ten days' space   the hero's monument,
And wrought with shining swords   the earthen rampart wall,
So that the wisest men   worthy might deem it.
Then in that cairn they placed   necklets and rings and gems
Which from the dragon's hoard   brave men had taken.
Back to the earth they gave   treasures of ancient folk,
Gold to the gloomy mould,   where it now lieth
Useless to sons of men   as it e'er was of yore.
Then round the mound there rode   twelve manly warriors,
Chanting their bitter grief,   singing the hero dead,
Mourning their noble king   in fitting words of woe !
They praised his courage high   and his proud, valiant deeds,
Honoured him worthily,   as it is meet for men
Duly to praise in words   their friendly lord and king
When his soul wanders forth   far from its fleshly home.
So all the Geat chiefs,   Beowulf's bodyguard,
Wept for their leader's fall :   sang in their loud laments
That he of earthly kings   mildest to all men was,
Gentlest, most gracious,   most keen to win glory."

CHAPTER II : THE DREAM OF MAXEN WLEDIG

The Position of Constantine

IT would seem that the Emperor Constantine the Great loomed very large in the eyes of mediæval England. Even in Anglo-Saxon times many legends clustered round his name, so that Cynewulf, the religious poet of early England, wrote the poem of " Elene " mainly on the subject of his conversion. The story of the Vision of the Holy Cross with the inscription *In hoc signo vinces* was inspiring to a poet to whom the heathen were a living reality, not a distant abstraction ; and Constantine's generosity to the Church of Rome and its bishop Sylvester added another element of attraction to his character in the mediæval mind. It is hardly surprising that other legends of his conversion and generosity should have sprung up, which differ entirely from the earlier and more authentic record. Thus " the moral Gower " has preserved for us an alternative legend of the cause of Constantine's conversion, which forms a good illustration of the virtue of pity in the " Confessio Amantis." Whence this later legend sprang we have no knowledge, for nothing in the known history of Constantine warrants our regarding him as a disciple of mercy, but its existence shows that the mediæval mind was busied with his personality. Another most interesting proof of his importance to Britain is given in the following legend of " The Dream of Maxen Wledig," preserved in the " Mabinogion." This belongs to the Welsh patriotic legends, and tends to glorify the marriage of the British Princess Helena with the Roman emperor, by representing it as pre-ordained by Fate. The fact that the hero of the Welsh saga is the Emperor Maxentius instead of Constantius detracts little from the interest of the legend, which is only one instance of the well-known theme of the lover led by dream, or vision, or magic glass to the home and heart of the beloved.

The Emperor Maxen Wledig

The Emperor Maxen Wledig was the most powerful occupant of the throne of the Cæsars who had ever ruled Europe from the City of the Seven Hills. He was the most handsome man in his dominions, tall and strong and skilled in all manly exercises ; withal he was gracious and friendly to all his vassals and tributary kings, so that he was universally beloved. One day he announced his wish to go hunting, and was accompanied on his expedition down the Tiber valley by thirty-two vassal kings, with whom he enjoyed the sport heartily. At noon the heat was intense, they were far from Rome, and all were weary. The emperor proposed a halt, and they dismounted to take rest. Maxen lay down to sleep with his head on a shield, and soldiers and attendants stood around making a shelter for him from the sun's rays by a roof of shields hung on their spears. Thus he fell into a sleep so deep that none dared to awake him. Hours passed by, and still he slumbered, and still his whole retinue waited impatiently for his awakening. At length, when the evening shadows began to lie long and black on the ground, their impatience found vent in little restless movements of hounds chafing in their leashes, of spears clashing, of shields dropping from the weariness of their holders, and horses neighing and prancing; and then Maxen Wledig awoke suddenly with a start. "Ah, why did you arouse me ?" he asked sadly. "Lord, your dinner hour is long past—did you not know ?" they said. He shook his head mournfully, but said no word, and, mounting his horse, turned it

43

and rode in unbroken silence back to Rome, with his head sunk on his breast. Behind him rode in dismay his retinue of kings and tributaries, who knew nothing of the cause of his sorrowful mood.

The Emperor's Malady

From that day the emperor was changed, changed utterly. He rode no more, he hunted no more, he paid no heed to the business of the empire, but remained in seclusion in his own apartments and slept. The court banquets continued without him, music and song he refused to hear, and though in his sleep he smiled and was happy, when he awoke his melancholy could not be cheered or his gloom lightened. When this condition of things had continued for more than a week it was determined that the emperor must be aroused from this dreadful state of apathy, and his groom of the chamber, a noble Roman of very high rank—indeed, a king, under the emperor—resolved to make the endeavour.

"My lord," said he, "I have evil tidings for you. The people of Rome are beginning to murmur against you, because of the change that has come over you. They say that you are bewitched, that they can get no answers or decisions from you, and all the affairs of the empire go to wrack and ruin while you sleep and take no heed. You have ceased to be their emperor, they say, and they will cease to be loyal to you."

The Dream of the Emperor

Then Maxen Wledig roused himself and said to the noble: "Call hither my wisest senators and councillors, and I will explain the cause of my melancholy, and perhaps they will be able to give me relief." Accordingly the senators came together, and the emperor

44

ascended his throne, looking so mournful that the whole Senate grieved for him, and feared lest death should speedily overtake him. He began to address them thus:

"Senators and Sages of Rome, I have heard that my people murmur against me, and will rebel if I do not arouse myself. A terrible fate has fallen upon me, and I see no way of escape from my misery, unless ye can find one. It is now more than a week since I went hunting with my court, and when I was wearied I dismounted and slept. In my sleep I dreamt, and a vision cast its spell upon me, so that I feel no happiness unless I am sleeping, and seem to live only in my dreams. I thought I was hunting along the Tiber valley, lost my courtiers, and rode to the head of the valley alone. There the river flowed forth from a great mountain, which looked to me the highest in the world; but I ascended it, and found beyond fair and fertile plains, far vaster than any in our Italy, with mighty rivers flowing through the lovely country to the sea. I followed the course of the greatest river, and reached its mouth, where a noble port stood on the shores of a sea unknown to me. In the harbour lay a fleet of well-appointed ships, and one of these was most beautifully adorned, its planks covered with gold or silver, and its sails of silk. As a gangway of carved ivory led to the deck, I crossed it and entered the vessel, which immediately sailed out of the harbour into the ocean. The voyage was not of long duration, for we soon came to land in a wondrously beautiful island, with scenery of varied loveliness. This island I traversed, led by some secret guidance, till I reached its farthest shore, broken by cliffs and precipices and mountain ranges, while between the mountains and the sea I saw a fair and fruitful land traversed by a silvery, winding river, with a castle at its

45

mouth. My longing drew me to the castle, and when I came to the gate I entered, for the dwelling stood open to every man, and such a hall as was therein I have never seen for splendour, even in Imperial Rome. The walls were covered with gold, set with precious gems, the seats were of gold and the tables of silver, and two fair youths, whom I saw playing chess, used pieces of gold on a board of silver. Their attire was of black satin embroidered with gold, and golden circlets were on their brows. I gazed at the youths for a moment, and next became aware of an aged man sitting near them. His carved ivory seat was adorned with golden eagles, the token of Imperial Rome ; his ornaments on arms and hands and neck were of bright gold, and he was carving fresh chessmen from a rod of solid gold. Beside him sat, on a golden chair, a maiden (the loveliest in the whole world she seemed, and still seems, to me). White was her inner dress under a golden overdress, her crown of gold adorned with rubies and pearls, and a golden girdle encircled her slender waist. The beauty of her face won my love in that moment, and I knelt and said : ' Hail, Empress of Rome ! ' but as she bent forward from her seat to greet me I awoke. Now I have no peace and no joy except in sleep, for in dreams I always see my lady, and in dreams we love each other and are happy ; therefore in dreams will I live, unless ye can find some way to satisfy my longing while I wake."

The Quest for the Maiden

The senators were at first greatly amazed, and then one of them said : " My lord, will you not send out messengers to seek throughout all your lands for the maiden in the castle ? Let each group of messengers search for one year, and return at the end of the year

The Dream of the Emperor

"There came from heaven a leaping flame, which touched
the surface of the ground here and there"

[Page 61]

with tidings. So shall you live in good hope of success from year to year." The messengers were sent out accordingly, with wands in their hands and a sleeve tied on each cap, in token of peace and of an embassy; but though they searched with all diligence, after three years three separate embassies had brought back no news of the mysterious land and the beauteous maiden.

Then the groom of the chamber said to Maxen Wledig : "My lord, will you not go forth to hunt, as on the day when you dreamt this enthralling dream ?" To this the emperor agreed, and rode to the place in the valley where he had slept. " Here," he said, " my dream began, and I seemed to follow the river to its source." Then the groom of the chamber said : "Will you not send messengers to the river's source, my lord, and bid them follow the track of your dream ?" Accordingly thirteen messengers were sent, who followed the river up until it issued from the highest mountain they had ever seen. " Behold our emperor's dream !" they exclaimed, and they ascended the mountain, and descended the other side into a most beautiful and fertile plain, as Maxen Wledig had seen in his dream. Following the greatest river of all (probably the Rhine), the ambassadors reached the great seaport on the North Sea, and found the fleet waiting with one vessel larger than all the others ; and they entered the ship and were carried to the fair island of Britain. Here they journeyed westward, and came to the mountainous land of Snowdon, whence they could see the sacred isle of Mona (Anglesey) and the fertile land of Arvon lying between the mountains and the sea. " This," said the messengers, " is the land of our master's dream, and in yon fair castle we shall find the maiden whom our emperor loves."

The Finding of the Maiden

So they went through the lovely land of Arvon to the castle of Caernarvon, and in that lordly fortress was the great hall, with the two youths playing chess, the venerable man carving chessmen, and the maiden in her chair of gold. When the ambassadors saw the fair Princess Helena they fell on their knees before her and said : " Empress of Rome, all hail ! " But Helena half rose from her seat in anger as she said : " What does this mockery mean ? You seem to be men of gentle breeding, and you wear the badge of messengers : whence comes it, then, that ye mock me thus ? " But the ambassadors calmed her anger, saying : " Be not wroth, lady : this is no mockery, for the Emperor of Rome, the great lord Maxen Wledig, has seen you in a dream, and he has sworn to wed none but you. Which, therefore, will you choose, to accompany us to Rome, and there be made empress, or to wait here until the emperor can come to you ? " The princess thought deeply for a time, and then replied : " I would not be too credulous, or too hard of belief. If the emperor loves me and would wed me, let him find me in my father's house, and make me his bride in my own home."

The Dream Realized

After this the thirteen envoys departed, and returned to the emperor in such haste that when their horses failed they gave no need, but took others and pressed on. When they reached Rome and informed Maxen Wledig of the success of their mission he at once gathered his army and marched across Europe towards Britain. When the Roman emperor had crossed the sea he conquered Britain from Beli the son of Manogan, and made his way to Arvon. On entering the castle he saw first the two youths, Kynon and Adeon, playing chess, then their father, Eudav, the son of Caradoc, and then his beloved, the beauteous Helena, daughter of Eudav. "Empress of Rome, all hail!" Maxen Wledig said; and the princess bent forward in her chair and kissed him, for she knew he was her destined husband. The next day they were wedded, and the Emperor Maxen Wledig gave Helena as dowry all Britain for her father, the son of the gallant Caradoc, and for herself three castles, Caernarvon, Caerlleon, and Caermarthen, where she dwelt in turn; and in one of them was born her son Constantine, the only British-born Emperor of Rome. To this day in Wales the old Roman roads that connected Helena's three castles are known as " Sarn Helen."

CHAPTER III : THE STORY OF CONSTANTINE AND ELENE

The Greatness of Constantine Provokes Attack

IN the year 312, the sixth year after Constantine had become emperor, the Roman Empire had increased on every hand, for Constantine was a mighty leader in war, a gracious and friendly lord in peace ; he was a true king and ruler, a protector of all men. So mightily did he prosper that his enemies assembled great armies against him, and a confederation to overthrow him was made by the terrible Huns, the famous Goths, the brave Franks, and the warlike Hugas. This powerful confederation sent against Constantine an overwhelming army of Huns, whose numbers seemed to be countless, and yet the Hunnish leaders feared, when they knew that the emperor himself led the small Roman host.

The Eve of the Battle

The night before the battle Constantine lay sadly in the midst of his army, watching the stars, and dreading the result of the next day's conflict ; for his warriors were few compared with the Hunnish multitude, and even Roman discipline and devotion might not win the day against the mad fury of the barbarous Huns. At last, wearied out, the emperor slept, and a vision came to him in his sleep. He seemed to see, standing by him, a beautiful shining form, a man more glorious than the sons of men, who, as Constantine sprang up ready helmed for war, addressed him by name. The darkness of night fled before the heavenly light that shone from the angel, and the messenger said :

THE MORNING OF BATTLE

"O Constantinus, the Ruler of Angels,
The Lord of all glory, the Master of heaven's hosts,
Claims from thee homage. Be not thou affrighted,
Though armies of aliens array them for battle,
Though terrible warriors threaten fierce conflict.
Look thou to the sky, to the throne of His glory ;
There seest thou surely the symbol of conquest."

Elene.

Vision of the Cross

Constantine looked up as the angel bade him, and saw, hovering in the air, a cross, splendid, glorious, adorned with gems and shining with heavenly light. On its wood letters were engraved, gleaming with unearthly radiance :

"With this shalt thou conquer the foe in the conflict,
And with it shalt hurl back the host of the heathen."

Elene.

Constantine is Cheered

Constantine read these words with awe and gladness, for indeed he knew not what deity had thus favoured him, but he would not reject the help of the Unknown God ; so he bowed his head in reverence, and when he looked again the cross and the angel had disappeared, and around him as he woke was the greyness of the rising dawn. The emperor summoned to his tent two soldiers from the troops, and bade them make a cross of wood to bear before the army. This they did, greatly marvelling, and Constantine called a standard-bearer, to whom he gave charge to bear forward the Standard of the Cross where the danger was greatest and the battle most fierce.

The Morning of Battle

When the day broke, and the two armies could see each other, both hosts arrayed themselves for battle, in serried ranks of armed warriors, shouting their war-cries.

> "Loud sang the trumpets to stern-minded foemen :
> The dewy-winged eagle watched them march onward,
> The horny-billed raven rejoiced in the battle-play,
> The sly wolf, the forest-thief, soon saw his heart's desire
> As the fierce warriors rushed at each other.
> Great was the shield-breaking, loud was the clamour,
> Hard were the hand-blows, and dire was the downfall,
> When first the heroes felt the keen arrow-shower.
> Soon did the Roman host fall on the death-doomed Huns,
> Thrust forth their deadly spears over the yellow shields,
> Broke with their battle-glaives breasts of the foemen."
>
> *Elene.*

The Cross is Raised

Then, when the battle was at its height, and the Romans knew not whether they would conquer or die fighting to the last, the standard-bearer raised the Cross, the token of promised victory, before all the host, and sang the chant of triumph. Onward he marched, and the Roman host followed him, pressing on resistless as the surging waves. The Huns, bewildered by the strange rally, and dreading the mysterious sign of some mighty god, rolled back, at first slowly, and then more and more quickly, till sullen retreat became panic rout, and they broke and fled. Multitudes were cut down as they fled, other multitudes were swept away by the devouring Danube as they tried to cross its current ; some, half dead, reached the other side, and saved their lives in fortresses, guarding the steep cliffs beyond the Danube. Few, very few they were who ever saw their native land again.

There was great rejoicing in the Roman army and in the Roman camp when Constantine returned in triumph with the wondrous Cross borne before him.

52

CONSTANTINE'S CONVERSION

He passed on to the city, and the people of Rome gazed with awe on the token of the Unknown God who had saved their city, but none would say who that God might be.

A Council Summoned

The emperor summoned a great council of all the wisest men in Rome, and when all were met he raised the Standard of the Cross in the midst and said :

> " Can any man tell me, by spells or by ancient lore,
> Who is the gracious God, giver of victory,
> Who came in His glory, with the Cross for His token,
> Who rescued my people and gave me the victory,
> Scattered my foemen and put the fierce Huns to flight,
> Showed me in heaven His sign of deliverance,
> The loveliest Cross of light, gleaming in glory ? "
>
> *Elene.*

At first no man could give him any answer—perhaps none dared—till after a long silence the wisest of all arose and said he had heard that the Cross was the sign of Christ the King of Heaven, and that the knowledge of His way was only revealed to men in baptism. When strict search was made some Christians were found, who preached the way of life to Constantine, and rejoiced that they might tell before men of the life and death, the Resurrection and Ascension of Jesus Christ, who redeemed mankind from the bonds of evil ; and then Constantine, being fully instructed and convinced, was baptized and became the first Christian emperor.

Constantine Desires to Find our Saviour's Cross

Constantine's heart, however, was too full of love for his new Lord to let him rest satisfied without some visible token of Christ's sojourn on earth. He longed to have, to keep for his own, one thing at least which Jesus had touched during His life, and his thoughts turned chiefly to that Cross which had been to himself both the sign of triumph and the guide to the way of life. Thus he again called together his Christian teachers, and inquired more closely where Christ had suffered.

"In Judæa, outside the walls of Jerusalem, He died on the Cross," they told him.

"Then there, near that city, so blest and so curst, we must seek His precious Cross," cried Constantine.

Summons his Mother Elene

Forthwith he summoned from Britain his mother, the British Princess Elene, and when she had been taught the truth, had been converted and baptized, he told her of his heart's desire, and begged her to journey to Jerusalem and seek the sacred Cross.

Elene herself, when she heard Constantine's words, was filled with wonder, and said: "Dear son, thy words have greatly rejoiced my heart, for know that I, too, have seen a vision, and would gladly seek the Holy Cross, where it lies hidden from the eyes of men."

Elene's Vision

"Now will I tell thee the brightest of visions,
Dreamt at the midnight when men lay in slumber.
Hovering in heaven saw I a radiant Cross,
Gloriously gold-adorned, shining in splendour;
Starry gems shone on it at the four corners,
Flashed from the shoulder-span five gleaming jewels.
Angels surrounded it, guarding it gladly.
Yet in its loveliness sad was that Cross to see,
For 'neath the gold and gems fast blood flowed from it,
Till it was all defiled with the dark drops."

Dream of the Rood.

ELENE UNDERTAKES THE QUEST

In this dream of Elene's the Cross spoke to her, and told her of the sad fate which had made of that hapless tree the Cross on which the Redeemer of mankind had released the souls of men from evil, on which He had spread out His arms to embrace mankind, had bowed His head, weary with the strife, and had given up His soul. All creation wept that hour, for Christ was on the Cross.

> " Yet His friends came to him, left not His corpse alone,
>   Took down the Mighty King from His sharp sufferings—
>   Humbly I bowed myself down to the hands of men.
>   Sadly they laid Him down in His dark rock-hewn grave,
>   Sadly they sang for Him dirges for death-doomed ones,
>   Sadly they left Him there as His fair corpse grew cold.
>   We, the three Crosses, stood mournful in loneliness,
>   Till evil-thinking men felled us all three to ground,
>   Sank us deep into earth, sealed us from sight of man."
>   *Dream of the Rood.*

She Undertakes the Quest

As Constantine had been guided by the heavenly vision of the True Cross, so now Elene would journey to the land of the Jews and find the reality of that Holy Cross. Her will and that of her son were one in this matter, so that before long the whole city resounded with the bustle and clamour of preparation, for Elene was to travel with the pomp and retinue befitting the mother of the Emperor of Rome.

> " There by the Wendel Sea stood the wave-horses.
>   Proudly the plunging ships sought out the ocean path.
>   Line followed after line of the tall brine-ploughs.
>   Forth went the water-steeds o'er the sea-serpent's road
>   Bright shields on the bulwarks oft broke the foaming surge.
>   Ne'er saw I lady lead such a fair following ! "
>   *Elene.*

She Comes to Judæa

Queen Elene had a prosperous voyage, and, after touching at the land of the Greeks, reached in due time the country of Judæa, and so, with good hope, came to Jerusalem. There, in the emperor's name, she summoned to an assembly all the oldest and wisest Jews, a congregation of a thousand venerable rabbis, learned in all the books of the Law and the Prophets, and proud that they were the Chosen People in a world of heathens, aliens from the True God. These she addressed at first with a blending of flattery and re-proach—flattery for the Chosen People, reproach for their perversity of wickedness—and, finally, peremptorily demanded an answer to any question she might ask of them. The Jews withdrew and deliberated sadly whether they durst refuse the request of so mighty a person as the emperor's mother, and, deciding that they durst not, returned to the hall where Elene sat in splendour on her throne and announced their readiness to reply to all her questions. Elene, however, bade them first lessen their numbers. They chose five hundred to reply for them, and on these she poured such bitter reproaches that they at last exclaimed :

> " Lady, we learnt of yore laws of the Hebrew folk
> Which all our fathers learnt from the true ark of God.
> Lady, we know not now why thou thus blamest us ;
> How has the Jewish race done grievous wrong to thee ? "
> *Elene.*

She Cross-questions the Rabbis

Elene only replied : "Go ye away, and choose out from among these five hundred those whose wisdom is great enough to show them without delay the answer to all things I require"; and again they left he presence. When they were alone, one of them, named Judas, said : "I know what this queen requires : she will demand to know from us where the Cross is concealed on which the Lord of the Christians was crucified ; but if we tell this secret I know well that the Jews will cease to bear rule on the earth, and our holy scriptures will be forgotten.   For my grandfather Zacchæus, as he lay dying, bade me confess the truth if ever man should inquire concerning the Holy Tree ; and when I asked how our nation had failed to recognise the Holy and Just One, he told me that he had always withdrawn himself from the evil deeds of his generation, and their leaders had been blinded by their own unrighteousness, and had slain the Lord of Glory.   And he ended :

> "'Thus I and my father secretly held the Faith.
> Now warn I thee, my son, speak not thou mockingly
> Of the true Son of God reigning in glory :
> For whom my Stephen died, and the Apostle Paul.'
> *Elene.*

Now," said Judas, "since things are so, decide ye what we shall reveal, or what conceal, if this queen asks us."

One Appointed to Answer her

The other elders replied : "Do what seems to thee best, since thou alone knowest this.   Never have we heard of these strange secrets.   Do thou according to thy great wisdom."

While they still deliberated came the heralds with silver trumpets, which they blew, proclaiming aloud :

> "The mighty Queen calls you, O men, to the Council,
> That she may hear from you of your decision.
> Great is the need ye have of all your wisdom."
> *Elene.*

Slowly and reluctantly the Jewish rabbis returned to the council-chamber, and listened to Elene as she

57

plied them with questions about the ancient prophecies and the death of Christ; but to all her inquiries they professed entire ignorance, until, in her wrath, the queen threatened them with death by fire. Then they led forward Judas, saying : " He can reveal the mysteries of Fate, for he is of noble race, the son of a prophet. He will tell thee truth, O Queen, as thy soul loveth." Thus Elene let the other Jews go in peace, and took Judas for a hostage.

She Threatens him

Now Elene greeted Judas and said :

> " Lo, thou perverse one, two things lie before thee,
> Or death or life for thee : choose which thou wilt."
> *Elene.*

Judas replied to her, since he could not escape :

> " If the starved wanderer lost on the barren moors
> Sees both a stone and bread, easily in his reach,
> Which, O Queen, thinkest thou he will reject ? "
> *Elene.*

Thereupon Elene said : "If thou wouldst dwell in heaven with the angels, reveal to me where the True Cross lies hidden." Now Judas was very sad, for his choice lay between death and the revealing of the fateful secret, but he still tried to evade giving an answer, protesting that too long a time had passed for the secret to be known. Elene retorted that the Trojan War was a still more ancient story, and yet was still well known ; but Judas replied that men are bound to remember the valiant deeds of nations ; he himself had never even heard the story of which she spoke. This obstinacy angered the queen greatly, and she demanded to be taken at once to the hill of Calvary, that she might purify it, for the sake of Him who died there ; but Judas only repeated :

> "I know not the place, nor aught of that field."
>
> *Elene.*

Queen Elene was yet more enraged by his stubborn denials, and determined to obtain by force an answer to her questions. Calling her servants, she bade them thrust Judas into a deep dry cistern, where he lay, starving, bound hand and foot, for seven nights and days. On the seventh day his stubborn spirit yielded, and Judas lifted up his voice and called aloud, saying :

> " Now I beseech you all by the great God of heaven
> That you will lift me up out of this misery.
> I will tell all I know of that True Holy Cross,
> Now I no longer can hide it for heavy pain.
> Hunger has daunted me through all these dreary days.
> Foolish was I of yore ; late I confess it."
>
> *Elene.*

He Guides her to Calvary

The message was brought to Elene where she waited to hear tidings, and she bade her servants lift the weakened Judas from the dark pit ; then they led him, half dead with hunger, out of the city to the hill of Calvary. There Judas prayed to the God whom he now feared and worshipped for a sign, some token to guide them in their search for the Holy Cross. As he prayed a sweet-smelling vapour, curling upwards like the incense-wreaths around the altar, rose to the skies from the summit of the hill. The sign was manifest to all, and Judas gave thanks to God for His great mercy ; then, bidding the wondering soldiers help him, he began to dig. By this time all men knew what they sought, and each wished to uncover the holy relic, so that all dug with great zeal, until, under twenty feet of earth, they uncovered three crosses, so well preserved that they lay in the earth just as the Jews had hidden them.

Three Crosses Found

Judas and all rejoiced greatly at this marvel, and, reverently raising the three crosses, they bore them into the city, and laid them at the feet of Queen Elene, whose first rapture of joy was speedily turned to perplexity as she realised that she knew not which was that sacred Cross on which the King of Angels had suffered. " For," she said, " two thieves were crucified with him." But even Judas could not clear her doubts.

> " Lo we have heard of this from all the holy books,
> That there were with him two in His deep anguish.
> They hung in death by Him ; He was Himself the third.
> Heaven was all darkened o'er at that dread moment.
> Say, if thou rightly canst, which of these crosses
> Is that blest Tree of Fate which bore the Heaven's King."
> *Elene.*

A Miracle to Reveal our Saviour's Cross

Judas, however, suggested that the crosses should be carried to the midst of the city, and that they should pray for another miracle to reveal the truth. This was done at dawn, and the triumphant band of Christians raised hymns of prayer and praise until the ninth hour ; then came a mighty crowd bearing a young man lifeless on his bier. At Judas's command they laid down the bier, and he, praying to God, solemnly raised in turn each of the crosses and held it above the dead man's head. Lifeless still he lay as Judas raised the first two, but when he held above the corpse the third, the True Cross, the dead man arose instantly, body and soul reunited, one in praising God, and the whole multitude broke out into shouts of thanksgiving to the

The Queen's dilemma

"What raptures of rejoicing there were!"

Lord of Hosts, and the sacred relic was restored to the loving care of the queen.

The Nails Sought for

Nevertheless Elene's longing was still unsatisfied. She called Judas (whose new name in baptism was Cyriacus) and begged him to fulfil her desires, and to pray to God that she might find the nails which had pierced the Lord of Life, where they lay hidden from men in the ground of Calvary. Leading her out of the town, Cyriacus again prayed on Mount Calvary that God would send forth a token and reveal the secret. As he prayed there came from heaven a leaping flame, brighter than the sun, which touched the surface of the ground here and there, and kindled in each place a tiny star. When they dug at the spots where the stars shone they found each nail shining visibly and casting a radiance of its own in the dark earth. So Elene had obtained her heart's desire, and had now the True Cross and the Holy Nails.

Good News Brought to Constantine

Word of his mother's success was sent to the Emperor Constantine, and he was asked what should be done with these glorious relics. He bade Elene build in Jerusalem a glorious church, and make therein a beautiful shrine of silver, where the Holy Cross should be guarded for all generations by priests who should watch it day and night. This was done, but the nails were still Elene's possession, and she was at a loss how to preserve these holy relics, when the devout Cyriacus, now ordained Bishop of Jerusalem, went to her and said : "O lady and queen, take these precious nails for thy son the emperor. Make with them rings for his horse's bridle. Victory shall ever go with them ; they shall be called Holy to God, and he shall be called blessed whom that horse bears." The advice pleased the queen, and she had wrought a glorious bridle, adorned with the Holy Nails, and sent it to her son. Constantine received it with all reverence, and ordained that April 24, the day of the miracle of revelation, should henceforth be kept in honour as " Holy Cross Day." Thus were the emperor's zeal and the royal mother's devotion rewarded, and Christendom was enriched by some of its most precious treasures, the True Cross and the Holy Nails.

CHAPTER IV : THE COMPASSION OF CONSTANTINE

Youth of Constantine

CONSTANTINE THE GREAT was the eldest son of the Roman Emperor Constantius and the British Princess Helena, or Elena, and was brought up as a devout worshipper of the many gods of Rome. The lad grew up strong and handsome, of a tall and majestic figure, skilled in all warlike exercises, and, as he fought in the civil wars between the various Roman emperors, he showed himself a bold and prudent general in battle, a friendly and popular leader in time of peace. The popularity of the youthful Constantine was dangerous to him, and he needed, and showed, great skill in evading the deadly jealousy of the old Emperor Diocletian, and the hatred of his father's rival, Galerius. At last, however, his position became so dangerous that Constantius felt his son's life was no longer safe, and earnestly begged him to visit his native land of Britain, where Constantius had just been proclaimed emperor and had defeated the wild Caledonians. The excuse given was that Constantius was in bad health and needed his son ; but not until the young man was actually in Britain would his anxious father avow that he feared for his son's life.

Acclaimed Emperor

When the half-British Constantius died, Constantine, who was the favourite of the Roman soldiery of the west, was at once acclaimed as emperor by his devoted troops. He professed unwillingness to accept the honour, and it is said that he even tried in vain to escape on horseback from the affectionate solicitations of his soldiers. Seeing the uselessness of further protest,

Constantine accepted the imperial title, and wrote to Galerius claiming the throne and justifying his acceptance of the unsought dignity thrust upon him. Galerius acquiesced in the inevitable, and granted Constantine the inferior title of "Cæsar," with rule over Western Europe, and the wise prince was content to wait until favouring circumstances should destroy his rivals and give him that sole sway over the Roman Empire for which he was so well fitted. He had now reached the age of thirty, had fought valiantly in the wars in Egypt and Persia, and had risen by merit to the rank of tribune. His marriage with Fausta, the daughter of the Emperor Maximian, and his elevation to the rank of Augustus brought him nearer to the attainment of his ambition ; and at length the defeat and death of his rivals placed him at the head of the world-wide empire of Rome. It is to some period previous to Constantine's elevation to the supreme authority that we must refer the following story, told by Gower in his " Confessio Amantis " as an example of that true charity which is the mother of pity, and makes a man's heart so tender that,

> "Though he might himself relieve,
> Yet he would not another grieve,"

but in order to give pleasure to others would bear his own trouble alone.

Becomes a Leper

The noble Constantine, Emperor of Rome, was in the full flower of his age, goodly to look upon, strong and happy, when a great and sudden affliction came upon him : leprosy attacked him. The horrible disease showed itself first in his face, so that no concealment was possible, and if he had not been the emperor he would have been driven out to live in the forests and wilds. The leprosy spread from his face till it entirely covered his body, and became so bad that he could no longer ride out or show himself to his people. When all cures had been tried and had failed, Constantine withdrew himself from his lords, gave up all use of arms, abandoned his imperial duties, and shut himself in his palace, where he lived such a secluded life in his own apartments that Rome had, as it were, no lord, and all men throughout the empire talked of his illness and prayed their gods to heal him. When everything seemed to be in vain, Constantine yielded to the prayer of his council, that he would summon all the doctors, learned men, and physicians from every realm to Rome, that they might consider his illness and try if any cure could be found for his malady.

Rewards Offered for his Cure

A proclamation went forth throughout the world and great rewards were offered to any man who should heal the emperor. Tempted by the rewards and the great fame to be won, there came leeches and physicians from Persia and Arabia, and from every land that owned the sway of Rome, philosophers from Greece and Egypt, and magicians and sorcerers from the unexplored desert of the east. But, though Constantine tried all the remedies suggested or recommended by the wise men, his leprosy grew no better, but rather worse, and even magic could give him no help.

Again the learned men assembled and consulted what they should advise, for all were loath to abandon the emperor in his great distress, but they were all at a loss. They sat in silence, till at last one very old and very wise man, a great physician from Arabia, arose and said :

A Desperate Remedy

"Now that all else has failed, and naught is of any avail, I will tell of a remedy of which I have heard. It will, I believe, certainly cure our beloved emperor, but it is very terrible, and therefore I was loath to name it till every other means had been tried and failed, for it is a cruel thing for any man to do. Let the Emperor dip himself in a full bath of the blood of infants and children, seven years old or under, and he shall be healed, and his leprosy shall fall from him; for this malady is not natural to his body, and it demands an unnatural cure."

Constantine Assents Regretfully

The proposal was a terrible one to the assembly, and many would not agree to it at first, but when they considered that nothing else would heal the emperor they at length gave way, and sent two from among themselves to bring the news to Constantine, who was waiting for them in his darkened room. He was horrified when he heard the counsel they brought, and at first utterly refused to carry out so evil a plan; but because his life was very dear to his people, and because he felt that he had a great work to do in the world, he ultimately agreed, with many tears, to try the terrible remedy.

A Cruel Proclamation

Thereupon the council drew up letters, under the emperor's hand and seal, and sent them out to all the world, bidding all mothers with children of seven years of age or under to bring them with speed to Rome, that there the blood of the innocents might prove healing to the emperor's malady. Alas! what weeping and

66

wailing there was among the mothers when they heard this cruel decree ! How they cried, and clasped their babes to their breasts, and how they called Constantine more cruel than Herod, who killed the Holy Innocents ! The eastern ruler, they said, slew only the infants of one poor village, but their emperor, more ruthless, claimed the lives of all the young children of his whole empire.

Constantine is Conscience-stricken

But though the mothers lamented bitterly, they must needs bow to the emperor's decree, whether they were lief or loath, and thus a great multitude gathered in the great courtyard of the imperial palace at Rome : women nursing sucking-babes at the breast, or holding toddling infants by the hand, or with little children running by their sides, and all so heart-broken and woebegone that many swooned for very grief. The mothers wailed aloud, the children cried, and the tumult grew until Constantine heard it, where he sat lonely and wretched in his darkened room. He looked out of his window on the mournful sight in the courtyard, and was roused as from a trance, saying to himself : "O Divine Providence, who hast formed all men alike, lo ! the poor man is born, lives, suffers, and dies, just as does the rich ; to wise man and fool alike come sickness and health ; and no man may avoid that fortune which Nature's law hath ordained for him. Likewise to all men are Nature's gifts of strength and beauty, of soul and reason, freely and fully given, so that the poor child is born as capable of virtue as the king's son ; and to each man is given free will to choose virtue or vice. Yet thou givest to men diversity of rank, wealth or poverty, lordship or servitude, not always according to their deserts ; so much the more virtuous should that man be to whom thou hast put other men in subjection, men who are nevertheless his fellows and wear his likeness. Thou, O God, who hast put Nature and the whole universe under law, wouldst have all men rule themselves by law, and thou hast said that a man must do to others such things as he would have done to himself."

His Noble Resolve

Thus Constantine spoke within himself as he stood by the window and looked upon the weeping mothers and children, the very sentinels of his palace pitying them, and trying in vain to comfort them ; and a strife grew strong within him between his natural longing for healing and deliverance from this loathsome disease which had darkened his life, and the pity he felt for these poor creatures, and his horror at the thought of so much human blood to be shed for himself alone. The great moaning of the woeful mothers came to him, and the pitiful crying of the children, and he thought : "What am I that my health is to outweigh the lives and happiness of so many of my people ? Is my life of more value to the world than those of all the children who must shed their blood for my healing ? Surely each babe is as precious as Constantine the Emperor !" Thus his heart grew so tender and so full of compassion that he chose rather to die by this terrible sickness than to commit so great a slaughter of innocent children, and he renounced all other physicians, and trusted himself wholly to God's care.

He Announces his Determination

He at once summoned his council, and announced to them his resolution, giving as his reason, " He that will be truly master must be ever servant to pity ! "

and without delay the anxious mothers were told that their children were free and safe, for the emperor had renounced the cure, and needed their blood no longer. What raptures of rejoicing there were, what outpouring of blessing on the emperor, what songs of praise and thanks from the women wild with joy, cannot be fully told ; and yet greater grew their joy and thankfulness when Constantine, calling his high officials, bade them take all his gathered treasures and distribute them among the poor women, that they might feed and clothe their children, and so return home untouched by any loss, and recompensed in some degree for their sufferings. Thus did Constantine obey the behests of pity, and try to atone for the wrong to which he had consented in his heart, and which he had so nearly done to his people.

The Victims Sent Home Happy

Home to all parts of the Roman Empire went the women, bearing with them their happy children, and the rich gifts they had received. Each one thanked and blessed the emperor, and sang his praises, where before she had passed with tears and bitter curses on his head ; each woman shared her joy with her neighbours ; and the very children learnt from their mothers and fathers to pray for the healing of their great lord, who had given up his own will and sacrificed his own cure for gentle pity's sake. Thus the whole world prayed for Constantine's healing.

A Vision

Lo ! it never yet was known that charity went unrequited and this Constantine now learnt in his own glad experience ; for that same night, as he lay asleep, God sent to him a vision of two strangers, men of noble face and form, whom he reverenced greatly, and who said to him : " O Constantine, because thou hast obeyed the voice of pity, thou hast deserved pity ; therefore shalt thou find such mercy, that God, in His great pity, will save thee. Double healing shalt thou receive, first for thy body, and next for thy woeful soul ; both alike shall be made whole. And that thou mayst not despair, God will grant thee a sign—thy leprosy shall not increase till thou hast sent to Mount Celion, to Sylvester and all his clergy. There they dwell in secret for dread of thee, who hast been a foe to the law of Christ, and hast destroyed those who preach in His Holy Name. Now thou hast appeased God somewhat by thy good deed, since thou hast had pity on the innocent blood, and hast spared it ; for this thou shalt find teaching, from Sylvester, to the salvation of both body and soul. Thou wilt need no other leech." The emperor, who had listened with eagerness and awe, now spoke : " Great thanks I owe to you, my lords, and I will indeed do as ye have said ; but one thing I would pray you—what shall I tell Sylvester of the name or estate of those who send me to him ? " The two strangers said : " We are the Apostles Peter and Paul, who endured death here in thy city of Rome for the Holy Name of Christ, and we bid Sylvester teach and baptize thee into the true faith. So shall the Roman Empire become the kingdom of the Lord and of His Christ." So saying, they blessed him, and passed into the heavens out of his sight, and Constantine awoke from his slumber and knew that he had seen a vision. He called aloud eagerly, and his servants waiting in an outer room ran in to him quickly, for there was urgency in his voice. To them Constantine told his vision and the command which was laid upon him.

They filled the great vessel of silver with pure water

" Havelok sat up surprised "

CONSTANTINE BAPTIZED

Sylvester Summoned

Messengers rode in hot haste to Mount Celion, and inquired long and anxiously for Sylvester. At last they found him, a holy and venerable man, and summoned him, saying : " The Emperor calls for thee : come, therefore, at once." Sylvester's clergy were greatly affrighted, not knowing what this summons might mean, and dreading the death of their dear bishop and master ; but he went forth gladly, not knowing to what fate he was going. When he was brought to the palace the emperor greeted him kindly, and told him all his dream, and the command of the Apostles Peter and Paul, and ended with these words : " Now I have done as the vision bade, and have fetched thee here : tell me, I pray, the glad tidings which shall bring healing to my body and soul." When Sylvester heard this speech he was filled with joy and wonder, and thanked God for the vision He had sent to the emperor, and then he began to preach to him the Christian faith : he told of the Fall of Man, and the redemption of the world by the death and resurrection of Jesus Christ, of the Ascension of Jesus and His return at the Day of Judgment, of the justice of God, who will judge all men impartially according to their works, good or bad, and of the life of joy or misery to come. As Sylvester taught, the monarch listened and believed, and, when the tale was ended, announced his conversion to the true faith, and said he was ready, with his whole heart and soul, to be baptized.

Constantine Baptized

At the emperor's command, they took the great vessel of silver which had been made for the children's blood, and Sylvester bade them fill it with pure water from the well. When that was done with all haste, he bade Constantine stand therein, so that the water reached to his chin. As the holy rite began, a great light like the sun's rays shone from heaven into the place, and upon Constantine ; and as the sacred words were being read there fell now and again from his body scales like those of a fish, till there was nothing left of his horrible disease ; and thus in baptism Constantine was purified in body and soul.

CHAPTER V : HAVELOK THE DANE

The Origin of the Story

THE Danish occupation of England has left a very strong mark on our country in various ways—on its place-names, its racial characteristics, its language, its literature, and, in part, on its ideals. The legend of Havelok the Dane, with its popularity and widespread influence, is one result of Danish supremacy. It is thought that the origin of the legend, which contains a twofold version of the common story of the cruel guardian and the persecuted heir, is to be found in Wales ; but, however that may be, it is certain that in the continual rise and fall of small tribal kingdoms, Celtic or Teutonic, English or Danish, the circumstances out of which the story grew must have been common enough. Kings who died leaving helpless heirs to the guardianship of ambitious and wicked nobles were not rare in the early days of Britain, Wales, or Denmark ; the murder of the heir and the usurpation of the kingdom by the cruel regent were no unusual occurrences. The opportunity of localising the early legend seems to have come with the growing fame of Anlaf, or Olaf, Sihtricson, who was known to the Welsh as Abloec or Habloc. His adventurous life included a threefold expulsion from his inheritance of Northumbria, a marriage with the daughter of King Constantine III. of Scotland, and a family kinship with King Athelstan of England. In Anlaf Curan (as he was called) we have an historical hero on whom various romantic stories were gradually fathered, because of his adventurous life and his strong personality. These stories finally crystalized in a form which shows the English and Danish love of physical prowess (Havelok is the strongest man in the kingdom), as well as a certain cruelty of revenge which is more peculiarly Danish.   There is resentment of the Norman predominance to be found in the popularity of a story which shows the kitchen-boy excelling all the nobles in manly exercises, and the heiress to the kingdom wedded in scorn, as so many Saxon heiresses were after the Conquest, to a mere scullion.   There can be no doubt, however, that Havelok stood to mediæval England as a hero of the strong arm, a champion of the populace against the ruling race, and that his royal birth and dignity were a concession to historic facts and probabilities, not much regarded by the common people.   The story, again, showed another truly humble hero, Grim the fisher, whose loyalty was supposed to account for the special trading privileges of his town, Grimsby.   In Grim the story found a character who was in reality a hero of the poor and lowly, with the characteristic devotion of the tribesman to his chief, of the vassal to his lord, a devotion which was handed on from father to son, so that a second generation continued the services, and received the rewards, of the father who risked life and all for the sake of his king's heir.

The reader will not fail to notice the characteristic anachronisms which give to life in Saxon England in the tenth century the colour of the Norman chivalry of the thirteenth.

Havelok and Godard

In Denmark, long ago, lived a good king named Birkabeyn, rich and powerful, a great warrior and a man of mighty prowess, whose rule was undisputed over the whole realm.   He had three children—two daughters, named Swanborow and Elfleda the Fair, and one young and goodly son, Havelok, the heir to all

his dominions.   All too soon came the day that no
man can avoid, when Death would call King Birkabeyn
away, and he grieved sore over his young children to
be left fatherless and unprotected ; but, after much
reflection, and prayers to God for wisdom to help
his choice, he called to him Jarl Godard, a trusted
counsellor and friend, and committed into his hands
the care of the realm and of the three royal children,
until Havelok should be of age to .be knighted and
rule the land himself.   King Birkabeyn felt that such a
charge was too great a temptation for any man unbound
by oaths of fealty and honour, and although he did not
distrust his friend, he required Godard to swear,

> " By altar and by holy service book,
>   By bells that call the faithful to the church,
>   By blessed sacrament, and sacred rites,
>   By Holy Rood, and Him who died thereon,
>   That thou wilt truly rule and keep my realm,
>   Wilt guard my babes in love and loyalty,
>   Until my son be grown, and dubbèd knight:
>   That thou wilt then resign to him his land,
>   His power and rule, and all that owns his sway."

Jarl Godard took this most solemn oath at once,
with many protestations of affection and whole-hearted
devotion to the dying king and his heir, and King
Birkabeyn died happy in the thought that his children
would be well cared for during their helpless youth.

When the funeral rites were celebrated Jarl Godard
assumed the rule of the country, and, under pretext of
securing the safety of the royal children, removed them
to a strong castle, where no man was allowed access to
them, and where they were kept so closely that the
royal residence became a prison in all but name.
Godard, finding Denmark submit to his government
without resistance, began to adopt measures to rid

75

himself of the real heirs to the throne, and gave orders that food and clothes should be supplied to the three children in such scanty quantities that they might die of hardship; but since they were slow to succumb to this cruel, torturing form of murder, he resolved to slay them suddenly, knowing that no one durst call him to account. Having steeled his heart against all pitiful thoughts, he went to the castle, and was taken to the inner dungeon where the poor babes lay shivering and weeping for cold and hunger. As he entered, Havelok, who was even then a bold lad, greeted him courteously, and knelt before him, with clasped hands, begging a boon.

"Why do you weep and wail so sore?" asked Godard.

"Because we are so hungry," answered Havelok. "We have so little food, and we have no servants to wait on us; they do not give us half as much as we could eat; we are shivering with cold, and our clothes are all in rags. Woe to us that we were ever born! Is there in the land no more corn with which men can make bread for us? We are nearly dead from hunger."

These pathetic words had no effect on Godard, who had resolved to yield to no pity and show no mercy. He seized the two little girls as they lay cowering together, clasping one another for warmth, and cut their throats, letting the bodies of the hapless babies fall to the floor in a pool of blood; and then, turning to Havelok, aimed his knife at the boy's heart. The poor child, terrified by the awful fate of the two girls, knelt again before him and begged for mercy:

> "Fair lord, have mercy on me now, I pray!
> Look on my helpless youth, and pity me!
> Oh, let me live, and I will yield you all—
> My realm of Denmark will I leave to you,

And swear that I will ne'er assail your sway.
Oh, pity me, lord! be compassionate!
And I will flee far from this land of mine,
And vow that Birkabeyn was ne'er my sire!"

Jarl Godard was touched by Havelok's piteous speech, and felt some faint compassion, so that he could not slay the lad himself; yet he knew that his only safety was in Havelok's death.

"If I let him go," thought he, "Havelok will at last work me woe! I shall have no peace in my life, and my children after me will not hold the lordship of Denmark in safety, if Havelok escapes! Yet I cannot slay him with my own hands. I will have him cast into the sea with an anchor about his neck: thus at least his body will not float."

Godard left Havelok kneeling in terror, and, striding from the tower, leaving the door locked behind him, he sent for an ignorant fisherman, Grim, who, he thought, could be frightened into doing his will. When Grim came he was led into an ante-room, where Godard, with terrible look and voice, addressed him thus:

"Grim, thou knowest thou art my thrall." "Yea, fair lord," quoth Grim, trembling at Godard's stern voice. "And I can slay thee if thou dost disobey me." "Yea, lord; but how have I offended you?" "Thou hast not yet; but I have a task for thee, and if thou dost it not, dire punishment shall fall upon thee." "Lord, what is the work that I must do?" asked the poor fisherman. "Tarry: I will show thee." Then Godard went into the inner room of the tower, whence he returned leading a fair boy, who wept bitterly. "Take this boy secretly to thy house, and keep him there till dead of night; then launch thy boat, row out to sea, and fling him therein with an anchor round his neck, so that I shall see him never again."

Grim looked curiously at the weeping boy, and said: "What reward shall I have if I work this sin for you?"

Godard replied: "The sin will be on my head, as I am thy lord and bid thee do it; but I will make thee a freeman, noble and rich, and my friend, if thou wilt do this secretly and discreetly."

Thus reassured and bribed, Grim suddenly took the boy, flung him to the ground, and bound him hand and foot with cord which he took from his pockets. So anxious was he to secure the boy that he drew the cords very tight, and Havelok suffered terrible pain; he could not cry out, for a handful of rags was thrust into his mouth and over his nostrils, so that he could hardly breathe. Then Grim flung the poor boy into a horrible black sack, and carried him thus from the castle, as if he were bringing home broken food for his family. When Grim reached his poor cottage, where his wife Leve was waiting for him, he slung the sack from his shoulder and gave it to her, saying, "Take good care of this boy as of thy life. I am to drown him at midnight, and if I do so my lord has promised to make me a free man and give me great wealth."

When Dame Leve heard this she sprang up and flung the lad down in a corner, and nearly broke his head with the crash against the earthen floor. There Havelok lay, bruised and aching, while the couple went to sleep, leaving the room all dark but for the red glow from the fire. At midnight Grim awoke to do his lord's behest, and Dame Leve, going to the living-room to kindle a light, was terrified by a mysterious gleam as bright as day which shone around the boy on the floor and streamed from his mouth. Leve hastily called Grim to see this wonder, and

78

together they released Havelok from the gag and bonds and examined his body, when they found on the right shoulder the token of true royalty, a cross of red gold.

"God knows," quoth Grim, "that this is the heir of our land. He will come to rule in good time, will bear sway over England and Denmark, and will punish the cruel Godard." Then, weeping sore, the loyal fisherman fell down at Havelok's feet, crying, "Lord, have mercy on me and my wife! We are thy thralls, and never will we do aught against thee. We will nourish thee until thou canst rule, and will hide thee from Godard; and thou wilt perchance give me my freedom in return for thy life."

At this unexpected address Havelok sat up surprised, and rubbed his bruised head and said : "I am nearly dead, what with hunger, and thy cruel bonds, and the gag. Now bring me food in plenty!" "Yea, lord," said Dame Leve, and bustled about, bringing the best they had in the hut; and Havelok ate as if he had fasted for three days; and then he was put to bed, and slept in peace while Grim watched over him.

However, Grim went the next morning to Jarl Godard and said : "Lord, I have done your behest, and drowned the boy with an anchor about his neck. He is safe, and now, I pray you, give me my reward, the gold and other treasures, and make me a freeman as you have promised." But Godard only looked fiercely at him and said : "What, wouldst thou be an earl? Go home, thou foul churl, and be ever a thrall! It is enough reward that I do not hang thee now for insolence, and for thy wicked deeds. Go speedily, else thou mayst stand and palter with me too long." And Grim shrank quietly away, lest Godard should slay him for the murder of Havelok.

79

Now Grim saw in what a terrible plight he stood, at the mercy of this cruel and treacherous man, and he took counsel with himself and consulted his wife, and the two decided to flee from Denmark to save their lives. Gradually Grim sold all his stock, his cattle, his nets, everything that he owned, and turned it into good pieces of gold ; then he bought and secretly fitted out and provisioned a ship, and at last, when all was ready, carried on board Havelok (who had lain hidden all this time), his own three sons and two daughters ; then when he and his wife had gone on board he set sail, and, driven by a favourable wind, reached the shores of England.

Goldborough and Earl Godrich

Meanwhile in England a somewhat similar fate had befallen a fair princess named Goldborough. When her father, King Athelwold, lay dying all his people mourned, for he was the flower of all fair England for knighthood, justice, and mercy ; and he himself grieved sorely for the sake of his little daughter, soon to be left an orphan. "What will she do ?" moaned he. "She can neither speak nor walk ! If she were only able to ride, to rule England, and to guard herself from shame, I should have no grief, even if I died and left her alone, while I lived in the joy of paradise !"

Then Athelwold summoned a council to be held at Winchester, and asked the advice of the nobles as to the care of the infant Goldborough. They with one accord recommended Earl Godrich of Cornwall to be made regent for the little princess ; and the earl, on being appointed, swore with all solemn rites that he would marry her at twelve years old to the highest, the best, fairest, and strongest man alive, and in the meantime would train her in all royal virtues and customs. So King Athelwold died, and was buried with great lamentations, and Godrich ruled the land as regent. He was a strict but just governor, and England had great peace, without and within, under his severe rule, for all lived in awe of him, though no man loved him. Goldborough grew and throve in all ways, and became famous through the land for her gracious beauty and gentle and virtuous demeanour. This roused the jealousy of Earl Godrich, who had played the part of king so long that he almost believed himself King of England, and he began to consider how he could secure the kingdom for himself and his son. Thereupon he had Goldborough taken from Winchester, where she kept royal state, to Dover, where she was imprisoned in the castle, and strictly secluded from all her friends ; there she remained, with poor clothes and scanty food, awaiting a champion to uphold her right.

Havelok Becomes Cook's Boy

When Grim sailed from Denmark to England he landed in the Humber, at the place now called Grimsby, and there established himself as a fisherman. So successful was he that for twelve years he supported his family well, and carried his catches of fish far afield, even to Lincoln, where rare fish always brought a good price. In all this time Grim never once called on Havelok for help in the task of feeding the family ; he reverenced his king, and the whole household served Havelok with the utmost deference, and often went with scanty rations to satisfy the boy's great appetite. At length Havelok began to think how selfishly he was living, and how much food he consumed, and was filled with shame when he realized how his foster-father toiled unweariedly while he did nothing to help. In his remorseful meditations it became clear to him that,

81

though a king's son, he ought to do some useful work. "Of what use," thought he, is my great strength and stature if I do not employ it for some good purpose? There is no shame in honest toil. I will work for my food, and try to make some return to Father Grim, who has done so much for me. I will gladly bear his baskets of fish to market, and I will begin to-morrow."

On the next day, in spite of Grim's protests, Havelok carried a load of fish equal to four men's burden to Grimsby market, and sold it successfully, returning home with the money he received; and this he did day by day, till a famine arose and fish and food both became scarce. Then Grim, more concerned for Havelok than for his own children, called the youth to him and bade him try his fortunes in Lincoln, for his own sake and for theirs; he would be better fed, and the little food Grim could get would go further among the others if Havelok were not there. The one obstacle in the way was Havelok's lack of clothes, and Grim overcame that by sacrificing his boat's sail to make Havelok a coarse tunic. That done, they bade each other farewell, and Havelok started for Lincoln, barefooted and bareheaded, for his only garment was the sailcloth tunic. In Lincoln Havelok found no friends and no food for two days, and he was desperate and faint with hunger, when he heard a call : " Porters, porters ! hither to me ! " Roused to new vigour by the chance of work, Havelok rushed with the rest, and bore down and hurled aside the other porters so vigorously that he was chosen to carry provisions for Bertram, the earl's cook ; and in return he received the first meal he had eaten for nearly three days.

On the next day Havelok again overthrew the porters, and, knocking down at least sixteen, secured the work. This time he had to carry fish, and his basket

" Havelok again overthrew the porters "

" 'Welcome, dear lord!' "

was so laden that he bore nearly a cartload, with which he ran to the castle. There the cook, amazed at his strength, first gave him a hearty meal, and the· offered him good service under himself, with food and lodging for his wages. This offer Havelok accepted, and was installed as cook's boy, and employed in all the lowest offices—carrying wood, water, turf, hewing logs, lifting, fetching, carrying—and in all he showed himself a wonderfully strong worker, with unfailing good temper and gentleness, so that the little children all loved the big, gentle, fair-haired youth who worked so quietly and played with them so merrily. When Havelok's old tunic became worn out, his master, the cook, took pity on him and gave him a new suit, and then it could be seen how handsome and tall and strong a youth this cook's boy really was, and his fame spread far and wide round Lincoln Town.

Havelok and Goldborough

At the great fair of Lincoln, sports of all kinds were indulged in, and in these Havelok took his part, for the cook, proud of his mighty scullion, urged him to compete in all the games and races. As Earl Godrich had summoned his Parliament to meet that year at Lincoln, there was a great concourse of spectators, and even the powerful Earl Regent himself sometimes watched the sports and cheered the champions. The first contest was "putting the stone," and the stone chosen was so weighty that none but the most stalwart could lift it above the knee—none could raise it to his breast. This sport was new to Havelok, who had never seen it before, but when the cook bade him try his strength he lifted the stone easily and threw it more than twelve feet. This mighty deed caused his fame to be spread, not only among the poor servants with whom Havelok was classed, but also among the barons, their masters, and Havelok's Stone became a landmark in Lincoln. Thus Godrich heard of a youth who stood head and shoulders taller than other men, and was stronger, more handsome—and yet a mere common scullion. The news brought him a flash of inspiration : " Here is the highest, strongest, best man in all England, and him shall Goldborough wed. I shall keep my vow to the letter, and England must fall to me, for Goldborough's royal blood will be lost by her marriage with a thrall, the people will refuse her obedience, and England will cast her out."

Godrich therefore brought Goldborough to Lincoln, received her with bell-ringing and seemly rejoicing, and bade her prepare for her wedding. This the princess refused to do until she knew who was her destined husband, for she said she would wed no man who was not of royal birth. Her firmness drove Earl Godrich to fierce wrath, and he burst out : " Wilt thou be queen and mistress over me ? Thy pride shall be brought down : thou shalt have no royal spouse : a vagabond and scullion shalt thou wed, and that no later than to-morrow ! Curses on him who speaks thee fair ! " In vain the princess wept and bemoaned herself : the wedding was fixed for the morrow morn.

The next day at dawn Earl Godrich sent for Havelok, the mighty cook's boy, and asked him : " Wilt thou take a wife ? "

" Nay," quoth Havelok, " that will I not. I cannot feed her, much less clothe and lodge her. My very garments are not my own, but belong to the cook, my master." Godrich fell upon Havelok and beat him furiously, saying, " Unless thou wilt take the wench I give thee for wife I will hang or blind thee " ; and so, in great fear, Havelock agreed to the wedding. At

84

once Goldborough was brought, and forced into an immediate marriage, under penalty of banishment or burning as a witch if she refused. And thus the unwilling couple were united by the Archbishop of York, who had come to attend the Parliament.

Never was there so sad a wedding! The people murmured greatly at this unequal union, and pitied the poor princess, thus driven to wed a man of low birth; and Goldborough herself wept pitifully, but resigned herself to God's will. All men now acknowledged with grief that she and her husband could have no claim to the English throne, and thus Godrich seemed to have gained his object. Havelok and his unwilling bride recognised that they would not be safe near Godrich, and as Havelok had no home in Lincoln to which he could take the princess, he determined to go back to his faithful foster-father, Grim, and put the fair young bride under his loyal protection. Sorrowfully, with grief and shame in their hearts, Havelok and Goldborough made their way on foot to Grimsby, only to find the loyal Grim dead; but his five children were alive and in prosperity. When they saw Havelok and his wife they fell on their knees and saluted them with all respect and reverence. In their joy to see their king again, these worthy fisherfolk forgot their newly won wealth, and said: "Welcome, dear lord, and thy fair lady! What joy is ours to see thee again, for thy subjects are we, and thou canst do with us as thou wilt. All that we have is thine, and if thou wilt dwell with us we will serve thee and thy wife truly in all ways!" This greeting surprised Goldborough, who began to suspect some mystery, and she was greatly comforted when brothers and sisters busied themselves in lighting fires, cooking meals, and waiting on her hand and foot, as if she had been indeed a king's wife. Havelok, however, said nothing to explain the mystery, and Goldborough that night lay awake bewailing her fate as a thrall's bride, even though he was the fairest man in England.

The Revelation and Return to Denmark

As Goldborough lay sleepless and unhappy she became aware of a brilliant light shining around Havelok, and streaming from his mouth ; and while she feared and wondered an angelic voice cried to her :

> " Fair Princess, cease this grief and heavy moan !
> For Havelok, thy newly wedded spouse,
> Is son and heir to famous kings : the sign
> Thou findest in the cross of ruddy gold
> That shineth on his shoulder.   He shall be
> Monarch and ruler of two mighty realms ;
> Denmark and England shall obey his rule,
> And he shall sway them with a sure command.
> This shalt thou see with thine own eyes, and be
> Lady and Queen, with Havelok, o'er these lands."

This angelic message so gladdened Goldborough that she kissed, for the first time, her unconscious husband, who started up from his sleep, saying, " Dear love, sleepest thou ? I have had a wondrous dream. I thought I sat on a lofty hill, and saw all Denmark before me. As I stretched out my arms I embraced it all, and the people clung to my arms, and the castles fell at my feet ; then I flew over the salt sea with the Danish people clinging to me, and I closed all fair England in my hand, and gave it to thee, dear love! Now what can this mean ?"

Goldborough answered joyfully : " It means, dear heart, that thou shalt be King of Denmark and of England too : all these realms shall fall into thy power, and thou shalt be ruler in Denmark within one year. Now do thou follow my advice, and let us go to Denmark, taking with us Grim's three sons, who will accompany thee for love and loyalty ; and have no fear, for I know thou wilt succeed."

The next morning Havelok went to church early, and prayed humbly and heartily for success in his enterprise and retribution on the false traitor Godard ; then, laying his offering on the altar before the Cross, he went away glad in heart. Grim's three sons, Robert the Red, William Wendut, and Hugh the Raven, joyfully consented to go with Havelok to Denmark, to attack with all their power the false Jarl Godard and to win the kingdom for the rightful heir. Their wives and families stayed in England, but Goldborough would not leave her husband, and after a short voyage the party landed safely on the shores of Denmark, in the lands of Jarl Ubbe, an old friend of King Birkabeyn, who lived far from the court now that a usurper held sway in Denmark.

Havelok and Ubbe

Havelok dared not reveal himself and his errand until he knew more of the state of parties in the country, and he therefore only begged permission to live and trade there, giving Ubbe, as a token of good-will and a tribute to his power, a valuable ring, which the jarl prized greatly. Ubbe, gazing at the so-called merchant's great stature and beauty, lamented that he was not of noble birth, and planned to persuade him to take up the profession of arms. At first, however, he simply granted Havelok permission to trade, and invited him and Goldborough to a feast, promising them safety and honour under his protection. Havelok dreaded lest his wife's beauty might place them in jeopardy, but he dared not refuse the invitation, which was pointedly given to both ; accordingly, when they went to Ubbe's hall, Goldborough was escorted by Robert the Red and William Wendut.

87

Ubbe received them with all honour, and all men marvelled at Goldborough's beauty, and Ubbe's wife loved Goldborough at first sight as her husband did Havelok, so that the feast passed off with all joy and mirth, and none dared raise a hand or lift his voice against the wandering merchant whom Ubbe so strangely favoured. But Ubbe knew that when once Havelok and his wife were away from his protection there would be little safety for them, since the rough Danish nobles would think nothing of stealing a trader's fair wife, and many a man had cast longing eyes on Goldborough's loveliness. Therefore when the feast was over, and Havelok took his leave, Ubbe sent with him a body of ten knights and sixty men-at-arms, and recommended them to the magistrate of the town, Bernard Brown, a true and upright man, bidding him, as he prized his life, keep the strangers in safety and honour. Well it was that Ubbe and Bernard Brown took these precautions, for late at night a riotous crowd came to Bernard's house clamouring for admittance. Bernard withstood the angry mob, armed with a great axe, but they burst the door in by hurling a huge stone ; and then Havelok joined in the defence. He drew out the great beam which barred the door, and crying, " Come quickly to me, and you shall stay here ! Curses on him who flees ! " began to lay about him with the big beam, so that three fell dead at once. A terrible fight followed, in which Havelok, armed only with the beam, slew twenty men in armour, and was then sore beset by the rest of the troop, aiming darts and arrows at his unarmoured breast. It was going hardly with him, when Hugh the Raven, hearing and understanding the cries of the assailants, called his brothers to their lord's aid, and they all joined the fight so furiously that, long ere day, of the sixty men who had attacked the inn not one remained alive.

"With great joy they fell on their knees"

"On a miserable jade with his face to the tail"

HAVELOK AND UBBE

In the morning news was brought to Jarl Ubbe that his stranger guest had slain sixty of the best of his soldiery.

"What can this mean?" said Ubbe. "I had better go and see to it myself, for any messenger would surely treat Havelok discourteously, and I should be full loath to do that." He rode away to the house of Bernard Brown, and asked the meaning of its damaged and battered appearance.

"My lord," answered Bernard Brown, "last night at moonrise there came a band of sixty thieves who would have plundered my house and bound me hand and foot. When Havelok and his companions saw it they came to my aid, with sticks and stones, and drove out the robbers like dogs from a mill. Havelok himself slew three at one blow. Never have I seen a warrior so good! He is worth a thousand in a fray. But alas! he is grievously wounded, with three deadly gashes in side and arm and thigh, and at least twenty smaller wounds. I am scarcely harmed at all, but I fear he will die full soon."

Ubbe could scarcely believe so strange a tale, but all the bystanders swore that Bernard told nothing but the bare truth, and that the whole gang of thieves, with their leader, Griffin the Welshman, had been slain by the hero and his small party. Then Ubbe bade them bring Havelok, that he might call a leech to heal his wounds, for if the stranger merchant should live Jarl Ubbe would without fail dub him knight; and when the leech had seen the wounds he said the patient would make a good and quick recovery. Then Ubbe offered Havelok and his wife a dwelling in his own castle, under his own protection, till Havelok's grievous wounds were healed. There, too, fair Goldborough would be under the care of Ubbe's wife, who would cherish her as her own daughter. This kind offer was accepted gladly, and they all went to the castle, where a room was given them next to Ubbe's own.

At midnight Ubbe woke, aroused by a bright light in Havelok's room, which was only separated from his own by a slight wooden partition. He was vexed, suspecting his guest of midnight wassailing, and went to inquire what villainy might be hatching. To his surprise, both husband and wife were sound asleep, but the light shone from Havelok's mouth, and made a glory round his head. Utterly amazed at the marvel, Ubbe went away silently, and returned with all the garrison of his castle to the room where his guests still lay sleeping. As they gazed on the light Havelok turned in his sleep, and they saw on his shoulder the golden cross, shining like the sun, which all men knew to be the token of royal birth. Then Ubbe exclaimed : "Now I know who this is, and why I loved him so dearly at first sight : this is the son of our dead King Birkabeyn. Never was man so like another as this man is to the dead king : he is his very image and his true heir." With great joy they fell on their knees and kissed him eagerly, and Havelok awoke and began to scowl furiously, for he thought it was some treacherous attack ; but Ubbe soon undeceived him.

> "'Dear lord,' quoth he, 'be thou in naught dismayed,
> For in thine eyes methinks I see thy thought—
> Dear son, great joy is mine to live this day !
> My homage, lord, I freely offer thee :
> Thy loyal men and vassals are we all,
> For thou art son of mighty Birkabeyn,
> And soon shalt conquer all thy father's land,
> Though thou art young and almost friendless here.
> To-morrow will we swear our fealty due,
> And dub thee knight, for prowess unexcelled.'"

Now Havelok knew that his worst danger was over,

and he thanked God for the friend He had sent him, and left to the good Jarl Ubbe the management of his cause. Ubbe gathered an assembly of as many mighty men of the realm, and barons, and good citizens, as he could summon; and when they were all assembled, wondering what was the cause of this imperative summons, Ubbe arose and said:

"Gentles, bear with me if I tell you first things well known to you. Ye know that King Birkabeyn ruled this land until his death-day, and that he left three children—one son, Havelok, and two daughters—to the guardianship of Jarl Godard: ye all heard him swear to keep them loyally and treat them well. But ye do not know how he kept his oath! The false traitor slew both the maidens, and would have slain the boy, but for pity he would not kill the child with his own hands. He bade a fisherman drown him in the sea; but when the good man knew that it was the rightful heir, he saved the boy's life and fled with him to England, where Havelok has been brought up for many years. And now, behold! here he stands. In all the world he has no peer, and ye may well rejoice in the beauty and manliness of your king. Come now and pay homage to Havelok, and I myself will be your leader!"

Jarl Ubbe turned to Havelok, where he stood with Goldborough beside him, and knelt before him to do homage, an example which was followed by all present. At a second and still larger assembly held a fortnight later a similar oath of fealty was sworn by all, Havelok was dubbed knight by the noble Ubbe, and a great festival was celebrated, with sports and amusements for the populace. A council of war and vengeance was held with the great nobles.

The Death of Godard

Havelok, now acknowledged King of Denmark, was unsatisfied until he had punished the treacherous Godard, and he took a solemn oath from his soldiers that they would never cease the search for the traitor till they had captured him and brought him bound to judgment. After all, Godard was captured as he was hunting. Grim's three sons, now knighted by King Havelok, met him in the forest, and bade him come to the king, who called on him to remember and account for his treatment of Birkabeyn's children. Godard struck out furiously with his fists, but Sir Robert the Red wounded him in the right arm. When Godard's men joined in the combat, Robert and his brothers soon slew ten of their adversaries, and the rest fled ; returning, ashamed at the bitter reproaches of their lord, they were all slain by Havelok's men. Godard was taken, bound hand and foot, placed on a miserable jade with his face to the tail, and so led to Havelok. The king refused to be the judge of his own cause, and entrusted to Ubbe the task of presiding at the traitor's trial. No mercy was shown to the cruel Jarl Godard, and he was condemned to a traitor's death, with torments of terrible barbarity. The sentence was carried out to the letter, and Denmark rejoiced in the punishment of a cruel villain.

Death of Godrich

Meanwhile Earl Godrich of Cornwall had heard with great uneasiness that Havelok had become King of Denmark, and intended to invade England with a mighty army to assert his wife's right to the throne. He recognised that his own device to shame Goldborough had turned against him, and that he must now fight for his life and the usurped dominion he held over England. Godrich summoned his army to Lincoln for the defence of the realm against the Danes, and called out every man fit to bear weapons, on pain or becoming thrall if they failed him. Then he thus addressed them :

> " Friends, listen to my words, and you will know
>   'Tis not for sport, nor idle show, that I
>   Have bidden you to meet at Lincoln here.
>   Lo ! here at Grimsby foreigners are come
>   Who have already won the Priory.
>   These Danes are cruel heathen, who destroy
>   Our churches and our abbeys : priests and nuns
>   They torture to the death, or lead away
>   To serve as slaves the haughty Danish jarls.
>   Now, Englishmen, what counsel will ye take ?
>   If we submit, they will rule all our land,
>   Will kill us all, and sell our babes for thralls,
>   Will take our wives and daughters for their own.
>   Help me, if ever ye loved English land,
>   To fight these heathen and to cleanse our soil
>   From hateful presence of these alien hordes.
>   I make my vow to God and all the saints
>   I will not rest, nor houseled be, nor shriven,
>   Until our realm be free from Danish foe !
>   Accursed be he who strikes no blow for home ! "

The army was inspired with valour by these courageous words, and the march to Grimsby began at once, with Earl Godrich in command. Havelok's men marched out gallantly to meet them, and when the battle joined many mighty deeds of valour were done, especially by the king himself, his foster-brothers, and Jarl Ubbe. The battle lasted long and was very fierce and bloody, but the Danes gradually overcame the resistance of the English, and at last, after a great hand-to-hand conflict, King Havelok captured Godrich. The traitor earl, who had lost a hand in the fray, was sent

93

bound and fettered to Queen Goldborough, who kept him, carefully guarded, until he could be tried by his peers, since (for all his treason) he was still a knight.

When the English recognised their rightful lady and queen they did homage with great joy, begging mercy for having resisted their lawful ruler at the command of a wicked traitor; and the king and queen pardoned all but Godrich, who was speedily brought to trial at Lincoln. He was sentenced to be burnt at the stake, and the sentence was carried out amid general rejoicings.

Now that vengeance was satisfied, Havelok and his wife thought of recompensing the loyal helpers who had believed in them and supported them through the long years of adversity. Havelok married one of Grim's daughters to the Earl of Chester, and the other to Bertram, the good cook, who became Earl of Cornwall in the place of the felon Godrich and his disinherited children; the heroic Ubbe was made Regent of Denmark for Havelok, who decided to stay and rule England, and all the noble Danish warriors were rewarded with gifts of gold, and lands and castles. After a great coronation feast, which lasted for forty days, King Havelok dismissed the Danish regent and his followers, and after sad farewells they returned to their own country. Havelok and Goldborough ruled England in peace and security for sixty years, and lived together in all bliss, and had fifteen children, who all became mighty kings and queens.

CHAPTER VI : HOWARD THE HALT

Introduction

IN every society and in all periods the obligations of family affection and duty to kinsmen have been recognised as paramount. In the early European communities a man's first duty was to stand by his kinsman in strife and to avenge him in death, however unrighteous the kinsman's quarrel might be.

How pitiful is the aged Priam's lament that he must needs kiss the hands that slew his dear son Hector, and, kneeling, clasp the knees of his son's murderer ! How sad is Cuchulain's plaint that his son Connla must go down to the grave unavenged, since his own father slew him, all unwitting ! One remembers, too, Beowulf's words : "Better it is for every man that he avenge his friend than that he mourn him much ! " Since, then, family affection, the laws of honour and duty, and every recognised standard of life demanded that a kinsman should obtain a full wergild (or money payment) for his relative's death, unless he chose to take up the blood-feud against the murderer's family, we can hardly wonder that some of the heroes of early European literature are heroes of vengeance. Orestes and Electra are Greek embodiments of the idea of the sacredness of vengeance for murdered kinsfolk, and similar feelings are revealed in Gudrun's revenge for the murder of Siegfried in the " Nibelungenlied." To the Teutonic or Celtic warrior there would be heroism of a noble type in a just vengeance fully accomplished, and this heroism would be more easily recognised when the wrongdoer was rich and powerful, the avenger old, poor, and friendless. While admitting that the hero of vengeance belongs to and represents only one side of the civilisation of a somewhat barbaric community, we

95

must allow that the elements of dogged perseverance, dauntless courage, and resolute loyalty in some degree redeemed the ferocity and cruelty of the blood-feud he waged against the ill-doer.

It is certain that in the popular Icelandic saga of "Howard the Halt" tradition has recorded with minute detail of approbation the story of a man and woman, old, weak, friendless, who, in spite of terrible odds, succeeded in obtaining a late but sufficing vengeance for the cruel slaughter of their only son, the murderer being the most powerful man of the region. The part here assigned to the woman indicates the firm hold which the blood-feud had gained on the imagination of the Norsemen.

Icelandic Ghosts

The story possesses a further interest as revealing the unique character of the Icelandic ghost or phantom. In other literatures the spirit returned from the dead is a thin, immaterial, disembodied essence, a faint shadow of its former self; in Icelandic legend the spirit returns in full possession of its body, but more evil-disposed to mankind than before death. It fights and wrestles, pummels its adversary black and blue, it is huge and bloated and hideous, it tries to strangle men, and leaves finger-marks on their throats. If the ghosts are those of drowned men, they come home every night dripping with sea-water, and crowd the family from the fire and from the hall. Apparently they are evil spirits animating the dead body, and nothing but the utter destruction of the body avails to drive away the malignant spirit.

The Story. Howard and Thorbiorn

Thus runs the saga of "Howard the Halt":

About the year 1000, when the Christian faith had

hardly yet been heard of in Iceland, there dwelt at
Bathstead, on the shores of Icefirth, in that far-distant
land, a mighty chieftain, of royal descent and great
wealth, named Thorbiorn. Though not among the
first settlers of Iceland, he had appropriated much un-
claimed land, and was one of the leading men of the
country-side, but was generally disliked for his arrogance
and injustice. Thorkel, the lawman and arbitrator of
Icefirth, was weak and easily cowed, so Thorbiorn's
wrongdoing remained unchecked ; many a maiden had
he betrothed to himself, and afterwards rejected, and
many a man had he ousted from his lands, yet no redress could be obtained, and no man was bold enough
to attack so great a chieftain or resist his will. Thorbiorn's house at Bathstead was one of the best in the
district, and his lands stretched down to the shores of
the firth, where he had made a haven with a jetty for
ships. His boathouse stood a little back above a ridge
of shingle, and beside a deep pool or lagoon. The
household of Thorbiorn included Sigrid, a fair maiden,
young and wealthy, who was his housekeeper ; Vakr,
an ill-conditioned and malicious fellow, Thorbiorn's
nephew ; and a strong and trusted serving-man named
Brand. Besides these there were house-carles in plenty,
and labourers, all good fighting-men.

Not far from Bathstead, at Bluemire, dwelt an old
Viking called Howard. He was of honourable descent,
and had won fame in earlier Viking expeditions, but
since he had returned lamed and nearly helpless from
his last voyage he had aged greatly, and men called
him Howard the Halt. His wife, Biargey, however,
was an active and stirring woman, and their only son,
Olaf, bade fair to become a redoubtable warrior. Though
only fifteen, Olaf had reached full stature, was tall, fair,
handsome, and stronger than most men. He wore his

fair hair long, and always went bareheaded, for his great bodily strength defied even the bitter winter cold of Iceland, and he faced the winds clad in summer raiment only. With all his strength and beauty, Olaf was a loving and obedient son to Howard and Biargey, and the couple loved him as the apple of their eye.

Olaf Meets Sigrid

The men of Icefirth were wont to drive their sheep into the mountains during the summer, leave them there till autumn, and then, collecting the scattered flocks, to restore to each man his own branded sheep. One autumn the flocks were wild and shy, and it was found that many sheep had strayed in the hills. When those that had been gathered were divided Thorbiorn had lost at least sixty wethers, and was greatly vexed. Some weeks later Olaf Howardson went alone into the hills, and returned with all the lost sheep, having sought them with great toil and danger. Olaf drove the rest of the sheep home to their grateful owners, and then took Thorbiorn's to Bathstead. Reaching the house at noonday, he knocked on the door, and as all men sat at their noontide meal, the housekeeper, the fair Sigrid, went forth herself and saw Olaf.

She greeted him courteously and asked his business, and he replied, "I have brought home Thorbiorn's wethers which strayed this autumn," and then the two talked together for a short time. Now Thorbiorn was curious to know what the business might be, and sent his nephew Vakr to see who was there; he went secretly and listened to the conversation between Sigrid and Olaf, but heard little, for Olaf was just saying, "Then I need not go in to Thorbiorn; thou, Sigrid, canst as well tell him where his sheep are now"; then he simply bade her farewell and turned away.

Olaf and Sigrid

"Howard leaves the house of Thorbiorn"

THORBIORN INSULTS OLAF

Vakr ran back into the hall, shouting and laughing, till Thorbiorn asked : "How now, nephew ! Why makest thou such outcry ? Who is there ? "

"It was Olaf Howardson, the great booby of Bluemire, bringing back the sheep thou didst lose in the autumn."

"That was a neighbourly deed," said Thorbiorn.

"Ah ! but there was another reason for his coming, I think," said Vakr. "He and Sigrid had a long talk together, and I saw her put her arms round his neck ; she seemed well pleased to greet him."

"Olaf may be a brave man, but it is rash of him to anger me thus, by trying to steal away my housekeeper," said Thorbiorn, scowling heavily. Olaf had no thanks for his kindness, and was ill received whenever he came ; yet he came often to see Sigrid, for he loved her, and tried to persuade her to wed him. Thorbiorn hated him the more for his open wooing, which he could not forbid.

Thorbiorn Insults Olaf

The next year, when harvest was over, and the sheep were brought home, again most of the missing sheep belonged to Thorbiorn, and again Olaf went to the mountains alone and brought back the stray ones. All thanked him, except the master of Bathstead, to whom Olaf drove back sixty wethers. Thorbiorn had grown daily more enraged at Olaf's popularity, his strength and beauty, and his evident love for Sigrid, and now chose this opportunity of insulting the bold youth who rivalled him in fame and in public esteem.

Olaf reached Bathstead at noon, and seeing that all men were in the hall, he entered, and made his way to the daïs where Thorbiorn sat ; there he leaned on his axe, and gazed steadily at the master, who gave him no

99

single word of greeting. Then every one kept silence, watching them both.

At last Olaf broke the stillness by asking : "Why are you all dumb ? There is no honour to those who say naught. I have stood here long enough and had no word of courteous greeting. Master Thorbiorn, I have brought home thy missing sheep."

Vakr answered spitefully : "Yes, we all know that thou hast become the Icefirth sheep-drover ; and we all know that thou hast come to claim some share of the sheep, as any other beggar might. Kinsman Thorbiorn, thou hadst better give him some little alms to satisfy him !"

Olaf flushed angrily as he answered : "Nay, it is not for that I came ; but, Thorbiorn, I will not seek thy lost sheep a third time." And as he turned and strode indignantly from the hall Vakr mocked and jeered at him. Yet Olaf passed forth in silence.

The third year Olaf found and brought home all men's sheep but Thorbiorn's ; and then Vakr spread the rumour that Olaf had stolen them, since he could not otherwise obtain a share of them. This rumour came at last to Howard's ears, and he upbraided Olaf, saying, when his son praised their mutton, "Yes, it is good, and it is really ours, not Thorbiorn's. It is terrible that we have to bear such injustice."

Olaf said nothing, but, seizing the leg of mutton, flung it across the room ; and Howard smiled at the wrath which his son could no longer suppress ; perhaps, too, Howard longed to see Olaf in conflict with Thorbiorn.

Olaf and the Wizard's Ghost

While Howard was still upbraiding Olaf a widow entered, who had come to ask for help in a difficult matter. Her dead husband (a reputed wizard) returned to his house night after night as a dreadful ghost, and no man would live in the house. Would Howard come and break the spell and drive away the dreadful nightly visitant ?

"Alas !" replied Howard, " I am no longer young and strong. Why do you not ask Thorbiorn ? He accounts himself to be chief here, and a chieftain should protect those in his country-side."

"Nay," said the widow. "I am only too glad if Thorbiorn lets me alone. I will not meddle with him."

Then said Olaf : " Father, I will go and try my strength with this ghost, for I am young and stronger than most, and I deem such a matter good sport."

Accordingly Olaf went back with the widow, and slept in the hall that night, with a skin rug over him. At nightfall the dead wizard came in, ghastly, evil-looking, and terrible, and tore the skin from over Olaf ; but the youth sprang up and wrestled with the evil creature, who seemed to have more than mortal strength. They fought grimly till the lights died out, and the struggle raged in the darkness up and down the hall, and finally out of doors. In the yard round the house the dead wizard fell, and Olaf knelt upon him and broke his back, and thought him safe from doing any mischief again. When Olaf returned to the hall men had rekindled the lights, and all made much of him, and tended his bruises and wounds, and counted him a hero indeed. His fame spread through the whole district, and he was greatly beloved by all men ; but Thorbiorn hated him more than ever.

Soon another quarrel arose, when a stranded whale, which came ashore on Howard's land, was adjudged to Thorbiorn. The lawman, Thorkel, was summoned to decide to whom the whale belonged, and came to view it. " It is manifestly theirs," said he falteringly, for he dreaded Thorbiorn's wrath. "Whose saidst thou?" cried Thorbiorn, coming to him menacingly, with drawn sword. "Thine," said Thorkel, with downcast eyes; and Thorbiorn triumphantly claimed and took the whale, though the injustice of the decree was evident. Yet Olaf felt no ill-will to Thorbiorn, for Sigrid's sake, but contrived to render him another service.

Olaf's Second Fight with the Ghost

Brand the Strong, Thorbiorn's shepherd, could not drive his sheep one day. Olaf met him trying to get his frightened wethers home: it seemed an impossible task, because an uncanny human form, with waving arms, stood in a narrow bend of the path and drove them back and scattered them. Brand told Olaf all the tale, and when the two went to look, Olaf saw that the enemy was the ghost of the dead wizard whom he had fought before. "Which wilt thou do," said Olaf, "fight the wizard or gather thy sheep?"

"I have no wish to fight the ghost; I will find my scattered sheep," said Brand; "that is the easier task."

Then Olaf ran at the ghost, who awaited him at the top of a high bank, and he and the wizard wrestled again with each other till they fell from the bank into a snowdrift, and so down to the seashore. There Olaf, whose strength had been tried to the utmost, had the upper hand, and again broke the back of the dead wizard; but, seeing that that had been of no avail before, he took the body, swam out to sea with it, and sank it deep in the firth. Ever after men believed that this part of the coast was dangerous to ships.

Brand thanked the youth much for his help, and when he reached Bathstead related what Olaf had done for him. Thorbiorn said nothing, but Vakr sneered, and called Brand a coward for asking help of Olaf.

OLAF MEETS THORBIORN

The strife grew keen between them, almost to blows, and was only settled by Thorbiorn, who forbade Brand to praise Olaf or to accept help from him. His ill-will grew so evident to all men that Howard the Halt decided, in spite of Olaf's reluctance, to remove to a homestead on the other side of the firth, away from Thorbiorn's neighbourhood.

Olaf Meets Thorbiorn

That summer Thorbiorn decided to marry. He wooed a maiden who was sister of the wise Guest, who dwelt at the Mead, and Guest agreed to the match, on condition that Thorbiorn should renounce his injustice and evil ways; to this Thorbiorn assented, and the wedding was held shortly after. Thorbiorn had said nothing to his household of his proposed marriage, and Sigrid first heard of it when the wedding was over, and the bridal party would soon be riding home to Bathstead. Sigrid was very wroth that she must give up her control of the household to another, and refused to stay to serve under Thorbiorn's wife; accordingly she withdrew from Bathstead to a kinsman's house, taking all her goods with her. Thorbiorn raged furiously on his return, when he found that she was gone, for her wealth made a great difference to his comfort, and threatened dire punishment to all who had helped her. Olaf continued his wooing of Sigrid, and went to see her often in her kinsman's abode, and they loved each other greatly.

One day when Olaf had been seeking some lost sheep he made his way to Sigrid's house, to talk with her as usual. As they stood near the house together and talked Sigrid looked suddenly anxious and said :

" I see Thorbiorn and Vakr coming in a boat over the firth with weapons beside them, and I see the gleam of Thorbiorn's great sword Warflame. I fear they have done, or will do, some evil deed, and therefore I pray thee, Olaf, not to stay and meet them. He has hated thee for a long time, and the help thou didst give me to leave Bathstead did not mend matters. Go thy way now, and do not fall in with them."

"I am not afraid," said Olaf. "I have done Thorbiorn no wrong, and I will not flee before him. He is only one man, as I am."

"Alas!" Sigrid replied, "how canst thou, a stripling of eighteen, hope to stand before a grown man, a mighty champion, armed with a magic sword? Thy words and thoughts are brave, as thou thyself art, but the odds are too great for thee: they are two to one, since Vakr, ever spiteful and malicious, will not stand idle while thou art in combat with Thorbiorn."

"Well," said Olaf, "I will not avoid them, but I will not seek a contest. If it must be so, I will fight bravely; thou shalt hear of my deeds."

"No, that will never be; I will not live after thee to ask of them," said Sigrid.

"Farewell now; live long and happily!" said Olaf; and so they bade each other farewell, and Olaf left her there, and went down to the shore where his sheep lay. Thorbiorn and Vakr had just landed, and they greeted each other, and Olaf asked them their errand. "We go to my mother," said Vakr.

"Let us go together," replied Olaf, "for my way is the same in part. But I am sorry that I must needs drive my sheep home, for Icefirth sheep-drovers will become proud if a great man like thee should join the trade, Thorbiorn."

"Nay, I do not mind that," said Thorbiorn; so they all went on together; and as he went Olaf caught up a crooked cudgel with which to herd his sheep; he noticed, too, that Thorbiorn and Vakr kept trying to lag behind him, and he took care that they all walked abreast.

The Combat

When the three came near the house of Thordis, Vakr's mother, where the ways divided, Thorbiorn said : " Now, nephew Vakr, we need no longer delay what we would do." And then Olaf knew that he had fallen into their snare. He ran up a bank beside the road, and the two set on him from below, and he defended himself at first manfully with the crooked cudgel ; but Thorbiorn's sword Warflame sliced this like a stalk of flax, and Olaf had to betake himself to his axe, and the fight went on for long.

A New Enemy Comes

The noise of the fray reached the ears of Thordis, Vakr's mother, in her house, so that she sent a boy to learn the cause, and when he told her that Olaf Howardson was fighting against Thorbiorn and Vakr she bade her second son go to the help of his kinsfolk.

" I will not go," said he. " I would rather fight for Olaf than for them. It is a shame for two to set on one man, and they such great champions too. I will not be the third ; I will not go."

" Now I know that thou art a coward," sneered his mother. " Daughter, not son, thou art, too timid to help thy kinsfolk. I will show thee that I am a braver daughter than thou a son ! "

Olaf's Death

By these words Thordis so enraged her son that he seized his axe and rushed from the house down the hill towards Olaf, who could not see the new-comer, because he stood with his back to the house. Coming close to

Olaf, the new assailant drove the axe in deep between his shoulders, and when Olaf felt the blow he turned, and with a mighty stroke slew his last enemy. Thereupon Thorbiorn thrust Olaf through with the sword Warflame, and he died. Then Thorbiorn took Olaf's teeth, which he smote from his jaw, wrapped them in a cloth, and carried them home.

The news of the slaughter was at once told by Thorbiorn (for so long as homicide was not concealed it was not considered murder), and told fairly, so that all men praised Olaf for his brave defence, and lamented his death. But when men sought for the fair Sigrid she could not be found, and was seen no more from that day. She had loved Olaf greatly, had seen him fall, and could not live when he was dead ; but no man knew where she died or was buried.

The terrible news of Olaf's death came to Howard, and he sighed heavily and took to his bed for grief, and remained bedridden for twelve months, leaving his wife Biargey to manage the daily fishing and the farm. Men thought that Olaf would be for ever unavenged, because Howard was too feeble, and his adversary too mighty and too unjust.

Howard Claims Wergild for Olaf

When a year had passed away Biargey came to Howard where he lay in his bed, and bade him arise and go to Bathstead. Said she :

" I would have thee claim wergild for our son, since a man that can no longer fight may well prove his valour by word of mouth, and if Thorbiorn should show any sign of justice thou shalt not claim too much."

Howard replied : " I know it is a bootless errand to ask justice from Thorbiorn, but I will do thy will in this matter."

HOWARD AT THE THING

So Howard went heavily, walking as an old man, to Bathstead, and, after the usual greetings, said :

"I have come to thee, Thorbiorn, on a great matter —to claim wergild for my dead son Olaf, whom thou didst slay guiltless."

Thorbiorn answered : "I have never yet paid a wergild, though I have slain many men—some say innocent men. But I am sorry for thee, since thou hast lost a brave son, and I will at least give thee something. There is an old horse named Dodderer out in the pastures, grey with age, sore-backed, too old to work ; but thou canst take him home, and perhaps he will be some good, when thou hast fed him up."

Now Howard was angered beyond speech. He reddened and turned straight to the door ; and as he went down the hall Vakr shouted and jeered ; but Howard said no word, good or bad. He returned home, and took to his bed for another year.

Howard at the Thing

In the second year Biargey again urged Howard to try for a wergild. She suggested that he should follow Thorbiorn to the Thing and try to obtain justice, for men loathed Thorbiorn's evil ways, and Howard would be sure to have many sympathizers. Howard was loath to go. "Thorbiorn, my son's slayer, has mocked me once ; shall he mock me again where all the chieftains are assembled ? I will not go to endure such shame !"

To his surprise, Biargey urged her will, saying : "Thou wilt have friends, I know, since Guest will be there, and he is a just man, and will strive to bring about peace between thee and Thorbiorn. And hearken to me, and heed my words, husband ! If Thorbiorn is condemned to pay thee money, and there is a large ring of assessors, it may be that when thou and he are in the ring together he will do something to grieve thee sorely. Then look thou well to it! If thy heart be light, make thou no peace; I am somewhat fore-sighted, and I know that then Olaf shall be avenged. But if thou be heavy-hearted, then do thou be recon-ciled to Thorbiorn, for I know that Olaf shall lie unatoned for."

Howard replied: "Wife, I understand thee not, nor thy words, but this I know: I would do and bear all things if I might but obtain due vengeance for Olaf's death."

At last Howard, impressed by his wife's half-pro-phetic words, roused himself, and rode away to the Thing; here he found shelter with a great chieftain, Steinthor of Ere, who was kind to the old man, and gave Howard a place in his booth. Steinthor praised Olaf's courage and manful defence, and bade his followers cherish the old man, and not arouse his grief for his dead son.

Howard and Thorbiorn

As the days wore on Howard did nothing towards obtaining compensation for his great loss, until Steinthor asked him why he took no action in the matter. Howard replied that he felt helpless against Thorbiorn's evil words and deeds; but Steinthor bade him try to win Guest to his side—then he would succeed. Howard took heart, and set off for the booth which Thorbiorn shared with Guest; but unhappily Guest was not there when Howard came. Thorbiorn greeted him and asked what matter had brought him, and Howard replied:

"My grief for Olaf is yet deep in my heart; still I remember his death; and now again I come to claim a wergild for him."

Thorbiorn answered: "Come to me at home in my

own country, and I may do somewhat for thee, but I will not have thee whining against me here."

Howard said : "If thou wilt do nothing here, I have proved that thou wilt do still less in thine own country ; but I had hoped for help from other chieftains."

Thorbiorn burst out wrathfully : "See ! He will stir up other men against me ! Get thee gone, old man, or thou shalt not escape a beating."

Now Howard was greatly angered, and said: "Yes, old I am—too old and feeble to win respect ; but the days have been when I would not have endured such wrong ; yea, and if Olaf were still alive thou wouldst not have flouted me thus." As he left Thorbiorn's sight his grief and anger were so great that he did not notice Guest returning, but went heavily to Steinthor's booth, where he told all Thorbiorn's injustice, and won much sympathy.

Guest and Howard

When Guest had entered the booth he sat down beside Thorbiorn and said :

"Who was the man whom I met leaving the booth just now ?"

"A wise question for a wise man to ask ! How can I tell ? So many come and go," said Thorbiorn.

"But this was an old man, large of stature, lame in one knee ; yet he looked a brave warrior, and he was so wrathful that he did not know where he went. He seemed a man likely to be lucky, too, and not one to be lightly wronged."

"That must have been old Howard the Halt," said Thorbiorn. "He is a man from my district, who has come after me to the Thing."

"Ah ! Was it his brave son Olaf whom thou didst slay guiltless ?"

"Yes, certainly," returned Thorbiorn.

"How hast thou kept the promise of better ways which thou didst make when thou didst marry my sister?" he asked; and Thorbiorn sat silent. "This wrong must be amended," said Guest, and sent an honourable man to bring Howard to him. Howard at first refused to face Thorbiorn again, but at last reluctantly consented to meet Guest, and when the latter had greeted him in friendly and honourable fashion he told the whole story, from the time of Thorbiorn's first jealousy of Olaf.

Guest was horrified. "Heard ever man such injustice!" he cried. "Now, Thorbiorn, choose one of two things: either my sister shall no longer be thy wife, or thou shalt allow me to give judgment between Howard and thee."

Guest's Judgment and the Payment of the Wergild

Thorbiorn agreed to leave the matter in Guest's hands, and many men were called to make a ring as assessors, that all might be legally done, and Thorbiorn and Howard stood together in the ring. Then Guest gave judgment: "Thorbiorn, I cannot condemn thee to pay Howard all thou owest—with all thy wealth, thou hast not money enough for that; but for slaying Olaf thou shalt pay a threefold wergild. For the other wrongs thou hast done him, I, thy brother-in-law, will try to atone by gifts, and friendship, and all honour in my power, as long as we both live; and if he will come home to stay with me he shall be right welcome."

Thorbiorn agreed to the award, saying carelessly: "I will pay him at home in my own country, if he will come to me when I have more leisure."

"No," said Guest, who distrusted Thorbiorn, "thou shalt pay here, and now, fully; and I myself will pay
110

"The silver rolled in all directions from his cloak"

"Thorbiorn lifted the huge stone"

one wergild, to help thee in atonement." When this was agreed Howard sat down in the ring, and Guest gave him the one wergild (a hundred of silver), which Howard received in the skirt of his cloak ; and then Thorbiorn paid one wergild slowly, coin by coin, and said he had no more money ; but Guest bade him pay it all.

Then Thorbiorn drew out a cloth and untied it, saying, " He will surely count himself paid in full if I give him this ! " and he flung into the old man's face, as he sat on the ground, the teeth of the dead Olaf, saying, " Here are thy son's teeth ! "

Howard sprang up, bleeding, mad with rage and grief. The silver rolled in all directions from his cloak as he came to his feet, but he heeded it not at all. Blinded with blood, and furious, he broke through the ring of assessors, dashed one of them to earth, and rushed away like a young man ; but when he came to Steinthor's booth he lay as if dead, and spoke to no man.

Guest would have no more to do with Thorbiorn. " Thou hast no equal for cruelty and evil ; thou shalt surely repent it," he said ; and he rode to Bathstead, took his sister away, with all her wealth, and broke off his alliance with Thorbiorn, caring nothing for the shame he put upon so unjust a man.

Howard went home, told Biargey all that had happened, and took to his bed again, a poor, old, helpless, miserable man ; but his wife, who saw her presage beginning to come true, kept up her courage, rowed out fishing every day, and guided the household for yet another year.

Biargey and her Brethren

That summer, one day, as Biargey was rowed out to the fishing as usual, she saw Thorbiorn's boat coming up the firth, and bade her man take up the lines and go to meet him, and row round the cutter, while she talked with Thorbiorn. As Biargey's little boat approached the cutter Thorbiorn stopped his vessel, for he saw that she would speak with him, and her boat circled round the cutter while she asked his business, and learnt that he was going with Vakr to meet a brother and nephew of his, to bring them to Bathstead, and that he expected to be away from home for a week. The little skiff had now passed completely round the motionless cutter, and Olaf's mother, having learnt all she wanted, bade her rower quit Thorbiorn; the little boat shot swiftly and suddenly away, leaving Thorbiorn with an uneasy sense of witchcraft. So disquieted did he feel that he would have pursued her and drowned "the old hag," as he called her, had he not been prevented by Brand the Strong, who had been helped in his need by Olaf.

As the little craft shot away Biargey smiled mysteriously, and said to her rower: "Now I feel sure that Olaf my son will be avenged. I have work to do: let us not go home yet."

"Where, then, shall we go?" asked the man.

"To my brother Valbrand."

Valbrand

Now Valbrand was an old man who had been a mighty warrior in his youth, but had now settled down to a life of quiet and peace; he had, however, two promising sons, well-grown and manly youths. When Valbrand saw his sister he came to meet her, saying:

"Welcome, sister! Seldom it is that we see thee. Wilt thou abide with us this night, or is thine errand one that craves haste?"

"I must be home to-night," she replied, and added

mysteriously : " But there is help I would fain ask of thee. Wilt thou lend me thy seal-nets ? We have not enough to catch such fish as we need."

Valbrand answered: " Willingly, and thou shalt choose for thyself. Here are three, one old and worn out, two new and untried ; which wilt thou take ? "

" I will have the new ones, but I do not need them yet ; keep them ready for the day when I shall send and ask for them," Biargey replied, and bade Valbrand farewell, and rowed away to her next brother.

Thorbrand and Asbrand

When Howard's wife came to her brother Thorbrand she was well received by him and his two sons, and here she asked for the loan of a trout-net, since she had not enough to catch the fish. Thorbrand offered her her choice—one old and worn out, or two new and untried nets ; and again Biargey chose the new ones, and bade them be ready when the messenger came.

From her third brother, Asbrand, who had only one son, Biargey asked a turf-cutter, as hers was not keen enough to cut all she wanted ; again she was offered her choice, and chose the new, untried cutter, instead of the old, rusty, notched one. Then Biargey bade farewell to Asbrand, refusing his offer of hospitality, and went home to Howard, and told him of her quests and the promises she had received. The old couple knew what the promises meant, but they said nothing to each other about it.

The Arousing of Howard

When seven days had passed Biargey came to Howard, saying : " Arise now, and play the man, if thou wilt ever win vengeance for Olaf. Thou must do it

113

now or never, since now the opportunity has come.
Knowest thou not that to-day Thorbiörn returns to
Bathstead, and thou must meet him to-day? And
have I not found helpers for thee in my nephews?
Thou wilt not need to face the strife alone."

Hereupon Howard sprang up joyfully from his bed,
and was no longer lame or halt, nor looked like an old
man, but moved briskly, clad himself in good armour,
and seemed a mighty warrior. His joy broke forth in
words, and he chanted songs of gladness in vengeance,
and joy in strife, and evil omen to the death-doomed
foe. Thus gladly, with spear in hand, he went forth to
find his enemy and avenge his son; but he turned and
kissed his brave wife farewell, for he said: "It may
well be that we shall not meet again." Biargey said:
"Nay, we shall meet again, for I know that thou
bearest a bold heart and a strong arm, and wilt do
valiantly."

Howard Gathers his Friends

Howard and one fighting-man took their boat and
rowed to Valbrand's house, and saw him and his sons
making hay. Valbrand greeted Howard well, for he
had not seen him for long, and begged him to stay
there, but Howard would not. "I am in haste, and
have come to fetch the two new seal-nets thou didst
lend to my wife," he said; and Valbrand understood him
well. He called to his sons, "Come hither, lads; here
is your kinsman Howard, with mighty work on hand,"
and the two youths ran up hastily, leaving their hay-
making. Valbrand went to the house, and returned
bearing good weapons, which he gave to his sons,
bidding them follow their kinsman Howard and help
in his vengeance.

They three went down to the boat, took their

seats beside Howard's man, and rowed to Asbrand's
house. There Howard asked for the promised new
turf-cutter, and Asbrand's son, a tall and manly youth,
joined the party. At their next visit, to Thorbrand's
house, Howard asked for the two trout-nets, and
Thorbrand's two sons, with one stout fighting-man,
came gladly with their kinsman.

Howard's Plan

As they rowed away together one of the youths
asked : " Why is it that thou hast no sword or axe, Uncle
Howard ? " Howard replied : " It may be that we shall
meet Thorbiorn, and when the meeting is over I shall
not be a swordless man, but it is likely that I shall have
Warflame, that mighty weapon, the best of swords ; and
here I have a good spear."

These words seemed to them all a good omen, and as
they rowed towards Bathstead they saw a flock of ravens,
which encouraged them yet more, since the raven was the
bird of Odin, the haunter of fields of strife and bloodshed.

When they reached Bathstead they sprang on the
jetty, carried their boat over the ridge of shingle to the
quiet pool by the boathouse, and hid themselves where
they could see, but remain themselves unseen. Howard
took command, and appointed their places, bidding them
be wary, and not stir till he gave the word.

Thorbiorn's Return

Late that evening, just before dusk, Thorbiorn and
Vakr came home, bringing their kinsmen with them, a
party of ten in all. They had no suspicion of any
ambush, and Thorbiorn said to Vakr : " It is a fine night,
and dry, Vakr ; we will leave the boat here—she will
take no hurt through the night—and thou shalt carry
our swords and spears up to the boathouse."

Vakr obeyed, and bore all the weapons to the boat-house. Howard's men would have slain him then, but Howard forbade, and let him return to the jetty for more armour. When Vakr had gone back Howard sent to the boathouse for the magic sword, Warflame ; drawing it, he gripped it hard and brandished it, for he would fain avenge Olaf with the weapon which had slain him. When Vakr came towards the ambush a second time he was laden with shields and helmets. Howard's men sprang up to take him, and he turned to flee as he saw and heard them. But his foot slipped, and he fell into the pool, and lay there weighed down by all the armour, till he died miserably—a fitting end for one so ignoble and cruel.

Thorbiorn's Death

Howard's men shouted and waved their weapons, and ran down to the beach to attack their enemies ; but Thorbiorn, seeing them, flung himself into the sea, swimming towards a small rocky islet. When Howard saw this he took Warflame between his teeth, and, old as he was, plunged into the waves and pursued Thorbiorn. The latter had, however, a considerable start, and was both younger and stronger than his adversary, so that he was already on the rock and prepared to dash a huge stone at Howard, when the old man reached the islet. Now there seemed no hope for Howard, but still he clung fiercely to the rock and strove to draw himself up on the land. Thorbiorn lifted the huge stone to cast at his foe, but his foot slipped on the wet rocks, and he fell backward ; before he could recover his footing Howard rushed forward and slew him with his own sword Warflame, striking out his teeth, as Thorbiorn had done to Olaf.

When Howard swam back to Bathstead, and they

told him that in all six of Thorbiorn's men were dead, while he had only lost one serving-man, he rejoiced greatly; but his vengeance was not satisfied until he had slain yet another brother of Thorbiorn's.

Steinthor Shelters Howard

Then, with the news of this great revenge to be told, Howard and his kinsmen took refuge with that Steinthor who had given him help and shelter during the Thing.

"Who are ye, and what tidings do ye bring?" asked Steinthor as the little party of seven entered his hall.

"I am Howard, and these are my kinsmen," said Howard. "We tell the slaying of Thorbiorn and his brothers, his nephews and his house-carles, eight in all."

Steinthor exclaimed in surprise: "Art thou that Howard, old and bedridden, who didst seem like to die last year at the Thing, and hast thou done these mighty deeds with only these youths to aid thee? This is a great marvel, nearly as wondrous as thy restoration to youth and health. Great enmity will ye have aroused against you!"

Said Howard: "Bethink thee that thou didst promise me thy help if I should ever need it. Therefore have I come to thee now, because I have some little need of aid."

Steinthor laughed. "A little help! When dost thou think thou wilt need much, if this be not the time? But bide ye all here in honour, and I will set the matter right, since thou and these thy helpers have done so valiantly."

The Thing and Guest's Award

Howard and his kinsmen abode long with their host, until the Thing met again; then Steinthor rode away, leaving the uncle and nephews under good safeguard.

It was a great meeting, with many cases to judge. When the matter of the death of Thorbiorn's family was brought up Steinthor spoke on Howard's behalf, and offered to let Guest again give judgment, since he had done so before. This offer was accepted by Thorbiorn's surviving kinsfolk, and Guest, as before, gave a fair award.

Since a threefold wergild was still due to Howard for the slaying of Olaf, three of the eight dead need not be paid for. Thorbiorn, Vakr, and that brother of his slain by Olaf should continue unatoned for, because they were evildoers, and fell in an unrighteous quarrel of their own seeking; moreover, the slaying of Howard's serving-man cancelled one wergild; there remained, therefore, but one wergild for Howard to pay—one hundred of silver—which was paid out of hand. In addition to this, Howard must change his dwelling, and his nephews must travel abroad for some years. This sentence pleased all men greatly, and they broke up the Thing in great content, and Howard rode home at the head of a goodly company to his stout-hearted wife Biargey, who had kept his house and lands in good order all this time. They made a great feast, and gave rich gifts to all their friends and kinsmen; then when the farewells were over the exiles went abroad and did valiantly in Norway; but Howard sold his lands and moved to another part of the island. There he prospered greatly; and when he died his memory was handed down as that of a mighty warrior and a valiant and prudent man.

CHAPTER VII : ROLAND, THE HERO OF EARLY FRANCE

The Roland Legends

CHARLES THE GREAT, King of the Franks, world-famous as Charlemagne, won his undying renown by innumerable victories for France and for the Church. Charles as the head of the Holy Roman Empire and the Pope as the head of the Holy Catholic Church equally dominated the imagination of the mediæval world. Yet in romance Charlemagne's fame has been eclipsed by that of his illustrious nephew and vassal, Roland, whose crowning glory has sprung from his last conflict and heroic death in the valley of Roncesvalles.

> " Oh for a blast of that dread horn,
> On Fontarabian echoes borne,
> That to King Charles did come,
> When Roland brave, and Olivier,
> And every paladin and peer
> On Roncesvalles died."
>
> *Scott.*

Briefly, the historical facts are these : In A.D. 778 Charles was returning from an expedition into Spain, where the dissensions of the Moorish rulers had offered him the chance of extending his borders while he fought for the Christian faith against the infidel. He had taken Pampeluna, but had been checked before Saragossa, and had not ventured beyond the Ebro ; he was now making his way home through the Pyrenees. When the main army had safely traversed the passes, the rear was suddenly attacked by an overwhelming body of mountaineers, Gascons and Basques, who, resenting the violation of their mountain sanctuaries, and longing for plunder, drove the

119

Frankish rearguard into a little valley (now marked by the chapel of Ibagneta and still called Roncesvalles), and there slew every man.

The Historic Basis

The whole romantic legend of Roland has sprung from the simple words in a contemporary chronicle, " In which battle was slain Roland, prefect of the marches of Brittany." [1]

This same fight of Roncesvalles was the theme of an archaic poem, the " Song of Altobiscar," written about 1835. In it we hear the exultation of the Basques as they see the knights of France fall beneath their onslaughts. The Basques are on the heights—they hear the trampling of a mighty host which throngs the narrow valley below : its numbers are as countless as the sands of the sea, its movement as resistless as the waves which roll those sands on the shore. Awe fills the bosoms of the mountain tribesmen, but their leader is undaunted. " Let us unite our strong arms ! " he cries aloud. " Let us tear our rocks from their beds and hurl them upon the enemy ! Let us crush and slay them all ! " So said, so done : the rocks roll plunging into the valley, slaying whole troops in their descent. " And what mangled flesh, what broken bones, what seas of blood ! Soon of that gallant band not one is left alive ; night covers all, the eagles devour the flesh, and the bones whiten in this valley to all eternity ! "

A Spanish Version

So runs the " Song of Altobiscar." But Spain too claims part of the honour of the day of Roncesvalles.

---

[1] *See* " Myths and Legends of the Middle Ages," by H. Guerber.

ROLAND IN FRENCH LITERATURE

True, Roland was in reality slain by Basques, not by Spaniards ; but Spain, eager to share the honour, has glorified a national hero, Bernardo del Carpio, who, in the Spanish legend, defeats Roland in single combat and wins the day.

The Italian Orlando

Italy has laid claim to Roland, and in the guise of Orlando, Orlando Furioso, Orlando Innamorato, has made him into a fantastic, chivalrous knight, a hero of many magical adventures.

Roland in French Literature

Noblest of all, however, is the development of the "Roland Saga" in French literature ; for, even setting aside much legendary lore and accumulated tradition, the Roland of the old epic is a perfect hero of the early days of feudalism, when chivalry was in its very beginnings, before the cult of the Blessed Virgin Mary added the grace of courtesy to its heroism. Evidently Roland had grown in importance before the "Chanson de Roland" took its present form, for we find the rearguard skirmish magnified into a great battle, which manifestly contains recollections of later Saracen invasions and Gascon revolts. As befits the hero of an epic, Roland is now of royal blood, the nephew of the great emperor, who has himself increased in age and splendour ; this heroic Roland can obviously only be overcome by the treachery of one of the Franks themselves, so there appears the traitor Ganelon (a Romance version of a certain Danilo or Nanilo), who is among the Twelve Peers what Judas was among the Apostles; the mighty Saracens, not the insignificant Basques, are now the victors ; and the vengeance taken by Charlemagne on the Saracens and on the traitor is boldly added to history, which leaves the disaster unavenged. Thus the bare fact was embroidered over gradually by the historical imagination, aided by patriotism, until a really national hero was evolved out of an obscure Breton count.

The "Chanson de Roland"

The "Song of Roland," as we now have it, seems to be a late version of an Anglo-Norman poem, made by a certain Turoldus or Thorold ; and it must bear a close resemblance to that chant which fired the soldiers of William the Norman at Hastings, when

> "Taillefer, the noble singer,
>   On his war-horse swift and fiery,
>   Rode before the Norman host ;
>   Tossed his sword in air and caught it,
>   Chanted loud the death of Roland,
>   And the peers who perished with him
>   At the pass of Roncevaux."
> *Roman de Rou.*

The "Song of Roland" bears an intimate relation to the development of European thought, and the hero is doubly worth our study as hero and as type of national character. Thus runs the story :

The Story

The Emperor Charles the Great, Carolus Magnus, or Charlemagne, had been for seven years in Spain, and had conquered it from sea to sea, except Saragossa, which, among its lofty mountains, and ruled by its brave king Marsile, had defied his power. Marsile still held to his idols, Mahomet, Apollo, and Termagaunt, dreading in his heart the day when Charles would force him to become a Christian.

AN EMBASSY TO CHARLEMAGNE

The Saracen Council

The Saracen king gathered a council around him, as he reclined on a seat of blue marble in the shade of an orchard, and asked the advice of his wise men.

> " ' My lords,' quoth he, 'you know our grievous state.
> The mighty Charles, great lord of France the fair,
> Has spread his hosts in ruin o'er our land.
> No armies have I to resist his course,
> No people have I to destroy his hosts.
> Advise me now, what counsel shall I take
> To save my race and realm from death and shame ? ' "

Blancandrin's Advice

A wily emir, Blancandrin, of Val-Fonde, was the only man who replied. He was wise in counsel, brave in war, a loyal vassal to his lord.

> " ' Fear not, my liege,' he answered the sad king.
> ' Send thou to Charles the proud, the arrogant,
> And offer fealty and service true,
> With gifts of lions, bears, and swift-foot hounds,
> Seven hundred camels, falcons, mules, and gold—
> As much as fifty chariots can convey—
> Yea, gold enough to pay his vassals all.
> Say thou thyself will take the Christian faith,
> And follow him to Aix to be baptized.
> If he demands thy hostages, then I
> And these my fellows give our sons to thee,
> To go with Charles to France, as pledge of truth.
> Thou wilt not follow him, thou wilt not yield
> To be baptized, and so our sons must die;
> But better death than life in foul disgrace,
> With loss of our bright Spain and happy days.'
> So cried the pagans all ; but Marsile sat
> Thoughtful, and yet at last accepted all."

An Embassy to Charlemagne

Now King Marsile dismissed the council with words of thanks, only retaining near him ten of his most famous barons, chief of whom was Blancandrin ; to them he said : " My lords, go to Cordova, where Charles is at this time. Bear olive-branches in your hands, in token of peace, and reconcile me with him. Great shall be your reward if you succeed. Beg Charles to have pity on me, and I will follow him to Aix within a month, will receive the Christian law, and become his vassal in love and loyalty."

" Sire," said Blancandrin, " you shall have a good treaty ! "

The ten messengers departed, bearing olive-branches in their hands, riding on white mules, with reins of gold and saddles of silver, and came to Charles as he rested after the siege of Cordova, which he had just taken and sacked.

Reception by Charlemagne

Charlemagne was in an orchard with his Twelve Peers and fifteen thousand veteran warriors of France. The messengers from the heathen king reached this orchard and asked for the emperor ; their gaze wandered over groups of wise nobles playing at chess, and groups of gay youths fencing, till at last it rested on a throne of solid gold, set under a pine-tree and overshadowed with eglantine. There sat Charles, the king who ruled fair France, with white flowing beard and hoary head, stately of form and majestic of countenance. No need was there of usher to cry : " Here sits Charles the King."

The ambassadors greeted Charlemagne with all honour, and Blancandrin opened the embassy thus :

" Peace be with you from God the Lord of Glory whom you adore ! Thus says the valiant King Marsile : He has been instructed in your faith, the way of salvation, and is willing to be baptized ; but you have been

"Here sits Charles the King!"

"Ganelon rode away"

too long in our bright Spain, and should return to Aix. There will he follow you and become your vassal, holding the kingdom of Spain at your hand. Gifts have we brought from him to lay at your feet, for he will share his treasures with you ! "

He is Perplexed

Charlemagne raised his hands in thanks to God, but then bent his head and remained thinking deeply, for he was a man of prudent mind, cautious and far-seeing, and never spoke on impulse. At last he said proudly: " Ye have spoken fairly, but Marsile is my greatest enemy : how can I trust your words ? "

Blancandrin replied : " He will give hostages, twenty of our noblest youths, and my own son will be among them. King Marsile will follow you to the wondrous springs of Aix-la-Chapelle, and on the feast of St. Michael will receive baptism in your court."

Thus the audience ended. The messengers were feasted in a pavilion raised in the orchard, and the night passed in gaiety and good-fellowship.

He Consults his Twelve Peers

In the early morning Charlemagne arose and heard Mass ; then, sitting beneath a pine-tree, he called the Twelve Peers to council. There came the twelve heroes, chief of them Roland and his loyal brother-in-arms Oliver ; there came Archbishop Turpin ; and, among a thousand loyal Franks, there came Ganelon the traitor. When all were seated in due order Charlemagne began :

" My lords and barons, I have received an embassy of peace from King Marsile, who sends me great gifts and offers, but on condition that I leave Spain and return to Aix. Thither will he follow me, to receive the Faith, become a Christian and my vassal. Is he to be trusted ?"

" Let us beware," cried all the Franks.

Roland Speaks

Roland, ever impetuous, now rose without delay, and spoke : " Fair uncle and sire, it would be madness to trust Marsile. Seven years have we warred in Spain, and many cities have I won for you, but Marsile has ever been treacherous. Once before when he sent messengers with olive-branches you and the French foolishly believed him, and he beheaded the two counts who were your ambassadors to him. Fight Marsile to the end, besiege and sack Saragossa, and avenge those who perished by his treachery."

Ganelon Objects

Charlemagne looked out gloomily from under his heavy brows, he twisted his moustache and pulled his long white beard, but said nothing, and all the Franks remained silent, except Ganelon, whose hostility to Roland showed clearly in his words :

" Sire, blind credulity were wrong and foolish, but follow up your own advantage. When Marsile offers to become your vassal, to hold Spain at your hand and to take your faith, any man who urges you to reject such terms cares little for our death ! Let pride no longer be your counsellor, but hear the voice of wisdom."

The aged Duke Naimes, the Nestor of the army, spoke next, supporting Ganelon : " Sire, the advice of Count Ganelon is wise, if wisely followed. Marsile lies at your mercy ; he has lost all, and only begs for pity. It would be a sin to press this cruel war, since he offers full guarantee by his hostages. You need

126

only send one of your barons to arrange the terms of peace."

This advice pleased the whole assembly, and a murmur was heard : "The Duke has spoken well."

"Who Shall Go to Saragossa?"

> " ' My lords and peers, whom shall we send
> To Saragossa to Marsile ? '
> ' Sire, let me go,' replied Duke Naimes ;
> ' Give me your glove and warlike staff.'
> ' No ! ' cried the king, ' my counsellor,
> Thou shalt not leave me unadvised—
> Sit down again ; I bid thee stay.'

> " ' My lords and peers, whom shall we send
> To Saragossa to Marsile ? '
> ' Sire, I can go,' quoth Roland bold.
> ' That canst thou not,' said Oliver ;
> ' Thy heart is far too hot and fierce—
> I fear for thee.   But I will go,
> If that will please my lord the King.'
> ' No ! ' cried the king, ' ye shall not go.
> I swear by this white flowing beard
> No peer shall undertake the task.'

> " ' My lords and peers, whom shall we send ? '
> Archbishop Turpin rose and spoke :
> ' Fair sire, let me be messenger.
> Your nobles all have played their part ;
> Give me your glove and warlike staff,
> And I will show this heathen king
> In frank speech how a true knight feels.'
> But wrathfully the king replied :
> ' By this white beard, thou shalt not go !
> Sit down, and raise thy voice no more.' "

Roland Suggests Ganelon

"Knights of France," quoth Charlemagne, "choose me now one of your number to do my errand to Marsile, and to defend my honour valiantly, if need be."

"Ah," said Roland, "then it must be Ganelon, my stepfather; for whether he goes or stays, you have none better than he!"

This suggestion satisfied all the assembly, and they cried: "Ganelon will acquit himself right manfully. If it please the King, he is the right man to go."

Charlemagne thought for a moment, and then, raising his head, beckoned to Ganelon. "Come hither, Ganelon," he said, "and receive this glove and staff, which the voice of all the Franks gives to thee."

Ganelon is Angry

"No," replied Ganelon, wrathfully. "This is the work of Roland, and I will never forgive him, nor his friends, Oliver and the other Peers. Here, in your presence, I bid them defiance!"

"Your anger is too great," said Charlemagne; "you will go, since it is my will also."

"Yes, I shall go, but I shall perish as did your two former ambassadors. Sire, forget not that your sister is my wife, and that Baldwin, my son, will be a valiant champion if he lives. I leave to him my lands and fiefs. Sire, guard him well, for I shall see him no more."

"Your heart is too tender," said Charlemagne. "You must go, since such is my command."

He Threatens Roland

Ganelon, in rage and anguish, glared round the council, and his face drew all eyes, so fiercely he looked at Roland.

"Madman," said he, "all men know that I am thy stepfather, and for this cause thou hast sent me to Marsile, that I may perish! But if I return I will be revenged on thee."

128

GANELON IS SENT

"Madness and pride," Roland retorted, "have no terrors for me; but this embassy demands a prudent man, not an angry fool: if Charles consents, I will do his errand for thee."

"Thou shalt not. Thou art not my vassal, to do my work, and Charles, my lord, has given me his commands. I go to Saragossa; but there will I find some way to vent my anger."

Now Roland began to laugh, so wild did his step-father's threats seem, and the laughter stung Ganelon to madness. "I hate you," he cried to Roland; "you have brought this unjust choice on me." Then, turning to the emperor: "Mighty lord, behold me ready to fulfil your commands."

But is Sent

"Fair Lord Ganelon," spoke Charlemagne, "bear this message to Marsile. He must become my vassal and receive holy baptism. Half of Spain shall be his fief; the other half is for Count Roland. If Marsile does not accept these terms I will besiege Saragossa, capture the town, and lead Marsile prisoner to Aix, where he shall die in shame and torment. Take this letter, sealed with my seal, and deliver it into the king's own right hand."

Thereupon Charlemagne held out his right-hand glove to Ganelon, who would fain have refused it. So reluctant was he to grasp it that the glove fell to the ground. "Ah, God!" cried the Franks, "what an evil omen! What woes will come to us from this embassy!" "You shall hear full tidings," quoth Ganelon. "Now, sire, dismiss me, for I have no time to lose." Very solemnly Charlemagne raised his hand and made the sign of the Cross over Ganelon, and gave him his blessing, saying, "Go, for the honour of Jesus

Christ, and for your Emperor." So Ganelon took his leave, and returned to his lodging, where he prepared for his journey, and bade farewell to the weeping retainers whom he left behind, though they begged to accompany him. "God forbid," cried he, "that so many brave knights should die! Rather will I die alone. You, sirs, return to our fair France, greet well my wife, guard my son Baldwin, and defend his fief!"

He Plots with Marsile's Messengers

Then Ganelon rode away, and shortly overtook the ambassadors of the Moorish king, for Blancandrin had delayed their journey to accompany him, and the two envoys began a crafty conversation, for both were wary and skilful, and each was trying to read the other's mind. The wily Saracen began:

> " ' Ah ! what a wondrous king is Charles !
> How far and wide his conquests range !
> The salt sea is no bar to him :
> From Poland to far England's shores
> He stretches his unquestioned sway;
> But why seeks he to win bright Spain ? '
> ' Such is his will,' quoth Ganelon ;
> ' None can withstand his mighty power ! '

> " ' How valiant are the Frankish lords
> But how their counsel wrongs their king
> To urge him to this long-drawn strife—
> They ruin both themselves and him ! '
> ' I blame not them,' quoth Ganelon,
> ' But Roland, swollen with fatal pride.
> Near Carcassonne he brought the King
> An apple, crimson streaked with gold :
> " Fair sire," quoth he, " here at your feet
> I lay the crowns of all the kings."
> If he were dead we should have peace ! '

GANELON WITH THE SARACENS

> "'How haughty must this Roland be,
> Who fain would conquer all the earth !
> Such pride deserves due chastisement !
> What warriors has he for the task ?'
> 'The Franks of France,' quoth Ganelon,
> 'The bravest warriors 'neath the sun !
> For love alone they follow him
> (Or lavish gifts which he bestows)
> To death, or conquest of the world !'"

To Betray Roland

The bitterness in Ganelon's tone at once struck Blancandrin, who cast a glance at him and saw the Frankish envoy trembling with rage. He suddenly addressed Ganelon in whispered tones : "Hast thou aught against the nephew of Charles ? Wouldst thou have revenge on Roland ? Deliver him to us, and King Marsile will share with thee all his treasures." Ganelon was at first horrified, and refused to hear more, but so well did Blancandrin argue and so skilfully did he lay his snare that before they reached Saragossa and came to the presence of King Marsile it was agreed that Roland should be destroyed by their means.

Ganelon with the Saracens

Blancandrin and his fellow ambassadors conducted Ganelon into the presence of the Saracen king, and announced Charlemagne's peaceable reception of their message and the coming of his envoy. "Let him speak : we listen," said Marsile.

Ganelon then began artfully : "Peace be to you in the name of the Lord of Glory whom we adore ! This is the message of King Charles : You shall receive the Holy Christian Faith, and Charles will graciously grant you one-half of Spain as a fief ; the other half he intends for his nephew Roland (and a haughty partner you will find him !). If you refuse he will take Saragossa, lead you captive to Aix, and give you there to a shameful death."

Marsile's Anger

Marsile's anger was so great at this insulting message that he sprang to his feet, and would have slain Ganelon with his gold-adorned javelin ; but he, seeing this, half drew his sword, saying :

> " 'Sword, how fair and bright thou art !
> Come thou forth and view the light.
> Long as I can wield thee here
> Charles my Emperor shall not say
> That I die alone, unwept.
> Ere I fall Spain's noblest blood
> Shall be shed to pay my death.' "

The Saracen Council

However, strife was averted, and Ganelon received praise from all for his bold bearing and valiant defiance of his king's enemy. When quiet was restored he repeated his message and delivered the emperor's letter, which was found to contain a demand that the caliph, Marsile's uncle, should be sent, a prisoner, to Charles, in atonement for the two ambassadors foully slain before. The indignation of the Saracen nobles was intense, and Ganelon was in imminent danger, but, setting his back against a pine-tree, he prepared to defend himself to the last. Again the quarrel was stayed, and Marsile, taking his most trusted leaders, withdrew to a secret council, whither, soon, Blancandrin led Ganelon. Here Marsile excused his former rage, and, in reparation, offered Ganelon a superb robe of marten's fur, which was accepted ; and then began the tempting of the traitor. First demanding a pledge of secrecy, Marsile

132

pitied Charlemagne, so aged and so weary with rule. Ganelon praised his emperor's prowess and vast power. Marsile repeated his words of pity, and Ganelon replied that as long as Roland and the Twelve Peers lived Charlemagne needed no man's pity and feared no man's power ; his Franks, also, were the best living warriors. Marsile declared proudly that he could bring four hundred thousand men against Charlemagne's twenty thousand French ; but Ganelon dissuaded him from any such expedition.

Ganelon Plans Treachery

> " ' Not thus will you overcome him ;
> Leave this folly, turn to wisdom.
> Give the Emperor so much treasure
> That the Franks will be astounded.
> Send him, too, the promised pledges,
> Sons of all your noblest vassals.
> To fair France will Charles march homeward,
> Leaving (as I will contrive it)
> Haughty Roland in the rearguard.
> Oliver, the bold and courteous,
> Will be with him : slay those heroes,
> And King Charles will fall for ever ! '
> ' Fair Sir Ganelon,' quoth Marsile,
> ' How must I entrap Count Roland ? '
> ' When King Charles is in the mountains
> He will leave behind his rearguard
> Under Oliver and Roland.
> Send against them half your army :
> Roland and the Peers will conquer,
> But be wearied with the struggle—
> Then bring on your untired warriors.
> France will lose this second battle,
> And when Roland dies, the Emperor
> Has no right hand for his conflicts—
> Farewell all the Frankish greatness !
> Ne'er again can Charles assemble
> Such a mighty host for conquest,
> And you will have peace henceforward ! ' "

Welcomed by Marsile

Marsile was overjoyed at the treacherous advice, and embraced and richly rewarded the felon knight. The death of Roland and the Peers was solemnly sworn between them, by Marsile on the book of the Law of Mahomet, by Ganelon on the sacred relics in the pommel of his sword. Then, repeating the compact between them, and warning Ganelon against treason to his friends, Marsile dismissed the treacherous envoy, who hastened to return and put his scheme into execution.

Ganelon Returns to Charles

In the meantime Charles had retired as far as Valtierra, on his way to France, and there Ganelon found him, and delivered the tribute, the keys of Saragossa, and a false message excusing the absence of the caliph. He had, so Marsile said, put to sea with three hundred thousand warriors who would not renounce their faith, and all had been drowned in a tempest, not four leagues from land. Marsile would obey King Charles's commands in all other respects. "Thank God!" cried Charlemagne. "Ganelon, you have done well, and shall be well rewarded!"

The French Camp. Charles Dreams

Now the whole Frankish army marched towards the Pyrenees, and, as evening fell, found themselves among the mountains, where Roland planted his banner on the topmost summit, clear against the sky, and the army encamped for the night; but the whole Saracen host had also marched and encamped in a wood not far from the Franks. Meanwhile, as Charlemagne slept he had dreams of evil omen. Ganelon, in his dreams, seized

134

the imperial spear of tough ash-wood, and broke it, so that the splinters flew far and wide. In another dream he saw himself at Aix attacked by a leopard and a bear, which tore off his right arm ; a greyhound came to his aid, but he knew not the end of the fray, and slept unhappily.

A Morning Council

When morning light shone, and the army was ready to march, the clarions of the host sounded gaily, and Charlemagne called his barons around him.

> " ' My lords and Peers, ye see these strait defiles :
> Choose ye to whom the rearguard shall be given.'
> ' My stepson Roland,' straight quoth Ganelon.
> ' 'Mid all the Peers there is no braver knight :
> In him will lie the safety of your host.'
> Charles heard in wrath, and spoke in angry tones :
> ' What fiendish rage has prompted this advice ?
> Who then will go before me in the van ? '
> The traitor tarried not, but answered swift :
> ' Ogier the Dane will do that duty best.' "

When Roland heard that he was to command the rearguard he knew not whether to be pleased or not. At first he thanked Ganelon for naming him. "Thanks, fair stepfather, for sending me to the post of danger. King Charles shall lose no man nor horse through my neglect." But when Ganelon replied sneeringly, "You speak the truth, as I know right well," Roland's gratitude turned to bitter anger, and he reproached the villain. "Ah, wretch ! disloyal traitor ! thou thinkest perchance that I, like thee, shall basely drop the glove. But thou shalt see ! Sir King, give me your bow. I will not let my badge of office fall, as thou didst, Ganelon, at Cordova. No evil omen shall assail the host through me."

135

Roland for the Rearguard

Charlemagne was very loath to grant his request, but on the advice of Duke Naimes, most prudent of counsellors, he gave to Roland his bow, and offered to leave with him half the army. To this the champion would not agree, but would only have twenty thousand Franks from fair France. Roland clad himself in his shining armour, laced on his lordly helmet, girt himself with his famous sword Durendala, and hung round his neck his flower-painted shield ; he mounted his good steed Veillantif, and took in hand his bright lance with the white pennon and golden fringe ; then, looking like the Archangel St. Michael, he rode forward, and easy it was to see how all the Franks loved him and would follow where he led. Beside him rode the famous Peers of France, Oliver the bold and courteous, the saintly Archbishop Turpin, and Count Gautier, Roland's loyal vassal. They chose carefully the twenty thousand French for the rearguard, and Roland sent Gautier with one thousand of their number to search the mountains. Alas! they never returned, for King Almaris, a Saracen chief, met and slew them all among the hills ; and only Gautier, sorely wounded and bleeding to death, returned to Roland in the final struggle.

Charlemagne spoke a mournful "Farewell" to his nephew and the rearguard, and the mighty army began to traverse the gloomy ravine through the dark masses of rocks, and to emerge on the other side of the Pyrenees. All wept, most for joy to set eyes on that dear land of fair France, which for seven years they had not seen ; but Charles, with a sad foreboding of disaster, hid his eyes beneath his cloak and wept in silence.

THE SARACEN PURSUIT

Charles is Sad

"What grief weighs on your mind, sire?" asked the wise Duke Naimes, riding up beside Charlemagne.

"I mourn for my nephew. Last night in a vision I saw Ganelon break my trusty lance—this Ganelon who has sent Roland to the rear. And now I have left Roland in a foreign land, and, O God! if I lose him I shall never find his equal!" And the emperor rode on in silence, seeing naught but his own sad foreboding visions.

The Saracen Pursuit

Meanwhile King Marsile, with his countless Saracens, had pursued so quickly that the van of the heathen army soon saw waving the banners of the Frankish rear. Then as they halted before the strife began, one by one the nobles of Saragossa, the champions of the Moors, advanced and claimed the right to measure themselves against the Twelve Peers of France. Marsile's nephew received the royal glove as chief champion, and eleven Saracen chiefs took a vow to slay Roland and spread the faith of Mahomet.

"Death to the rearguard! Roland shall die! Death to the Peers! Woe to France and Charlemagne! We will bring the Emperor to your feet! You shall sleep at St. Denis! Down with fair France!" Such were their confident cries as they armed for the conflict; and on their side no less eager were the Franks.

"Fair Sir Comrade," said Oliver to Roland, "methinks we shall have a fray with the heathen."

"God grant it," returned Roland. "Our duty is to hold this pass for our king. A vassal must endure for his lord grief and pain, heat and cold, torment and death; and a knight's duty is to strike mighty blows, that men may sing of him, in time to come, no evil songs.   Never shall such be sung of me."

Oliver Descries the Saracens

Hearing a great tumult, Oliver ascended a hill and looked towards Spain, where he perceived the great pagan army, like a gleaming sea, with shining hauberks and helms flashing in the sun.   "Alas ! we are betrayed ! This treason is plotted by Ganelon, who put us in the rear," he cried.   "Say no more," said Roland ; "blame him not in this : he is my stepfather."

Now Oliver alone had seen the might of the pagan array, and he was appalled by the countless multitudes of the heathens.   He descended from the hill and appealed to Roland.

Roland will not Blow his Horn

     "'Comrade Roland, sound your war-horn,
     Your great Olifant, far-sounding :
     Charles will hear it and return here.'
     'Cowardice were that,' quoth Roland ;
     'In fair France my fame were tarnished.
     No, these Pagans all shall perish
     When I brandish Durendala.'

     "'Comrade Roland, sound your war-horn :
     Charles will hear it and return here.'
     'God forbid it,' Roland answered,
     'That it e'er be sung by minstrels
     I was asking help in battle
     From my King against these Pagans.
     I will ne'er do such dishonour
     To my kinsmen and my nation.
     No, these heathen all shall perish
     When I brandish Durendala.'

     "'Comrade Roland, sound your war-horn :
     Charles will hear it and return here.
     See how countless are the heathen
     And how small our Frankish troop is !'

" The saintly Archbishop Turpin "

" Charlemagne heard it again "

TURPIN BLESSES THE KNIGHTS

' God forbid it,' answered Roland,
That our fair France be dishonoured
Or by me or by my comrades—
Death we choose, but not dishonour ! ' "

Roland was a valiant hero, but Oliver had prudence
as well as valour, and his advice was that of a good and
careful general. Now he spoke reproachfully.

It is Too Late

"Ah, Roland, if you had sounded your magic horn
the king would soon be here, and we should not
perish ! Now look to the heights and to the mountain
passes : see those who surround us. None of us will
see the light of another day ! "

"Speak not so foolishly," retorted Roland. "Accursed
be all cowards, say I." Then, softening his tone a little,
he continued : " Friend and comrade, say no more.
The emperor has entrusted to us twenty thousand
Frenchmen, and not a coward among them. Lay on
with thy lance, Oliver, and I will strike with Durendala. If I die men shall say: ' This was the sword of a
noble vassal.' "

Turpin Blesses the Knights

Then spoke the brave and saintly Archbishop Turpin.
Spurring his horse, he rode, a gallant figure, to the
summit of a hill, whence he called aloud to the Frankish
knights :

" ' Fair sirs and barons, Charles has left us here
To serve him, or at need to die for him.
See, yonder come the foes of Christendom,
And we must fight for God and Holy Faith.
Now, say your shrift, and make your peace with Heaven ;
I will absolve you and will heal your souls ;
And if you die as martyrs, your true home
Is ready midst the flowers of Paradise ! ' "

The Frankish knights, dismounting, knelt before Turpin, who blessed and absolved them all, bidding them, as penance, to strike hard against the heathen.

Then Roland called his brother-in-arms, the brave and courteous Oliver, and said : " Fair brother, I know now that Ganelon has betrayed us for reward, and Marsile has bought us ; but the payment shall be made with our swords, and Charlemagne will terribly avenge us."

"Montjoie! Montjoie!"

While the two armies yet stood face to face in battle array Oliver replied : " What good is it to speak ? You would not sound your horn, and Charles cannot help us ; he is not to blame. Barons and lords, ride on and yield not. In God's name fight and slay, and remember the war-cry of our Emperor." And at the words the war-cry of " Montjoie ! Montjoie ! " burst from the whole army as they spurred against the advancing heathen host.

The Fray

Great was the fray that day, deadly was the combat, as the Moors and Franks crashed together, shouting their cries, invoking their gods or saints, wielding with utmost courage sword, lance, javelin, scimitar, or dagger. Blades flashed, lances were splintered, helms were cloven in that terrible fight of heroes. Each of the Twelve Peers did mighty feats of arms. Roland himself slew the nephew of King Marsile, who had promised to bring Roland's head to his uncle's feet, and bitter were the words that Roland hurled at the lifeless body of his foe, who had but just before boasted that Charlemagne should lose his right hand. Oliver slew the heathen king's brother, and one by one the Twelve

Peers proved their mettle on the twelve champions of
King Marsile, and left them dead or mortally wounded
on the field. Wherever the battle was fiercest and the
danger greatest, where help was most needed, there
Roland spurred to the rescue, swinging Durendala,
and, falling on the heathen like a thunderbolt of war,
turned the tide of battle again and yet again.

> " Red was Roland, red with bloodshed :
> Red his corselet, red his shoulders,
> Red his arm, and red his charger."

Like the red god Mars he rode through the battle ;
and as he went he met Oliver, with the truncheon of
a spear in his grasp.

> " ' Friend, what hast thou there ? ' cried Roland.
> ' In this game 'tis not a distaff,
> But a blade of steel thou needest.
> Where is now Hauteclaire, thy good sword,
> Golden-hilted, crystal-pommeled ? '
> ' Here,' said Oliver ; ' so fight I
> That I have not time to draw it.'
> ' Friend,' quoth Roland, ' more I love thee
> Ever henceforth than a brother.' "

The Saracens Perish

Thus the battle continued, most valiantly contested
by both sides, and the Saracens died by hundreds and
thousands, till all their host lay dead but one man, who
fled wounded, leaving the Frenchmen masters of the
field, but in sorry plight—broken were their swords and
lances, rent their hauberks, torn and bloodstained their
gay banners and pennons, and many, many of their
brave comrades lay lifeless. Sadly they looked round on
the heaps of corpses, and their minds were filled with
grief as they thought of their companions, of fair France
which they should see no more, and of their emperor
who even now awaited them while they fought and died

141

tor him. Yet they were not discouraged ; loudly their cry re-echoed, "Montjoie ! Montjoie !" as Roland cheered them on, and Turpin called aloud : "Our men are heroes ; no king under heaven has better. It is written in the Chronicles of France that in that great land it is our king's right to have valiant soldiers."

A Second Saracen Army

While they sought in tears the bodies of their friends, the main army of the Saracens, under King Marsile in person, came upon them ; for the one fugitive who had escaped had urged Marsile to attack again at once, while the Franks were still weary. The advice seemed good to Marsile, and he advanced at the head of a hundred thousand men, whom he now hurled against the French, in columns of fifty thousand at a time ; and they came on right valiantly, with clarions sounding and trumpets blowing.

> "'Soldiers of the Lord,' cried Turpin,
> 'Be ye valiant and steadfast,
> For this day shall crowns be given you
> Midst the flowers of Paradise.
> In the name of God our Saviour,
> Be ye not dismayed nor frighted,
> Lest of you be shameful legends
> Chanted by the tongue of minstrels.
> Rather let us die victorious,
> Since this eve shall see us lifeless !—
> Heaven has no room for cowards !
> Knights, who nobly fight, and vainly,
> Ye shall sit amid the holy
> In the blessed fields of Heaven.
> On then, Friends of God, to glory !'"

And the battle raged anew, with all the odds against the small handful of French, who knew they were doomed, and fought as though they were "fey." [1]

[1] Marked out for death.

THE SECOND ARMY DEFEATED

Gloomy Portents

Meanwhile the whole course of nature was disturbed. In France there were tempests of wind and thunder, rain and hail; thunderbolts fell everywhere, and the earth shook exceedingly. From Mont St. Michel to Cologne, from Besançon to Wissant, not one town could show its walls uninjured, not one village its houses unshaken. A terrible darkness spread over all the land, only broken when the heavens split asunder with the lightning-flash. Men whispered in terror: " Behold the end of the world! Behold the great Day of Doom! " Alas! they knew not the truth: it was the great mourning for the death of Roland.

Many French Knights Fall

In this second battle the French champions were weary, and before long they began to fall before the valour of the newly arrived Saracen nobles. First died Engelier the Gascon, mortally wounded by the lance of that Saracen who swore brotherhood to Ganelon; next Samson, and the noble Duke Anseis. These three were well avenged by Roland and Oliver and Turpin. Then in quick succession died Gerin and Gerier and other valiant Peers at the hands of Grandoigne, until his death-dealing career was cut short by Durendala. Another desperate single combat was won by Turpin, who slew a heathen emir " as black as molten pitch."

The Second Army Defeated

Finally this second host of the heathens gave way and fled, begging Marsile to come and succour them; but now of the victorious French there were but sixty valiant champions left alive, including Roland, Oliver, and the fiery prelate Turpin.

A Third Appears

Now the third host of the pagans began to roll forward upon the dauntless little band, and in the short breathing-space before the Saracens again attacked them Roland cried aloud to Oliver:

> "'Fair Knight and Comrade, see these heroes,
> Valiant warriors, lying lifeless!
> I must mourn for our fair country
> France, left widowed of her barons.
> Charles my King, why art thou absent?
> Brother mine, how shall we send him
> Mournful tidings of our struggle?'
> 'How I know not,' said his comrade.
> 'Better death than vile dishonour.'"

Roland Willing to Blow his Horn

> "'Comrade, I will blow my war-horn:
> Charles will hear it in the passes
> And return with all his army.'
> Oliver quoth: ''Twere disgraceful
> To your kinsmen all their life-days.
> When I urged it, then you would not;
> Now, to sound your horn is shameful,
> And I never will approve it.'"

Oliver Objects. They Quarrel

> "'See, the battle goes against us:
> Comrade, I shall sound my war-horn.'
> Oliver replied: 'O coward!
> When I urged it, then you would not.
> If fair France again shall greet me
> You shall never wed my sister;
> By this beard of mine I swear it!'

> "'Why so bitter and so wrathful?'
> Oliver returned: ''Tis thy fault;
> Valour is not kin to madness,
> Temperance knows naught of fury.

THE HORN IS BLOWN

You have killed these noble champions,
You have slain the Emperor's vassals,
You have robbed us of our conquests.
Ah, your valour, Count, is fatal !
Charles must lose his doughty heroes,
And your league with me must finish
With this day in bitter sorrow.' "

Turpin Mediates

Archbishop Turpin heard the dispute, and strove to calm the angry heroes. " Brave knights, be not so enraged. The horn will not save the lives of these gallant dead, but it will be better to sound it, that Charles, our lord and emperor, may return, may avenge our death and weep over our corpses, may bear them to fair France, and bury them in the sanctuary, where the wild beasts shall not devour them." " That is well said," quoth Roland and Oliver.

The Horn is Blown

Then at last Roland put the carved ivory horn, the magic Olifant, to his lips, and blew so loudly that the sound echoed thirty leagues away. " Hark ! our men are in combat !" cried Charlemagne ; but Ganelon retorted : " Had any but the king said it, that had been a lie."

A second time Roland blew his horn, so violently and with such anguish that the veins of his temples burst, and the blood flowed from his brow and from his mouth. Charlemagne, pausing, heard it again, and said : "That is Roland's horn ; he would not sound it were there no battle." But Ganelon said mockingly : "There is no battle, for Roland is too proud to sound his horn in danger. Besides, who would dare to attack Roland, the strong, the valiant, great and wonderful Roland ? No man. He is doubtless hunting, and

145

laughing with the Peers. Your words, my liege, do out show how old and weak and doting you are. Ride on, sire ; the open country lies far before you."

When Roland blew the horn for the third time he had hardly breath to awaken the echoes ; but still Charlemagne heard. " How faintly comes the sound ! There is death in that feeble blast ! " said the emperor ; and Duke Naimes interrupted eagerly : " Sire, Roland is in peril ; some one has betrayed him—doubtless he who now tries to beguile you ! Sire, rouse your host, arm for battle, and ride to save your nephew."

Ganelon Arrested

Then Charlemagne called aloud : " Hither, my men. Take this traitor Ganelon and keep him safe till my return." And the kitchen folk seized the felon knight, chained him by the neck, and beat him ; then, binding him hand and foot, they flung him on a sorry nag, to be borne with them till Charles should demand him at their hands again.

Charles Returns

With all speed the whole army retraced their steps, turning their faces to Spain, and saying : " Ah, if we could find Roland alive what blows we would strike for him ! " Alas ! it was too late ! Too late !

How lofty are the peaks, how vast and shadowy the mountains ! How dim and gloomy the passes, how deep the valleys ! How swift the rushing torrents ! Yet with headlong speed the Frankish army hastens back, with trumpets sounding in token of approaching help, all praying God to preserve Roland till they come. Alas ! they cannot reach him in time ! Too late ! Too late !

ROLAND FIGHTS DESPERATELY

Roland Weeps for his Comrades

Now Roland cast his gaze around on hill and
valley, and saw his noble vassals and comrades lie
dead. As a noble knight he wept for them, saying:

> "'Fair Knights, may God have mercy on your souls!
> May He receive you into Paradise
> And grant you rest on banks of heavenly flowers!
> Ne'er have I known such mighty men as you.
> Fair France, that art the best of all dear lands,
> How art thou widowed of thy noble sons!
> Through me alone, dear comrades, have you died,
> And yet through me no help nor safety comes.
> God have you in His keeping! Brother, come,
> Let us attack the heathen and win death,
> Or grief will slay me! Death is duty now.'"

He Fights Desperately

So saying, he rushed into the battle, slew the only son
of King Marsile, and drove the heathen before him as
the hounds drive the deer. Turpin saw and applauded.
"So should a good knight do, wearing good armour
and riding a good steed. He must deal good strong
strokes in battle, or he is not worth a groat. Let a
coward be a monk in some cloister and pray for the
sins of us fighters."

Marsile in wrath attacked the slayer of his son, but
in vain; Roland struck off his right hand, and Marsile
fled back mortally wounded to Saragossa, while his
main host, seized with panic, left the field to Roland.
However, the caliph, Marsile's uncle, rallied the ranks,
and, with fifty thousand Saracens, once more came
against the little troop of Champions of the Cross,
the three poor survivors of the rearguard.

Roland cried aloud: "Now shall we be martyrs for
our faith. Fight boldly, lords, for life or death! Sell
yourselves dearly! Let not fair France be dishonoured

in her sons. When the Emperor sees us dead with our slain foes around us he will bless our valour."

Oliver Falls

The pagans were emboldened by the sight of the three alone, and the caliph, rushing at Oliver, pierced him from behind with his lance. But though mortally wounded Oliver retained strength enough to slay the caliph, and to cry aloud: "Roland! Roland! Aid me!" then he rushed on the heathen army, doing heroic deeds and shouting "Montjoie! Montjoie!" while the blood ran from his wound and stained the earth blood-red. At this woeful sight Roland swooned with grief, and Oliver, faint from loss of blood, and with eyes dimmed by fast-coming death, distinguished not the face of his dear friend; he saw only a vague figure drawing near, and, mistaking it for an enemy, raised his sword Hauteclaire and gave Roland one last terrible blow, which clove the helmet, but harmed not the head. The blow roused Roland from his swoon, and, gazing tenderly at Oliver, he gently asked him:

> "'Comrade and brother, was that blow designed
> To slay your Roland, him who loves you so?
> There is no vengeance you would wreak on me.'
> 'Roland, I hear you speak, but see you not.
> God guard and keep you, friend; but pardon me
> The blow I struck, unwitting, on your head.'
> 'I have no hurt,' said Roland; 'I forgive
> Here and before the judgment-throne of God.'"

And Dies

Now Oliver felt the pains of death come upon him. Both sight and hearing were gone, his colour fled, and, dismounting, he lay upon the earth; there, humbly confessing his sins, he begged God to grant him rest in Paradise, to bless his lord Charlemagne and the fair

"Turpin fell forward dying"

"The angels of God descended around him"

land of France, and to keep above all men his comrade Roland, his best-loved brother-in-arms. This ended, he fell back, his heart failed, his head drooped low, and Oliver the brave and courteous knight lay dead on the blood-stained earth, with his face turned to the east. Roland lamented him in gentle words : " Comrade, alas for thy valour ! Many days and years have we been comrades : no ill didst thou to me, nor I to thee : now thou art dead, 'tis pity that I live ! "

Turpin is Mortally Wounded. The Horn Again

Turpin and Roland now stood together for a time, and were joined by the brave Count Gautier, whose thousand men had been slain, and he himself grievously wounded ; he now came, like a loyal vassal, to die with his lord Roland, and was slain in the first discharge of arrows which the Saracens shot. Taught by experience, the pagans kept their distance, and wounded Turpin with four lances, while they stood some yards away from the heroes. But when Turpin felt himself mortally wounded he plunged into the throng of the heathen, killing four hundred before he fell, and Roland fought on with broken armour, and with ever-bleeding head, till in a pause of the deadly strife he took his horn and again sent forth a feeble dying blast.

Charles Answers the Horn

Charlemagne heard it, and was filled with anguish. " Lords, all goes ill : I know by the sound of Roland's horn he has not long to live ! Ride on faster, and let all our trumpets sound, in token of our approach." Then sixty thousand trumpets sounded, so that mountains echoed it and valleys replied, and the heathen heard it and trembled. " It is Charlemagne ! Charles is coming ! " they cried. " If Roland lives till he comes the war will begin again, and our bright Spain is lost." Thereupon four hundred banded together to slay Roland; but he rushed upon them, mounted on his good steed Veillantif, and the valiant pagans fled. But while Roland dismounted to tend the dying archbishop they returned and cast darts from afar, slaying Veillantif, the faithful war-horse, and piercing the hero's armour. Still nearer and nearer sounded the clarions of Charlemagne's army in the defiles, and the Saracen host fled for ever, leaving Roland alone, on foot, expiring, amid the dying and the dead.

Turpin Blesses the Dead

Roland made his way to Turpin, unlaced his golden helmet, took off his hauberk, tore his own tunic to bind up his grievous wounds, and then gently raising the prelate, carried him to the fresh green grass, where he most tenderly laid him down.

> "' Ah, gentle lord,' said Roland, ' give me leave
> To carry here our comrades who are dead,
> Whom we so dearly loved ; they must not lie
> Unblest ; but I will bring their corpses here
> And thou shalt bless them, and me, ere thou die.'
> ' Go,' said the dying priest, ' but soon return.
> Thank God ! the victory is yours and mine ! ' "

With great pain and many delays Roland traversed the field of slaughter, looking in the faces of the dead, till he had found and brought to Turpin's feet the bodies of the eleven Peers, last of all Oliver, his own dear friend and brother, and Turpin blessed and absolved them all. Now Roland's grief was so deep and his weakness so great that he swooned where he stood, and the archbishop saw him fall and heard his cry of pain. Slowly and painfully Turpin struggled to his feet, and, bending over Roland, took Olifant, the curved ivory horn ; inch by inch the dying archbishop tottered towards a little mountain stream, that the few drops he could carry might revive Roland.

He Dies

However, his weakness overcame him before he reached the water, and he fell forward dying. Feebly he made his confession, painfully he joined his hands in prayer, and as he prayed his spirit fled. Turpin, the faithful champion of the Cross, in teaching and in battle, died in the service of Charlemagne. May God have mercy on his soul !

When Roland awoke from his swoon he looked for Turpin, and found him dead, and, seeing Olifant, he guessed what the archbishop's aim had been, and wept for pity. Crossing the fair white hands over Turpin's breast, he sadly prayed :

> " ' Alas ! brave priest, fair lord of noble birth,
> Thy soul I give to the great King of Heaven !
> No mightier champion has He in His hosts,
> No prophet greater to maintain the Faith,
> No teacher mightier to convert mankind
> Since Christ's Apostles walked upon the earth !
> May thy fair soul escape the pains of Hell
> And Paradise receive thee in its bowers ! ' "

Roland's Last Fight

Now death was very near to Roland, and he felt it coming upon him while he yet prayed and commended himself to his guardian angel Gabriel. Taking in one hand Olifant, and in the other his good sword Durendala, Roland climbed a little hill, one bowshot within the realm of Spain. There under two pine-trees he found four marble steps, and as he was about to climb them, fell swooning on the grass very near his end. A lurking Saracen, who had feigned death, stole from his covert, and, calling aloud, "Charles's nephew is vanquished! I will bear his sword back to Arabia," seized Durendala as it lay in Roland's dying clasp. The attempt roused Roland, and he opened his eyes, saying, "Thou art not of us," then struck such a blow with Olifant on the helm of the heathen thief that he fell dead before his intended victim.

He Tries to Break his Sword

Pale, bleeding, dying, Roland struggled to his feet, bent on saving his good blade from the defilement of heathen hands. He grasped Durendala, and the brown marble before him split beneath his mighty blows ; but the good sword stood firm, the steel grated but did not break, and Roland lamented aloud that his famous sword must now become the weapon of a lesser man. Again Roland smote with Durendala, and clove the block of sardonyx, but the good steel only grated and did not break, and the hero bewailed himself aloud, saying, "Alas ! my good Durendala, how bright and pure thou art ! How thou flamest in the sunbeams, as when the angel brought thee ! How many lands hast thou conquered for Charles my King, how many champions slain, how many heathen converted! Must I now leave thee to the pagans ? May God spare fair France this shame ! " A third time Roland raised the sword and struck a rock of blue marble, which split asunder, but the steel only grated—it would not break ; and the hero knew that he could do no more.

His Last Prayer

Then he flung himself on the ground under a pine-tree with his face to the earth, his sword and Olifant beneath him, his face to the foe, that Charlemagne and the Franks might see when they came that he died

"Under the trees lay the body of Roland"

Aude the Fair falls dead at the Emperor's feet

victorious. He made his confession, prayed for mercy, and offered to Heaven his glove, in token of submission for all his sins. "*Mea culpa!* O God! I pray for pardon for all my sins, both great and small, that I have sinned from my birth until this day." So he held up towards Heaven his right-hand glove, and the angels of God descended around him. Again Roland prayed:

> "'O very Father, who didst never lie,
> Didst bring St. Lazarus from the dead again,
> Didst save St. Daniel from the lion's mouth,
> Save Thou my soul and keep it from all ills
> That I have merited by all my sins!'"

He Dies

Again he held up to Heaven his glove, and St. Gabriel received it; then, with head bowed and hands clasped, the hero died, and the waiting cherubim, St. Raphael, St. Michael, and St. Gabriel, bore his soul to Paradise.

So died Roland and the Peers of France.

Charles Arrives

Soon after Roland's heroic spirit had passed away the emperor came galloping out of the mountains into the valley of Roncesvalles, where not a foot of ground was without its burden of death.

Loudly he called: "Fair nephew, where art thou? Where is the archbishop? And Count Oliver? Where are the Peers?"

Alas! of what avail was it to call? No man replied, for all were dead; and Charlemagne wrung his hands, and tore his beard and wept, and his army bewailed their slain comrades, and all men thought of vengeance. Truly a fearful vengeance did Charles take, in that terrible battle which he fought the next day against the

Emir of Babylon, come from oversea to help his vassal Marsile, when the sun stood still in heaven that the Christians might be avenged on their enemies ; in the capture of Saragossa and the death of Marsile, who, already mortally wounded, turned his face to the wall and died when he heard of the defeat of the emir ; but when vengeance was taken on the open enemy Charlemagne thought of mourning, and returned to Roncesvalles to seek the body of his beloved nephew.

The emperor knew well that Roland would be found before his men, with his face to the foe. Thus he advanced a bowshot from his companions and climbed a little hill, there found the little flowery meadow stained red with the blood of his barons, and there at the summit, under the trees, lay the body of Roland on the green grass. The broken blocks of marble bore traces of the hero's dying efforts, and Charlemagne raised Roland, and, clasping the hero in his arms, lamented over him.

His Lament

    " ' The Lord have mercy, Roland, on thy soul !
    Never again shall our fair France behold
    A knight so worthy, till France be no more !

    " ' The Lord have mercy, Roland, on thy soul !
    That thou mayest rest in flowers of Paradise
    With all His glorious Saints for evermore !
    My honour now will lessen and decay,
    My days be spent in grief for lack of thee,
    My joy and power will vanish. There is none,
    Comrade or kinsman, to maintain my cause.

    " ' The Lord have mercy, Roland, on thy soul !
    And grant thee place in Paradise the blest,
    Thou valiant youth, thou mighty conqueror !
    How widowed lies our fair France and how lone !
    How will the realms that I have swayed rebel
    Now thou art taken from my weary age !

THE TRAITOR PUT TO DEATH

So deep my woe that fain would I die too
And join my valiant Peers in Paradise
While men inter my weary limbs with thine!'"[1]

The Dead Buried

The French army buried the dead with all honour,
where they had fallen, except the bodies of Roland,
Oliver, and Turpin, which were carried to Blaye, and
interred in the great cathedral there ; and then Charlemagne returned to Aix.

Aude the Fair

As Charles the Great entered his palace a beauteous
maiden met him, Aude the Fair, the sister of Oliver and
betrothed bride of Roland.   She asked eagerly :
" Where is Roland the mighty captain, who swore to
take me for his bride ? "
" Alas ! dear sister and friend," said Charlemagne,
weeping and tearing his long white beard, " thou askest
tidings of the dead.   But I will replace him : thou
shalt have Louis, my son, Count of the Marches."
" These words are strange," exclaimed Aude the
Fair.   " God and all His saints and angels forbid that
I should live when Roland my love is dead."   Thereupon she lost her colour and fell at the emperor's
feet ; he thought her fainting, but she was dead.   God
have mercy on her soul !

The Traitor Put to Death

Too long it would be to tell of the trial of Ganelon
the traitor.   Suffice it that he was torn asunder by wild
horses, and his name remains in France a byword for
all disloyalty and treachery.

[1] The poetical quotations are from the " Chanson de Roland."

155

CHAPTER VIII : THE COUNTESS CATHLEEN

Celtic Mysticism

IN all Celtic literature there is recognisable a certain spirit which seems to be innate in the very character of the people, a spirit of mysticism and acknowledgment of the supernatural. It carries with it a love of Nature, a delight in beauty, colour and harmony, which is common to all the Celtic races. But with these characteristics we find in Ireland a spiritual beauty, a passion of self-sacrifice, unknown in Wales or Brittany. Hence the early Irish heroes are frequently found renouncing advantages, worldly honour, and life itself, at the bidding of some imperative moral impulse. They are the knights-errant of early European chivalry, which was a much deeper and more real inspiration than the carefully cultivated artificial chivalry of centuries later. Cuchulain, Diarmuit, Naesi all pay with their lives for their obedience to the dictates of honour and conscience. And in women, for whom in those early days sacrifice of self was the only way of heroism, the surrender even of eternal bliss was only the sublimation of honour and chivalry ; and this was the heroism of the Countess Cathleen.

The Cathleen Legend

The legend is old, so old that its root has been lost and we know not who first imagined it ; but the idea, the central incident, doubtless goes back to Druid times, when a woman might well have offered herself up to the cruel gods to avert their wrath and stay the plagues which fell upon her people. Under a like impulse Curtius sprang into the gulf in the Forum, and Decius devoted himself to death to win the safety of

156

the Roman army. In each case the powers, evil or beneficent, were supposed to be appeased by the offering of a human life. When Christianity found this legend of sacrifice popular among the heathen nations, it was comparatively easy to adopt it and give it a yet wider scope, by making the sacrifice spiritual rather than physical, and by finally rewarding the hero with heavenly joys. It is to be noted, too, that even at this early period there is a certain glorification of chicanery : the fiend fulfils his side of the contract, but God Himself breaks the other side. This becomes a regular feature in all tales that relate dealings with the Evil One : all Devil's Bridges, Devil's Dykes, and the Faust legends show that Satan may be trusted to keep his word, while the saints invariably kept the letter and broke the spirit. To so primitive a tale as that of " The Countess Cathleen " the pettifogging quibbles of later saints are utterly unknown : God saves her soul because it is His will to reward such abnegation of self, and even the Evil One dare not question the Divine Will.

The Story. Happy Ireland

Once, long ago, as the Chronicles tell us, Ireland was known throughout Europe as " The Isle of Saints," for St. Patrick had not long before preached the Gospel, the message of good tidings, to the warring inhabitants, to tribes of uncivilised Celts, and to marauding Danes and Vikings. He had driven out the serpent-worshippers, and consecrated the Black Stone of Tara to the worship of the True God ; he had convinced the High King of the truth and reasonableness of the doctrine of the Trinity by the illustration of the shamrock leaf, and had overthrown the great idols and purified the land. Therefore the fair shores and fertile vales of Erin, the clustered islets, dropped like jewels in the azure seas, the mist-covered, heather-clad hill-sides, even the barren mountain-tops and the patches of firm ground scattered in the solitudes of fathomless bogs, were homes of pious Culdee or lonely hermit. There was still strife in Ireland, for king fought with king, and heathen marauders still vexed the land ; but many warlike Irish clans or " septs " turned their ardour for fight to religious conflicts, and often every man of a tribe became a monk, so that great abbeys and tribal monasteries and schools were built on the hills where, in former days, stood the chieftain's stronghold (*rath* or *dun*, as Irish legends name it), with its earth mounds and wooden palisades. Holy psalms and chants replaced the boastful songs of the old bards, whilst warriors, accustomed to regard fighting and hunting as the only occupations worthy of a freeborn man, now peacefully illuminated manuscripts or wrought at useful handicrafts. Yet still in secret they dreaded and tried to appease the wrath of the Dagda, Brigit of the Holy Fire, Ængus the Ever-Young, and the awful Washers of the Ford, the Choosers of the Slain ; and to this dread was now joined the new fear of the cruel demons who obeyed Satan, the Prince of Evil.

The Young Countess

At this time there dwelt in Ireland the Countess Cathleen, young, good, and beautiful. Her eyes were as deep, as changeful, and as pure as the ocean that washed Erin's shores ; her yellow hair, braided in two long tresses, was as bright as the golden circlet on her brow or the yellow corn in her garners ; and her step was as light and proud and free as that of the deer in her wide domains. She lived in a stately castle in the midst of great forests, with the cottages of her tribesmen around her gates, and day by day and year by

year she watched the changing glories of the mighty
woods, as the seasons brought new beauties, till her
soul was as lovely as the green woods and purple
hills around. The Countess Cathleen loved the dim,
mysterious forest, she loved the tales of the ancient
gods, and of

> "Old, unhappy, far-off things,
> And battles long ago ; "
>
> *Wordsworth.*

but more than all she loved her clansmen and vassals :
she prayed for them at all the holy hours, and taught
and tended them with loving care, so that in no place in
Ireland could be found a happier tribe than that which
obeyed her gentle rule.

Dearth and Famine

One year there fell upon Ireland, erewhile so happy
a great desolation—"For Scripture saith, an ending to
all good things must be "[1]—and the happiness of the
Countess Cathleen's tribe came to an end in this wise :
A terrible famine fell on the land ; the seed-corn rotted
in the ground, for rain and never-lifting mists filled
the heavy air and lay on the sodden earth ; then when
spring came barren fields lay brown where the shooting
corn should be ; the cattle died in the stall or fell from
weakness at the plough, and the sheep died of hunger
in the fold ; as the year passed through summer
towards autumn the berries failed in the sun-parched
woods, and the withered leaves, fallen long before the
time, lay rotting on the dank earth ; the timid wild
things of the forest, hares, rabbits, squirrels, died in
their holes or fell easy victims to the birds and beasts
of prey ; and these, in their turn, died of hunger in the
famine-stricken forests.

[1] C. Kingsley.

"I searched all day : the mice and rats and hedgehogs
Seemed to be dead, and I could hardly hear
A wing moving in all the famished woods." [1]

Distress of the Peasants

A cry of bitter agony and lamentation rose from the
starving Isle of Saints to the gates of Heaven, and fell
back unheard ; the sky was hard as brass above, and
the earth was barren beneath, and men and women
died in despair, their shrivelled lips still stained green
by the dried grass and twigs they had striven to eat.

"I passed by Margaret Nolan's : for nine days
Her mouth was green with dock and dandelion ;
And now they wake her."

The Misery Increases

In vain the High King of Ireland proclaimed a
universal peace, and wars between quarrelling tribes
stopped and foreign pirates ceased to molest the land,
and chief met chief in the common bond of misery ;
in vain the rich gave freely of their wealth—soon there
was no distinction between rich and poor, high and low,
chief and vassal, for all alike felt the grip of famine, all
died by the same terrible hunger. Soon many of the
great monasteries lay desolate, their stores exhausted,
their portals open, while the brethren, dead within, had
none to bury them ; the lonely hermits died in their
little beehive-shaped cells, or fled from the dreadful
solitude to gather in some wealthy abbey which could
still feed its monks ; and isle and vale which had
echoed their holy chants knew the sounds no more.
Over all, unlifting, unchanging, brooded the deadly
vapour, bearing the plague in its heavy folds, and
filling the air with a sultry lurid haze.

[1] The poetical quotations throughout this story are taken, by
permission, from Mr. W. B. Yeats's play " The Countess Cathleen."

CATHLEEN'S WIDE CHARITY

"There is no sign of change—day copies day,
Green things are dead—the cattle too are dead
Or dying—and on all the vapour hangs
And fattens with disease, and glows with heat."

Cathleen Heartbroken for her People

Round the castle of the Countess Cathleen there was great stir and bustle, for her tender heart was wrung with the misery of her people, and her prayers for them ascended to God unceasingly. So thin she grew and so worn that the physicians bade her servants bring harp and song to charm away the sadness that weighed upon her spirit; but all in vain! Neither the well-loved legends of the ancient gods, nor her harp, nor the voice of her bards could bring her relief—nothing but the attempt to save her people. From the earliest days of the famine her house and her stores were ever ready to supply the wants of the homeless, the poor, the suffering; her wealth was freely spent for food for the starving while supplies could yet be bought either near or in distant baronies; and when known supplies failed her lavish offers tempted the churlish farmers, who still hoarded grain that they might enrich themselves in the great dearth, to sell some of their garnered stores. When she could no longer induce them to part with their grain, her own winter provisions, wine and corn, were distributed generously to all who asked for relief, and none ever left her castle without succour.

Her Wide Charity

Thus passed the early months of bitter starvation, and the Countess Cathleen's name was borne far and wide through Ireland, accompanied with the blessings of all the rescued; and round her castle, from every district, gathered a mighty throng of poor—not only her own clansmen—who all looked to her for a daily dole of

161

food and drink to keep some life in them until the
pestilential mists should pass away. The wholesome
cold of winter would purify the air and bring new hope
and promise of new life in the coming year. Alas !
the winter drew on apace and still the poisonous
yellow vapours hung heavily over the land, and still the
deadly famine clutched each feeble heart and weakened
the very springs of life, and the winter frosts slew more
than the summer heats, so feeble were the people and so
weakened.

Lawlessness Breaks Out

At last, even in the Isle of Saints, the bonds of right
and wrong were loosened, all respect for property
vanished in the universal desolation, and men began to
rob and plunder, to trust only to the right of might,
thinking that their poor miserable lives were of more
value than aught else, than conscience and pity and
honesty. Thus Cathleen lost by barefaced robbery
much of what she still possessed of flocks and herds, or
scanty fruit and corn. Her servants would gladly have
pursued the robbers and regained the spoils, but Cathleen forbade it, for she pitied the miserable thieves, and
thought no evil of them in this bitter dearth. By this
time she had distributed all her winter stores, and had
only enough to feed her poor pensioners and her household with most scanty rations ; and she herself shared
equally with them, for the most earnest entreaties of her
faithful servants could not induce her to fare better than
they in anything. Soon there would be nothing left for
daily distribution, and her heart almost broke as she saw
the misery of her helpless dependents ; they looked to
her as an angel of pity and deliverance, while she knew
herself to be as helpless as they. Day by day Cathleen
went among them, with her pitifully scanty doles of

" Day by day Cathleen went among them "

The Peasant's Story

food, cheering them by her words and smiles, and by her very presence ; and each day she went to her chapel, where she could cast aside the mask of cheerfulness she wore before her people, and prayed to the Blessed Virgin Mary and all the saints to show her how to save her own tribe and all the land.

Cathleen Has an Inspiration

As the Countess knelt long before the altar one noon-tide she passed from her prayers into a deep sleep, and sank down on the altar steps. In the troubled depths of her mind a thought arose, which came to her as an inspiration from Heaven itself. She awoke and sprang up joyfully, exclaiming aloud : "Thanks be to Our Lady and to all the saints ! To them alone the blessed thought is due. Thus can I save my poor until the dearth is over."

Then Cathleen left her oratory with such a light heart as she had not felt since the terrible visitation began, and the gladness in her face was so new and wonderful that all her servants noticed the change, and her old foster-mother, who loved the Countess with the utmost devotion, shuddered at the thought that perhaps her darling had come under the power of the ancient gods and would be bewitched away to Tir-nan-og, the land of never-dying youth. Fearfully old Oona watched Cathleen's face as she passed through the hall, and Cathleen saw the anxious gaze, and came and laid her hand on the old woman's shoulder, saying, " Nay, fear not, nurse ; the saints have heard my prayer and put it into my heart to save all these helpless ones." Then she crossed the hall to her own room, and called a servant, saying, " Send hither quickly Fergus my steward."

She Summons her Steward

Shortly afterwards the steward came, Fergus the White, an old grey-haired man, who had been foster-brother to Cathleen's grandfather. He had seen three generations pass away, he had watched the change from heathenism to Christianity, and of all the chief's family, to which his loyal devotion had ever clung, there remained but this one young girl, and he loved her as his own child. Fergus did obeisance to his liege lady, and kissed her hand kneeling as he asked:

"What would the Countess Cathleen with her steward? Shall I render my account of lands and wealth?"

Demands to Know what Wealth she Owns

"How much have I in lands?" the Countess asked. And Fergus answered in surprise: "Your lands are worth one hundred thousand pounds."

"Of what value is the timber in my forests?" "As much again."

"What is the worth of my castles and my fair residences?" continued the Countess Cathleen. And Fergus still replied: "As much more," though in his heart he questioned why his lady wished to know now, while the famine made all riches seem valueless.

"How much gold still unspent lies in thy charge in my treasure-chests?"

"Lady, your stored gold is three hundred thousand pounds, as much as all your lands and forests and houses are worth."

The Countess Cathleen thought for an instant, and then, as one who makes a momentous decision, spoke firmly, though her lips quivered as she gave utterance to her thought:

THE STEWARD RELUCTANTLY OBEYS

"Go Far and Buy Food"

" Then, Fergus, take my bags of coin and go. Leave here my jewels and some gold, for I may hear of some stores of grain hoarded by niggard farmers, and may induce them to sell, if not for the love of God, then for the love of gold. Take, too, authority from me, written and sealed with my seal, to sell all my lands and timber, and castles, except this one alone where I must dwell. Send a man, trustworthy and speedy, to the North, to Ulster, where I hear the famine is less terrible, and let him buy what cattle he can find, and drive them back as soon as may be."

> " Keeping this house alone, sell all I have ;
> Go to some distant country, and come again
> With many herds of cows and ships of grain."

The Steward Reluctantly Obeys

The ancient steward, Fergus the White, stood at first speechless with horror and grief, but after a moment of silence his sorrow found vent in words, and he besought his dear lady not to sell everything, her ancient home, her father's lands, her treasured heirlooms, and leave herself no wealth for happier times. All his persuasions were useless, for Cathleen would not be moved ; she bade him " Farewell " and hastened his journey, saying, " A cry is in mine ears ; I cannot rest." So there was no help for it. A trusty man was despatched to Ulster to buy up all the cattle (weak and famine-stricken as they would be) in the North Country ; while Fergus himself journeyed swiftly to England, which was still prosperous and fertile, untouched by the deadly famine, and knowing nothing of the desolation of the sister isle, to which the English owed so much of their knowledge of the True Faith.

Buys Stores in England

In England Fergus spent all the gold he brought with him, and then sold all the Countess Cathleen bade him sell—lands, castles, forests, pastures, timber—all but one lonely castle in the desolate woods, where she dwelt among her own people, with the dying folk thronging round her gates and in her halls. Good bargains Fergus made also, for he was a shrewd and loyal steward, and the saints must have touched the hearts of the English merchants, so that they gave good prices for all, or perhaps they did not realize the dire distress that prevailed in Ireland. However that may have been, Fergus prospered in his trading, and bought grain, and wine, and fat oxen and sheep, so that he loaded many ships with full freights of provisions, enough to carry the starving peasantry through the famine year till the next harvest. At last all his money was spent, all his ships were laden, everything was ready, and the little fleet lay in harbour, only awaiting a fair wind, which, unhappily, did not come.

His Return Delayed

First of all Fergus waited through a deadly calm, when the sails hung motionless, drooping, with no breath of air to stir them, when the fog that brooded over the shores of England never lifted and all sailing was impossible ; then the winds dispersed the fog, and Fergus, forgetting caution in his great anxiety to return, hastily set sail for his own land, and there came fierce tempests and contrary winds, so that his little fleet was driven back, and one or two ships went down with all their stores of food. Fergus wept to see his lady's wealth lost in the wintry sea, but he dared not venture again, and though he chafed and fretted at the delay, it was nearly two months after he reached England before he could sail back to his young mistress and her starving countrymen. The trusty messenger who had been sent to buy cattle had succeeded beyond his own expectation ; he also had made successful bargains, and had found more cattle than he believed were still alive in Ireland. He had bought all, and was driving them slowly towards the Countess Cathleen's forest dwelling. Their progress was so slow, because of their weakness and the scanty fodder by the way, that no news of them came to Cathleen, and she knew not that while corn and cattle were coming with Fergus across the sea, food was also coming to her slowly through the barren ways of her own native land. None of this she knew, and despair would have filled her heart, but for her faith in God and her belief in the great inspiration that had been given to her.

Deepening Misery in Ireland

Meanwhile terrible things had been happening in Ireland. As in England in later days, " men said openly that Christ and His saints slept"; they thought with longing of the mighty old gods, for the new seemed powerless, and they yearned for the friendly " good people " who had fled from the sound of the church bell. Thus many minds were ready to revolt from the Christian faith if they had not feared the life after death and the endless torments of the Christian Hell. Some few, desperate, even offered secret worship to the old heathen gods, and true love to the One True God had grown cold.

Two Mysterious Strangers

Now on the very day on which Fergus sailed for England, and his comrade departed to Ulster, two mysterious

167

and stately strangers suddenly appeared in Erin. Whence they came no man knew, but they were first seen near the wild seashore of the west, and the few poor inhabitants thought they had been put ashore by some vessel or wrecked on that dangerous coast. Aliens they certainly were, for they talked with each other in a tongue that none understood, and they appeared as if they did not comprehend the questions asked of them. Thus they passed away from the western coasts, and made their way inland ; but when they next appeared, in a village not far from Dublin, they had greatly changed : they wore magnificent robes and furs, with splendid jewelled gloves on their hands, and golden circlets, set with gleaming rubies, bound their brows ; their black steeds showed no trace of weakness and famine as they rode through the woods and carefully noted the misery everywhere.

Their Strange Story

At last they alighted at the little lodge, where a forester's widow gladly received them ; and their royal dress, lofty bearing and strange language accorded ill with the mean surroundings and the scanty accommodation of that little hut. The dead forester had been one of the Countess Cathleen's most faithful vassals, and his holding was but a short distance from the castle, so that the strangers could, unobserved, watch the life of the little village. As time passed they told their hostess they were merchants, simple traders from a distant country, trafficking in very precious gems ; but they had no wares for exchange, and no gems to show ; they made no inquiries or researches, bargained with no man, seemed to do no business ; they were the most unusual merchants ever seen in Ireland, and the strangeness of their behaviour troubled men's minds.

PROFESSED ERRAND OF MERCY

Mysterious Behaviour

Day by day they ate, unquestioning, the coarse food their poor hostess set before them, and the black bread which was the best food obtainable in those terrible days, but they added to it wine, rich and red, from their own private store, and they paid her lavishly in good red gold, so that she wondered that any men should stay in the famine-stricken country when they could so easily leave it at their will. Gradually, too, speaking now in the Irish tongue, they began to ask her cautious questions of the people, of the land, of the famine, how men lived and how they died, and so they heard of the exceeding goodness of the Countess Cathleen, whose bounty had saved so many lives, and was still saving others, though the deadly pinch of famine grew sorer with the passing days. To their hostess they admired Cathleen's goodness, and were loud in her praises, but they looked askance at one another and their brows were black with discontent.

Professed Errand of Mercy

Then one day the kingly merchants told the poor widow who harboured them that they too were the friends of the poor and starving ; they were servants of a mighty prince, who in his compassion and mercy had sent them on a mission to Ireland to help the afflicted peasants to fight against famine and death. They said that they themselves had no food to give, only wine and gold in plenty, so that men might exert themselves and search for food to buy. Their hostess, hearing this, and knowing that there were still some niggards who refused to part with their mouldering heaps of corn, setting the price so high that no man could buy, called down the blessing of God and Mary

169

and all the saints upon their heads, for if they would distribute their gold to all, or even buy the corn themselves and distribute it, men need no longer die of hunger.

A New Traffic

When she prayed for a blessing on the two strangers they smiled scornfully and impatiently ; and the elder said, cunningly :

> "Alas ! we know the evils of mere charity,
> And would devise a more considered way.
> Let each man bring one piece of merchandise."

"Ah, sirs ! " replied the hostess, "then your compassion, your gold and your goodwill are of no avail. Think you, after all these weary months, that any man has merchandise left to sell ? They have sold long ago all but the very clothes they wear, to keep themselves alive till better days come. Such offers are mockery of our distress."

"We mock you not," said the elder merchant. "All men have the one precious thing we wish to buy, and have come hither to find ; none has already lost or sold it."

"What precious treasure can you mean ? Men in Ireland now have only their lives, and can barely cherish those," said the poor woman, wondering greatly and much afraid.

Buyers of Souls

The elder merchant continued gazing at her with a crafty smile and an eye ever on the alert for tokens of understanding. "Poor as they are, Irishmen have still one thing that we will purchase, if they will sell : their souls, which we have come to obtain for our mighty Prince, and with the great price that we shall pay in

pure gold men can well save their lives till the starving
time is over. Why should men die a cruel, lingering
death or drag through weary months of miserable half-
satisfied life when they may live well and merrily at
the cost of a soul, which is no good but to cause fear
and pain ? We take men's souls and liberate them from
all pain and care and remorse, and we give in exchange
money, much money, to procure comforts and ease ;
we enrol men as vassals of our great lord, and he is no
hard taskmaster to those who own his sway."

Slow Trade at First

When the poor widow heard these dreadful words
she knew that the strangers were demons come to
tempt men's souls and to lure them to Hell. She
crossed herself, and fled from them in fear, praying to
be kept from temptation ; and she would not return to
her little cottage in the forest, but stayed in the village
warning men against the evil demons who were tempting the starving people, till she too died of the famine,
and her house was left wholly to the strangers. Yet
the merchants fared ever well, better than before her
departure, and those who ventured to the forest
dwelling found good food and rich wine, which the
strangers sometimes gave to their visitors, with crafty
hints of abundance to be easily obtained. Then when
timid individuals asked the way to win these comforts
the strangers began their tempting, and represented the
ease to be gained by the sale of men's souls. One man,
bolder than the rest, made a bargain with the demons
and gave them his soul for three hundred crowns of
gold, and from that time he in his turn became a
tempter. He boasted of his wealth, of the rich food
the merchants gave him at times, of the potent wine
he drank from their generously opened bottles, and,

best of all, he vaunted his freedom from pity, conscience, or remorse.

Trade Increases

Gradually many people came to the forest dwelling and trafficked with the demon merchants. The purchase of souls went on busily, and the demons paid prices varying according to the worth of the soul and the record of its former sins ; but to all who sold they gave food and wine, and in gloating over their gold, and satisfying hunger and thirst, men forgot to ask whence came this food and wine and the endless stores of coin. Now many people ventured into the forest to deal with the demons, and the narrow track grew into a broad beaten way with the numbers of those who came, and all returned fed and warmed, and bearing bags heavy with coin, and the promise of abundant food and easy service. Those who had sold their souls rioted with the money, for the demons gave them food, and they bought wine from the inexhaustible stores of the evil merchants. The poor, lost people knew that there was no hope for them after death, and they tried by all means to keep themselves alive and to enjoy what was yet left to them ; but their mirth was fearful and they durst not stop to think.

Cathleen Hears of the Demon Traders

At first the Countess Cathleen knew nothing of the terrible doings of the demons, for she never passed beyond her castle gates, but spent her time in prayer for her people's safety and for the speedy return of her messengers ; but when the starving throng of pensioners at her gates grew daily less, and there were fewer claimants for the pitiful allowance which was all she had to give, she wondered if some other mightier helper had come

172

to Ireland.   But she could hear of none, and soon the
shameless rioting and drunkenness in the village came
to her knowledge, and she wondered yet more whence
her clansmen obtained the means for their excesses, for
she felt instinctively that the origin of all this rioting
must be evil.   Cathleen therefore called to her an old
peasant, whose wife had died of hunger in the early
days of the famine, so that he himself had longed to
die and join her ; but when he came to her she was
horror-struck by the change in him.   Now he came
flushed with wine, with defiant look and insolent bearing, and his face was full of evil mirth as he tried to
answer soberly the Countess's questions.

"Why do the villagers and strangers no longer
come to me for food ?   I have but little now to give,
but all are welcome to share it with me and my
household."

The Peasant's Story

"They do not come, O Countess, because they are
no longer starving.   They have better food and wine,
and abundance of money to buy more."

"Whence then have they obtained the money, the
food, and the wine for the drinking-bouts, the tumult
of which reaches me even in my oratory ?"

"Lady, they have received all from the generous
merchants who are in the forest dwelling where old
Mairi formerly lived ; she is dead now, and these noble
strangers keep open house in her cottage night and
day ; they are so wealthy that they need not stint their
bounty, and so powerful that they can find good food,
enough for all who go to them.   Since Brigit died
(your old servant, lady) her husband and son work no
more, but serve the strange merchants, and urge
all men to join them ; and I, and many others, have

done so, and we are now wealthy" (here he showed the Countess a handful of gold) "and well fed, and have wine as much as heart can desire."

"But do you give them nothing in return for all their generosity? Are they so noble that they ask nothing in requital of their bounty?"

"Good Gold for Souls"

"Oh, yes, we give them something, but nothing of importance, nothing we cannot spare. They are merchants of souls, and buy them for their king, and they pay good red gold for the useless, painful things. I have sold my soul to them, and now I weep no more for my wife; I am gay, and have wine enough and gold enough to help me through this dearth!"

"Alas!" sighed the Countess, "and what when you too die?" The old peasant laughed at her grief as he said: "Then, as now, I shall have no soul to trouble me with remorse or conscience"; and the Countess covered her eyes with her hand and beckoned silently that he should go. In her oratory, whither she betook herself immediately, she prayed with all her spirit that the Virgin and all the saints would inspire her to defeat the demons and to save her people's souls.

Cathleen Tries to Check the Traffic

Next day Cathleen called together all the people in the village, her own tribesmen and strangers. She offered them again a share of all she had, and the daily rations she could distribute, but told them that all must share alike and that she had nothing but the barest necessaries to give—scanty portions of corn and meal, with milk from one or two famine-stricken cows her servants had managed to keep alive. To this she added that she had sent two trusty messengers for help, one to Ulster for cattle, and Fergus to England for corn and wine ; they must return soon, she felt sure, with abundant supplies, if men would patiently await their return.

In Vain

But all was useless. Her messengers had sent no word of their return, and the abundant supplies at the forest cottage were more easily obtained, and were less carefully regulated, than those of the Countess Cathleen. The merchants, too, were ever at hand with their cunning wiles, and their active, persuasive dupes, who would gladly bring all others into their own soulless condition. The wine given by the demons warmed the hearts of all who drank, and the deceived peasants dreamed of happiness when the famine was over, and so the passionate appeal of the Countess failed, and the sale of souls continued merrily. The noise of revelry grew daily louder and more riotous, and the drinkers cared nothing for the death or departure of their dearest friends ; while those who died, died drunken and utterly reckless, or full of horror and despair, reviling the crafty merchants who had deceived them with promises of life and happiness. The evil influence clung all about the countryside, and seemed in league with the pitiless powers of Nature against the souls of men, till at last the stricken Countess, putting her trust in God, sought out the forest lodge where the demon merchants dwelt, trafficking for souls. The way was easy to find now, for a broad beaten track led to the dwelling, and as the evil spirits saw Cathleen coming slowly along the path their wicked eyes gleamed and their clawlike hands worked convulsively in their jewelled gloves, for they hoped she had come to sell her pure soul.

She Visits the Demons

"What does the Countess Cathleen wish to obtain from two poor stranger merchants?" said the elder with an evil smile; and the younger, bowing deeply, said: "Lady, you may command us in all things, save what touches our allegiance to our king." Cathleen replied: "I have no merchandise to barter, nothing for trade with you, for you buy such things as I will never sell: you buy men's souls for Hell. I come only to beg that you will release the poor souls whom you have bought for Satan's kingdom, and will have mercy on my ignorant people and deceive them no more. I have yet some gold unspent and jewels unsold: take all there is, but let my people go free." Then the merchants laughed aloud scornfully, and rejected her offer. "Would you have us undo our work? Have we toiled, then, for naught to extend our master's sway? Have we won for him so many souls to dwell for ever in his kingdom and do his work, and shall we give them back for your entreaties? We have gold enough, and food and wine enough, fair lady. The souls we have bought we keep, for our master gives us honour and rank proportioned to the number of souls we win for him, and you may see by the golden circlets round our brows that we are princes of his kingdom, and have brought him countless souls. Nevertheless, there is one most rare and precious thing which could redeem these bartered souls of Ireland's peasants, things of little worth."

They Make a Proposal

"Oh, what is that?" said the Countess. "If I have it, or can in any way procure it, tell me, that I may redeem these deluded people's souls."

" Thieves have broken into the treasure-chamber "

" Cathleen signed the bond "

FALSE TIDINGS

"You have it now, fair saint. It is one pure soul, precious as multitudes of more sin-stained souls. Our master would far rather have a perfect and flawless pearl for his diadem than myriads of these cracked and flawed crystals. Your soul, most saintly Countess, would redeem the souls of all your tribe, if you would sell it to our king ; it would be the fairest jewel in his crown. But think not to save your people otherwise, and beguile them no longer with false promises of help : your messenger to Ulster lies sick of ague in the Bog of Allen, and no food comes from England."

False Tidings

"We saw a man
Heavy with sickness in the Bog of Allen
Whom you had bid buy cattle. Near Fair Head
We saw your grain ships lying all becalmed
In the dark night, and not less still than they
Burned all their mirrored lanterns in the sea."

When Cathleen heard of the failure of her messengers to bring food it seemed as if all hope were indeed over, and the demons smiled craftily upon her as she turned silently to go, and laughed joyously to each other when she had left their presence. Now they had good hope to win her for their master ; but they knew that their time was short, since help was not far away.

"Last night, closed in the image of an owl,
I hurried to the cliffs of Donegal,
And saw, creeping on the uneasy surge,
Those ships that bring the woman grain and meal ;
They are five days from us.
I hurried east,
A grey owl flitting, flitting in the dew,
And saw nine hundred oxen toil through Meath,
Driven on by goads of iron ; they too, brother,
Are full five days from us. Five days for traffic."

Cathleen's Despair

The Countess then went back in bitter grief to her desolate castle, where only faithful old servants now waited in the halls, and whispered together in the dark corners, and, kneeling in her oratory, she prayed far into the night for light in her darkness. As she prayed before the altar she slept for very weariness, and was aroused by a sudden furious knocking, and an outcry of "Thieves! Thieves!" Cathleen rose quickly from the altar steps, and met her foster-mother, Oona, at the door of the oratory; and Oona cried aloud: "Thieves have broken into the treasure-chamber, and nothing is left!" Cathleen asked if this were true, and discovered that not a single coin, not a single gem was left: the demons had stolen all. And while the servants still mourned over the lost treasures of the house there came another cry of "Thieves! Thieves!" and an old peasant rushed in, exclaiming that all the food was gone. That, alas! was true: the few sacks of meal which supplied the scanty daily fare were emptied and the bags flung on the floor. Now indeed the last poor resource was gone.

A Desperate Decision

When the Countess heard of this last terrible misfortune a great light broke upon her mind with a blinding flash, and showed her a way to save others, even at the cost of her own salvation. It seemed God's answer to her prayer for guidance, and she resolved to follow the inspiration thus sent into her mind. She decided now what she would do; her mind was made up, and the light which shines from extreme sacrifice of self was so bright upon her face that her old nurse and her servants, wailing around her, were awe-stricken and durst not question or check her. She returned to her oratory door, and, standing on the steps, looking down on her weeping domestics, she cried :

> " I am desolate,
> For a most sad resolve wakes in my heart ;
> But always I have faith.   Old men and women,
> Be silent ;   God does not forsake the world.
> Mary Queen of Angels
> And all you clouds and clouds of saints, farewell ! "

With one last long gaze at the little altar of her oratory she resolutely closed the door and turned away.

She Revisits the Demons

The next day the merchants in their forest lodge were still buying souls, and giving food and wine to the starving peasants who sold.   They were buying men and women, sinful, terrified, afraid to die, eager to live ; buying them more cheaply than before because of the increase of sin and terror.   Bargains were being struck and bartering was in full progress, when suddenly all the peasants stopped, shamefaced, as one said, " Here comes the Countess Cathleen," and down the track she was seen approaching slowly.   One by one the peasants slunk away, and the demon merchants were quite alone when Cathleen entered the little cottage where they sat, with bags of coin on the table before them and on the ground beside them.   Again they greeted her with mocking respect, and asked to know her will.

" Merchants, do you still buy souls for Hell ? "

" Lady, our traffic prospers, for the famine lies long on the land, and men would fain live till better days come again.   Besides, we can give them food and wine and wealth for future years ; and all in exchange for a mere soul, a little breath of wind."

"Perhaps the Countess Cathleen has come to deal with us," said the younger.

"Merchant, you are right; I have come to bring you merchandise. I have a soul to sell, so costly that perhaps the price is beyond your means."

The elder merchant replied joyfully : " No price is beyond our means, if only the soul be worth the price ; if it be a pure and stainless soul, fit to join the angels and saints in Paradise, our master will gladly pay all you ask. Whose is the soul, and what is the price ?"

Her Terms

"The people starve, therefore the people go
    Thronging to you. I hear a cry come from them,
    And it is in my ears by night and day :
    And I would have five hundred thousand crowns,
    To find food for them till the dearth go by ;
    And have the wretched spirits you have bought
    For your gold crowns, released, and sent to God.
    The soul that I would barter is my soul."

The Bond Signed

When the demons heard this, and knew that Cathleen was willing to give her own soul as ransom for the souls of others, they were overjoyed, their eyes flashed, the rubies of their golden crowns shot out fiery gleams, and their fingers clutched the air as if they already held her stainless soul. This would be a great triumph to their master, and they would win great honour in Hell when they brought him a soul worth far, far more than large abundance of ordinary sinful souls. Very carefully they watched while the trembling Countess signed the bond which gave her soul to Hell, very gladly they paid down the money for which she had stipulated, and very joyously they saw the signs of speedy death in her face, knowing, as they did, how soon the coming relief would show her sacrifice to have been unnecessary, though now it was irrevocable.

General Lamentation

Sadly but resolutely she turned away, followed by her servants bearing the bags of gold, and as she passed through the village a rumour ran before her of what she had done. All men were sobered by the terrible tidings, and the redeemed people waited for her coming, and followed her weeping and lamenting, for now their souls were free again, and they recognised the great sacrifice she had made for them ; but it was too late to save her, though now all would have died for her. Cathleen passed on into her castle, and there in the courtyard she distributed the money to all her people, and bade them dwell quietly in obedience till her steward returned. She herself, she said, could not stay ; she must go on a long and dark journey, for her people's need had broken her heart and conquered her ; she was no longer her own, but belonged to the dark lord of Hell ; she could not bid them pray for her, nor could she pray for herself.

Cathleen Fades Away

Her people, who knew the great price at which she had redeemed them, besought the Blessed Virgin and all the saints to have mercy on her ; and all the souls she had released, on earth and in Heaven, prayed for her night and day, and the blessed saints interceded for her. Yet from day to day the Countess Cathleen faded, and the demons, ceasing all other traffic, lurked in waiting to catch her soul as she died. Night and day her heart-broken foster-mother Oona tended her ; but she grew feebler, till it seemed that she would die before Fergus returned.

The Steward Returns

On the fifth day, however, glad tidings came. Fergus had landed, and sent word that he was bringing corn and meal as quickly as possible; also a wandering peasant brought a message that nine hundred oxen were within one day's journey of her castle; and when the gentle Cathleen heard this, and knew that her people were safe, she died with a smile on her lips and thanks to God for her people on her tongue. That same night a great tempest broke over the land, which drove away the pestilential mists, and left the country free from evil influences, for with the morning men found the forest lodge crushed beneath the fallen trees, and the two demon merchants vanished. All gathered round the castle and mourned for the Countess Cathleen, for none knew how it would go with her spirit; they feared that the evil demons had borne her soul to Hell. All had prayed for her, but there had been no sign, no token of forgiveness. Nevertheless their prayers were heard and answered.

The Demons Cheated

In the next night, when the great storm had passed away and the vapours no longer filled the air, when Fergus had distributed food and wine, and the oxen had been apportioned to every family, so that plenty reigned in every house, when only Cathleen's castle lay desolate, shrouded in gloom, the faithful old nurse Oona, watching by the body of her darling, had a glorious vision. She saw the splendid armies of the angels who guard mankind from evil, she saw the saints who had suffered and overcome, and amid them was the Countess Cathleen, happy with saints and angels in the bliss of Paradise; for her love had redeemed her own soul as well as the

souls of others, and God had pardoned her sin because
of her self-sacrifice.

> " The light beats down : the gates of pearl are wide,
>   And she is passing to the floor of peace,
>   And Mary of the seven times wounded heart
>   Has kissed her lips, and the long blessed hair
>   Has fallen on her face ; the Light of Lights
>   Looks always on the motive, not the deed,
>   The Shadow of Shadows on the deed alone."

CHAPTER IX : CUCHULAIN, THE CHAMPION OF IRELAND

Introduction

AMONG all the early literatures of Europe, there are two which, at exactly opposite corners of the continent, display most strikingly similar characteristics, characteristics which apparently point to some racial affinity in the peoples who produced them. These literatures are the Greek and the Irish. It has been maintained with much ingenuity that the Greeks oi Homer, the early Britons, and the Irish Celts were all of one stock, as shown by the many points they had in common. It is certain that in customs, manner of life, ethics, ideas of religion, and methods of warfare a striking similarity may be seen between the Greeks as described by Homer and the Britons as Julius Cæsar knew them, or the Irish as their own legends reveal them. We must expect to find in their myths and legends a certain resemblance of Celtic ideas to Greek ideas ; and if the great Achilles sulks in his tent because he is unjustly deprived of his captive, the fair Briseis, we shall not be surprised to find the Champion of Erin quarrelling over his claim to precedence. The contest between the heroes for the armour of dead Achilles is paralleled by this contest between the three greatest warriors oi Ireland for the special dish of honour called the "Champion's Portion," a distinction which also recalls Greek life.

Cuchulain, the Irish Achilles

The resemblance of the Cuchulain legend to the story of Achilles is so strong that Cuchulain is often called "the Irish Achilles," but there are elements of humour and pathos in his story which the tale of Achilles cannot

184

show, and in reckless courage, power of inspiring dread, sense of personal merit, and frankness of speech the Irish hero is not inferior to the mighty Greek. The way in which Cuchulain established his claim to be regarded as Chief Champion of Erin is related in the following story, which shows some primitive Celtic features found again in Welsh legends and other national folk-tales.

The Youth of Cuchulain

Cuchulain was the nephew of King Conor of Ulster, son of his sister Dechtire, and men say his father was no mortal man, but the great god Lugh of the Long Hand. When Cuchulain was born he was brought up by King Conor himself and the wisest men of Ireland ; when five years old, he beat all the other boys in games and warlike exercises, and on the day on which he was seven he assumed the arms of a warrior, so much greater was he than the sons of mortal men. Cuchulain had overheard his tutor, Cathbad the Druid, say to the older youths, " If any young man take arms to-day, his name will be greater than any other name in Ireland, but his span of life will be short," and as he loved fame above long life, he persuaded his uncle, King Conor, to invest him with the weapons of manhood. His fame soon spread all over Ireland, for his warlike deeds were those of a proved warrior, not of a child of nursery age, and by the time Cuchulain was seventeen he was in reality without peer among the champions of Ulster, or of all Ireland.

Cuchulain's Marriage

When the men of Ulster remembered Cuchulain's divine origin, they would fain have him married, so that he might not die childless ; and for a year they searched

185

all Erin for a fit bride for so great a champion. Cuchulain, however, went wooing for himself, to the dun of Forgall the Wily, a Druid of great power. Forgall had two daughters, of whom the younger, Emer, was the most lovely and virtuous maiden to be found in the country, and she became Cuchulain's chosen bride. Gallant was his wooing, and merry and jesting were her answers to his suit, for though Emer loved Cuchulain at first sight she would not accept him at once, and long they talked together. Finally Emer consented to wed Cuchulain when he had undergone certain trials and adventures for a year, and had accomplished certain feats, a test which she imposed on her lover, partly as a trial of his worthiness and constancy and partly to satisfy her father Forgall, who would not agree to the marriage. When Cuchulain returned triumphant at the end of the year, he rescued Emer from the confinement in which her father had placed her, and won her at the sword's point; they were wedded, and dwelt at Armagh, the capital of Ulster, under the protection of King Conor.

Bricriu's Feast

It happened that at Conor's court was one chief who delighted in making mischief, as Thersites among the Grecian leaders. This man, Bricriu of the Bitter Tongue, came to King Conor and invited him and all the heroes of the Red Branch, the royal bodyguard of Ulster, to a feast at his new dwelling, for he felt sure he could find some occasion to stir up strife at a feast. King Conor, however, and the Red Branch heroes, distrusted Bricriu so much that they refused to accept the invitation, unless Bricriu would give sureties that, having received his guests, he would leave the hall before the feasting began. Bricriu, who had expected some such condition, readily agreed, and before going home to prepare his feast took measures for stirring up strife among the heroes of Ulster.

Bricriu's Falsehood

Before Bricriu left Armagh he went to the mighty Laegaire and with many words of praise said : "All good be with you, O Laegaire, winner of battles ! Why should you not be Champion of Ireland for ever ?"

"I can be, if I will," said Laegaire.

"Follow my advice, and you shall be head of all the champions of Ireland," said cunning Bricriu.

"What is your counsel ?" asked Laegaire.

"King Conor is coming to a feast in my house," said Bricriu, "and the Champion's Bit will be a splendid portion for any hero. That warrior who obtains it at this feast will be acclaimed Chief Champion of Erin. When the banquet begins do you bid your chariot-driver rise and claim the hero's portion for you, for you are indeed worthy of it, and I hope that you may get what you so well deserve !"

"Some men shall die if my right is taken from me," quoth Laegaire ; but Bricriu only laughed and turned away.

Bricriu Meets Conall Cearnach

Bricriu next met Conall Cearnach, Cuchulain's cousin, one of the chiefs of the Red Branch.

"May all good be with you, Conall the Victorious," quoth he. "You are our defence and shield, and no foe dare face you in battle. Why should you not be Chief Champion of Ulster ?"

"It only depends on my will," said Conall ; and then Bricriu continued his flattery and insidious suggestions until he had stirred up Conall to command his charioteer to claim the Champion's Portion at Bricriu's feast. Very joyous was Bricriu, and very evilly he smiled as he turned away when he had roused the ambition of Conall Cearnach, for he revelled in the prospect of coming strife.

Bricriu Meets Cuchulain

"May all good be with you, Cuchulain," said Bricriu, as he met the youthful hero. "You are the chief defence of Erin, our bulwark against the foe, our joy and darling, the hero of Ulster, the favourite of all the maidens of Ireland, the greatest warrior of our land! We all live in safety under the protection of your mighty hand, so why should you not be the Chief Champion of Ulster? Why will you leave the Hero's Portion to some less worthy warrior?"

"By the god of my people, I will have it, or slay any bold man who dares to deprive me of it," said Cuchulain.

Thereupon Bricriu left Cuchulain and travelled to his home, where he made his preparations for receiving the king, as if nothing were further from his thoughts than mischief-making and guile.

The Feast and the Quarrel

When King Conor and his court had entered Bricriu's house at Dundrum, and were sitting at the feast, Bricriu was forced by his sureties to leave the hall, for men feared his malicious tongue, and as he went to his watch-tower he turned and cried:

"The Champion's Portion at my feast is worth having; let it be given to the best hero in Ulster."

The carving and distribution of the viands began, and when the Champion's Portion was brought forward it was claimed by three chariot-drivers, Laegaire's, Conall's, and Cuchulain's, each on behalf of his master; and when no decision was made by King Conor the three heroes claimed it, each for himself. But Laegaire and Conall united in defying Cuchulain and ridiculing his claim, and a great fight began in the hall, till all men shook for fear; and at last King Conor intervened, before any man had been wounded.

"Put up your swords," he said. "The Champion's Portion at this feast shall be divided among the three, and we will ask King Ailill and Queen Meave of Connaught to say who is the greatest champion." This plan pleased every one but Bricriu, who saw his hopes of fomenting strife disappear.

The Women's Quarrel

Just at that moment the women rose and quitted the hall to breathe the fresh air, and Bricriu spied his opportunity. Going down from his watch-tower, he met Fedelm, the wife of Laegaire, with her fifty maidens, and said to her:

"All good be with you to-night, Fedelm of the Fresh Heart! Truly in beauty, in birth, in dignity, no woman in Ulster is your equal. If you enter my hall first to-night, you will be queen of the Ulster women."

Fedelm walked on merrily enough, but determined that she would soon re-enter the hall, and certainly before any other woman. Bricriu next met Lendabair the Favourite, Conall's wife, and gave her similar flattery and a similar prophecy, and Lendabair also determined to be first back at the house and first to enter the hall.

Then Bricriu waited till he saw Emer, Cuchulain's fair wife. "Health be with you, Emer, wife of the best man in Ireland! As the sun outshines the stars, so do you outshine all other women! You should of right enter the house first, for whoever does so will be queen of the women of Ulster, and none has a better claim to be their queen than Cuchulain's wife, Forgall's fair daughter."

The Husbands Intervene

The three fair women, each with her train of fifty maidens, watched one another carefully, and when one turned back towards the house the others accompanied her, step for step ; and the noise of their returning footsteps as they raced along alarmed their husbands. Sencha, the king's wise counsellor, reassured them, saying, " It is only a woman's quarrel ; Bricriu has stirred up enmity among the wives of the heroes "; and as he spoke Emer reached the hall, having suddenly outrun the others ; but the doors were shut. Then followed bitter complaints from Fedelm and Lendabair, both united against Emer, as their husbands had been against Cuchulain. Again King Conor was forced to call for silence, since each hero was supporting his own wife's claims to be queen of the Ulster women. The strife was only calmed by the promise that the claim to the highest place should be settled by Ailill and Meave of Connaught, who would be impartial judges.

The Heroes Journey to Connaught

Bricriu's feast lasted for three days longer, and then King Conor and the Red Branch heroes returned to Armagh. There the dispute about the Championship began again, and Conor sent the heroes to Cruachan, in Connaught, to obtain a judgment from King Ailill. " If he does not decide, go to Curoi of Munster, who is a just and wise man, and will find out the best hero by wizardry and enchantments." When Conor had decided thus, Laegaire and Conall, after some disputa-

"All three drove furiously towards Cruachan"

"Three monstrous cats were let into the room"

tion as to who should start first, had their chariots got ready and drove towards Cruachan, but Cuchulain stayed amusing himself and the women in Armagh. When his chariot-driver reproached him with losing the Champion's Portion through laziness Cuchulain replied : "I never thought about it, but there is still time to win it. Yoke my steeds to the chariot." By this time, however, the other two heroes were far, very far, in advance, with the chief men of Ulster following them.

Cuchulain's Steeds

Cuchulain had quite lately won two mighty magic steeds, which arose from two lonely lakes—the Grey of Macha, his best-beloved horse, and the Black Sainglain. The struggle between the hero and these magic steeds had been terrible before he had been able to tame them and reduce them to submission ; now he had them yoked to his chariot, and when he had once started he soon came up with the other two heroes, and all three drove furiously towards Cruachan, with all the warriors of Ulster behind them.

Queen Meave Watches the Heroes

The noise of the advancing war-chariots reached Queen Meave at Cruachan, and she wondered greatly to hear thunder from a clear sky ; but her fair daughter, looking from her window, said : "Mother, I see chariots coming."

"Who comes in the first ?" asked Queen Meave.

"I see a big stout man, with reddish gold hair and long forked beard, dressed in purple with gold adornments ; and his shield is bronze edged with gold ; he bears a javelin in his hand."

"That man I know well," answered her mother.

"He is mighty Laegaire, the Storm of War, the Knife of Victory; he will slay us all, unless he comes in peace."

"I see another chariot," quoth the princess, "bearing a fair man with long wavy hair, a man of clear red and white complexion, wearing a white vest and a cloak of blue and crimson. His shield is brown, with yellow bosses and a bronze edge."

"That is valiant Conall the Victorious," quoth Meave. "Small chance shall we have if he comes in anger."

"Yet a third chariot comes, wherein stands a dark, sad youth, most handsome of all the men of Erin; he wears a crimson tunic, brooched with gold, a long white linen cloak, and a white, gold-embroidered hood. His hair is black, his look draws love, his glance shoots fire, and the hero-light gleams around him. His shield is crimson, with a silver rim, and images of beasts shine on it in gold."

Terror in Connaught

"Alas! that is the hero Cuchulain," said Meave. "He is more to be feared than all others. His voice in anger tells the doom of men; his wrath is fatal. Truly we are but dead if we have aroused Cuchulain's wrath." After a pause: "Tell me, daughter, are there yet other chariots?"

"The men of Ulster follow in chariots so numerous that the earth quakes beneath them, and their sound is as thunder, or the dashing waves of the sea."

Now Queen Meave was terrified in good earnest, but hoped by a hearty welcome to turn aside the wrath of the heroes of Ulster; thus when they arrived at the dun of Cruachan they found the best of receptions, and all the Red Branch warriors were feasted for three days and nights.

THE FIRST TEST

Conor Explains the Matter

After three days Ailill of Connaught asked their business, and King Conor related to him everything as it had occurred—the feast, the dispute for the Champion's Portion, the women's quarrel, and the decision to be judged by King Ailill. This angered Ailill, who was a peaceable man.

"It was no friend of mine who referred you to me, for I shall surely incur the hatred of two heroes," quoth he.

"You are the best judge of all," replied King Conor.

"Then I must have time—three days and nights—to decide," said Ailill.

"We can spare our heroes so long," quoth Conor, and therewith the Ulster men returned to Armagh, leaving the three claimants to the Championship at Cruachan.

The First Test

That night Ailill put them to an unexpected test. Their feast was served to them in a separate room, and the king went to his protectors, the Fairy People of the Hills, in the Good People's Hill at Cruachan, and begged some help in his judgment. They willingly aided him, and three magic beasts, in the shape of monstrous cats, were let into the room where the heroes feasted. When they saw them Laegaire and Conall rose up from their meal, clambered up among the rafters, and stayed there all night. Cuchulain waited till one attacked him, and then drawing his sword, struck the monster. It showed no further sign of fight, and Cuchulain kept watch all night, till the magic beasts disappeared at daybreak. When Ailill came into the room and saw the heroes as they had spent the night he laughed as he said :

" Are you not content to yield the Championship to Cuchulain ? "

" Indeed no," said Conall and Laegaire. " We are used to fighting men, not monstrous beasts."

The Second Test

The next day King Ailill sent the heroes to his own foster-father, Ercol, to spend a night with him, that he also might test them. When they arrived, and had feasted, Laegaire was sent out that night to fight the witches of the valley. Fierce and terrible were these witches, and they beat Laegaire, and took his arms and armour.

When Conall went to fight them the witches beat him and took his spear, but he kept his sword and brought it back with honour. Cuchulain, who was the youngest, went last, and he too was being beaten, when the taunts of his chariot-driver, who was watching, aroused him, and he beat the witches, and bore off in triumph their cloaks of battle. Yet even after this the other two heroes would not acknowledge Cuchulain's superiority.

Ercol's Defeat

The next day Ercol fought with each champion separately, and conquered both Laegaire and Conall, terrifying the former so much that he fled to Cruachan and told Meave and Ailill that Ercol had killed the other two. When Cuchulain arrived victorious, with Ercol tied captive at his chariot-wheels, he found all men mourning for him and Conall as for the dead.

Meave's Plan to Avoid Strife in Cruachan

Now indeed Ailill was in great perplexity, for he durst not delay his decision, and he dreaded the wrath

194

of the two disappointed heroes. He and Queen Meave consulted long together, and at length Meave promised to relieve him of the responsibility of judgment. Summoning Laegaire to the king's room, she said : ,

"Welcome, O Laegaire! You are greatest of the warriors of Ulster. To you we give the headship of the heroes of Ireland and the Champion's Portion, and to your wife the right to walk first of all the women of Ulster. In token thereof we give you this cup of bronze with a silver bird embossed, to be seen by no man till you be come to King Conor in the Red Branch House at Armagh. Then show your cup and claim your right, and none will dispute it with you."

So Laegaire went away well pleased, and they sent for Conall. To him they gave a silver cup, with a bird embossed in gold, and to him they pretended to adjudge the Championship, and Conall left them well content.

Cuchulain, who was playing chess, refused to attend the King of Connaught when he was summoned, and Queen Meave had to entreat him to come to their private room. There they gave him a golden cup, with a bird designed in precious gems, with many words of flattery for Cuchulain and his fair and noble wife, Emer.

The Return of the Champions

Now the heroes, each well content, bade farewell to the court at Cruachan, and drove back to Armagh, but none durst ask how they had sped. That evening, at the banquet, when the Champion's Portion was set aside, Laegaire arose and claimed it, showing as proof that his claim was just the bronze cup he brought from Queen Meave.

But alas! Conall the Victorious had a silver cup, and while he was exulting in this proof of his rightful claim

195

to the championship Cuchulain produced his golden cup, and the dispute began all over again. King Conor would have allowed Cuchulain's claim, but Laegaire vowed that his rival had bribed Ailill and Meave with great treasures to give him the golden cup, and neither Laegaire nor Conall would yield him the victory or accept the judgment as final. "Then you must go to Curoi," said the king, and to that they all agreed.

The Champions Visit Curoi

The next day the three champions drove to Kerry, where Curoi dwelt in a magic dun. He was away from home planning enchantments to test them, for he knew they were coming, but his wife welcomed them, and bade them watch the dun for one night each, beginning with Laegaire, as the eldest. Laegaire took up his sentinel's post outside the dun, and Curoi's wife worked the charm which prevented entrance after nightfall. The night was long and silent, and Laegaire thought he would have a quiet watch, when he saw a great shadow arise from the sea.

The Giant Fights Laegaire and Conall

This shadow took the shape of a huge giant, whose spears were mighty branch-stripped oaks, which he hurled at Laegaire. They did not touch him, however, and Laegaire made some show of fight ; but the giant took him up, squeezed him so tightly as nearly to slay him, and then threw him over the magic wall of the dun, where the others found him lying half dead. All men thought that he had sprung with a mighty leap over the wall, since no other entrance was to be found, and Laegaire kept silence and did not explain to them.

Conall, who took the watch the second night, fared exactly as Laegaire had done, and likewise did not

196

" The dragon sank towards him, opening its terrible jaws "

"The body of Uath arose"

confess how he had been thrown over the wall of the dun, nor what became of the giant in the dawn.

Cuchulain's Trials

The third night was Cuchulain's watch, and he took his post outside the dun, and the gates and wall were secured by magic spells, so that none could enter. Vainly he watched till midnight, and then he thought he saw nine grey shadowy forms creeping towards him.

"Who goes there?" he cried. "If you be friends, stop ; if foes, come on ! " Then the nine shadowy foes raised a shout, and fell upon the hero ; but he fought hard and slew them, and beheaded them. A second and a third time similar groups of vague, shadowy foemen rushed at him, and he slew them all in like manner, and then, wearied out, sat down to rest.

The Dragon

Later on in the night, as he was still watching, he heard a heavy sound, like waves surging in the lake, and when he roused himself to see what it was he beheld a monstrous dragon. It was rising from the water and flying towards the dun, and seemed ready to devour everything in its way. When the dragon perceived him it soared swiftly into the air, and then gradually sank towards him, opening its terrible jaws. Cuchulain sprang up, giving his wonderful hero-leap, and thrust his arm into the dragon's mouth and down its throat ; he found its heart, tore it out, and saw the monster fall dead on the ground. He then cut off its scaly head, which he added to those of his former enemies.

The Giant Worsted by Cuchulain

Towards daybreak, when feeling quite worn out and very sleepy, he became slowly aware of a great

197

shadow coming to him westward from the sea. The shadow, as before, became a giant, who greeted him in a surly tone with, "This is a bad night." "It will be worse yet for you," said Cuchulain. The giant, as he had done with the other heroes, threw oaks, but just missed him ; and when he tried to grapple with him the hero leaped up with drawn sword. In his anger the hero-light shone round him, and he sprang as high as the giant's head, and gave him a stroke that brought him to his knees. "Life for life, Cuchulain," said the giant, and vanished at once, leaving no trace.

Cuchulain Re-enters the Dun

Now Cuchulain would gladly have returned to the fort to rest, but there seemed no way of entrance, and the hero was vexed at his own helplessness, for he thought his comrades had jumped over the magic walls. Twice he boldly essayed to leap the lofty wall, and twice he failed ; then in his wrath his great strength came upon him, the hero-light shone round him, and he took a little run and, leaning on his spear, leaped so high and so far that he alighted in the middle of the court, just before the door of the hall.

As he sighed heavily and wearily, Curoi's wife said : "That is the sigh of a weary conqueror, not of a beaten man " ; and Cuchulain went in and sat down to rest.

The Decision

The next morning Curoi's wife asked the champions : "Are you content that the Championship should go to Cuchulain ? I know by my magic skill what he has endured in the past night, and you must see that you are not equal to him."

"Nay, that we will not allow," quoth they. "It was one of Cuchulain's friends among the People of the Hills who came to conquer us and to give him the Championship. We are not content, and we will not give up our claim, for the fight was not fair."

" Go home now to Armagh, is Curoi's word, and wait there until he himself brings his decision," said Curoi's wife. So they bade her farewell, and went back to the Red Branch House in Armagh, with the dispute still unsettled ; but they agreed to await peaceably Curoi's decision, and abide by it when he should bring it.

Uath, the Stranger

Some time after this, when Curoi had made no sign of giving judgment, it happened that all the Ulster heroes were in their places in the Red Branch House, except Cuchulain and his cousin Conall. As they sat in order of rank in the hall they saw a terrible stranger coming into the room. He was gigantic in stature, hideous of aspect, with ravening yellow eyes. He wore a skin roughly sewn together, and a grey cloak over it, and he sheltered himself from the light with a spreading tree torn up by the roots. In his hand he bore an enormous axe, with keen and shining edge. This hideous apparition strode up the hall and leant against a carved pillar beside the fire.

" Who are you ? " asked one chieftain in sport. " Are you come to be our candlestick, or would you burn the house down ? Is this the place for such as you ? Go farther down the hall ! "

" My name is Uath, the Stranger, and for neither of those things am I come. I seek that which I cannot find in the whole world, and that is a man to keep the agreement he makes with me."

The Agreement

" What is the agreement ? " asked King Conor.

199

"Behold my axe !" quoth the stranger. "The man who will grasp it to-day may cut my head off with it, provided that I may, in like manner, cut off his head to-morrow. Now you men of Ulster, heroes of the Red Branch, have won the palm through the wide world for courage, honour, strength, truth, and generosity ; do you, therefore, find me a man to keep this agreement. King Conor is excepted, because of his royal dignity, but no other. And if you have no champion who dare face me, I will say that Ulster has lost her courage and is dishonoured."

"It is not right for a whole province to be disgraced for lack of a man to keep his word," said King Conor, "but I fear we have no such champions here."

Laegaire Accepts the Challenge

"By my word," said Laegaire, who had listened attentively to the whole conversation, "there will be a champion this very moment. Stoop down, fellow, and let me cut off your head, that you may take mine to-morrow."

Then Uath chanted magic spells over the axe as he stroked the edge, and laid his neck on a block, and Laegaire hewed so hard that the axe severed the head from the body and struck deep into the block. Then the body of Uath arose, took up the head and the axe, and strode away down the hall, all people shrinking out of its way, and so it passed out into the night.

"If this terrible stranger returns to-morrow he will slay us all," they whispered, as they looked pityingly at Laegaire, who was trying in vain to show no signs of apprehension.

Laegaire and Conall Disgraced

When the next evening came, and men sat in the

CUCHULAIN ACCEPTS THE CHALLENGE

Red Branch House, talking little and waiting for what would happen, in came Uath, the Stranger, as well and sound as before the terrible blow, bearing his axe, and eager to return the stroke. Alas! Laegaire's heart had failed him and he did not come, and the stranger jeered at the men of Ulster because their great champion durst not keep his agreement, nor face the blow he should receive in return for one he gave.

The men of Ulster were utterly ashamed, but Conall Cearnach, the Victorious, was present that night, and he made a new agreement with Uath. Conall gave a blow which beheaded Uath, but again, when the stranger returned whole and sound on the following evening, the champion was not to be found : Conall would not face the blow.

Cuchulain Accepts the Challenge

When Uath found that a second hero of Ulster had failed him he again taunted them all with cowardice and promise-breaking.

"What! is there not one man of courage among you Ulstermen? You would fain have a great name, but have no courage to earn it! Great heroes are you all! Not one among you has bravery enough to face me! Where is that childish youth Cuchulain! A poor miserable fellow he is, but I would like to see if his word is better to be relied on than the word of these two great heroes."

"A youth I may be," said Cuchulain, "but I will keep my word without any agreement."

Uath laughed aloud. "Yes! that is likely, is it not? And you with so great a fear of death!"

Thereupon the youth leapt up, caught the deadly axe, and severed the giant's head as he stood with one stroke.

Cuchulain Stands the Test

The next day the Red Branch heroes watched Cuchulain to see what he would do. They would not have been surprised if he had failed like the others, who now were present. The champion, however, showed no signs of failing or retreat. He sat sorrowfully in his place, waiting for the certain death that must come, and regretting his rashness, but with no thought of breaking his word.

With a sigh he said to King Conor as they waited: "Do not leave this place till all is over. Death is coming to me very surely, but I must fulfil my agreement, for I would rather die than break my word."

Towards the close of day Uath strode into the hall exultant.

"Where is Cuchulain?" he cried.

"Here I am," was the reply.

"Ah, poor boy! your speech is sad to-night, and the fear of death lies heavy on you; but at least you have redeemed your word and have not failed me."

The youth rose from his seat and went towards Uath, as he stood with the great axe ready, and knelt to receive the blow.

Curoi's Decision and Cuchulain's Victory

The hero of Ulster laid his head on the block; but Uath was not satisfied. "Stretch out your neck better," said he.

"You are playing with me, to torment me," said Cuchulain. "Slay me now speedily, for I did not keep you waiting last night."

However, he stretched out his neck as Uath bade, and the stranger raised his axe till it crashed upwards through the rafters of the hall, like the crash of trees falling in a

202

storm. When the axe came down with a terrific sound all men looked fearfully at Cuchulain. The descending axe had not even touched him ; it had come down with the blunt side on the ground, and the youth knelt there unharmed. Smiling at him, and leaning on his axe, stood no terrible and hideous stranger, but Curoi of Kerry, come to give his decision at last.

" Rise up, Cuchulain," said Curoi. " There is none among all the heroes of Ulster to equal you in courage and loyalty and truth. The Championship of the Heroes of Ireland is yours from this day forth, and the Champion's Portion at all feasts ; and to your wife I adjudge the first place among all the women of Ulster. Woe to him who dares to dispute this decision ! " Thereupon Curoi vanished, and the Red Branch warriors gathered around Cuchulain, and all with one voice acclaimed him the Champion of the Heroes of all Ireland—a title which has clung to him until this day.

CHAPTER X : THE TALE OF GAMELYN

The "Wicked Brothers" Theme

THE tale of "Gamelyn" is a variant of the old fairy-tale subject of the Wicked Elder Brothers, one of the oldest and most interesting versions of which may still be read in the Biblical story of Joseph and his brethren. Usually a father dies leaving three sons, of whom the two elder are worthless and the youngest rises to high honour, whereupon the elder brothers try to kill the youngest from envy at his good fortune. A similar root-idea is found in "Cinderella" and other fairy-tales of girls, but in these there may usually be found a cruel stepmother and two contemptuous stepsisters—a noteworthy variation which seems to point to some deep-rooted idea that the ties of blood are stronger among women than among men.

Literary Influence of the "Gamelyn" Story

The story of "Gamelyn" has two great claims to our attention : it is, through Lodge's "Euphues' Golden Legacy," the ultimate source of Shakespeare's *As You Like It*, and it seems to be the earliest presentment in English literature of the figure of "the noble outlaw." In fact, Gamelyn is probably the literary ancestor of "bold Robin Hood," and stands for an English ideal of justice and equity, against legal oppression and wickedness in high places. He shows, too, the love of free life, of the merry greenwood and the open road, which reappears after so many centuries in the work of Robert Louis Stevenson.

The Story

In the reign of King Edward I. there dwelt in Lincolnshire, near the vast expanse of the Fens, a noble gentleman, Sir John of the Marches. He was now old, but was still a model of all courtesy and a "very perfect gentle knight." He had three sons, of whom the youngest, Gamelyn, was born in his father's old age, and was greatly beloved by the old man; the other two were much older than he, and John, the eldest, had already developed a vicious and malignant character. Gamelyn and his second brother, Otho, reverenced their father, but John had no respect or obedience for the good gentleman, and was the chief trouble of his declining years, as Gamelyn was his chief joy.

The Father Feels his End Approaching

At last old age and weakness overcame the worthy old Sir John, and he was forced to take to his bed, where he lay sadly meditating on his children's future, and wondering how to divide his possessions justly among the three. There was no difficulty of inheritance or primogeniture, for all the knight's lands were held in fee-simple, and not in entail, so that he might bequeath them as he would. Sir John of the Marches, fearing lest he should commit an injustice, sent throughout the district for wise knights, begging them to come hastily, if they wished to see him alive, and help him. When the country squires and lords, his near neighbours, heard of his grave condition, they hurried to the castle, and gathered in the bedchamber, where the dying knight greeted them thus: "Lords and gentlemen, I warn you in truth that I may no longer live; by the will of God death lays his hand upon me." When they heard this they tried to encourage him, by bidding him remember that God can provide a remedy for every disease, and the good knight received their kindly words without dispute. "That God can send remedy for an ill I will never deny ; but I beseech you, for my sake, to divide my lands among my three sons. For the love of God deal justly, and forget not my youngest, Gamelyn. Seldom does any heir to an estate help his brothers after his father's death."

How Shall he Dispose of his Estate?

The friends whom Sir John had summoned deliberated long over the disposal of the estate. The majority wished to give all to the eldest son, but a strong minority urged the claims of the second, but all agreed that Gamelyn might wait till his eldest brother chose to give him a share of his father's lands. At last it was decided to divide the inheritance between the two elder sons, and the knights returned to the chamber where the brave old knight lay dying, and told him their decision. He summoned up strength enough to protest against their plan of distribution, and said :

> " ' Nay, by St. Martin, I can yet bequeath
> My lands to whom I wish : they still are mine.
> Then hearken, neighbours, while I make my will.
> To John, my eldest son, and heir, I leave
> Five ploughlands, my dead father's heritage ;
> My second, Otho, ploughlands five shall hold,
> Which my good right hand won in valiant strife ;
> All else I own, in lands and goods and wealth,
> To Gamelyn, my youngest, I devise ;
> And I beseech you, for the love of God,
> Forsake him not, but guard his helpless youth
> And let him not be plundered of his wealth.' "

Then Sir John, satisfied with having proclaimed his will, died with Christian resignation, leaving his little son Gamelyn in the power of the cruel eldest brother, now, in his turn, Sir John.

"Go and do your own baking!"

"Lords, for Christ's sake help poor Gamelyn out of prison!"

GAMELYN RESISTS

The Cruel Eldest Son

Since the boy was a minor, the new knight, as natural guardian, assumed the control of Gamelyn's land, vassals, education, and nurture ; and full evilly he discharged his duties, for he clothed and fed him badly, and neglected his lands, so that his parks and houses, his farms and villages, fell into ruinous decay. The boy, when he grew older, noticed this and resented it, but did not realize the power in his own broad limbs and mighty sinews to redress his wrongs, though by the time he fully understood his injuries no man would dare to face him in fight when he was angry, so strong a youth had he become.

Gamelyn Resists

While Gamelyn, one day, walking in the hall, mused on the ruin of all his inheritance, Sir John came blustering in, and, seeing him, called out : "How now : is dinner ready ?" Enraged at being addressed as if he were a mere servant, he replied angrily : "Go and do your own baking ; I am not your cook."

Sir John almost doubted the evidence of his ears. "What, my dear brother, is that the way to answer ? Thou hast never addressed me so before !"

"No," replied Gamelyn ; "until now I have never considered all the wrong you have done me. My parks are broken open, my deer are driven off ; you have deprived me of my armour and my steeds ; all that my father bequeathed to me is falling into ruin and decay. God's curse upon you, false brother !"

Sir John was now enraged beyond all measure, and shouted : "Stand still, vagabond, and hold thy peace ! What right hast thou to speak of land or vassals ? Thou shalt learn to be grateful for food and raiment."

"A curse upon him that calls me vagabond! I am no worse than yourself; I am the son of a lady and a good knight."

Gamelyn Terrifies the Household

In spite of all his anger, Sir John was a cautious man, with a prudent regard for his own safety. He would not risk an encounter with Gamelyn, but summoned his servants and bade them beat him well, till he should learn better manners. But when the boy understood his brother's intention he vowed that he would not be beaten alone—others should suffer too, and Sir John not the least. Thereupon, leaping on to the wall, he seized a pestle which lay there, and so boldly attacked the timid servants, though they were armed with staves, that he drove them in flight, and laid on furious strokes which quenched the small spark of courage in them. Sir John had not even that small amount of bravery: he fled to a loft and barred the door, while Gamelyn cleared the hall with his pestle, and scoffed at the cowardly grooms who fled so soon from the strife they had begun. When he sought for his brother he could not see him at first, but afterwards perceived his sorry countenance peeping from a window. "Brother," said Gamelyn, "come a little nearer, and I will teach you how to play with staff and buckler."

"Nay, by St. Richard, I will not descend till thou hast put down that pestle. Brother, be no more enraged, and I will make peace with thee. I swear it by the grace of God!"

"I was forced to defend myself," said Gamelyn, "or your menials would have injured and degraded me: I could not let grooms beat a good knight's son; but now grant me one boon, and we shall soon be reconciled."

A WRESTLING MATCH

Sir John's Guile

"Yes, certainly, brother; ask thy boon, and I will grant it readily. But indeed I was only testing thee, for thou art so young that I doubted thy strength and manliness. It was only a pretence of beating that I meant."

"This is my request," said the boy: "if there is to be peace between us you must surrender to me all that my father bequeathed me while he was alive."

To this Sir John consented with apparent willingness, and even promised to repair the decayed mansions and restore the lands and farms to their former prosperity; but though he feigned content with the agreement and kissed his brother with outward affection yet he was inwardly meditating plans of treachery against the unsuspecting youth.

A Wrestling Match

Shortly after this quarrel between the brothers a wrestling competition was announced, the winner of which would become the owner of a fine ram and a ring of gold, and Gamelyn determined to try his powers. Accordingly he begged the loan of "a little courser" from Sir John, who offered him his choice of all the steeds in the stable, and then curiously questioned him as to his errand. The lad explained that he wished to compete in the wrestling match, hoping to win honour by bearing away the prize; then, springing on the beautiful courser that was brought him ready saddled, he spurred his horse and rode away merrily, while the false Sir John locked the gate behind him, praying that he might get his neck broken in the contest. The boy rode along, rejoicing in his youth and strength, singing as he went, till he drew near the appointed place, and then he suddenly heard a man's voice lamenting aloud and crying, "Wellaway! Alas!" and saw a venerable yeoman wringing his hands. "Good man," said Gamelyn, "why art thou in such distress? Can no man help thee?"

A Dreaded Champion

"Alas!" said the yeoman. "Woe to the day on which I was born! The champion wrestler here has overthrown my two stalwart sons, and unless God help them they must die of their grievous hurts. I would give ten pounds to find a man to avenge on him the injuries done to my dear sons."

"Good man, hold my horse while my groom takes my coat and shoes, and I will try my luck and strength against this doughty champion."

"Thank God!" said the yeoman. "I will do it at once; I will guard thy coat and shoes and good steed safely—and may Jesus Christ speed thee well!"

Gamelyn Enters

When Gamelyn entered the ring, barefooted and stripped for wrestling, all men gazed curiously at the rash youth who dared to challenge the stalwart champion, and the great man himself, rising from the ground, strolled across to meet Gamelyn and said haughtily: "Who is thy father, and what is thy name? Thou art, forsooth, a young fool to come here!"

Gamelyn answered equally haughtily: "Thou knewest well my father while he lived: he was Sir John of the Marches, and I am his youngest son, Gamelyn."

The champion replied: "Boy, I knew thy father well in his lifetime, and I have heard of thee, and nothing good: thou hast always been in mischief."

GAMELYN DEFEATS THE CHAMPION

"Now I am older thou shalt know me better," said Gamelyn.

Defeats the Champion

The wrestling had lasted till late in the evening, and the moon was shining on the scene when Gamelyn and the champion began their struggle. The wrestler tried many wily tricks, but the boy was ready for them all, and stood steady against all that his opponent could do. Then, in his turn, he took the offensive, grasped his adversary round the waist, and cast him so heavily to the ground that three ribs were broken, and his. left arm. Then the victor said mockingly :

"Shall we count that a cast, or not reckon it ?"

"By heaven ! whether it be one or no, any man in thy hand will never thrive," said the champion painfully.

The yeoman, who had watched the match with great anxiety, now broke out with blessings : "Blessed be thou, young sir, that ever thou wert born !" and now taunting the fallen champion, said : "It was young 'Mischief' who taught thee this game."

"He is master of us all," said the champion. "In all my years of wrestling I have never been mishandled so cruelly."

Now the victor stood in the ring, ready for more wrestling, but no man would venture to compete with him, and the two judges who kept order and awarded the prizes bade him retire, for no other competitor could be found to face him.

But he was a little disappointed at this easy victory.

"Is the fair over ? Why, I have not half sold my wares," he said.

The champion was still capable of grim jesting. "Now, as I value my life, any purchaser of your wares is a fool ; you sell so dearly."

" Not at all," broke in the yeoman ; " you have bought your share full cheap, and made a good bargain."

He Wins the Prizes

While this short conversation had been going on the judges had returned to their seats, and formally awarded the prize to Gamelyn, and now came to him, bearing the ram and the ring for his acceptance.

Gamelyn took them gladly, and went home the next morning, followed by a cheering crowd of admirers ; but when the cowardly Sir John saw the people he bolted the castle doors against his more favourite and successful brother.

He Overcomes his Brother's Servants

The porter, obeying his master's commands, refused Gamelyn entrance ; and the youth, enraged at this insult, broke down the door with one blow, caught the fleeing porter, and flung him down the well in the courtyard. His brother's servants fled from his anger, and the crowd that had accompanied him swarmed into courtyard and hall, while the knight took refuge in a little turret.

" Welcome to you all," said Gamelyn. " We will be masters here and ask no man's leave. Yesterday I left five tuns of wine in the cellar ; we will drain them dry before you go. If my brother objects (as he well may, for he is a miser) I will be butler and caterer and manage the whole feast. Any person who dares to object may join the porter in the well."

Naturally no objections were raised, and Gamelyn and his friends held high revel for a week, while Sir John lay hidden in his turret, terrified at the noise and revelry, and dreading what his brother might do to him now he had so great a following.

GAMELYN CONSENTS TO BE BOUND

A Reckoning with Sir John

However, the guests departed quietly on the eighth day, leaving Gamelyn alone, and very sorrowful, in the hall where he had held high revel. As he stood there, musing sadly, he heard a timid footstep, and saw his brother creeping towards him. When he had attracted Gamelyn's attention he spoke out loudly : "Who made thee so bold as to destroy all my household stores ?"

"Nay, brother, be not wroth," said the youth quietly. "If I have used anything I have paid for it fully beforehand. For these sixteen years you have had full use and profit of fifteen good ploughlands which my father left me ; you have also the use and increase of all my cattle and horses ; and now all this past profit I abandon to you, in return for the expense of this feast of mine."

Then said the treacherous Sir John : "Hearken, my dear brother : I have no son, and thou shalt be my heir—I swear by the holy St. John."

"In faith," said Gamelyn, "if that be the case, and if this offer be made in all sincerity, may God reward you ! " for it was impossible for his generous disposition to suspect his brother of treachery and to fathom the wiles of a crafty nature ; hence it happened that he was so soon and easily beguiled.

Gamelyn Allows Himself to be Chained

Sir John hesitated a moment, and then said doubtfully: "There is one thing I must tell you, Gamelyn. When you threw my porter into the well I swore in my wrath that I would have you bound hand and foot. That is impossible now without your consent, and I must be forsworn unless you will let yourself be bound for a moment, as a mere form, just to save me from the sin of perjury."

213

So sincere Sir John seemed, and so simple did the whole thing appear, that Gamelyn consented at once. "Why, certainly, brother, you shall not be forsworn for my sake." So he sat down, and the servants bound him hand and foot ; and then Sir John looked mockingly at him as he said : "So now, my fine brother, I have you caught at last." Then he bade them bring fetters and rivet them on Gamelyn's limbs, and chain him fast to a post in the centre of the hall. Then he was placed on his feet with his back to the post and his hands manacled behind him, and as he stood there the false brother told every person who entered that Gamelyn had suddenly gone mad, and was chained for safety's sake, lest he should do himself or others some deadly hurt. For two long days and nights he stood there bound, with no food or drink, and grew faint with hunger and weariness, for his fetters were so tight that he could not sit or lie down ; bitterly he lamented the carelessness which made him fall such an easy prey to his treacherous brother's designs.

Adam Spencer to the Rescue

When all others had left the hall Gamelyn appealed to old Adam Spencer, the steward of the household, a loyal old servant who had known Sir John of the Marches, and had watched the boy grow up. "Adam Spencer," quoth he, "unless my brother is minded to slay me, I am kept fasting too long. I beseech thee, for the great love my father bore thee, get the keys and release me from my bonds. I will share all my free land with thee if thou wilt help me in this distress."

The poor old servant was greatly perplexed. He knew not how to reconcile his grateful loyalty to his dead master with the loyalty due to his present lord, and he said doubtfully : "I have served thy brother for sixteen years,

and if I release thee now he will rightly call me a traitor."
" Ah, Adam ! thou wilt find him a false rogue at the last,
as I have done. Release me, dear friend Adam, and I
will be true to my agreement, and will keep my covenant
to share my land with thee." By these earnest words
the steward was persuaded, and, waiting till Sir John
was safely in bed, managed to obtain possession of the
keys and release Gamelyn, who stretched his arms and
legs and thanked God for his liberty. " Now," said he,
" if I were but well fed no one in this house should
bind me again to-night." So Adam took him to a
private room and set food before him ; eagerly he
ate and drank till his hunger was satisfied and he began
to think of revenge. " What is your advice, Adam ?
Shall I go to my brother and strike off his head ? He
well merits it."

A Plan of Escape

" No," answered Adam, " I know a better plan than
that. Sir John is to give a great feast on Sunday to
many Churchmen and prelates ; there will be present a
great number of abbots and priors and other holy men.
Do you stand as if bound by your post in the hall, and
beseech them to release you. If they will be surety for
you, your liberty will be gained with no blame to me ; if
they all refuse, you shall cast aside the unlocked chains,
and you and I, with two good staves, can soon win your
freedom. Christ's curse on him who fails his comrade ! "

" Yes," quoth Gamelyn, " evil may I thrive if I fail
in my part of the bargain ! But if we must needs help
them to do penance for their sins, you must warn me,
brother Adam, when to begin."

" By St. Charity, master, I will give you good
warning. When I wink at you be ready to cast away
your fetters at once and come to me."

215

"This is good advice of yours, Adam, and blessings on your head. If these haughty Churchmen refuse to be surety for me I will give them good strokes in payment."

A Great Feast

Sunday came, and after mass many guests thronged to the feast in the great hall; they all stared curiously at Gamelyn as he stood with his hands behind him, apparently chained to his post, and Sir John explained sadly that he, after slaying the porter and wasting the household stores, had gone mad, and was obliged to be chained, for his fury was dangerous. The servants carried dainty dishes round the table, and beakers of rich wines, but though Gamelyn cried aloud that he was fasting no food was brought to him. Then he spoke pitifully and humbly to the noble guests: "Lords, for Christ's sake help a poor captive out of prison." But the guests were hard-hearted, and answered cruelly, especially the abbots and priors, who had been deceived by Sir John's false tales. So harshly did they reply to the youth's humble petition that he grew angry. "Oh," said he, "that is all the answer I am to have to my prayer! Now I see that I have no friends. Cursed be he that ever does good to abbot or prior!"

The Banquet Disturbed

Adam Spencer, busied about the removal of the cloth, looked anxiously at Gamelyn, and saw how angry he grew. He thought little more of his service, but, making a pretext to go to the pantry, brought two good oak staves, and stood them beside the hall door. Then he winked meaningly at Gamelyn, who with a sudden shout flung off his chains, rushed to the hall door, seized a staff, and began to lay about him lustily, whirling his weapon as lightly as if it had been a holy-water sprinkler. There was a dreadful commotion in the hall, for the portly Churchmen tried to escape, but the mere laymen loved Gamelyn, and drew aside to give him free play, so that he was able to scatter the prelates. Now he had no pity on these cruel Churchmen, as they had been without pity for him ; he knocked them over, battered them, broke their arms and legs, and wrought terrible havoc among them ; and during this time Adam Spencer kept the door so that none might escape. He called aloud to Gamelyn to respect the sanctity of men of Holy Church and shed no blood, but if he should by chance break arms and legs there would be no sacrilege, because no blood need be shed.

Sir John in Chains

Thus Gamelyn worked his will, laying hands on monks and friars, and sent them home wounded in carts and waggons, while some of them muttered : " We were better at home, with mere bread and water, than here where we have had such a sorry feast ! " Then Gamelyn turned his attention to his false brother, who had been unable to escape, seized him by the neck, broke his backbone with one blow from his staff, and thrust him, sitting, into the fetters that yet hung from the post where Gamelyn had stood. " Sit there, brother, and cool thy blood," said Gamelyn, as he and Adam sat down to a feast, at which the servants waited on them eagerly, partly from love and partly from fear.

The Sheriff's Men Appear

Now the sheriff happened to be only five miles away, and soon heard the news of this disturbance, and how Gamelyn and Adam had broken the king's peace ; and, as his duty was, he determined to arrest the law-breakers. Twenty-four of his best men were sent to the castle to gain admittance and arrest Gamelyn and his steward ; but the new porter, a devoted adherent of Gamelyn, denied them entrance till he knew their errand ; when they refused to tell it, he sent a servant to rouse Gamelyn and warn him that the sheriff's men stood before the gate.

> "Then answered Gamelyn : 'Good porter, go ;
> Delay my foes with fair speech at the gate
> Till I relieve thee with some cunning wile.
> If I o'erlive this strait, I will requite
> Thy truth and loyalty. Adam,' quoth he,
> 'Our foes are on us, and we have no friend—
> The sheriff's men surround us, and have sworn
> A mighty oath to take us : we must go
> Whither our safety calls us.' He replied :
> 'Go where thou wilt, I follow to the last
> Or die forlorn : but this proud sheriff's troop
> Will flee before our onset, to the fens.' "

The Sheriff Arrives

As Gamelyn and Adam looked round for weapons the former saw a cart-staff, a stout post used for propping up the shafts ; this he seized, and ran out at the little postern gate, followed by Adam with another staff. They caught the sheriff's twenty-four bold men in the rear, and when Gamelyn had felled three, and Adam two, the rest took to their heels. "What !" said Adam as they fled. "Drink a draught of my good wine ! I am steward here." "Nay," they shouted back ; "such wine as yours scatters a man's brains far too thoroughly." Now this little fray was hardly ended before the sheriff came in person with a great troop. Gamelyn knew not what to do, but Adam again had a plan ready. "Let us stay no longer, but go to the greenwood : there we shall at least be at liberty." The advice suited Gamelyn, and each drank a draught of wine, mounted his steed, and

213

W.H.MARGETSON

"Then cheer thee, Adam"

"Come from the seat of justice"

lightly rode away, leaving the empty nest for the sheriff, with no eggs therein. However, that officer dismounted, entered the hall, and found Sir John fettered and nearly dying. He released him, and summoned a leech, who healed his grievous wound, and enabled him to do more mischief.

Gamelyn Goes to the Greenwood

Meanwhile Adam wandered with Gamelyn in the greenwood, and found it very hard work, with little food. He complained aloud to his young lord:

> " 'Would I were back in mine old stewardship—
> Full blithe were I, the keys to bear and keep!
> I like not this wild wood, with wounding thorns,
> And nought of food or drink, or restful ease.'
> 'Ah! Adam,' answered Gamelyn, 'in sooth
> Full many a good man's son feels bitter woe!
> Then cheer thee, Adam.' "

As they spoke sadly together Gamelyn heard men's voices near by, and, looking through the bushes, saw seven score young men, sitting round a plentiful feast, spread on the green grass. He rejoiced greatly, bidding Adam remember that " Boot cometh after bale," and pointing out to him the abundance of provisions near at hand. Adam longed for a good meal, for they had found little to eat since they came to the greenwood. At that moment the master-outlaw saw them in the underwood, and bade his young men bring to him these new guests whom God had sent: perchance, he said, there were others besides these two. The seven bold youths who started up to do his will cried to the two new-comers: "Yield and hand us your bows and arrows!" "Much sorrow may he have who yields to you," cried Gamelyn. "Why, with five more ye would be only twelve, and I could fight you all." When the outlaws saw how boldly he bore himself they changed their tone, and said mildly : "Come to our master, and tell him thy desire." "Who is your master ?" quoth Gamelyn. "He is the crowned king of the outlaws," quoth they ; and the two strangers were led away to the chief.

The master-outlaw, sitting on a rustic throne, with a crown of oak-leaves on his head, asked them their business, and Gamelyn replied : "He must needs walk in the wood who may not walk in the town. We are hungry and faint, and will only shoot the deer for food, for we are hard bestead and in great danger."

Gamelyn Joins the Outlaws

The outlaw leader had pity on their distress, and gave them food ; and as they ate ravenously the outlaws whispered one to another : "This is Gamelyn !" "This is Gamelyn !" Understanding all the evils that had befallen him, their leader soon made Gamelyn his second in command ; and when after three weeks the outlaw king was pardoned and allowed to return home, Gamelyn was chosen to succeed him and was crowned king of the outlaws. So he dwelt merrily in the forest, and troubled not himself about the world outside.

The Law at Work

Meanwhile the treacherous Sir John had recovered, and in due course had become sheriff, and indicted his brother for felony. As Gamelyn did not appear to answer the indictment he was proclaimed an outlaw and wolf's-head, and a price was set upon his life. Now his bondmen and vassals were grieved at this, for they feared the cruelty of the wicked sheriff ; they therefore sent messengers to Gamelyn to tell him the ill news, and deprecate his wrath. The youth's anger

rose at the tidings, and he promised to come and beard
Sir John in his hall and protect his own tenants.

Gamelyn Arrested

It was certainly a stroke of rash daring thus to venture into the county where his brother was sheriff, but
he strode boldly into the moot-hall, with his hood
thrown back, so that all might recognise him, and cried
aloud : "God save all you lordings here present ! But,
thou broken-backed sheriff, evil mayst thou thrive !
Why hast thou done me such wrong and disgrace as
to have me indicted and proclaimed an outlaw ?"
Sir John did not hesitate to use his legal powers, but,
seeing his brother was quite alone, had him arrested
and cast into prison, whence it was his intention that
only death should release him.

Otho as Surety

All these years the second brother, Otho, had lived
quietly on his own lands and taken no heed of the
quarrels of the two others ; but now, when news came
to him of Sir John's deadly hatred to their youngest
brother, and Gamelyn's desperate plight, he was deeply
grieved, roused himself from his peaceful life, and rode
to see if he could help his brother. First he besought
Sir John's mercy for the prisoner, for the sake of
brotherhood and family love ; but he only replied
that Gamelyn must stay imprisoned till the justice
should hold the next assize. Then Otho offered to be
bail, if only his young brother might be released from his
bonds and brought from the dismal dungeon where he
lay. To this Sir John finally consented, warning Otho
that if the accused failed to appear before the justice
he himself must suffer the penalty for the breach
of bail. "I agree," said Otho. "Have him released at

once, and deliver him to me." Then Gamelyn was set free on his brother's surety, and the two rode home to Otho's house, talking sadly of all that had befallen, and how Gamelyn had become king of the outlaws. The next morning Gamelyn asked Otho's permission to go to the greenwood and see how his young men fared, but Otho pointed out so clearly how dreadful would be the consequences to him if he did not return that the young man vowed :

> " ' I swear by James, the mighty saint of Spain,
> That I will not desert thee, nor will fail
> To stand my trial on the appointed day,
> If God Almighty give me strength and health
> And power to keep my vow. I will be there,
> That I may show what bitter hate Sir John,
> My cruel brother, holds against me.' "

Gamelyn Goes to the Woods

Thereupon Otho bade him go. "God shield thee from shame ! Come when thou seest it is the right time, and save us both from blame and reproach." So Gamelyn went gaily to the merry greenwood, and found his company of outlaws ; and so much had they to tell of their work in his absence, and so much had he to relate of his adventures, that time slipped by, and he soon fell again into his former mode of life, and his custom of robbing none but Churchmen, fat abbots and priors, monks and canons, so that all others spoke good of him, and called him the " courteous outlaw."

The Term Expires

Gamelyn stood one day looking out over the woods and fields, and it suddenly came to his mind with a pang of self-reproach that he had forgotten his promise to Otho, and the day of the assize was very near. He called his young men (for he had learned not to trust himself to the honour or loyalty of his brother the sheriff), and bade them prepare to accompany him to the place of assize, sending Adam on as a scout to learn tidings. Adam returned in great haste, bringing sad news. The judge was in his place, a jury empanelled to condemn Gamelyn to death, bribed thereto by the wicked sheriff, and Otho was fettered in the gaol in place of his brother. The news enraged Gamelyn, but Adam Spencer was even more infuriated; he would gladly have held the doors of the moot-hall and slain every person inside except Otho; but his master's sense of justice was too strong for that. "Adam," he said, "we will not do so, but will slay the guilty and let the innocent escape. I myself will have some conversation with the justice in the hall; and meanwhile do ye, my men, hold the doors fast. I will make myself justice to-day, and thou, Adam, shalt be my clerk. We will give sentence this day, and God speed our new work!" All his men applauded this speech and promised him obedience, and the troop of outlaws hastened to surround the hall.

Gamelyn in the Court

Once again Gamelyn strode into the moot-hall in the midst of his enemies, and was recognised by all. He released Otho, who said gently: "Brother, thou hast nearly overstayed the time; the sentence has been given against me that I shall be hanged."

"Brother," said Gamelyn, "this day shall thy foes and mine be hanged: the sheriff, the justice, and the wicked jurors." Then Gamelyn turned to the judge, who sat as if paralysed in his seat of judgment, and said:

> "'Come from the seat of justice: all too oft
>   Hast thou polluted law's clear stream with wrong;
>   Too oft hast taken reward against the poor;
>   Too oft hast lent thine aid to villainy,

And given judgment 'gainst the innocent.
Come down and meet thine own meed at the bar,
While I, in thy place, give more rightful doom
And see that justice dwells in law for once.' "

A Scene

The justice sat still, dumb with astonishment, and Gamelyn struck him fiercely, cut his cheek, and threw him over the bar so that his arm broke ; and no man durst withstand the outlaw, for fear of his company standing at the doors. The youth sat down in the judge's seat, with Otho beside him, and Adam in the clerk's desk ; and he placed in the dock the false sheriff, the justice, and the unjust jurors, and accused them of wrong and attempted murder. In order to keep up the forms of law, he empanelled a jury of his own young men, who brought in a verdict of " Guilty," and the prisoners were all condemned to death and hanged out of hand, though the false sheriff attempted to appeal to the brotherly affection of which he had shown so little.

Honour from the King

After this high-handed punishment of their enemies Gamelyn and his brother went to lay their case before King Edward, and he forgave them, in consideration of all the wrongs and injuries Gamelyn had suffered ; and before they returned to their distant county the king made Otho sheriff of the county, and Gamelyn chief forester of all his free forests ; his band of outlaws were all pardoned, and the king gave them posts according to their capabilities. Now Gamelyn and his brother settled down to a happy, peaceful life. Otho, having no son, made Gamelyn his heir, and the latter married a beauteous lady, and lived with her in joy till his life's end.

CHAPTER XI : WILLIAM OF CLOUDESLEE

Introduction

THE outlaw of mediæval England has always possessed a potent charm for the minds of less rebellious persons. No doubt now the attraction has somewhat waned, for in the exploration of distant lands and the study of barbaric tribes men can find that breadth of outlook, that escape from narrow conventionalities, which they could formerly gain only by the cult of the " noble outlaw." The romance of life for many a worthy citizen must have been found in secret sympathy with Robin Hood and his merry band of banished men, robbing the purse-proud to help the needy and gaily defying law and authority.

To the poor, however, the outlaw was something more than an easy entrance to the realms of romance ; he was a real embodiment of the spirit of liberty. Of all the unjust laws which the Norman conquerors laid upon England, perhaps the most bitterly resented were the forest laws, and resistance to them was the most popular form of national independence. Hence it follows that we find outlaw heroes popular very early in our history—heroes who stand in the mind of the populace for justice and true liberty against the oppressive tyranny of subordinate officials, and who are always taken into favour by the king, the fount of true justice.

Famous Outlaws

There is some slight tinge of the " outlaw hero " in Hereward, but the outlaw period of that patriot's life is but an episode in his defence of England against William the Norman. There is a fully developed outlaw hero, the ideal of the type, in Robin Hood, but he has been somewhat idealized and ennobled by being transformed into a banished Earl of Huntingdon. Less known, but equally heroic, is William of Cloudeslee, the William Tell of England, whose fame is that of a good yeoman, a good archer, and a good patriot.

The Outlaws

In the green forest of Englewood, in the "North Countree," not ar from the fortified town of Carlisle, dwelt a merry band of outlaws. They were not evil-doers, but sturdy archers and yeomen, whose outlawry had been incurred only for shooting the king's deer. Indeed, to most men of that time—that is, to most men who were not in the royal service—the shooting of deer, and the pursuit of game in general, were not only venial offences, but the most natural thing in life. The royal claim to exclusive hunting in the vast forests of Epping, Sherwood, Needwood, Barnesdale, Englewood, and many others seemed preposterous to the yeomen who lived on the borders of the forests, and they took their risks and shot the deer and made venison pasty, convinced that they were wronging no one and risking only their own lives. They had the help and sympathy of many a man who was himself a law-abiding citizen, as well as the less understanding help of the town mob and the labourers in the country.

The Leaders

While the outlaws of merry Sherwood recognised no chief but Robin Hood and no foe but the Sheriff of Nottingham, the outlaws of Englewood were under the headship of three famous archers, brothers-in-arms sworn to stand by each other, but not brothers in blood. Their names were Adam Bell, William of Cloudeslee, and Clym of the Cleugh ; and of the three William of

Cloudeslee alone was married. His wife, fair Alice of Cloudeslee, dwelt in a strong house within the walls of Carlisle, with her three children, for they were not included in William's outlawry. It was possible thus for her to send her husband warning of any attack planned by the Sheriff of Carlisle on the outlaws, and she had saved him and his comrades from surprise already.

William Goes to Carlisle

When the blithe spring had come, and the forest was beautiful with its fresh green leaves, William began to long for his home and family ; he had not ventured into Carlisle for some time, and it was more than six months since he had seen his wife's face. Little wonder was it, then, that he announced his intention of visiting his home, at the risk of capture by his old enemy the Sheriff. In vain his comrades dissuaded him from the venture. Adam Bell was especially urgent in his advice that William should remain in the greenwood.

" You shall not go to Carlisle, brother, by my advice, nor with my consent. If the sheriff or the justice should know that you are in the town short would be your shrift and soon your span of life would end. Stay with us, and we will fetch you tidings of your wife."

William replied : " Nay, I must go myself ; I cannot rest content with tidings only. If all is well I will return by prime to-morrow, and if I fail you at that hour you may be sure I am taken or slain ; and I pray you guard well my family, if that be so."

Taking leave of his brother outlaws, William made his way unobserved into the town and came to his wife's dwelling. It was closely shut, with doors strongly bolted, and he was forced to knock long on the window before his wife opened the shutter to see who was the importunate visitor.

227

"Let me in quickly, my own Alice," he said. "I have come to see you and my three children. How have you fared this long time?"

"Alas!" she replied, hurriedly admitting him, and bolting the door again, "why have you come now, risking your dear life to gain news of us? Know you not that this house has been watched for more than six months, so eager are the sheriff and the justice to capture and hang you? I would have come to you in the forest, or sent you word of our welfare. I fear—oh, how I fear!—lest your coming be known!"

The Old Woman's Treachery

"Now that I am here, let us make merry," quoth William. "No man has seen me enter, and I would fain enjoy my short stay with you and my children, for I must be back in the forest by prime to-morrow. Can you not give a hungry outlaw food and drink?"

Then Dame Alice bustled about and prepared the best she had for her husband; and when all was ready a very happy little family sat down to the meal, husband and wife talking cheerily together, while the children watched in wondering silence the father who had been away so long and came to them so seldom.

There was one inmate of the house who saw in William's return a means of making shameful profit. She was an old bedridden woman, apparently paralysed, whom he had rescued from utter poverty seven years before. During all that time she had lain on a bed near the fire, had shared all the life of the family, and had never once moved from her couch. Now, while husband and wife talked together and the darkness deepened in the room, this old impostor slipped from her bed and glided stealthily out of the house.

228

News Brought to the Sheriff

It happened that the king's assize was being held just then in Carlisle, and the sheriff and his staunch ally the justice were sitting together in the Justice Hall. Thither this treacherous old woman hurried with all speed and pushed into the hall, forcing her way through the crowd till she came near the sheriff. "Ha! what would you, good woman?" asked he, surprised. "Sir, I bring tidings of great value." "Tell your tidings, and I shall see if they be of value or no. If they are I will reward you handsomely." "Sir, this night William of Cloudeslee has come into Carlisle, and is even now in his wife's house. He is all alone, and you can take him easily. Now what will you pay me, for I am sure this news is much to you?" "You say truth, good woman. That bold outlaw is the worst of all who kill the king's deer in his forest of Englewood, and if I could but catch him I should be well content. Dame, you shall not go without a recompense for your journey here and for your loyalty." The sheriff then bade his men give the old woman a piece of scarlet cloth, dyed in grain, enough for a gown, and the treacherous hag hid the gift under her cloak, hastened away to Alice's house, and slipped unperceived into her place again, hiding the scarlet cloth under the bed-coverings.

The Hue and Cry

Immediately he had heard of Cloudeslee's presence in Carlisle the sheriff sent out the hue and cry, and with all speed raised the whole town, for though none hated the outlaws men dared not refuse to obey the king's officer. The justice, too, joined the sheriff in the congenial task of capturing an outlaw whose condemnation was already pronounced. With all the forces at their disposal, sheriff and justice took their way towards the house where William and Alice, unconscious of the danger besetting them, still talked lovingly together.

Suddenly the outlaw's ears, sharpened by woodcraft and by constant danger, heard a growing noise coming nearer and nearer. He knew the sound of the footsteps of many people, and among the casual shuffling of feet recognised the ominous tramp of soldiers.

"Wife, we are betrayed," cried William. "Hither comes the sheriff to take me."

The Siege of the House

Alice ran quickly up to her bedchamber and opened a window looking to the back, and saw, to her despair, that soldiers beset the house on every side and filled all the neighbouring streets. Behind them pressed a great throng of citizens, who seemed inclined to leave the capture of the outlaw to the guard. At the same moment William from the front called to his wife that the sheriff and justice were besieging the house on that side.

"Alas! dear husband, what shall we do?" cried Alice. "Accursed be all treason! But who can have betrayed you to your foes? Go into my bedchamber, dear William, and defend yourself there, for it is the strongest room in the house. The children and I will go with you, and I will guard the door while you defend the windows."

The plan was speedily carried out, and while William took his stand by the window Alice seized a pole-axe and stationed herself by the door. "No man shall enter this door alive while I live," said she.

THE HOUSE IS BURNT

The Attack

From the window Cloudeslee could perceive his
mortal enemies the justice and the sheriff ; and drawing his good longbow, he shot with deadly aim fair at
the breast of the justice. It was well for the latter
then that he wore a suit of good chain-mail under his
robes ; the arrow hit his breast and split in three on the
mail.

"Beshrew the man that clad you with that mail
coat ! You would have been a dead man now if your
coat had been no thicker than mine," said William.

"Yield yourself, Cloudeslee, and lay down your bow
and arrows," said the justice. "You cannot escape, for
we have you safe."

"Never shall my husband yield ; it is evil counsel
you give," exclaimed the brave wife from her post at
the door.

The House is Burnt

The sheriff, who grew more angered as the hours
passed on and Cloudeslee was not taken, now cried
aloud : "Why do we waste time trifling here ? The
man is an outlaw and his life is forfeit. Let us burn
him and his house, and if his wife and children will
not leave him they shall all burn together, for it is
their own choice."

This cruel plan was soon carried out. Fire was set
to the door and wooden shutters, and the flames spread
swiftly ; the smoke rolled up in thick clouds into the
lofty bedchamber, where the little children, crouching
on the ground, began to weep for fear.

"Alas ! must we all die ? " cried fair Alice, grieving
for her children.

William opened the window and looked out, but

there was no chance of escape ; his foes filled every street and lane around the house. "Surely they will spare my wife and babes," he thought ; and, tearing the sheets from the bed, he made a rope, with which he let down to the ground his children, and last of all his weeping wife.

He called aloud to the sheriff : " Sir Sheriff, here have I trusted to you my chief treasures. For God's sake do them no harm, but wreak all your wrath on me !"

Gentle hands received Alice and her babes, and friendly citizens led them from the press ; but Alice went reluctantly, in utter grief, knowing that her husband must be burnt with his house or taken by his foes ; but for her children she would have stayed with him. William continued his wonderful archery, never missing his aim, till all his arrows were spent, and the flames came so close that his bowstring was burnt in two. Great blazing brands came falling upon him from the burning roof, and the floor was hot beneath his feet. "An evil death is this !" thought he. "Better it were that I should take sword and buckler and leap down amid my foes and so die, striking good blows in the throng of enemies, than stay here and let them see me burn."

Thereupon he leaped lightly down, and fought so fiercely that he nearly escaped through the throng, for the worthy citizens of Carlisle were not anxious to capture him ; but the soldiers, urged by the sheriff and justice, threw doors and windows upon him, hampered his blows, and seized and bound him, and cast him into a deep dungeon.

The Sheriff Gives Sentence

"Now, William of Cloudeslee," quoth the sheriff, "you shall be hanged with speed, as soon as I can have a new gallows made. So noted an outlaw merits no

"William continued his wonderful archery"

Adam Bell writes the letter

common gibbet ; a new one is most fitting. To-morrow
at prime you shall die. There is no hope of rescue, for
the gates of the town shall be shut. Your dear friends,
Adam Bell and Clym of the Cleugh, would be helpless
to save you, though they brought a thousand more like
themselves, or even all the devils in Hell."

Early next morning the justice arose, went to the
soldiers who guarded the gates, and forbade them to
open till the execution was over ; then he went to the
market-place and superintended the erection of a specially
lofty gallows, beside the pillory.

News is Brought to the Greenwood

Among the crowd who watched the gallows being
raised was a little lad, the town swineherd, who asked
a bystander the meaning of the new gibbet.

"It is put up to hang a good yeoman, William of
Cloudeslee, more's the pity ! He has done no wrong
but kill the King's deer, and that merits not hanging.
It is a foul shame that such injustice can be wrought in
the king's name."

The little lad had often met William of Cloudeslee
in the forest, and had carried him messages from his
wife ; William had given the boy many a dinner of
vension, and now he determined to help his friend if he
could. The gates were shut and no man could pass
out, but the boy stole along the wall till he found a
crevice, by which he clambered down outside. Then he
hastened to the forest of Englewood, and met Adam
Bell and Clym of the Cleugh.

"Come quickly, good yeomen ; ye tarry here too long.
While you are at ease in the greenwood your friend,
William of Cloudeslee, is taken, condemned to death, and
ready to be hanged. He needs your help this very hour."

Adam Bell groaned. "Ah ! if he had but taken our

advice he would have been here in safety with us now. In the greenwood there is no sorrow or care, but when William went to the town he was running into trouble." Then, bending his bow, he shot with unerring aim a hart, which he gave to the lad as recompense for his labour and goodwill.

The Outlaws Go to Carlisle

"Come," said Clym to Adam Bell, "let us tarry no longer, but take our bows and arrows and see what we can do. By God's grace we will rescue our brother, though we may abide it full dearly ourselves. We will go to Carlisle without delay."

The morning was fair as the two yeomen strode from the deep green shades of Englewood Forest along the hard white road leading to Carlisle Town. They were in time as yet, but when they drew near the wall they were amazed to see that no entrance or exit was possible ; the gates were shut fast.

Stepping back into the green thickets beside the road, the two outlaws consulted together. Adam Bell was for a valiant attempt to storm the gate, but Clym suddenly bethought him of a wiser plan.

Clym's Stratagem

Said he : "Let us pretend to be messengers from the king, with urgent letters to the justice. Surely that should win us admission. But alas ! I forgot. How can we bear out our pretence, for I am no learned clerk. I cannot write."

Quoth Adam Bell : "I can write a good clerkly hand. Wait one instant and I will speedily have a letter written ; then we can say we have the king's seal. The plan will do well enough, for I hold the gate-keeper no learned clerk, and this will deceive him."

234

THE OUTLAWS ENTER THE TOWN

Indeed, the letter which he quickly wrote and folded and sealed was very well and clearly written, and addressed to the Justice of Carlisle. Then the two bold outlaws hastened up the road and thundered on the town gates.

They Enter the Town

So long and loud they knocked that the warder came in great wrath, demanding who dared to make such clamour.

Adam Bell replied : " We are two messengers come straight from our lord the king." Clym of the Cleugh added : " We have a letter for the justice which we must deliver into his own hands. Let us in speedily to perform our errand, for we must return to the king in haste."

" No," the warder replied, " that I cannot do. No man may enter these gates till a false thief and outlaw be safely hanged. He is William of Cloudeslee, who has long deserved death."

Now Clym saw that matters were becoming desperate, and time was passing too quickly, so he adopted a more violent tone. " Ah, rascal, scoundrel, madman ! " quoth he. " If we be delayed here any longer thou shalt be hanged for a false thief ! To keep the king's messengers waiting thus ! Canst thou not see the king's seal ? Canst thou not read the address of the royal letter ? Ah, blockhead, thou shalt dearly abide this delay when my lord knows thereof."

Thus speaking, he flourished the forged letter, with its false seal, in the porter's face ; and the man, seeing the seal and the writing, believed what was told him. Reverently he took off his hood and bent the knee to the king's messengers, for whom he opened wide the gates, and they entered, walking warily.

They Keep the Gates

"At last we are within Carlisle walls, and glad thereof are we," said Adam Bell, "but when and how we shall go out again Christ only knows, who harrowed Hell and brought out its prisoners."

"Now if we had the keys ourselves we should have a good chance of life," said Clym, "for then we could go in and out at our own will." "Let us call the warder," said Adam. When he came running at their call both the yeomen sprang upon him, flung him to the ground, bound him hand and foot, and cast him into a dark cell, taking his bunch of keys from his girdle. Adam laughed and shook the heavy keys. "Now I am gate-ward of merry Carlisle. See, here are my keys. I think I shall be the worst warder they have had for three hundred years. Let us bend our bows and hold our arrows ready, and walk into the town to deliver our brother."

The Fight in the Market-place

When they came to the market-place they found a dense crowd of sympathizers watching pityingly the hangman's cart, in which lay William of Cloudeslee, bound hand and foot, with a rope round his neck. The sheriff and the justice stood near the gallows, and Cloudeslee would have been hanged already, but that the sheriff was hiring a man to measure the outlaw for his grave. "You shall have the dead man's clothes, good fellow, if you make his grave," said he.

Cloudeslee's courage was still undaunted. "I have seen as great a marvel ere now," quoth he, "as that a man who digs a grave for another may lie in it himself, in as short a time as from now to prime."

"You speak proudly, my fine fellow, but hanged you

shall be, if I do it with my own hand," retorted the sheriff furiously.

Now the cart moved a little nearer to the scaffold, and William was raised up to be ready for execution. As he looked round the dense mass of faces his keen sight soon made him aware of his friends. Adam Bell and Clym of the Cleugh stood at one corner of the market-place, with arrow on string, and their deadly aim bent at the sheriff and justice, whose horses raised them high above the murmuring throng. Cloudeslee showed no surprise, but said aloud : "Lo ! I see comfort, and hope tofare well in my journey. Yet if I might have my hands free I would care little what else befell me."

The Rescue

Now Adam said quietly to Clym : "Brother, do you take the justice, and I will shoot the sheriff. Let us both loose at once and leave them dying. It is an easy shot, though a long one."

Thus, while the sheriff yet waited for William to be measured for his grave, suddenly men heard the twang of bowstrings and the whistling flight of arrows through the air, and at the same moment both sheriff and justice fell writhing from their steeds, with the grey goose feathers standing in their breasts. All the by-standers fled from the dangerous neighbourhood, and left the gallows, the fatal cart, and the mortally wounded officials alone. The two bold outlaws rushed to release their comrade, cut his bonds, and lifted him to his feet. William seized an axe from a soldier and pursued the fleeing guard, while his two friends with their deadly arrows slew a man at each shot.

The Mayor of Carlisle

When the arrows were all used Adam Bell and Clym

237

of the Cleugh threw away their bows and took to sword and buckler. The fight continued till midday, for in the narrow streets the three comrades protected each other, and drew gradually towards the gate. Adam Bell still carried the keys at his girdle, and they could pass out easily if they could but once reach the gateway. By this time the whole town was in a commotion; again the hue and cry had been raised against the outlaws, and the Mayor of Carlisle came in person with a mighty troop of armed citizens, angered now at the fighting in the streets of the town.

The three yeomen retreated as steadily as they could towards the gate, but the mayor followed valiantly, armed with a pole-axe, with which he clove Cloudeslee's shield in two. He soon perceived the object of the outlaws, and bade his men guard the gates well, so that the three should not escape.

The Escape from Carlisle

Terrible was the din in the town now, for trumpets blew, church-bells were rung backward, women bewailed their dead in the streets, and over all resounded the clash of arms, as the fighting drew nigh the gate. When the gatehouse came in sight the outlaws were fighting desperately, with diminishing strength, but the thought of safety outside the walls gave them force to make one last stand. With backs to the gate and faces to the foe, Adam and Clym and William made a valiant onslaught on the townsfolk, who fled in terror, leaving a breathing-space in which Adam Bell turned the key, flung open the great ponderous gate, and flung it to again, when the three had passed through.

Adam and the Keys

As Adam locked the door they could hear inside

The fight at the gate

"Wait for me seven years, dear wife"

the town the hurrying footsteps of the rallying citizens, whose furious attack on the great iron-studded door came too late. The door was locked, and the three friends stood in safety outside, with their pleasant forest home within easy reach. The change of feeling was so intense that Adam Bell, always the man to seize the humorous point of a situation, laughed lightly. He called through the barred wicket :

"Here are your keys. I resign my office as warder —one half-day's work is enough for me ; and as I have resigned, and the former gate-ward is somewhat damaged and has disappeared, I advise you to find a new one. Take your keys, and much good may you get from them. Next time I advise you not to stop an honest yeoman from coming to see his own wife and have a chat with her."

Thereupon he flung the keys over the gate on the heads of the crowd, and the three brethren slipped away into the forest to their own haunts, where they found fresh bows and arrows in such abundance that they longed to be back in fair Carlisle with their foes before them.

William of Cloudeslee and his Wife Meet

While they were yet discussing all the details of the rescue they heard a woman's pitiful lament and the crying of little children. "Hark !" said Cloudeslee, and they all heard in the silence the words she said. It was William's wife, and she cried : "Alas ! why did I not die before this day ? Woe is me that my dear husband is slain ! He is dead, and I have no friend to lament with me. If only I could see his comrades and tell what has befallen him my heart would be eased of some of its pain."

William, as he listened, was deeply touched, and

walked gently to fair Alice, as she hid her face in her hands and wept. "Welcome, wife, to the greenwood!" quoth he. "By heaven, I never thought to see you again when I lay in bonds last night." Dame Alice sprang up most joyously. "Oh, all is well with me now you are here; I have no care or woe." "For that you must thank my dear brethren, Adam and Clym," said he; and Alice began to load them with her thanks, but Adam cut short the expression of her gratitude. "No need to talk about a little matter like that," he said gruffly. "If we want any supper we had better kill something, for the meat we must eat is yet running wild."

With three such good archers game was easily shot, and a merry meal was quickly prepared in the greenwood, and all joyfully partook of venison and other dainties. Throughout the repast William devotedly waited on his wife with deepest love and reverence, for he could not forget how she had defended him and risked her life to stand by him.

William's Proposed Visit to London

When the meal was over, and they reclined on the green turf round the fire, William began thoughtfully:
"It is in my mind that we ought speedily to go to London and try to win our pardon from the king. Unless we approach him before news can be brought from Carlisle he will assuredly slay us. Let us go at once, leaving my dear wife and my two youngest sons in a convent here; but I would fain take my eldest boy with me. If all goes well he can bring good news to Alice in her nunnery, and if all goes ill he shall bring her my last wishes. But I am sure I am not meant to die by the law." His brethren approved the plan, and they took fair Alice and her two youngest children to

240

the nunnery, and then the three famous archers with
the little boy of seven set out at their best speed for
London, watching the passers-by carefully, that no news
of the doings in Carlisle should precede them to the
king.

Outlaws in the Royal Palace

The three yeomen, on arriving in London, made
their way at once to the king's palace, and walked
boldly into the hall, regardless of the astonished and
indignant shouts of the royal porter. He followed
them angrily into the hall, and began reproaching
them and trying to induce them to withdraw, but to no
purpose. Finally an usher came and said : " Yeomen,
what is your wish ? Pray tell me, and I will help you
if I can ; but if you enter the king's presence thus
unmannerly you will cause us to be blamed. Tell me
now whence you come."

William fearlessly answered : "Sir, we will tell the
truth without deceit. We are outlaws from the king's
forests, outlawed for killing the king's deer, and we
come to beg for pardon and a charter of peace, to show
to the sheriff of our county."

The King and the Outlaws

The usher went to an inner room and begged to
know the king's will, whether he would see these outlaws or not. The king was interested in these bold
yeomen, who dared to avow themselves law-breakers,
and bade men bring them to audience with him. The
three comrades, with the little boy, on being introduced
into the royal presence, knelt down and held up their
hands, beseeching pardon for their offences.

" Sire, we beseech your pardon for our breach of
your laws. We are forest outlaws. who have slain your

fallow deer in many parts of your royal forests." "Your names? Tell me at once," said the king. "Adam Bell, Clym of the Cleugh, and William of Cloudeslee," they replied.

The king was very wrathful. "Are you those bold robbers of whom men have told me? Do you now dare to come to me for pardon? On mine honour I vow that you shall all three be hanged without mercy, as I am crowned king of this realm of England. Arrest them and lay them in bonds." There was no resistance possible, and the yeomen submitted ruefully to their arrest. Adam Bell was the first to speak. "As I hope to thrive, this game pleases me not at all," he said. "Sire, of your mercy, we beg you to remember that we came to you of our own free will, and to let us pass away again as freely. Give us back our weapons and let us have free passage till we have left your palace; we ask no more; we shall never ask another favour, however long we live."

The king was obdurate, however; he only replied: "You speak proudly still, but you shall all three be hanged."

The Queen Intercedes

The queen, who was sitting beside her husband, now spoke for the first time. "Sire, it were a pity that such good yeomen should die, if they might in any wise be pardoned." "There is no pardon," said the king. She then replied: "My lord, when I first left my native land and came into this country as your bride you promised to grant me at once the first boon I asked. I have never needed to ask one until to-day, but now, sire, I claim one, and I beg you to grant it." "With all my heart; ask your boon, and it shall be yours willingly." "Then, I pray you, grant me the lives of these good yeomen." "Madam, you might have had half my kingdom, and you ask a worthless trifle." "Sire, it seems not worthless to me ; I beg you to keep your promise." "Madam, it vexes me that you have asked so little ; yet since you will have these three outlaws, take them." The queen rejoiced greatly. "Many thanks, my lord and husband. I will be surety for them that they shall be true men henceforth. But, good my lord, give them a word of comfort, that they may not be wholly dismayed by your anger."

News Comes to the King

The king smiled at his wife. "Ah, madam ! you will have your own way, as all women will. Go, fellows, wash yourselves, and find places at the tables, where you shall dine well enough, even if it be not on venison pasty from the king's own forests."

The outlaws did reverence to the king and queen, and found seats with the king's guard at the lower tables in the hall. They were still satisfying their appetites when a messenger came in haste to the king ; and the three North Countrymen looked at one another uneasily, for they knew the man was from Carlisle. The messenger knelt before the king and presented his letters. "Sire, your officers greet you well."

"How fare they ? How does my valiant sheriff ? And the prudent justice ? Are they well ?"

"Alas ! my lord, they have been slain, and many another good officer with them."

"Who hath done this ?" questioned the king angrily.

"My lord, three bold outlaws, Adam Bell, Clym of the Cleugh, and William of Cloudeslee."

"What ! these three whom I have just pardoned ? Ah, sorely I repent that I forgave them ! I would give

243

a thousand pounds if I could have them hanged all three ; but I cannot."

The King's Test

As the king read the letters his anger and surprise increased. It seemed impossible that three men should overawe a whole town, should slay sheriff, justice, mayor, and nearly every official in the town, forge a royal letter with the king's seal, and then lock the gates and escape safely. There was no doubt of the fact, and the king raged impotently against his own foolish mercy in giving them a free pardon. It had been granted, however, and he could do nought but grieve over the ruin they had wrought in Carlisle. At last he sprang up, for he could endure the banquet no longer.

"Call my archers to go to the butts," he commanded. "I will see these bold outlaws shoot, and try if their archery is so fine as men say."

Accordingly the king's archers and the queen's archers arrayed themselves, and the three yeomen took their bows and looked well to their silken bowstrings ; and then all made their way to the butts where the targets were set up. The archers shot in turn, aiming at an ordinary target, but Cloudeslee soon grew weary of this childish sport, and said aloud : "I shall never call a man a good archer who shoots at a target as large as a buckler. We have another sort of butt in my country, and that is worth shooting at."

William of Cloudeslee's Archery

"Make ready your own butts," the king commanded, and the three outlaws went to a bush in a field close by and returned bearing hazel-rods, peeled and shining white. These rods they set up at four

244

hundred yards apart, and, standing by one, they said to the king : "We should account a man a fair archer if he could split one wand while standing beside the other." "It cannot be done ; the feat is too great," exclaimed the king. "Sire, I can easily do it," quoth Cloudeslee, and, taking aim very carefully, he shot, and the arrow split the wand in two. "In truth," said the king, "you are the best archer I have ever seen. Can you do greater wonders ?" "Yes," quoth Cloudeslee, "one thing more I can do, but it is a more difficult feat. Nevertheless I will try it, to show you our North Country shooting." "Try, then," the king replied ; "but if you fail you shall be hanged without mercy, because of your boasting."

Cloudeslee Shoots the Apple from his Son's Head

Now Cloudeslee stood for a few moments as if doubtful of himself, and the South Country archers watched him, hoping for a chance to retrieve their defeat, when William suddenly said : "I have a son, a dear son, seven years of age. I will tie him to a stake and place an apple on his head. Then from a distance of a hundred and twenty yards I will split the apple in two with a broad arrow." "By heaven !" the king cried, "that is a dreadful feat. Do as you have said, or by Him who died on the Cross I will hang you high. Do as you have said, but if you touch one hair of his head, or the edge of his gown, I will hang you and your two companions." "I have never broken my pledged word," said the North Country bowman, and he at once made ready for the terrible trial. The stake was set in the ground, the boy tied to it, with his face turned from his father, lest he should give a start and destroy his aim. Cloudeslee then paced the hundred and twenty yards, anxiously felt his string, bent his bow, chose his broadest arrow, and fitted it with care.

The Last Shot

It was an anxious moment. The throng of spectators felt sick with expectation, and many women wept and prayed for the father and his innocent son. But Cloudeslee showed no fear. He addressed the crowd gravely : "Good folk, stand all as still as may be. For such a shot a man needs a steady hand, and your movements may destroy my aim and make me slay my son. Pray for me."

Then, in an unbroken silence of breathless suspense, the bold marksman shot, and the apple fell to the ground, cleft into two absolutely equal halves. A cheer from every spectator burst forth deafeningly, and did not die down till the king beckoned for silence.

The King and Queen Show Favour

"God forbid that I should ever be your target," quoth he. "You shall be my chief forester in the North Country, with daily wage, and daily right of killing venison ; your two brethren shall become yeomen of my guard, and I will advance the fortunes ot your family in every way."

The queen smiled graciously upon William, and she bestowed a pension upon him, and bade him bring his wife, fair Alice, to court, to take up the post of chief woman of the bedchamber to the royal children.

Overwhelmed with these favours, the three yeomen became conscious of their own offences, more than they had told to the royal pair ; their awakened consciences sent them to a holy bishop, who heard their confessions, gave them penance and bade them live well for the future, and then absolved them. When they had returned to Englewood Forest and had broken up the outlaw band they came back to the royal court, and spent the rest of their lives in great favour with the king and queen.

CHAPTER XII : BLACK COLIN OF LOCH AWE

Introduction

IN considering the hero-myths of Scotland we are at once confronted with two difficulties. The first, and perhaps the greater, is this, that the only national heroes of Lowland Scotland are actual historical persons, with very little of the mythical character about them. The mention of Scottish heroes at once suggests Sir William Wallace, Robert Bruce, the Black Douglas, Sir Andrew Barton, and many more, whose exploits are matter of serious chronicle and sober record rather than subject of tradition and myth. These warriors are too much in reach of the fierce white searchlight of historic inquiry to be invested with mythical interest or to show any developments of ancient legend.

The second difficulty is of a different nature, and yet almost equally perplexing. In the old ballads and poems of the Gaelic Highlands there are mythical heroes in abundance, such as Fingal and Ossian, Comala, and a host of shadowy chieftains and warriors, but they are not distinctively Scotch. They are only Highland Gaelic versions of the Irish Gaelic hero-legends, Scotch embodiments of Finn and Oisin, whose real home was in Ireland, and whose legends were carried to the Western Isles and the Highlands by conquering tribes of Scots from Erin. These heroes are at bottom Irish, the champions of the Fenians and of the Red Branch, and in the Scotch legends they have lost much of their original beauty and chivalry.

The Highland Clans

It is rather in the private history of the country, as it were, than in its national records that we are likely to find a hero who will have something of the mythical in his story, something of the romance of the Middle Ages. The wars and jealousies of the clans, the adventures of a chief among hostile tribesmen, the raids and forays, the loves and hatreds of rival families, form a good background for a romantic legend ; and such a legend occurs in the story of Black Colin of Loch Awe, a warrior of the great Campbell clan in the fourteenth century. The tale is common in one form or another to all European lands where the call of the Crusades was heard, and the romantic Crusading element has to a certain extent softened the occasionally ferocious nature of Highland stories in general, so that there is no bloodthirsty vengeance, no long blood-feud, to be recorded of Black Colin Campbell.

The Knight of Loch Awe

During the wars between England and Scotland in the reigns of Edward I. and Edward II. one of the chief leaders in the cause of Scottish independence was Sir Nigel Campbell. The Knight of Loch Awe, as he was generally called, was a schoolfellow and comrade of Sir William Wallace, and a loyal and devoted adherent of Robert Bruce. In return for his services in the war of independence Bruce rewarded him with lands belonging to the rebellious MacGregors, including Glenurchy, the great glen at the head of Loch Awe through which flows the river Orchy. It was a wild and lonely district, and Sir Nigel Campbell had much conflict before he finally expelled the MacGregors and settled down peaceably in Glenurchy. There his son was born, and named Colin, and as years passed he won the nickname of Black Colin, from his swarthy complexion, or possibly from his character, which showed tokens of unusual fierceness and determination.

249

Black Colin's Youth

Sir Nigel Campbell, as all Highland chiefs did, sent his son to a farmer's family for fosterage. The boy became a child of his foster-family in every way ; he lived on the plain food of the clansmen, oatmeal porridge and oatcake, milk from the cows, and beef from the herds ; he ran and wrestled and hunted with his foster-brothers, and learnt woodcraft and warlike skill, broadsword play and the use of dirk and buckler, from his foster-father. More than all, he won a devoted following in the clan, for a man's foster-parents were almost dearer to him than his own father and mother, and his foster-brethren were bound to fight and die for him, and to regard him more than their own blood-relations. The foster-parents of Black Colin were a farmer and his wife, Patterson by name, living at Socach, in Glenurchy, and well and truly they fulfilled their trust.

He Goes on Crusade

In course of time Sir Nigel Campbell died, and Black Colin, his son, became Knight of Loch Awe, and lord of all Glenurchy and the country round. He was already noted for his strength and his dark complexion, which added to his beauty in the eyes of the maidens, and he soon found a lovely and loving bride. They dwelt on the Islet in Loch Awe, and were very happy for a short time, but Colin was always restless, because he would fain do great deeds of arms, and there was peace just then in the land.

At last one day a messenger arrived at the castle on the Islet bearing tidings that another crusade was on foot. This messenger was a palmer who had been in the Holy Land, and had seen all the holy places in Jerusalem.

250

THE TOKEN

He told Black Colin how the Saracens ruled the country, and hindered men from worshipping at the sacred shrines ; and he told how he had come home by Rome, where the Pope had just proclaimed another Holy War. The Pope had declared that his blessing would rest on the man who should leave wife and home and kinsfolk, and go forth to fight for the Lord against the infidel. As the palmer spoke Black Colin became greatly moved by his words, and when the old man had made an end he raised the hilt of his dirk and swore by the cross thereon that he would obey the summons and go on crusade.

The Lady of Loch Awe

Now Black Colin's wife was greatly grieved, and wept sorely, for she was but young, and had been wedded no more than a year, and it seemed to her hard that she must be left alone. She asked her husband : " How far will you go on this errand ? " " I will go as far as Jerusalem, if the Pope bids me, when I have come to Rome," said he. " Alas ! and how long will you be away from me ? " " That I know not, but it may be for years if the heathen Saracens will not surrender the Holy Land to the warriors of the Cross." " What shall I do during those long, weary years ? " asked she. " Dear love, you shall dwell here on the Islet and be Lady of Glenurchy till I return again. The vassals and clansmen shall obey you in my stead, and the tenants shall pay you their rents and their dues, and in all things you shall hold my land for me."

The Token

The Lady of Loch Awe sighed as she asked : " But if you die away in that distant land how shall I know ?

What will become of me if at last such woeful tidings should be brought ? "

"Wait for me seven years, dear wife," said Colin, "and if I do not return before the end of that time you may marry again and take a brave husband to guard your rights and rule the glen, for I shall be dead in the Holy Land."

"That I will never do. I will be the Lady of Glenurchy till I die, or I will become the bride of Heaven and find peace for my sorrowing soul in a nunnery. No second husband shall wed me and hold your land. But give me now some token that we may share it between us ; and you shall swear that on your deathbed you will send it to me ; so shall I know indeed that you are no longer alive."

"It shall be as you say," answered Black Colin, and he went to the smith of the clan and bade him make a massive gold ring, on which Colin's name was engraved, as well as that of the Lady of Loch Awe. Then, breaking the ring in two, Colin gave to his wife the piece with his name and kept the other piece, vowing to wear it near his heart and only to part with it when he should be dying. In like manner she with bitter weeping swore to keep her half of the ring, and hung it on a chain round her neck ; and so, with much grief and great mourning from the whole clan, Black Colin and his sturdy following of Campbell clansmen set out for the Holy Land.

The Journey

Sadly at first the little band marched away from all their friends and their homes ; bagpipes played their loudest marching tunes, and plaids fluttered in the breeze, and the men marched gallantly, but with heavy hearts, for they knew not when they would return, and they feared to find supplanters in their homes when they came back after many years. Their courage rose, however, as the miles lengthened behind them, and by the time they had reached Edinburgh and had taken ship at Leith all was forgotten but the joy of fighting and the eager desire to see Rome and the Pope, the Holy Land and the Holy Sepulchre. Journeying up the Rhine, the Highland clansmen made their way through Switzerland and over the passes of the Alps down into the pleasant land of Italy, where the splendour of the cities surpassed their wildest imaginations ; and so they came at last, with many other bands of Crusaders, to Rome.

The Crusade

At Rome the Knight of Loch Awe was so fortunate as to have an audience of the Pope himself, who was touched by the devotion which brought these stern warriors so far from their home. Black Colin knelt in reverence before the aged pontiff, whom he held in truth to be the Vicar of Christ on earth, and received his blessing, and commands to continue his journey to Rhodes, where the Knights of St. John would give him opportunity to fight for the faith. The small band of Campbells went on to Rhodes, and there took service with the Knights, and won great praise from the Grand Master ; but, though they fought the infidel, and exalted the standard of the Cross above the Crescent, Colin was still not at all satisfied. He left Rhodes after some years with a much-diminished band, and made his way as a pilgrim to Jerusalem. There he stayed until he had visited all the shrines in the Holy Land and prayed at every sacred spot. By this time the seven years of his proposed absence were ended, and he was still far from his home and the dear glen by Loch Awe.

The Lady's Suitor

While the seven years slowly passed away his sad and lonely wife dwelt in the castle on the Islet, ruling her lord's clan in all gentle ways, but fighting boldly when raiders came to plunder her clansmen. Yearly she claimed her husband's dues and watched that he was not defrauded of his rights. But though thus firm, she was the best help in trouble that her clan ever had, and all blessed the name of the Lady of Loch Awe.

So fair and gentle a lady, so beloved by her clan, was certain to have suitors if she were a widow, a·'d even before the seven years had passed away there were men who would gladly have persuaded her that her husband was dead and that she was free. She, however, steadfastly refused to hear a word of another marriage, saying : "When Colin parted from me he gave me two promises, one to return, if possible, within seven years, and the other to send me, on his deathbed, if he died away from me, a sure token of his death. I have not yet waited seven years, nor have I had the token of his death. I am still the wife of Black Colin of Loch Awe."

This steadfastness gradually daunted her suitors and they left her alone, until but one remained, the Baron Niel MacCorquodale, whose lands bordered on Glenurchy, and who had long cast covetous eyes on the glen and its fair lady, and longed no less for the wealth she was reputed to possess than for the power this marriage would give him.

The Baron's Plot

When the seven years were over the Baron MacCorquodale sought the Lady of Loch Awe again, wooing her for his wife. Again she refused, saying, "Until I have the token of my husband's death I will be wife to no other man." "And what is this token, lady?" asked the Baron, for he thought he could send a false one. "I will never tell that," replied the lady. "Do you dare to ask the most sacred secret between husband and wife? I shall know the token when it comes." The Baron was not a little enraged that he could not discover the secret, but he determined to wed the lady and her wealth notwithstanding; accordingly he wrote by a sure and secret messenger to a friend in Rome, bidding him send a letter with news that Black Colin was assuredly dead, and that certain words (which the Baron dictated) had come from him.

A Forged Letter

One day the Lady of Loch Awe, looking out from her castle, saw the Baron coming, and with him a palmer whose face was bronzed by Eastern suns. She felt that the palmer would bring tidings, and welcomed the Baron with his companion. "Lady, this palmer brings you sad news," quoth the Baron. "Let him tell it, then," replied she, sick with fear. "Alas! fair dame, if you were the wife of that gallant knight Colin of Loch Awe, you are now his widow," said the palmer sadly, as he handed her a letter. "What proof have you?" asked Black Colin's wife before she read the letter. "Lady, I talked with the soldier who brought the tidings," replied the stranger.

The letter was written from Rome to "The Right Noble Dame the Lady of Loch Awe," and told how news had come from Rhodes, brought by a man of Black Colin's band, that the Knight of Loch Awe had been mortally wounded in a fight against the Saracens.

Dying, he had bidden his clansmen return to their lady, but they had all perished but one, fighting for vengeance against the infidels. This man, who had held the dying Knight tenderly upon his knee, said that Colin bade his wife farewell, bade her remember his injunction to wed again and find a protector, gasped out, "Take her the token I promised ; it is here," and died ; but the Saracens attacked the Christians again, drove them back, and plundered the bodies of the slain, and when the one survivor returned to search for the precious token there was none ! The body was stripped of everything of value, and the clansman wound it in the plaid and buried it on the battlefield.

The Lady's Stratagem

There seemed no reason for the lady to doubt this news, and her grief was very real and sincere. She clad herself in mourning robes and bewailed her lost husband, but yet she was not entirely satisfied, for she still wore the broken half of the engraved ring on the chain round her neck, and still the promised death-token had not come. The Baron now pressed his suit with greater ardour than before, and the Lady of Loch Awe was hard put to it to find reasons for refusing him. It was necessary to keep him on good terms with the clan, for his lands bordered on those of Glenurchy, and he could have made war on the people in the glen quite easily, while the knowledge that their chief was dead would have made them a broken clan. So the lady turned to guile, as did Penelope of old in similar distress. "I will wed you, now that my Colin is dead," she replied at last, "but it cannot be immediately ; I must first build a castle that will command the head of Glenurchy and of Loch Awe. The MacGregors knew the best place for a house, there on Innis Eoalan ; there, where the ruins of MacGregor's White House now stand, will I build my castle. When it is finished the time of my mourning will be over, and I will fix the bridal day." With this promise the Baron had perforce to be contented, and the castle began to rise slowly at the head of Loch Awe ; but its progress was not rapid, because the lady secretly bade her men build feebly, and often the walls fell down, so that the new castle was very long in coming to completion.

Black Colin Hears the News

In the meantime all who loved Black Colin grieved to know that the Lady of Loch Awe would wed again, and his foster-mother sorrowed most of all, for she felt sure that her beloved Colin was not dead. The death-token had not been sent, and she sorely mistrusted the Baron MacCorquodale and doubted the truth of the palmer's message. At last, when the new castle was nearly finished and shone white in the rays of the sun, she called one of her sons and bade him journey to Rome to find the Knight of Loch Awe, if he were yet alive, and to bring sure tidings of his death if he were no longer living. The young Patterson set off secretly, and reached Rome in due course, and there he met Black Colin, just returned from Jerusalem. The Knight had at last realized that he had spent seven years away from his home, and that now, in spite of all his haste, he might reach Glenurchy too late to save his wife from a second marriage. He comforted himself, however, with the thought that the token was still safe with him, and that his wife would be loyal ; great, therefore, was his horror when he met his foster-brother and heard how the news of his death had been brought to the glen. He heard also how his wife had reluctantly promised to marry the Baron MacCorquodale, and had delayed

257

her wedding by stratagem, and he vowed that he would return to Glenurchy in time to spoil the plans of the wicked baron.

Black Colin's Return

Travelling day and night, Black Colin, with his faithful clansman, came near to Glenurchy, and sent his follower on in advance to bring back news. The youth returned with tidings that the wedding had been fixed for the next day, since the castle was finished and no further excuse for delay could be made. Then Colin's anger was greatly roused, and he vowed that the Baron MacCorquodale, who had stooped to deceit and forgery to gain his ends, should pay dearly for his baseness. Bidding his young clansman show no sign of recognition when he appeared, the Knight of Loch Awe sent him to the farm in the glen, where the anxious foster-mother eagerly awaited the return of the wanderer. When she saw her son appear alone she was plunged into despair, for she concluded, not that Black Colin was dead, but that he would return too late. When he, in the beggar's disguise which he assumed, came down the Glen he saw the smoke from the castle on the Islet, and said : " I see smoke from my house, and it is the smoke of a wedding feast in preparation, but I pray God who sent us light and love that I may reap the fruit of the love that is there."

The Foster-Mother's Recognition

The Knight then went to his foster-mother's house, knocked at the door, and humbly craved food and shelter, as a beggar. "Come in, good man," quoth the mistress of the house ; "sit down in the chimney-corner, and you shall have your fill of oatcake and milk." Colin sat down heavily, as if he were over-

"She looked earnestly into his face"

"The King blew a loud note on his bugle"

wearied, and the farmer's wife moved about slowly, putting before him what she had ; and the Knight saw that she did not recognise him, and that she had been weeping quite recently. "You are sad, I can see," he said. "What is the cause of your grief?" "I am not minded to tell that to a wandering stranger," she replied. "Perhaps I can guess what it is," he continued ; "you have lost some dear friend, I think." "My loss is great enough to give me grief," she answered, weeping. "I had a dear foster-son, who went oversea to fight the heathen. He was dearer to me than my own sons, and now news has come that he is dead in that foreign land. And the Lady of Loch Awe, who was his wife, is to wed another husband to-morrow. Long she waited for him, past the seven years he was to be away, and now she would not marry again, but that a letter has come to assure her of his death. Even yet she is fretting because she has not had the token he promised to send her ; and she will only marry because she dare no longer delay."

"What is this token?" asked Colin. "That I know not : she has never told," replied the foster-mother ; but oh ! if he were now here Glenurchy would never fall under the power of Baron MacCorquodale." "Would you know Black Colin if you were to see him?" the beggar asked meaningly ; and she replied : "I think I should, for though he has been away for years, I nursed him, and he is my own dear fosterling." "Look well at me, then, good mother of mine, for I am Colin of Loch Awe."

The mistress of the farm seized the beggar-man by the arm, drew him out into the light, and looked earnestly into his face ; then, with a scream of joy, she flung her arms around him, and cried : "O Colin ! Colin ! my dear son, home again at last ! Glad and glad I am to see you here in time! Weary have the years been since my nursling went away, but now you are home all will be well." And she embraced him and kissed him and stroked his hair, and exclaimed at his bronzed hue and his ragged attire.

The Foster-Mother's Plan

At last Colin stopped her raptures. "Tell me, mother, does my wife seem to wish for this marriage?" he asked; and his foster-mother answered: "Nay, my son, she would not wed now but that, thinking you are dead, she fears the Baron's anger if she continues to refuse him. But if you doubt her heart, follow my counsel, and you shall be assured of her will in this matter." "What do you advise?" asked he. She answered: "Stay this night with me here, and to-morrow go in your beggar's dress to the castle on the Islet. Stand with other beggars at the door, and refuse to go until the bride herself shall bring you food and drink. Then you can put your token in the cup the Lady of Loch Awe will hand you, and by her behaviour you shall learn if her heart is in this marriage or not." "Dear mother, your plan is good, and I will follow it," quoth Colin. "This night I will rest here, and on the morrow I will seek my wife."

The Beggar at the Wedding

Early next day Colin arose, clad himself in the disguise of a sturdy beggar, took a kindly farewell of his foster-mother, and made his way to the castle. Early as it was, all the servants were astir, and the whole place was in a bustle of preparation, while vagabonds of every description hung round the doors, begging for food and money in honour of the day. The new-comer acted much more boldly: he planted himself right in the open doorway and begged for food and drink in such a lordly tone that the servants were impressed by it, and one of them brought him what he asked—oatcake and butter-milk—and gave it to him, saying, " Take this and be-gone." Colin took the alms and drank the buttermilk, but put the cake into his wallet, and stood sturdily right in the doorway, so that the servants found it diffi-cult to enter. Another servant came to him with more food and a horn of ale, saying, " Now take this second gift of food and begone, for you are in our way here, and hinder us in our work."

The Beggar's Demand

But he stood more firmly still, with his stout travel-ling-staff planted on the threshold, and said : " I will not go." Then a third servant approached, who said : " Go at once, or it will be the worse for you. We have given you quite enough for one beggar. Leave quickly now, or you will get us and yourself into trouble." The disguised Knight only replied : " I will not go until the bride herself comes out to give me a drink of wine," and he would not move, for all they could say. The servants at last grew so perplexed that they went to tell their mistress about this importunate beggar. She laughed as she said : " It is not much for me to do on my last day in the old house," and she bade a servant attend her to the door, bringing a large jug full of wine.

The Token

As the unhappy bride came out to the beggar-man he bent his head in greeting, and she noticed his travel-stained dress and said : " You have come from far, good man"; and he replied : " Yes, lady, I have seen many distant lands." " Alas ! others have gone to see distant lands and have not returned," said she.

"If you would have a drink from the hands of the bride herself, I am she, and you may take your wine now"; and, holding a bowl in her hands, she bade the servant fill it with wine, and then gave it to Colin. "I drink to your happiness," said he, and drained the bowl. As he gave it back to the lady he placed within it the token, the half of the engraved ring. "I return it richer than I took it, lady," said he, and his wife looked within and saw the token.

The Recognition

Trembling violently, she snatched the tiny bit of gold from the bottom of the bowl, which fell to the ground and broke at her feet, and then she saw her own name engraved upon it. She looked long and long at the token, and then, pulling a chain at her neck, drew out her half of the ring with Colin's name engraved on it. "O stranger, tell me, is my husband dead?" she asked, grasping the beggar's arm. "Dead?" he questioned, gazing tenderly at her ; and at his tone she looked straight into his eyes and knew him. "My husband!" was all that she could say, but she flung her arms around his neck and was clasped close to his heart. The servants stood bewildered, but in a moment their mistress had turned to them, saying, "Run, summon all the household, bring them all, for this is my husband, Black Colin of Loch Awe, come home to me again." When all in the castle knew it there was great excitement and rejoicing, and they feasted bountifully, for the wedding banquet had been prepared.

The Baron's Flight

While the feast was in progress, and the happy wife sat by her long-lost husband and held his hand, as though she feared to let him leave her, a distant sound of bagpipes was heard, and the lady remembered that the Baron MacCorquodale would be coming for his wedding, which she had entirely forgotten in her joy. She laughed lightly to herself, and, beckoning a clansman, bade him go and tell the Baron that she would take no new husband, since her old one had come back to her, and that there would be questions to be answered when time served. The Baron MacCorquodale, in his wedding finery, with a great party of henchmen and vassals and pipers blowing a wedding march, had reached the mouth of the river which enters the side of Loch Awe ; the party had crossed the river, and were ready to take boat across to the Islet, when they saw a solitary man rowing towards them with all speed. "It is some messenger from my lady," said the Baron, and he waited eagerly to hear the message. With dreadful consternation he listened to the unexpected words as the clansman delivered them, and then bade the pipers cease their music. "We must return ; there will be no wedding to-day, since Black Colin is home again," quoth he ; and the crestfallen party retraced their steps, quickening them more and more as they thought of the vengeance of the long-lost chieftain ; but they reached their home in safety.

Castle Kilchurn

In the meantime Colin had much to tell his wife of his adventures, and to ask her of her life all these years. They told each other all, and Colin saw the false letter that had been sent to the Lady of Loch Awe, and guessed who had plotted this deceit. His anger grew against the bad man who had wrought this wrong and had so nearly gained his end, and he vowed that he would make the Baron dearly abide it. His wife calmed his fury somewhat by telling him how she had waited even beyond the seven years, and what stratagem she had used, and at last he promised not to make war on the Baron, but to punish him in other ways.

"Tell me what you have done with the rents of Glenurchy these seven years," said he. Then the happy wife replied : "With part I have lived, with part I have guarded the glen, and with part have I made a cairn of stones at the head of Loch Awe. Will you come with me and see it ? " And Colin went, deeply puzzled. When they came to the head of Loch Awe, there stood the new castle, on the site of the old house of the MacGregors ; and the proud wife laughed as she said : "Do you like my cairn of stones ? It has taken long to build." Black Colin was much pleased with the beautiful castle she had raised for him, and renamed it Kilchurn Castle, which title it still keeps. True to his vow, he took no bloody vengeance on the Baron MacCorquodale, but when a few years after he fell into his power the Knight of Loch Awe forced him to resign a great part of his lands to be united with those of Glenurchy.

CHAPTER XIII: THE MARRIAGE OF SIR GAWAYNE

Introduction

THE heroes of chivalry, from Roland the noble paladin to Spenser's Red-Cross Knight, have many virtues to uphold, and their characteristics are as varied as are the races which adopted chivalry and embodied it in their hero-myths. It is a far cry from the loyalty of Roland, in which love for his emperor is the predominant characteristic, to the tender and graceful reverence of Sir Calidore; but mediæval Wales, which has preserved the Arthurian legend most free from alien admixture, had a knight of courtesy quite equal to Sir Calidore. Courage was one quality on the possession of which these mediæval knights never prided themselves, because they could not imagine life without courage, but gentle courtesy was, unhappily, rare, and many a heroic legend is spoilt by the insolence of the hero to people of lower rank. Again, the legends often look lightly on the ill-treatment of maidens; yet the true hero is one who is never tempted to injure a defenceless woman. Similarly, a broken oath to a heathen or mere churl is excused as a trifling matter, but the ideal hero sweareth and breaketh not, though it be to his own hindrance.

Sir Gawayne

The true Knight of Courtesy is Sir Gawayne, King Arthur's nephew, who in many ways overshadows his more illustrious uncle. It is remarkable that the King Arthur of the mediæval romances is either a mere ordinary conqueror or a secondary figure set in the background to heighten the achievements of his more warlike followers. The latter is the conception of

265

Arthur which we find in this legend of the gentle and courteous Sir Gawayne.

King Arthur Keeps Christmas

One year the noble King Arthur was keeping his Christmas at Carlisle with great pomp and state. By his side sat his lovely Queen Guenever, the brightest and most beauteous bride that a king ever wedded, and about him were gathered the Knights of the Round Table. Never had a king assembled so goodly a company of valiant warriors as now sat in due order at the Round Table in the great hall of Carlisle Castle, and King Arthur's heart was filled with pride as he looked on his heroes. There sat Sir Lancelot, not yet the betrayer of his lord's honour and happiness, with Sir Bors and Sir Banier, there Sir Bedivere, loyal to King Arthur till death, there surly Sir Kay, the churlish steward of the king's household, and King Arthur's nephews, the young and gallant Sir Gareth, the gentle and courteous Sir Gawayne, and the false, gloomy Sir Mordred, who wrought King Arthur's overthrow. The knights and ladies were ranged in their fitting degrees and ranks, the servants and pages waited and carved and filled the golden goblets, and the minstrels sang to their harps lays of heroes of the olden time.

His Discontent

Yet in the midst of all this splendour the king was ill at ease, for he was a warlike knight and longed for some new adventure, and of late none had been known. Arthur sat moodily among his knights and drained the wine-cup in silence, and Queen Guenever, gazing at her husband, durst not interrupt his gloomy thoughts. At last the king raised his head, and, striking the table with his hand, exclaimed fiercely : " Are all my knights sluggards or cowards, that none of them goes forth to seek adventures? You are better fitted to feast well in hall than fight well in field. Is my fame so greatly decayed that no man cares to ask for my help or my support against evildoers? I vow here, by the boar's head and by Our Lady, that I will not rise from this table till some adventure be undertaken." "Sire, your loyal knights have gathered round you to keep the holy Yuletide in your court," replied Sir Lancelot; and Sir Gawayne said: "Fair uncle, we are not cowards, but few evildoers dare to show themselves under your rule; hence it is that we seem idle. But see yonder! By my faith, now cometh an adventure."

The Damsel's Request

Even as Sir Gawayne spoke a fair damsel rode into the hall, with flying hair and disordered dress, and, dismounting from her steed, knelt down sobbing at Arthur's feet. She cried aloud, so that all heard her: "A boon, a boon, King Arthur! I beg a boon of you!" "What is your request?" said the king, for the maiden was in great distress, and her tears filled his heart with pity. "What would you have of me?" "I cry for vengeance on a churlish knight, who has separated my love from me." "Tell your story quickly," said King Arthur; and all the knights listened while the lady spoke.

"I was betrothed to a gallant knight," she said, "whom I loved dearly, and we were entirely happy until yesterday. Then as we rode out together planning our marriage we came, through the moorland ways, unnoticing, to a fair lake, Tarn Wathelan, where stood a great castle, with streamers flying, and banners waving in the wind. It seemed a strong and goodly place, but alas! it stood on magic ground, and within

267

the enchanted circle of its shadow an evil spell fell on every knight who set foot therein. As my love and I looked idly at the mighty keep a horrible and churlish warrior, twice the size of mortal man, rushed forth in complete armour ; grim and fierce-looking he was, armed with a huge club, and sternly he bade my knight leave me to him and go his way alone. Then my love drew his sword to defend me, but the evil spell had robbed him of all strength, and he could do nought against the giant's club ; his sword fell from his feeble hand, and the churlish knight, seizing him, caused him to be flung into a dungeon. He then returned and sorely ill-treated me, though I prayed for mercy in the name of chivalry and of Mary Mother. At last, when he set me free and bade me go, I said I would come to King Arthur's court and beg a champion of might to avenge me, perhaps even the king himself. But the giant only laughed aloud. 'Tell the foolish king,' quoth he, 'that here I stay his coming, and that no fear of him shall stop my working my will on all who come. Many knights have I in prison, some of them King Arthur's own true men ; wherefore bid him fight with me, if he will win them back.' Thus, laughing and jeering loudly at you, King Arthur, the churlish knight returned to his castle, and I rode to Carlisle as fast as I could."

King Arthur's Vow

When the lady had ended her sorrowful tale all present were greatly moved with indignation and pity, but King Arthur felt the insult most deeply. He sprang to his feet in great wrath, and cried aloud : "I vow by my knighthood, and by the Holy Rood, that I will go forth to find that proud giant, and will never leave him till I have overcome him." The knights

268

applauded their lord's vow, but Queen Guenever looked doubtfully at the king, for she had noticed the damsel's mention of magic, and she feared some evil adventure for her husband. The damsel stayed in Carlisle that night, and in the morning, after he had heard Mass, and bidden farewell to his wife, King Arthur rode away. It was a lonely journey to Tarn Wathelan, but the country was very beautiful, though wild and rugged, and the king soon saw the little lake gleaming clear and cold below him, while the enchanted castle towered up above the water, with banners flaunting defiantly in the wind.

The Fight

The king drew his sword Excalibur and blew a loud note on his bugle. Thrice his challenge note resounded, but brought no reply, and then he cried aloud : " Come forth, proud knight ! King Arthur is here to punish you for your misdeeds ! Come forth and fight bravely. If you are afraid, then come forth and yield yourself my thrall."

The churlish giant darted out at the summons, brandishing his massive club, and rushed straight at King Arthur. The spell of the enchanted ground seized the king at that moment, and his hand sank down. Down fell his good sword Excalibur, down fell his shield, and he found himself ignominiously helpless in the presence of his enemy.

The Ransom

Now the giant cried aloud : " Yield or fight, King Arthur ; which will you do ? If you fight I shall conquer you, for you have no power to resist me ; you will be my prisoner, with no hope of ransom, will lose your land and spend your life in my dungeon with many other brave knights. If you yield I will hold you to ransom, but you must swear to accept the terms I shall offer."

"What are they," asked King Arthur. The giant replied : "You must swear solemnly, by the Holy Rood, that you will return here on New Year's Day and bring me a true answer to the question, ' What thing is it that all women most desire ?' If you fail to bring the right answer your ransom is not paid, and you are yet my prisoner. Do you accept my terms ?" The king had no alternative : so long as he stood on the enchanted ground his courage was overborne by the spell and he could only hold up his hand and swear by the Sacred Cross and by Our Lady that he would return, with such answers as he could obtain, on New Year's Day.

The King's Search

Ashamed and humiliated, the king rode away, but not back to Carlisle—he would not return home till he had fulfilled his task ; so he rode east and west and north and south, and asked every woman and maid he met the question the churlish knight had put to him. "What is it all women most desire ?" he asked, and all gave him different replies : some said riches, some splendour, some pomp and state ; others declared that fine attire was women's chief delight, yet others voted for mirth or flattery ; some declared that a handsome lover was the cherished wish of every woman's heart ; and among them all the king grew quite bewildered. He wrote down all the answers he received, and sealed them with his own seal, to give to the churlish knight when he returned to the Castle of Tarn Wathelan ; but in his own heart King Arthur felt that the true answer had not yet been given to him. He was sad as he turned and rode towards the giant's home on New Year's Day, for he feared to lose his liberty and lands, and the lonely journey seemed much more dreary than it had before, when he rode out from Carlisle so full of hope and courage and self-confidence.

The Loathly Lady

Arthur was riding mournfully through a lonely forest when he heard a woman's voice greeting him : "God save you, King Arthur ! God save and keep you ! " and he turned at once to see the person who thus addressed him. He saw no one at all on his right hand, but as he turned to the other side he perceived a woman's form clothed in brilliant scarlet; the figure was seated between a holly-tree and an oak, and the berries of the former were not more vivid than her dress, and the brown leaves of the latter not more brown and wrinkled than her cheeks. At first sight King Arthur thought he must be bewitched—no such nightmare of a human face had ever seemed to him possible. Her nose was crooked and bent hideously to one side, while her chin seemed to bend to the opposite side of her face ; her one eye was set deep under her beetling brow, and her mouth was nought but a gaping slit. Round this awful countenance hung snaky locks of ragged grey hair, and she was deadly pale, with a bleared and dimmed blue eye. The king nearly swooned when he saw this hideous sight, and was so amazed that he did not answer her salutation. The loathly lady seemed angered by the insult : " Now Christ save you, King Arthur ! Who are you to refuse to answer my greeting and take no heed of me ? Little of courtesy have you and your knights in your fine court in Carlisle if you cannot return a lady's greeting. Yet, Sir King, proud as you are, it may be that I can help you, loathly though I be ; but I will do nought for one who will not be courteous to me."

The Lady's Secret

King Arthur was ashamed of his lack of courtesy, and tempted by the hint that here was a woman who could help him. "Forgive me, lady," said he; "I was sorely troubled in mind, and thus, and not for want of courtesy, did I miss your greeting. You say that you can perhaps help me; if you would do this, lady, and teach me how to pay my ransom, I will grant anything you ask as a reward." The deformed lady said: "Swear to me, by Holy Rood, and by Mary Mother, that you will grant me whatever boon I ask, and I will help you to the secret. Yes, Sir King, I know by secret means that you seek the answer to the question, 'What is it all women most desire?' Many women have given you many replies, but I alone, by my magic power, can give you the right answer. This secret I will tell you, and in truth it will pay your ransom, when you have sworn to keep faith with me." "Indeed, O grim lady, the oath I will take gladly," said King Arthur; and when he had sworn it, with uplifted hand, the lady told him the secret, and he vowed with great bursts of laughter that this was indeed the right answer.

The Ransom

When the king had thoroughly realized the wisdom of the answer he rode on to the Castle of Tarn Wathelan, and blew his bugle three times. As it was New Year's Day, the churlish knight was ready for him, and rushed forth, club in hand, ready to do battle. "Sir Knight," said the king, "I bring here writings containing answers to your question; they are replies that many women have given, and should be right; these I bring in ransom for my life and lands." The

272

churlish knight took the writings and read them one by one, and each one he flung aside, till all had been read ; then he said to the king : "You must yield yourself and your lands to me, King Arthur, and rest my prisoner ; for though these answers be many and wise, not one is the true reply to my question ; your ransom is not paid, and your life and all you have is forfeit to me." "Alas ! Sir Knight," quoth the king, "stay your hand, and let me speak once more before I yield to you ; it is not much to grant to one who risks life and kingdom and all. Give me leave to try one more reply." To this the giant assented, and King Arthur continued : "This morning as I rode through the forest I beheld a lady sitting, clad in scarlet, between an oak and a holly-tree ; she says, 'All women will have their own way, and this is their chief desire.' Now confess that I have brought the true answer to your question, and that I am free, and have paid the ransom for my life and lands."

The Price of the Ransom

The giant waxed furious with rage, and shouted : "A curse upon that lady who told you this ! It must have been my sister, for none but she knew the answer. Tell me, was she ugly and deformed ?" When King Arthur replied that she was a loathly lady, the giant broke out : "I vow to heaven that if I can once catch her I will burn her alive ; for she has cheated me of being King of Britain. Go your ways, Arthur ; you have not ransomed yourself, but the ransom is paid and you are free.'

Gladly the king rode back to the forest where the loathly lady awaited him, and stopped to greet her. "I am free now, lady, thanks to you ! What boon do you ask in reward for your help ? I have promised to

273

grant it you, whatever it may be." "This is my boon, King Arthur, that you will bring some young and courteous knight from your court in Carlisle to marry me, and he must be brave and handsome too. You have sworn to fulfil my request, and you cannot break your word." These last words were spoken as the king shook his head and seemed on the point of refusing a request so unreasonable ; but at this reminder he only hung his head and rode slowly away, while the unlovely lady watched him with a look of mingled pain and glee.

King Arthur's Return

On the second day of the new year King Arthur came home to Carlisle. Wearily he rode along and dismounted at the castle, and wearily he went into his hall, where sat Queen Guenever. She had been very anxious during her husband's absence, for she dreaded magic arts, but she greeted him gladly and said : " Welcome, my dear lord and king, welcome home again ! What anxiety I have endured for you ! But now you are here all is well. What news do you bring, my liege ? Is the churlish knight conquered ? Where have you had him hanged, and where is his head ? Placed on a spike above some town-gate ? Tell me your tidings, and we will rejoice together." King Arthur only sighed heavily as he replied : " Alas ! I have boasted too much ; the churlish knight was a giant who has conquered me, and set me free on conditions." " My lord, tell me how this has chanced." " His castle is an enchanted one, standing on enchanted ground, and surrounded with a circle of magic spells which sap the bravery from a warrior's mind and the strength from his arm. When I came on his land and felt the power of his mighty charms, I was unable to

274

" He hung his head and rode slowly away "

"Lady, I will be a true and loyal husband"

resist him, but fell into his power, and had to yield myself to him. He released me on condition that I would fulfil one thing which he bade me accomplish, and this I was enabled to do by the help of a loathly lady ; but that help was dearly bought, and I cannot pay the price myself."

Sir Gawayne's Devotion

By this time Sir Gawayne, the king's favourite nephew, had entered the hall, and greeted his uncle warmly ; then, with a few rapid questions, he learnt the king's news, and saw that he was in some distress. " What have you paid the loathly lady for her secret, uncle ? " he asked. " Alas ! I have paid her nothing ; but I promised to grant her any boon she asked, and she has asked a thing impossible." " What is it ? " asked Sir Gawayne. "Since you have promised it, the promise must needs be kept. Can I help you to perform your vow ? " " Yes, you can, fair nephew Gawayne, but I will never ask you to do a thing so terrible," said King Arthur. "I am ready to do it, uncle, were it to wed the loathly lady herself." " That is what she asks, that a fair young knight should marry her. But she is too hideous and deformed ; no man could make her his wife." " If that is all your grief," replied Sir Gawayne, "things shall soon be settled; I will wed this ill-favoured dame, and will be your ransom." " You know not what you offer," answered the king. " I never saw so deformed a being. Her speech is well enough, but her face is terrible, with crooked nose and chin, and she has only one eye." "She must be an ill-favoured maiden ; but I heed it not," said Sir Gawayne gallantly, " so that I can save you from trouble and care." " Thanks, dear Gawayne, thanks a thousand times ! Now through your devotion

I can keep my word. To-morrow we must fetch your bride from her lonely lodging in the greenwood; but we will feign some pretext for the journey. I will summon a hunting party, with horse and hound and gallant riders, and none shall know that we go to bring home so ugly a bride." "Gramercy, uncle," said Sir Gawayne. "Till to-morrow I am a free man."

The Hunting Party

The next day King Arthur summoned all the court to go hunting in the greenwood close to Tarn Wathelan; but he did not lead the chase near the castle: the remembrance of his defeat and shame was too strong for him to wish to see the place again. They roused a noble stag and chased him far into the forest, where they lost him amid close thickets of holly and yew interspersed with oak copses and hazel bushes—bare were the hazels, and brown and withered the clinging oak leaves, but the holly looked cheery, with its fresh green leaves and scarlet berries. Though the chase had been fruitless, the train of knights laughed and talked gaily as they rode back through the forest, and the gayest of all was Sir Gawayne; he rode wildly down the forest drives, so recklessly that he drew level with Sir Kay, the churlish steward, who always preferred to ride alone. Sir Lancelot, Sir Stephen, Sir Banier, and Sir Bors all looked wonderingly at the reckless youth; but his younger brother, Gareth, was troubled, for he knew all was not well with Gawayne, and Sir Tristram, buried in his love for Isolde, noticed nothing, but rode heedlessly, wrapped in sad musings.

Sir Kay and the Loathly Lady

Suddenly Sir Kay reined up his steed, amazed; his eye had caught the gleam of scarlet under the trees, and
276

as he looked he became aware of a woman, clad in a dress of finest scarlet, sitting between a holly-tree and an oak. "Good greeting to you, Sir Kay," said the lady, but the steward was too much amazed to answer. Such a face as that of the lady he had never even imagined, and he took no notice of her salutation. By this time the rest of the knights had joined him, and they all halted, looking in astonishment on the mis-shapen face of the poor creature before them. It seemed terrible that a woman's figure should be surmounted by such hideous features, and most of the knights were silent for pity's sake ; but the steward soon recovered from his amazement, and his rude nature began to show itself. The king had not yet appeared, and Sir Kay began to jeer aloud. "Now which of you would fain woo yon fair lady ?" he asked. "It takes a brave man, for methinks he will stand in fear of any kiss he may get, it must needs be such an awesome thing. But yet I know not ; any man who would kiss this beau-teous damsel may well miss the way to her mouth, and his fate is not quite so dreadful after all. Come, who will win a lovely bride !" Just then King Arthur rode up, and at sight of him Sir Kay was silent ; but the loathly lady hid her face in her hands, and wept that he should pour such scorn upon her.

The Betrothal

Sir Gawayne was touched with compassion for this uncomely woman alone among these gallant and hand-some knights, a woman so helpless and ill-favoured, and he said : "Peace, churl Kay, the lady cannot help herself ; and you are not so noble and courteous that you have the right to jeer at any maiden ; such deeds do not become a knight of Arthur's Round Table. Besides, one of us knights here must wed this unfor-

277

tunate lady." "Wed her?" shouted Kay. "Gawayne, you are mad!" "It is true, is it not, my liege?" asked Sir Gawayne, turning to the king; and Arthur reluctantly gave token of assent, saying, "I promised her not long since, for the help she gave me in a great distress, that I would grant her any boon she craved, and she asked for a young and noble knight to be her husband. My royal word is given, and I will keep it; therefore have I brought you here to meet her." Sir Kay burst out with, "What? Ask me perchance to wed this foul quean? I'll none of her. Where'er I get my wife from, were it from the fiend himself, this hideous hag shall never be mine." "Peace, Sir Kay," sternly said the king; "you shall not abuse this poor lady as well as refuse her. Mend your speech, or you shall be knight of mine no longer." Then he turned to the others and said: "Who will wed this lady and help me to keep my royal pledge? You must not all refuse, for my promise is given, and for a little ugliness and deformity you shall not make me break my plighted word of honour." As he spoke he watched them keenly, to see who would prove sufficiently devoted, but the knights all began to excuse themselves and to depart. They called their hounds, spurred their steeds, and pretended to search for the track of the lost stag again; but before they went Sir Gawayne cried aloùd: "Friends, cease your strife and debate, for I will wed this lady myself. Lady, will you have me for your husband?" Thus saying, he dismounted and knelt before her.

The Lady's Words

The poor lady had at first no words to tell her gratitude to Sir Gawayne, but when she had recovered a little she spoke: "Alas! Sir Gawayne, I fear you do but jest.   Will you wed with one so ugly and deformed as I ?   What sort of wife should I be for a knight so gay and gallant, so fair and comely as the king's own nephew ?   What will Queen Guenever and the ladies of the Court say when you return to Carlisle bringing with you such a bride ?   You will be shamed, and all through me."   Then she wept bitterly, and her weeping made her seem even more hideous ; but King Arthur, who was watching the scene, said : "Lady, I would fain see that knight or dame who dares mock at my nephew's bride.   I will take order that no such unknightly discourtesy is shown in my court," and he glared angrily at Sir Kay and the others who had stayed, seeing that Sir Gawayne was prepared to sacrifice himself and therefore they were safe.   The lady raised her head and looked keenly at Sir Gawayne, who took her hand, saying : "Lady, I will be a true and loyal husband to you if you will have me ; and I shall know how to guard my wife from insult.   Come, lady, and my uncle will announce the betrothal."   Now the lady seemed to believe that Sir Gawayne was in earnest, and she sprang to her feet, saying : "Thanks to you !   A thousand thanks, Sir Gawayne, and blessings on your head !   You shall never rue this wedding, and the courtesy you have shown.   Wend we now to Carlisle."

The Journey to Carlisle

A horse with a side-saddle had been brought for Sir Gawayne's bride, but when the lady moved it became evident that she was lame and halted in her walk, and there was a slight hunch on her shoulders. Both of these deformities showed little when she was seated, but as she moved the knights looked at one another, shrugged their shoulders and pitied Sir Gawayne, whose courtesy had bound him for life to so deformed

279

a wife. Then the whole train rode away together, the bride between King Arthur and her betrothed, and all the knights whispering and sneering behind them. Great was the excitement in Carlisle to see that ugly dame, and greater still the bewilderment in the court when they were told that this loathly lady was Sir Gawayne's bride.

The Bridal

Only Queen Guenever understood, and she showed all courtesy to the deformed bride, and stood by her as her lady-of-honour when the wedding took place that evening, while King Arthur was groomsman to his nephew. When the long banquet was over, and bride and bridegroom no longer need sit side by side, the tables were cleared and the hall was prepared for a dance, and then men thought that Sir Gawayne would be free for a time to talk with his friends; but he refused. "Bride and bridegroom must tread the first dance together, if she wishes it," quoth he, and offered his lady his hand for the dance. "I thank you, sweet husband," said the grim lady as she took it and moved forward to open the dance with him; and through the long and stately measure that followed, so perfect was his dignity, and the courtesy and grace with which he danced, that no man dreamt of smiling as the deformed lady moved clumsily through the figures of the dance.

Sir Gawayne's Bride

At last the long evening was over, the last measure danced, the last wine-cup drained, the bride escorted to her chamber, the lights out, the guests separated in their rooms, and Gawayne was free to think of what he had done, and to consider how he had ruined his whole hope of happiness. He thought of his uncle's favour, of the poor lady's gratitude, of the blessing she had invoked upon him, and he determined to be gentle with her, though he could never love her as his wife. He entered the bride-chamber with the feeling of a man who has made up his mind to endure, and did not even look towards his bride, who sat awaiting him beside the fire. Choosing a chair, he sat down and looked sadly into the glowing embers and spoke no word.

"Have you no word for me, husband? Can you not even give me a glance?" asked the lady, and Sir Gawayne turned his eyes to her where she sat; and then he sprang up in amazement, for there sat no loathly lady, no ugly and deformed being, but a maiden young and lovely, with black eyes and long curls of dark hair, with beautiful face and tall and graceful figure. "Who are you, maiden?" asked Sir Gawayne; and the fair one replied: "I am your wife, whom you found between the oak and the holly-tree, and whom you wedded this night."

Sir Gawayne's Choice

"But how has this marvel come to pass?" asked he, wondering, for the fair maiden was so lovely that he marvelled that he had not known her beauty even under that hideous disguise. "It is an enchantment to which I am in bondage," said she. "I am not yet entirely free from it, but now for a time I may appear to you as I really am. Is my lord content with his loving bride?" asked she, with a little smile, as she rose and stood before him. "Content!" he said, as he clasped her in his arms. "I would not change my dear lady for the fairest dame in Arthur's court, not though she were Queen Guenever herself. I am the happiest knight that lives, for I thought to save my uncle and help a hapless lady, and I have won my own happiness thereby. Truly I shall never rue the day when I wedded you, dear heart." Long they sat and talked together, and then Sir Gawayne grew weary, and would fain have slept, but his lady said : "Husband, now a heavy choice awaits you. I am under the spell of an evil witch, who has given me my own face and form for half the day, and the hideous appearance in which you first saw me for the other half. Choose now whether you will have me fair by day and ugly by night, or hideous by day and beauteous by night. The choice is your own."

The Dilemma

Sir Gawayne was no longer oppressed with sleep ; the choice before him was too difficult. If the lady remained hideous by day he would have to endure the taunts of his fellows ; if by night, he would be unhappy himself. If the lady were fair by day other men might woo her, and he himself would have no love for her ; if she were fair to him alone, his love would make her look ridiculous before the court and the king. Nevertheless, acting on the spur of the moment, he spoke : "Oh, be fair to me only—be your old self by day, and let me have my beauteous wife to myself alone." "Alas! is that your choice?" she asked. "I only must be ugly when all are beautiful, I must be despised when all other ladies are admired ; 1 am as fair as they, but I must seem foul to all men. Is this your love, Sir Gawayne?" and she turned from him and wept. Sir Gawayne was filled with pity and remorse when he heard her lament, and began to realize that he was studying his own pleasure rather than his lady's feelings, and his courtesy and gentleness again won the upper hand. "Dear love, if you would rather that men should see you

"Now you have released me from the spell completely"

Queen Godhild prays ever for her son Horn

fair, I will choose that, though to me you will be always as you are now. Be fair before others and deformed to me alone, and men shall never know that the enchantment is not wholly removed."

Sir Gawayne's Decision

Now the lady looked pleased for a moment, and then said gravely: "Have you thought of the danger to which a young and lovely lady is exposed in the court? There are many false knights who would woo a fair dame, though her husband were the king's favourite nephew; and who can tell?—one of them might please me more than you. Sure I am that many will be sorry they refused to wed me when they see me to-morrow morn. You must risk my beauty under the guard of my virtue and wisdom, if you have me young and fair." She looked merrily at Sir Gawayne as she spoke; but he considered seriously for a time, and then said: "Nay, dear love, I will leave the matter to you and your own wisdom, for you are wiser in this matter than I. I remit this wholly unto you, to decide according to your will. I will rest content with whatsoever you resolve."

The Lady's Story

Now the fair lady clapped her hands lightly, and said: "Blessings on you, dear Gawayne, my own dear lord and husband! Now you have released me from the spell completely, and I shall always be as I am now, fair and young, till old age shall change my beauty as he doth that of all mortals. My father was a great duke of high renown who had but one son and one daughter, both of us dearly beloved, and both of goodly appearance. When I had come to an age to be married my father determined to take a new wife, and he wedded a witch-lady. She resolved to rid herself of his two children, and cast a spell upon us both, whereby I was transformed from a fair lady into the hideous monster whom you wedded, and my gallant young brother into the churlish giant who dwells at Tarn Wathelan. She condemned me to keep that awful shape until I married a young and courtly knight who would grant me all my will. You have done all this for me, and I shall be always your fond and faithful wife. My brother too is set free from the spell, and he will become again one of the truest and most gentle knights alive, though none can excel my own true knight, Sir Gawayne."

The Surprise of the Knights

The next morning the knight and his bride descended to the great hall, where many knights and ladies awaited them, the former thinking scornfully of the hideous hag whom Gawayne had wedded, the latter pitying so young and gallant a knight, tied to a lady so ugly. But both scorn and pity vanished when all saw the bride. "Who is this fair dame?" asked Sir Kay. "Where have you left your ancient bride?" asked another, and all awaited the answer in great bewilderment. "This is the lady to whom I was wedded yester evening," replied Sir Gawayne. "She was under an evil enchantment, which has vanished now that she has come under the power of a husband, and henceforth my fair wife will be one of the most beauteous ladies of King Arthur's court. Further, my lord King Arthur, this fair lady has assured me that the churlish knight of Tarn Wathelan, her brother, was also under a spell, which is now broken, and he will be once more a courteous and gallant knight, and the ground on which his fortress stands will have henceforth no magic power to quell the courage of any knight alive. Dear liege and uncle, when I wedded yesterday

284

the loathly lady I thought only of your happiness, and in that way I have won my own lifelong bliss."

King Arthur's joy at his nephew's fair hap was great, for he had grieved sorely over Gawayne's miserable fate, and Queen Guenever welcomed the fair maiden as warmly as she had the loathly lady, and the wedding feast was renewed with greater magnificence, as a fitting end to the Christmas festivities.

CHAPTER XIV: KING HORN

Introduction

AMONG the hero-legends which are considered to be of native English growth and to have come down to us from the times of the Danish invasions is the story of King Horn; but although "King Horn," like "Havelok the Dane," was originally a story of Viking raids, it has been so altered that the Norse element has been nearly obliterated. In all but the bare circumstances of the tale, "King Horn" is a romance of chivalry, permeated with the Crusading spirit, and reflecting the life and customs of the thirteenth century, instead of the more barbarous manners of the eighth or ninth centuries. The hero's desire to obtain knighthood and do some deed worthy of the honour, the readiness to leave his betrothed for long years at the call of honour or duty, the embittered feeling against the Saracens, are all typical of the romance of the Crusades. Another curious point which shows a later than Norse influence is the wooing of the reluctant youth by the princess, of which there are many instances in mediæval literature; it reveals a consciousness of feudal rank which did not exist in early times, and a certain recognition of the privileges of royal birth which were not granted before the days of romantic chivalry. King Horn himself is a hero of the approved chivalric type, whose chief distinguishing feature is his long indifference to the misfortunes of the sorely-tried princess to whom he was betrothed.

The Royal Family of Suddene

There once lived and ruled in the pleasant land of Suddene a noble king named Murry, whose fair consort, Queen Godhild, was the most sweet and gentle lady alive, as the king was a pattern of all knightly virtues. This royal pair had but one child, a son, named Horn, now twelve years old, who had been surrounded from his birth with loyal service and true devotion. He had a band of twelve chosen companions with whom he shared sports and tasks, pleasures and griefs, and the little company grew up well trained in chivalrous exercises and qualities. Childe Horn had his favourites among the twelve. Athulf was his dearest friend, a loving and devoted companion ; and next to him in Horn's affection stood Fikenhild, whose outward show of love covered his inward envy and hatred. In everything these two were Childe Horn's inseparable comrades, and it seemed that an equal bond of love united the three.

The Saracen Invasion

One day as King Murry was riding over the cliffs by the sea with only two knights in attendance he noticed some unwonted commotion in a little creek not far from where he was riding, and he at once turned his horse's head in that direction and galloped down to the shore. On his arrival in the small harbour he saw fifteen great ships of strange build, and their crews, Saracens all armed for war, had already landed, and were drawn up in warlike array. The odds against the king were terrible, but he rode boldly to the invaders and asked: "What brings you strangers here ? Why have you sought our land ?" A Saracen leader, gigantic of stature, spoke for them all and replied : "We are here to win this land to the law of Mahomet and to drive out the Christian law. We will slay all the inhabitants that believe on Christ. Thou thyself shalt be our first conquest, for thou shalt not leave this place alive." Thereupon the Saracens attacked

287

the little band, and though the three Christians fought valiantly they were soon slain. The Saracens then spread over the land, slaying, burning, and pillaging, and forcing all who loved their lives to renounce the Christian faith and become followers of Mahomet. When Queen Godhild heard of her husband's death and saw the ruin of her people she fled from her palace and all her friends and betook herself to a solitary cave, where she lived unknown and undiscovered, and continued her Christian worship while the land was overrun with pagans. Ever she prayed that God would protect her dear son, and bring him at last to his father's throne.

Horn's Escape

Soon after the king's death the Saracens had captured Childe Horn and his twelve comrades, and the boys were brought before the pagan emir. They would all have been slain at once or flayed alive, but for the beauty of Childe Horn, for whose sake their lives were spared. The old emir looked keenly at the lads, and said : "Horn, thou art a bold and valiant youth, of great stature for thine age, and of full strength, yet I know thou hast not yet reached thy full growth. If we release thee with thy companions, in years to come we shall dearly rue it, for ye will become great champions of the Christian law and will slay many of us. Therefore ye must die. But we will not slay you with our own hands, for ye are noble lads, and shall have one feeble chance for your lives. Ye shall be placed in a boat and driven out to sea, and if ye all are drowned we shall not grieve overmuch. Either ye must die or we, for I know we shall dearly abide your king's death if ye youths survive." Thereupon the lads were all taken to the shore, and, weeping and lamenting, were

288

thrust into a rudderless boat, which was towed out to sea and left helpless.

Arrival in Westernesse

The other boys sat lamenting and bewailing their fate, but Childe Horn, looking round the boat, found a pair of oars, and as he saw that the boat was in the grasp of some strong current he rowed in the same direction, so that the boat soon drifted out of sight of land. The other lads were a dismal crew, for they thought their death was certain, but Horn toiled hard at his rowing all night, and with the dawn grew so weary that he rested for a little on his oars. When the rising sun made things clear, and he could see over the crests of the waves, he stood up in the boat and uttered a cry of joy. "Comrades," cried he, "dear friends, I see land not far away. I hear the sweet songs of birds and see the soft green grass. We have come to some unknown land and have saved our lives." Then Athulf took up the glad tidings and began to cheer the forlorn little crew, and under Horn's skilful guidance the little boat grounded gently and safely on the sands of Westernesse. The boys sprang on shore, all but Childe Horn having no thought of the past night and the journey ; but he stood by the boat, looking sadly at it.

Farewell to the Boat.

> " ' Boat,' quoth he, ' which hast borne me on my way,
> Have thou good days beside a summer sea !
> May never wave prevail to sink thee deep !
> Go, little boat, and when thou comest home
> Greet well my mother, mournful Queen Godhild ;
> Tell her, frail skiff, her dear son Horn is safe.
> Greet, too, the pagan lord, Mahomet's thrall,
> The bitter enemy of Jesus Christ,

And bid him know that I am safe and well.
Say I have reached a land beyond the sea,
Whence, in God's own good time, I will return
Then he shall feel my vengeance for my sire.'"

Then sorrowfully he pushed the boat out into the ocean, and the ebbing tide bore it away, while Horn and his companions set their faces resolutely towards the town they could see in the distance.

King Ailmar and Childe Horn

As the little band were trudging wearily towards the town they saw a knight riding towards them, and when he came nearer they became aware that he must be some noble of high rank. When he halted and began to question them, Childe Horn recognised by his tone and bearing that this must be the king. So indeed it was, for King Ailmar of Westernesse was one of those noble rulers who see for themselves the state of their subjects and make their people happy by free, unrestrained intercourse with them. When the king saw the forlorn little company he said : " Whence are ye, fair youths, so strong and comely of body ? Never have I seen so goodly a company of thirteen youths in the realm of Westernesse. Tell me whence ye come, and what ye seek." Childe Horn assumed the office of spokesman, for he was leader by birth, by courage, and by intellect. " We are lads of noble families in Suddene, sons of Christians and of men of lofty station. Pagans have taken the land and slain our parents, and we boys fell into their hands. These heathen have slain and tortured many Christian men, but they had pity upon us, and put us into an old .boat with no sail or rudder. So we drifted all night, until I saw your land at dawn, and our boat came to the shore. Now we are in your power, and you may do with us what

290

you will, but I pray you to have pity on us and to feed us, that we may not perish utterly."

Ailmar's Decision

King Ailmar was touched as greatly by the simple boldness of the spokesman as by the hapless plight of the little troop, and he answered, smiling : " Thou shalt have nought but help and comfort, fair youth. But, I pray thee, tell me thy name." Horn answered readily : " King, may all good betide thee ! I am named Horn, and I have come journeying in a boat on the sea—now I am here in thy land." King Ailmar replied : " Horn ! That is a good name : mayst thou well enjoy it. Loud may this Horn sound over hill and dale till the blast of so mighty a Horn shall be heard in many lands from king to king, and its beauty and strength be known in many countries. Horn, come thou with me and be mine, for I love thee and will not forsake thee."

Childe Horn at Court

The king rode home, and all the band of stranger youths followed him on foot, but for Horn he ordered a horse to be procured, so that the lad rode by his side ; and thus they came back to the court. When they entered the hall he summoned his steward, a noble old knight named Athelbrus, and gave the lads in charge to him, saying, " Steward, take these foundlings of mine, and train them well in the duties of pages, and later of squires. Take especial care with the training of Childe Horn, their chief ; let him learn all thy knowledge of woodcraft and fishing, of hunting and hawking, of harping and singing ; teach him how to carve before me, and to serve the cup solemnly at banquets ; make him thy favourite pupil and train him to be a knight as good as thyself. His companions thou mayst put into other service, but Horn shall be my own page, and afterwards my squire." Athelbrus obeyed the king's command, and the thirteen youths soon found themselves set to learn the duties of court life, and showed themselves apt scholars, especially Childe Horn, who did his best to satisfy the king and his steward on every point.

The Princess Rymenhild

When Childe Horn had been at court for six years, and was now a squire, he became known to all courtiers, and all men loved him for his gentle courtesy and his willingness to do any service. King Ailmar made no secret of the fact that Horn was his favourite squire, and the Princess Rymenhild, the king's fair daughter, loved him with all her heart. She was the heir to the throne, and no man had ever gainsaid her will, and now it seemed to her unreasonable that she should not be allowed to wed a good and gallant youth whom she loved. It was difficult for her to speak alone with him, for she had six maiden attendants who waited on her continually, and Horn was engaged with his duties either in the hall, among the knights, or waiting on the king. The difficulties only seemed to increase her love, and she grew pale and wan, and looked miserable. It seemed to her that if she waited longer her love would never be happy, and in her impatience she took a bold step.

Athelbrus Deceives the Princess

She kept her chamber, called a messenger, and said to him : "Go quickly to Athelbrus the steward, and bid him come to me at once. Tell him to bring with him the squire Childe Horn, for I am lying ill in my room, and would be amused. Say I expect them quickly, for

I am sad in mind, and have need of cheerful converse."
The messenger bowed, and, withdrawing, delivered the
message exactly as he had received it to Athelbrus, who
was much perplexed thereby. He wondered whence
came this sudden illness, and what help Childe Horn
could give. It was an unusual thing for the squire to be
asked into a lady's bower, and still more so into that of
a princess, and Athelbrus had already felt some suspicion as to the sentiments of the royal lady towards
the gallant young squire. Considering all these things,
the cautious steward deemed it safer not to expose
young Horn to the risks that might arise from such an
interview, and therefore induced Athulf to wait upon
the princess and to endeavour to personate his more
distinguished companion. The plan succeeded beyond
expectation in the dimly lighted room, and the infatuated
princess soon startled the unsuspecting squire by a warm
and unreserved declaration of her affection. Recovering
from his natural amazement, he modestly disclaimed a
title to the royal favour and acknowledged his identity.

On discovering her mistake the princess was torn by
conflicting emotions, but finally relieved the pressure
of self-reproach and the confusion of maiden modesty
by overwhelming the faithful steward with denunciation
and upbraiding, until at last, in desperation, the poor
man promised, against his better judgment, to bring
about a meeting between his love-lorn mistress and the
favoured squire.

Athelbrus Summons Horn

When Rymenhild understood that Athelbrus would
fulfil her desire she was very glad and joyous; her
sorrow was turned into happy expectation, and she
looked kindly upon the old steward as she said: "Go
now quickly, and send him to me in the afternoon.

The king will go to the wood for sport and pastime, and Horn can easily remain behind; then he can stay with me till my father returns at eve. No one will betray us; and when I have met my beloved I care not what men may say."

Then the steward went down to the banqueting-hall, where he found Childe Horn fulfilling his duties as cup-bearer, pouring out and tasting the red wine in the king's golden goblet. King Ailmar asked many questions about his daughter's health, and when he learnt that her malady was much abated he rose in gladness from the table and summoned his courtiers to go with him into the greenwood. Athelbrus bade Horn tarry, and when the gay throng had passed from the hall the steward said gravely: "Childe Horn, fair and courteous, my beloved pupil, go now to the bower of the Princess Rymenhild, and stay there to fulfil all her commands. It may be thou shalt hear strange things, but keep rash and bold words in thy heart, and let them not be upon thy tongue. Horn, dear lad, be true and loyal now, and thou shalt never repent it."

Horn and Rymenhild

Horn listened to this unusual speech with great astonishment, but, since Sir Athelbrus spoke so solemnly, he laid all his words to heart, and thus, marvelling greatly, departed to the royal bower. When he had knocked at the door, and had been bidden to come in, entering, he found Rymenhild sitting in a great chair, intently regarding him as he came into the room. He knelt down to make obeisance to her, and kissed her hand, saying, "Sweet be thy life and soft thy slumbers, fair Princess Rymenhild! Well may it be with thy gentle ladies of honour! I am here at thy command, lady, for Sir Athelbrus, the steward, bade me come to

294

speak with thee. Tell me thy will, and I will fulfil all thy desires." She arose from her seat, and, bending towards him as he knelt, took him by the hand and lifted him up, saying, " Arise and sit beside me, Childe Horn, and we will drink this cup of wine together." In great astonishment the youth did as the princess bade, and sat beside her, and soon, to his utter amazement, Rymenhild avowed her love for him, and offered him her hand. "Have pity on me, Horn, and plight me thy troth, for in very truth I love thee, and have loved thee long, and if thou wilt I will be thy wife."

Horn Refuses the Princess

Now Horn was in evil case, for he saw full well in what danger he would place the princess, Sir Athelbrus, and himself if he accepted the proffer of her love. He knew the reason of the steward's warning, and tried to think what he might say to satisfy the princess and yet not be disloyal to the king. At last he replied : "Christ save and keep thee, my lady Rymenhild, and give thee joy of thy husband, whosoever he may be ! I am too lowly born to be worthy of such a wife ; I am a mere foundling, living on thy father's bounty. It is not in the course of nature that such as I should wed a king's daughter, for there can be no equal match between a princess and a landless squire."

Rymenhild was so disheartened and ashamed at this reply to her loving appeal that her colour changed, she turned deadly pale, began to sigh, flung her arms out wildly, and fell down in a swoon. Childe Horn lifted her up, full of pity for her deep distress, and began to comfort her and try to revive her. As he held her in his arms he kissed her often, and said :

"'Lady, dear love, take comfort and be strong!
For I will yield me wholly to thy guidance
If thou wilt compass one great thing for me.
Plead with King Ailmar that he dub me knight,
That I may prove me worthy of thy love.
Soon shall my knighthood be no idle dream,
And I will strive to do thy will, dear heart.'"

Now at these words Rymenhild awoke from her swoon, and made him repeat his promise. She said: "Ah! Horn, that shall speedily be done. Ere the week is past thou shalt be Sir Horn, for my father loves thee, and will grant the dignity most willingly to one so dear to him. Go now quickly to Sir Athelbrus, give him as a token of my gratitude this golden goblet and this ring; pray him that he persuade the king to dub thee knight. I will repay him with rich rewards for his gentle courtesy to me. May Christ help him to speed thee in thy desires!" Horn then took leave of Rymenhild with great affection, and found Athelbrus, to whom he delivered the gifts and the princess's message, which the steward received with due reverence.

Horn Becomes a Knight

This plan seemed to Athelbrus very good, for it raised Horn to be a member of the noble Order of Knights, and would give him other chances of distinguishing himself. Accordingly he went to the king as he sat over the evening meal, and spoke thus: "Sir King, hear my words, for I have counsel for thee. To-morrow is the festival of thy birth, and the whole realm of Westernesse must rejoice in its master's joy. Wear thou thy crown in solemn state, and I think it were nought amiss if thou shouldst knight young Horn, who will become a worthy defender of thy throne." "That were well done," said King Ailmar. "The youth pleases me, and I will knight him with my own sword. Afterwards he shall knight his twelve comrades the same day."

The next day the ceremony of knighting was performed with all solemnity, and at its close a great banquet was prepared and all men made merry. But Princess Rymenhild was somewhat sad. She could not descend to the hall and take her customary place, for this was a feast for knights alone, and she would not be without her betrothed one moment longer, so she sent a messenger to fetch Sir Horn to her bower.

Horn and Athulf Go to Rymenhild

Now that Horn was a newly dubbed knight he would not allow the slightest shadow of dishonour to cloud his conduct; accordingly, when he obeyed Rymenhild's summons he was accompanied by Athulf. "Welcome, Sir Horn and Sir Athulf," she cried, holding out her hands in greeting. "Love, now that thou hast thy will, keep thy plighted word and make me thy wife; release me from my anxiety and do as thou hast said."

> "'Dear Rymenhild, hold thou thyself at peace,'
> Quoth young Sir Horn; 'I will perform my vow.
> But first I must ride forth to prove my might;
> Must conquer hardships, and my own worse self,
> Ere I can hope to woo and wed my bride.
> We are but new-fledged knights of one day's growth,
> And yet we know the custom of our state
> Is first to fight and win a hero's name,
> Then afterwards to win a lady's heart.
> This day will I do bravely for thy love
> And show my valour and my deep devotion
> In prowess 'gainst the foes of this thy land.
> If I come back in peace, I claim my wife.'"

Rymenhild protested no longer, for she saw that where honour was concerned Horn was inflexible.

"My true knight," said she, "I must in sooth believe thee, and I feel that I may. Take this ring engraved with my name, wrought by the most skilled worker of our court, and wear it always, for it has magic virtues. The gems are of such saving power that thou shalt fear no strokes in battle, nor ever be cast down if thou gaze on this ring and think of thy love. Athulf, too, shall have a similar ring. And now, Horn, I commend thee to God, and may Christ give thee good success and bring thee back in safety!"

Horn's First Exploit

After taking an affectionate farewell of Rymenhild, Horn went down to the hall, and, seeing all the other new-made knights going in to the banquet, he slipped quietly away and betook himself to the stables. There he armed himself secretly and mounted his white charger, which pranced and reared joyfully as he rode away ; and Horn began to sing for joy of heart, for he had won his chief desire, and was happy in the love of the king's daughter. As he rode by the shore he saw a stranger ship drawn up on the beach, and recognised the banner and accoutrements of her Saracen crew, for he had never forgotten the heathens who had slain his father. "What brings you here?" he asked angrily, and as fearlessly as King Murry had done, and received the same answer : "We will conquer this land and slay the inhabitants." Then Horn's anger rose, he gripped his sword, and rushed boldly at the heathens, and slew many of them, striking off a head at each blow. The onslaught was so sudden that the Saracens were taken by surprise at first, but then they rallied and surrounded Horn, so that matters began to look dangerous for him. Then he remembered the betrothal ring, and looked on it, thinking earnestly of Rymenhild, his dear love, and

Horn kills the Saracen Leader

"Now, in her misery, she set the dagger to her heart"

such courage came to him that he was able to defeat the pagans and slay their leader. The others, sorely wounded—for none escaped unhurt—hurried on board ship and put to sea, and Horn, bearing the Saracen leader's head on his sword's point, rode back to the royal palace. Here he related to King Ailmar this first exploit of his knighthood, and presented the head of the foe to the king, who rejoiced greatly at Horn's valour and success.

Rymenhild's Dream

The next day the king and all the court rode out hunting, but Horn made an excuse to stay behind with the princess, and the false and wily Fikenhild was also left at home, and he crept secretly to Rymenhild's bower to spy on her. She was sitting weeping bitterly when Sir Horn entered. He was amazed. " Love, for mercy's sake, why weepest thou so sorely?" he asked; and she replied : " I have had a mournful dream. I dreamt that I was casting a net and had caught a great fish, which began to burst the net. I greatly fear that I shall lose my chosen fish." Then she looked sadly at Horn. But the young knight was in a cheery mood, and replied : " May Christ and St. Stephen turn thy dream to good ! If I am thy fish, I will never deceive thee nor do aught to displease thee, and hereto I plight thee my troth. But I would rather interpret thy dream otherwise. This great fish which burst thy net is some one who wishes us ill, and will do us harm soon." Yet in spite of Horn's brave words it was a sad betrothal, for Rymenhild wept bitterly, and her lover could not stop her tears.

Fikenhild's False Accusation

Fikenhild had listened to all their conversation with

growing envy and anger, and now he stole away silently, and met King Ailmar returning from the chase.

> "' King Ailmar,' said the false one, 'see, I bring
> A needed warning, that thou guard thyself,
> For Horn will take thy life ; I heard him vow
> To slay thee, or by sword or fire, this night.
> If thou demand what cause of hate he has,
> Know that the villain wooes thine only child,
> Fair Rymenhild, and hopes to wear thy crown.
> E'en now he tarries in the maiden's bower,
> As he has often done, and talks with her
> With guileful tongue, and cunning show of love.
> Unless thou banish him thou art not safe
> In life or honour, for he knows no law.' "

The king at first refused to believe the envious knight's report, but, going to Rymenhild's bower, he found apparent confirmation, for Horn was comforting the princess, and promising to wed her when he should have done worthy feats of arms. The king's wrath knew no bounds, and with words of harsh reproach he banished Horn at once, on pain of death. The young knight armed himself quickly and returned to bid farewell to his betrothed.

Horn's Banishment

"Dear heart," said he, "now thy dream has come true, and thy fish must needs break the net and be gone. The enemy whom I foreboded has wrought us woe. Farewell, mine own dear Rymenhild ; I may no longer stay, but must wander in alien lands. If I do not return at the end of seven years take thyself a husband and tarry no longer for me. And now take me in your arms and kiss me, dear love, ere I go !" So they kissed each other and bade farewell, and Horn called to him his comrade Athulf, saying, " True and faithful friend, guard well my dear love. Thou hast never forsaken me ; now do thou keep Rymenhild for me." Then he rode away, and, reaching the haven, hired a good ship and sailed for Ireland, where he took service with King Thurston, under the name of Cuthbert. In Ireland he became sworn brother to the king's two sons, Harold and Berild, for they loved him from the first moment they saw him, and were in no way jealous of his beauty and valour.

Horn Slays the Giant Emir

When Christmas came, and King Thurston sat at the banquet with all his lords, at noontide a giant strode into the hall, bearing a message of defiance. He came from the Saracens, and challenged any three Irish knights to fight one Saracen champion. If the Irish won the pagans would withdraw from Ireland ; if the Irish chiefs were slain the Saracens would hold the land. The combat was to be decided the next day at dawn. King Thurston accepted the challenge, and named Harold, Berild, and Cuthbert (as Horn was called) as the Christian champions, because they were the best warriors in Ireland ; but Horn begged permission to speak, and said : " Sir King, it is not right that one man should fight against three, and one heathen hound think to resist three Christian warriors. I will fight and conquer him alone, for I could as easily slay three of them." At last the king allowed Horn to attempt the combat alone, and spent the night in sorrowful musing on the result of the contest, while Horn slept well and arose and armed himself cheerily. He then aroused the king, and the Irish troop rode out to a fair and level green lawn, where they found the emir with many companions awaiting them. The combat began at once, and Horn gave blows so mighty that the pagan onlookers fell swooning through very fear, till Horn

said : "Now, knights, rest for a time, if it pleases you."
Then the Saracens spoke together, saying aloud that no
man had ever so daunted them before except King
Murry of Suddene.

This mention of his dead father aroused Horn, who
now realized that he saw before him his father's
murderers. His anger was kindled, he looked at his
ring and thought of Rymenhild, and then, drawing his
sword again, he rushed at the heathen champion. The
giant fell pierced through the heart, and his companions
fled to their ships, hotly pursued by Horn and his
company. Much fighting there was, and in the hot
strife near the ships the king's two sons, Harold and
Berild, were both slain.

Horn Refuses the Throne

Sadly they were laid on a bier and brought back
to the palace, their sorrowful father lamenting their
early death ; and when he had wept his fill the mournful king came into the hall where all his knights silently
awaited him. Slowly he came up to Horn as he sat a
little apart from the rest, and said : "Cuthbert, wilt
thou fulfil my desire ? My heirs are slain, and thou
art the best knight in Ireland for strength and beauty
and valour ; I implore thee to wed Reynild, my only
daughter (now, alas ! my only child), and to rule my
realm. Wilt thou do so, and lift the burden of my
cares from my weary shoulders ? " But Horn replied:
"O Sir King, it were wrong for me to receive thy fair
daughter and heir and rule thy realm, as thou dost
offer. I shall do thee yet better service, my liege,
before I die ; and I know that thy grief will change ere
seven years have passed away. When that time is
over, Sir King, give me my reward : thou shalt not
refuse me thy daughter when I desire her." To this

RYMENHILD'S DISTRESS

King Thurston agreed, and Horn dwelt in Ireland for seven years, and sent no word or token to Rymenhild all the time.

Rymenhild's Distress

In the meantime Princess Rymenhild was in great perplexity and trouble, for a powerful ruler, King Modi of Reynes, wooed her for his wife, and her own betrothed sent her no token of his life or love. Her father accepted the new suitor for her hand, and the day of the wedding was fixed, so that Rymenhild could no longer delay her marriage. In her extremity she besought Athulf to write letters to Horn, begging him to return and claim his bride and protect her ; and these letters she delivered to several messengers, bidding them search in all lands until they found Sir Horn and gave the letters into his own hand. Horn knew nought of this, till one day in the forest he met a weary youth, all but exhausted, who told how he had sought Horn in vain. When Horn declared himself, the youth broke out into loud lamentations over Rymenhild's unhappy fate, and delivered the letter which explained all her distress. Now it was Horn's turn to weep bitterly for his love's troubles, and he bade the messenger return to his mistress and tell her to cease her tears, for Horn would be there in time to rescue her from her hated bridegroom. The youth returned joyfully, but as his boat neared the shore of Westernesse a storm arose and the messenger was drowned ; so that Rymenhild, opening her tower door to look for expected succour, found her messenger lying dead at the foot of the tower, and felt that all hope was gone. She wept and wrung her hands, but nothing that she could do would avert the evil day.

Horn and King Thurston

As soon as Horn had read Rymenhild's letter he went to King Thurston and revealed the whole matter to him. He told of his own royal parentage, his exile, his knighthood, his betrothal to the princess, and his banishment ; then of the death of the Saracen leader who had slain King Murry, and the vengeance he had taken. Then he ended :

> "'King Thurston, be thou wise, and grant my boon ;
> Repay the service I have yielded thee ;
> Help me to save my princess from this woe.
> I will take counsel for fair Reynild's fate,
> For she shall wed Sir Athulf, my best friend,
> My truest comrade and my doughtiest knight.
> If ever I have risked my life for thee
> And proved myself in battle, grant my prayer.'"

To this the king replied : "Childe Horn, do what thou wilt."

Horn Returns on the Wedding-day

Horn at once invited Irish knights to accompany him to Westernesse to rescue his love from a hateful marriage, and many came eagerly to fight in the cause of the valiant Cuthbert who had defended Ireland for seven years. Thus it was with a goodly company that Horn took ship, and landed in King Ailmar's realm ; and he came in a happy hour, for it was the wedding-day of Princess Rymenhild and King Modi of Reynes. The Irish knights landed and encamped in a wood, while Horn went on alone to learn tidings. Meeting a palmer, he asked the news, and the palmer replied : "I have been at the wedding of Princess Rymenhild, and a sad sight it was, for the bride was wedded against her will, vowing she had a husband though he is a banished

man. She would take no ring nor utter any vows ; but
the service was read, and afterwards King Modi took
her to a strong castle, where not even a palmer was
given entrance. I came away, for I could not endure
the pity of it. The bride sits weeping sorely, and if
report be true her heart is like to break with grief."

Horn is Disguised as a Palmer

"Come, palmer," said Horn, "lend me your cloak
and scrip. I must see this strange bridal, and it may
be I shall make some there repent of the wrong they
have done to a helpless maiden. I will essay to enter."
The change was soon made, and Horn darkened his
face and hands as if bronzed with Eastern suns, bowed
his back, and gave his voice an old man's feebleness, so
that no man would have known him ; which done, he
made his way to King Modi's new castle. Here he
begged admittance for charity's sake, that he might
share the broken bits of the wedding feast ; but he was
churlishly refused by the porter, who would not be
moved by any entreaties. At last Horn lost all patience,
and broke open the door, and threw the porter out
over the drawbridge into the moat ; then, once more
assuming his disguise, he made his way into the hall
and sat down in the beggars' row.

The Recognition

Rymenhild was weeping still, and her stern husband
seemed only angered by her tears. Horn looked about
cautiously, but saw no sign of Athulf, his trusted
comrade ; for he was at this time eagerly looking for
his friend's coming from the lofty watch-tower, and
lamenting that he could guard the princess no longer.
At last, when the banquet was nearly over, Rymenhild
rose to pour out wine for the guests, as the custom was

then; and she bore a horn of ale or wine along the benches to each person there. Horn, sitting humbly on the ground, called out: "Come, courteous Queen, turn to me, for we beggars are thirsty folk." Rymenhild smiled sadly, and, setting down the horn, filled a bowl with brown ale, for she thought him a drunkard. "Here, drink this, and more besides, if thou wilt; I never saw so bold a beggar," she said. But Horn refused. He handed the bowl to the other beggars, and said: "Lady, I will drink nought but from a silver cup, for I am not what you think me. I am no beggar, but a fisher, come from afar to fish at thy wedding feast. My net lies near by, and has lain there for seven years, and I am come to see if it has caught any fish. Drink to me, and drink to Horn from thy horn, for far have I journeyed."

When the palmer spoke of fishing, and his seven-year-old net, Rymenhild felt cold at heart; she did not recognise him, but wondered greatly when he bade her drink "to Horn." She filled her cup and gave it to the palmer, saying, "Drink thy fill, and then tell me if thou hast ever seen Horn in thy wanderings." As the palmer drank, he dropped his ring into the cup; then he returned it to Rymenhild, saying, "Queen, seek out what is in thy draught." She said nothing then, but left the hall with her maidens and went to her bower, where she found the well-remembered ring she had given to Horn in token of betrothal. Greatly she feared that Horn was dead, and sent for the palmer, whom she questioned as to whence he had got the ring.

Horn's Stratagem

Horn thought he would test her love for him, since she had not recognised him, so he replied: "By St. Giles, lady, I have wandered many a mile, far into realms of the West, and there I found Sir Horn ready prepared to sail home to your land. He told me that he planned to reach the realm of Westernesse in time to see you before seven years had passed, and I embarked with him. The winds were favourable and we had a quick voyage, but, alas! he fell ill and died. When he lay dying he begged me piteously, 'Take this ring, from which I have never been parted, to my dear lady Rymenhild,' and he kissed it many times and pressed it to his breast. May God give his soul rest in Paradise!"

When Rymenhild heard those terrible tidings she sighed deeply and said: "O heart, burst now, for thou shalt never more have Horn, for love of whom thou hast been tormented so sorely!" Then she fell upon her bed, and grasped the dagger which she had concealed there; for if Horn did not come in time she had planned to slay both her hateful lord and herself that very night. Now, in her misery, she set the dagger to her heart, and would have slain herself at once, had not the palmer interrupted her. Rushing forward, he exclaimed: "Dear Queen and lady, I am Horn, thine own true love. Dost thou not recognise me? I am Childe Horn of Westernesse. Take me in thy arms, dear love, and kiss me welcome home." As Rymenhild stared incredulously at him, letting the dagger fall from her trembling hand, he hurriedly cast away his disguise, brushed off the disfiguring stain he had put on his cheeks, and stood up straight and strong, her own noble knight and lover. What joy they had together! How they told each other of all their adventures and troubles, and how they embraced and kissed each other!

Horn Slays King Modi

When their joy had become calmer, Horn said to his lady: "Dear Rymenhild, I must leave thee now, and return to my knights, who are encamped in the forest. Within an hour I will return to the feast and give the king and his guests a stern lesson." Then he flung away the palmer's cloak, and went forth in knightly array ; while the princess went up to the watch-tower, where Athulf still scanned the sea for some sign of Horn's coming. Rymenhild said : "Sir Athulf, true friend, go quickly to Horn, for he has arrived, and with him he brings a great army." The knight gladly hastened to the courtyard, mounted his steed, and soon overtook Horn. They were greatly rejoiced to meet again, and had much to tell each other and to plan for that day's work.

In the evening Horn and his army reached the castle, where they found the gates undone for them by their friends within, and in a short but desperate conflict King Modi and all the guests at the banquet were slain, except Rymenhild, her father, and Horn's twelve comrades. Then a new wedding was celebrated, for King Ailmar durst not refuse his daughter to the victor, and the bridal was now one of real rejoicing, though the king was somewhat bitter of mood.

Horn's Departure

When the hours wore on to midnight, Horn, sitting beside his bride, called for silence in the hall, and addressed the king thus : "Sir King, I pray thee listen to my tale, for I have much to say and much to explain. My name is in sooth Horn, and I am the son of King Murry of Suddene, who was slain by the Saracens. Thou didst cherish me and give me knighthood, and I proved myself a true knight on the very day when I was dubbed. Thou didst love me then, but evil men accused me to thee and I was banished. For seven years I have lived in a strange land ; but now that I have returned, I have won thy fair daughter as my bride. But I cannot dwell here in idleness while the heathen hold my father's land. I vow by the Holy Rood that I will not rest, and will not claim my wife, until I have purified Suddene from the infidel invaders, and can lay its crown at Rymenhild's feet. Do thou, O King, guard well my wife till my return."

The king consented to this proposal, and, in spite of Rymenhild's grief, Horn immediately bade her farewell, and with his whole army embarked for Suddene, this time accompanied by Athulf, but leaving the rest of his comrades for the protection of his wife.

The Apostate Knight

The wind blew fair for Suddene, and the fleet reached the port. The warriors disembarked, and marched inland, to encamp for the night in a wood, where they could be hidden. Horn and Athulf set out at midnight to endeavour to obtain news of the foe, and soon found a solitary knight sleeping. They awoke him roughly, saying, "Knight, awake! Why sleepest thou here? What dost thou guard?" The knight sprang lightly from the ground, saw their faces and the shining crosses on their shields, and cast down his eyes in shame, saying, "Alas! I have served these pagans against my will. In time gone by I was a Christian, but now I am a coward renegade, who forsook his God for fear of death at the hands of the Saracens! I hate my infidel masters, but I fear them too, and they have forced me to guard this district and keep watch against Horn's return. If he should come to his own again how glad I should be! These infidels slew his father, and drove him into exile, with his twelve comrades, among whom was my own son, Athulf, who loved the prince as his own life. If the prince is yet alive, and my son also, God grant that I may see them both again! Then would I joyfully die."

The Recognition

Horn answered quickly : " Sir Knight, be glad and rejoice, for here are we, Horn and Athulf, come to avenge my father and retake my realm from the heathen." Athulf's father was overcome with joy and shame ; he hardly dared to embrace his son, yet the bliss of meeting was so great that he clasped Athulf in his arms and prayed his forgiveness for the disgrace he had brought upon him. The two young knights said nothing of his past weakness, but told him all their own adventures, and at last he said : " What is your true errand hither ? Can you two alone slay the heathen ? Dear Childe Horn, what joy this will be to thy mother Godhild, who still lives in a solitary retreat, praying for thee and for the land ! " Horn broke in on his speech with " Blessed be the hour when I returned ! Thank God that my mother yet lives ! We are not alone, but I have an army of valiant Irish warriors, who will help me to regain my realm."

The Reconquest of Suddene

Now the king blew his horn, and his host marched out from the wood and prepared to attack the Saracens. The news soon spread that Childe Horn had returned, and many men who had accepted the faith of Mahomet for fear of death now threw off the hated religion, joined the true king's army, and were rebaptized. The war was not long, for the Saracens had made themselves universally hated, and the inhabitants rose against them ; so that in a short time the country was purged of the infidels, who were slain or fled to other lands. Then Horn brought his mother from her retreat, and

310

together they purified the churches which had been desecrated, and restored the true faith. When the land of Suddene was again a Christian realm King Horn was crowned with solemn rites, and a great coronation feast was held, which lasted too long for Horn's true happiness.

Fikenhild Imprisons Rymenhild

During Horn's absence from Westernesse, his comrades watched carefully over Rymenhild; but her father, who was growing old, had fallen much under the influence of the plausible Fikenhild. From the day when Fikenhild had falsely accused Horn to the king, Ailmar had held him in honour as a loyal servant, and now he had such power over the old ruler that when he demanded Rymenhild's hand in marriage, saying that Horn was dead in Suddene, the king dared not refuse, and the princess was bidden to make ready for a new bridal. For this day Fikenhild had long been prepared; he had built a massive fortress on a promontory, which at high tide was surrounded by the sea, but was easy of access at the ebb; thither he now led the weeping princess, and began a wedding feast which was to last all day, and to end only with the marriage ceremony at night.

Horn's Dream

That same night, before the feast, King Horn had a terrible dream. He thought he saw his wife taken on board ship; soon the ship began to sink, and Rymenhild held out her hands for rescue, but Fikenhild, standing in safety on shore, beat her back into the waves with his sword. With the agony of the sight Horn awoke, and, calling his comrade Athulf, said: "Friend, we must depart to-day. My wife is in danger

311

from false Fikenhild, whom I have trusted too much. Let us delay no longer, but go at once. If God will, I hope to release her, and to punish Fikenhild. God grant we come in time!" With some few chosen knights, King Horn and Athulf set out, and the ship drove darkling through the sea, they knew not whither. All the night they drifted on, and in the morning found themselves beneath a newly built castle, which none of them had seen before.

Horn's Disguise

While they were seeking to moor their boat to the shore, one of the castle windows looking out to sea opened, and they saw a knight standing and gazing seaward, whom they speedily recognised; it was Athulf's cousin, Sir Arnoldin, one of the twelve comrades, who had accompanied the princess thither in the hope that he might yet save her from Fikenhild; he was now looking, as a forlorn hope, over the sea, though he believed Horn was dead. His joy was great when he saw the knights, and he came out to them and speedily told them of Rymenhild's distress and the position of affairs in the castle. King Horn was not at a loss for an expedient even in this distress. He quickly disguised himself and a few of his comrades as minstrels, harpers, fiddlers, and jugglers. Then, rowing to the mainland, he waited till low tide, and made his way over the beach to the castle, accompanied by his disguised comrades. Outside the castle walls they began to play and sing, and Rymenhild heard them, and, asking what the sounds were, gave orders that the minstrels should be admitted. They sat on benches low down the hall, tuning their harps and fiddles, and watching the bride, who seemed unhappy and pale. When Horn sang a lay of true love and happi-

312

Horn and his followers disguised as minstrels

" Little John caught the horse by the bridle "

ness, Rymenhild swooned for grief, and the king was touched to the heart with bitter remorse that he had tried her constancy so long, and had allowed her to endure such hardships and misery for his sake.

Death of Fikenhild

King Horn now glanced down and saw the ring or betrothal on his finger, where he had worn it ever, except that fateful day when he had given it as a token of recognition to Rymenhild. He thought of his wife's sufferings, and his mind was made up. Springing from the minstrels' bench, he strode boldly up the hall, throwing off his disguise, and, shouting, "I am King Horn! False Fikenhild, thou shalt die!" he slew the villain in the midst of his men. Horn's comrades likewise flung off their disguise, and soon overpowered the few of the household who cared to fight in their dead master's cause. The castle was taken for King Ailmar, who was persuaded to nominate Sir Arnoldin his heir, and the baronage of Westernesse did homage to him as the next king. Horn and his fair wife begged the good old steward Sir Athelbrus to go with them to Suddene, and on the way they touched at Ireland, where Reynild, the king's fair daughter, was induced to look favourably on Sir Athulf and accept him for her husband. The land of King Modi, which had now no ruler, was committed to the care of Sir Athelbrus, and Horn and Rymenhild at last reached Suddene, where the people received their fair queen with great joy, and where they dwelt in happiness till their lives' end

CHAPTER XV: ROBIN HOOD

Introduction

ENGLAND during the twelfth, thirteenth, and fourteenth centuries was slowly taught the value of firm administrative government. In Saxon England, the keeping of the peace and the maintenance of justice had been left largely to private and family enterprise and to local and trading communities. In Norman England, the royal authority was asserted throughout the kingdom, though as yet the king had to depend in large measure upon the co-operation of his barons and the help of the burghers to supply the lack of a standing army and an adequate police. Under the Plantagenets, the older chivalry was slowly breaking up, and a new, wealthy burgher and trading community was rapidly gaining influence in the land ; whilst the clergy, corrupted by excess of wealth and power, had strained, almost to breaking, the controlling force of religion. It was therefore natural that in these latter days a class of men should arise to avail themselves of the unique opportunities of the time—men who, loving liberty and hating oppression, took the law into their own hands and executed a rough and ready justice between the rich and the poor which embodied the best traditions of knight-errantry, whilst they themselves lived a free and merry life on the tolls they exacted from their wealthy victims. Such a man may well have been the original Robin Hood, a man who, when once he had captured the popular imagination, soon acquired heroic reputation and was credited with every daring deed and every magnanimous action in two centuries of 'freebooting.'

Robin Hood Seeks a Guest

At one time Robin Hood lived in the noble forest of

Barnesdale, in Yorkshire. He had but few of his merry
men with him, for his headquarters were in the glorious
forest of Sherwood. Just now, however, the Sheriff of
Nottinghamshire was less active in his endeavours to put
down the band of outlaws, and the leader had wandered
farther north than usual. Robin's companions were his
three dearest comrades and most loyal followers, Little
John (so called because of his great stature), Will Scarlet,
Robin's cousin, and Much, the miller's son. These three
were all devoted to their leader, and never left his side,
except at such times as he sent them away on his business.

On this day Robin was leaning against a tree, lost in
thought, and his three followers grew impatient ; they
knew that before dinner could be served there were the
three customary Masses to hear, and their leader gave
no sign of being ready for Mass. Robin always heard
three Masses before his dinner, one of the Father, one
of the Holy Spirit, and the last of Our Lady, who was
his patron saint and protector. As the three yeomen
were growing hungry, Little John ventured to address
him. "Master, it would do you good if you would
dine early to-day, for you have fasted long." Robin
aroused himself and smiled. "Ah, Little John, methinks care for thine own appetite hath a share in that
speech, as well as care for me. But in sooth I care not
to dine alone. I would have a stranger guest, some
abbot or bishop or baron, who would pay us for our
hospitality. I will not dine till a guest be found, and
I leave it to you three to find him." Robin turned
away, laughing at the crestfallen faces of his followers,
who had not counted on such a vague commission ;
but Little John, quickly recovering himself, called to
him : "Master, tell us, before we leave you, where we
shall meet, and what sort of people we are to capture
and bring to you in the greenwood."

The Outlaws' Rules

"You know that already," said their master. "You are to do no harm to women, nor to any company in which a woman is travelling; this is in honour of our dear Lady. You are to be kind and gentle to husbandmen and toilers of all degrees, to worthy knights and yeomen, to gallant squires, and to all children and helpless people; but sheriffs (especially him of Nottingham), bishops, and prelates of all kinds, and usurers in Church and State, you may regard as your enemies, and may rob, beat, and despoil in any way. Meet me with your guest at our great trysting oak in the forest, and be speedy, for dinner must wait until the visitor has arrived." "Now may God send us a suitable traveller soon," said Little John, "for I am hungry for dinner now." "So am I," said each of the others, and Robin laughéd again. "Go ye all three, with bows and arrows in hand, and I will stay alone at the trysting tree and await your coming. As no man passes this way, you can walk up to the willow plantation and take your stand on Watling Street; there you will soon meet with likely travellers, and I will accept the first who appears. I will find means to have dinner ready against your return, and we will hope that our visitor's generosity will compensate us for the trouble of cooking his dinner."

Robin Hood's Guest

The three yeomen, taking their longbows in hand and arrows in their belts, walked up through the willow plantation to a place on Watling Street where another road crossed it; but there was no one in sight. As they stood with bows in hand, looking towards the forest of Barnesdale, they saw in the distance a knight riding in their direction. As he drew nearer they were struck by his appearance, for he rode as a man who had lost all interest in life; his clothes were disordered, he looked neither to right nor left, but drooped his head sadly, while one foot hung in the stirrup and the other dangled slackly in the air. The yeomen had never seen so doleful a rider; but, sad as he was, this was a visitor and must be taken to Robin; accordingly Little John stepped forward and caught the horse by the bridle.

Little John Escorts the Knight

The knight raised his head and looked blankly at the outlaw, who at once doffed his cap, saying, " Welcome, Sir Knight! I give you, on my master's behalf, a hearty welcome to the greenwood. Gentle knight, come now to my master, who hath waited three hours, fasting, for your approach before he would dine. Dinner is prepared, and only tarries your courteous appearance." The stranger knight seemed to consider this address carefully, for he sighed deeply, and then said : " I cry thee mercy, good fellow, for the delay, though I wot not how I am the cause thereof. But who is thy master? " Little John replied : " My master's name is Robin Hood, and I am sent to guide you to him." The knight said : " So Robin Hood is thy leader? I have heard of him, and know him to be a good yeoman; therefore I am ready to accompany thee, though, in good sooth, I had intended to eat my midday meal at Blythe or Doncaster to-day. But it matters little where a broken man dines ! "

Robin Hood's Feast

The three yeomen conducted the knight along the forest ways to the trysting oak where Robin awaited

317

them. As they went they observed that the knight was weeping silently for some great distress, but their courtesy forbade them to make any show of noticing his grief. When the appointed spot was reached, Robin stepped forward and courteously greeted his guest, with head uncovered and bended knee, and welcomed him gladly to the wild greenwood. "Welcome, Sir Knight, to our greenwood feast! I have waited three hours for a guest, and now Our Lady has sent you to me we can dine, after we have heard Mass." The knight said nothing but, "God save you, good Robin, and all your merry men"; and then very devoutly they heard the three Masses, sung by Friar Tuck. By this time others of the outlaw band had appeared, having returned from various errands, and a gay company sat down to a banquet as good as any the knight had ever eaten.

Robin Converses with the Knight

There was abundance of good things—venison and game of all kinds, swans and river-fowl and fish, with bread and good wine. Every one seemed joyous, and merry jests went round that jovial company, till even the careworn guest began to smile, and then to laugh outright. At this Robin was well pleased, for he saw that his visitor was a good man, and was glad to have lifted the burden of his care, even if only for a few minutes; so he smiled cheerfully at the knight and said: "Be merry, Sir Knight, I pray, and eat heartily of our food, for it is with great goodwill that we offer it to you." "Thanks, good Robin," replied the knight. "I have enjoyed my dinner to-day greatly; for three weeks I have not had so good a meal. If I ever pass by this way again I will do my best to repay you in kind; as good a dinner will I try to provide as you have given me."

318

THE KNIGHT'S POVERTY

Robin Demands Payment

The outlaw chief seemed to be affronted by this suggestion, and replied, with a touch of pride in his manner : " Thanks for your proffer, Sir Knight, but, by Heaven ! no man has ever yet deemed me a glutton. While I eat one dinner I am not accustomed to look eagerly for another—one is enough for me. But as for you, my guest, I think it only fitting that you should pay before you go ; a yeoman was never meant to pay for a knight's banquet." The knight blushed, and looked confused for a moment, and then said : "True, Robin, and gladly would I reward you for my entertainment, but I have no money worth offering ; even all I have would not be worthy of your acceptance, and I should be shamed in your eyes, and those of your men."

The Knight's Poverty

" Is that the truth ? " asked Robin, making a sign to Little John, who arose, and, going to the knight's steed, unstrapped a small coffer, which he brought back and placed before his master. "Search it, Little John," said he, and " You, sir, tell me the very truth, by your honour as a belted knight." " It is truth, on my honour, that I have but ten shillings," replied the knight, "and if Little John searches he will find no more." " Open the coffer," said Robin, and Little John took it away to the other side of the trysting oak, where he emptied its contents on his outspread cloak, and found exactly ten shillings. Returning to his master, who sat at his ease, drinking and gaily conversing with his anxious guest, Little John whispered : " The knight has told the truth," and thereupon Robin exclaimed aloud : " Sir Knight, I will not take one penny from you; you may rather borrow of me if you have need of more money, for ten shillings is but a miserable sum for a knight. But tell me now, if it be your pleasure, how you come to be in such distress." As he looked inquiringly at the stranger, whose blush had faded once, only to be renewed as he found his word of honour doubted, he noticed how thin and threadbare were his clothes and how worn his russet leather shoes; and he was grieved to see so noble-seeming a man in such a plight.

The Knight's Story

Yet Robin meant to fathom the cause of the knight's trouble, for then, perhaps, he would be able to help him, so he continued pitilessly: "Tell me just one word, which I will keep secret from all other men: were you driven by compulsion to take up knighthood, or urged to beg it by reason of the ownership of some small estate; or have you wasted your old inheritance with fines for brawling and strife, or in gambling and riotousness, or in borrowing at usury? All of these are fatal to a good estate."

The knight replied: "Alas! good Robin, none of these hath been my undoing. My ancestors have all been knights for over a hundred years, and I have not lived wastefully, but soberly and sparely. As short a time ago as last year I had over four hundred pounds saved, which I could spend freely among my neighbours, and my income was four hundred pounds a year from my land; but now my only possessions are my wife and children. This is the work of God's hand, and to Him I commit me to amend my estate in His own good time."

How the Money was Lost

"But how have you so soon lost this great wealth?"

"I have no money worth offering"

"Sir Richard knelt in courteous salutation"

asked Robin incredulously ; and the knight replied sadly : " Ah, Robin, you have no son, or you would know that a father will give up all to save his first-born. I have one gallant son, and when I went on the Crusade with our noble Prince Edward I left him at home to guard my lands, for he was twenty years old, and was a brave and comely youth. When I returned, after two years' absence, it was to find him in great danger, for in a public tournament he had slain in open fight a knight of Lancashire and a bold young squire. He would have died a shameful death had I not spent all my ready money and other property to save him from prison, for his enemies were mighty and unjust ; and even that was not enough, for I was forced to mortgage my estates for more money. All my land lies in pledge to the abbot of St. Mary's Abbey, in York, and I have no hope to redeem it. I was riding to York when your men found me."

The Sum Required

" For what sum is your land pledged ? " asked the master-outlaw ; and the knight replied : " The Abbot lent me four hundred pounds, though the value of the land is far beyond that." " What will you do if you fail to redeem your land ? " asked Robin. " I shall leave England at once, and journey once more to Jerusalem, and tread again the sacred Hill of Calvary, and never more return to my native land. That will be my fate, for I see no likelihood of repaying the loan, and I will not stay to see strangers holding my father's land. Farewell, my friend Robin, farewell to you all ! Keep the ten shillings ; I would have paid more if I could, but that is the best I can give you." " Have you no friends at home ? " asked Robin ; and the knight said : " Many friends I thought I had, sir. They were very kind and helpful in my days of prosperity, when I did not need them ; now they will not know me, so much has my poverty seemed to alter my face and appearance."

Robin Offers a Loan

This pitiful story touched the hearts of the simple and kindly outlaws ; they wept for pity, and cared not to hide their tears from each other, until Robin made them all pledge their guest in bumpers of good red wine. Then their chief asked, as if continuing his own train of thought: " Have you any friends who will act as sureties for the repayment of the loan ? " " None at all," replied the knight hopelessly, "but God Himself, who suffered on the Tree for us." This last reply angered Robin, who thought it savoured too much of companionship with the fat and hypocritical monks whom he hated, and he retorted sharply : " No such tricks for me ! Do you think I will take such a surety, or even one of the saints, in return for good solid gold ? Get some more substantial surety, or no gold shall you have from me. I cannot afford to waste my money."

The Knight Offers Surety

The knight replied, sighing heavily : " If you will not take these I have no earthly surety to offer ; and in Heaven there is only our dear Lady. I have served her truly, and she has never failed me till now, when her servant, the abbot, is playing me so cruel a trick." " Do you give Our Lady as your surety ? " said Robin Hood. " I would take her bond for any sum, for throughout all England you could find no better surety than our dear Lady, who has always been gracious to me. She is enough security. Go, Little John, to my treasury and bring me four hundred pounds, well counted, with no false or clipped coin therein."

THE BOND OF REPAYMENT

Robin Hood's Gifts

Little John, accompanied by Much, the careful treasurer of the band, went quickly to the secret place where the master-outlaw kept his gold. Very carefully they counted out the coins, testing each, to see that it was of full weight and value. Then, on the suggestion of Little John, they provided the knight with new clothing, even to boots and spurs, and finally supplied him with two splendid horses, one for riding and one to carry his baggage and the coffer of gold.

The guest watched all these preparations with bewildered eyes, and turned to Robin, crying, "Why have you done all this for me, a perfect stranger?" "You are no stranger, but Our Lady's messenger. She sent you to me, and Heaven grant you may prove true."

The Bond of Repayment

"God grant it," echoed the knight. "But, Robin, when shall I repay this loan, and where? Set me a day, and I will keep it." "Here," replied the outlaw, "under this greenwood tree, and in a twelvemonth's time; so will you have time to regain your friends and gather your rents from your redeemed lands. Now farewell, Sir Knight; and since it is not meet for a worthy knight to journey unattended, I will lend you also my comrade, Little John, to be your squire, and to do you yeoman service, if need be." The knight bade farewell to Robin and his generous followers, and was turning to ride away, when he suddenly stopped and addressed the master-outlaw: "In faith, good Robin, I had forgotten one thing. You know not my name. I am Sir Richard of the Lea, and my land lies in Uterysdale." "As for that," said Robin Hood, "I trouble not myself. You are Our Lady's messenger;

323

that is enough for me." So Sir Richard rode gladly away, blessing the generous outlaw who lent him money to redeem his land, and a stout yeoman to defend the loan.

Sir Richard's Journey

As the knight and his new servant rode on, Sir Richard called to his man, saying, "I must by all means be in York to-morrow, to pay the abbot of St. Mary's four hundred pounds; if I fail of my day I shall lose my land and lordship for ever"; and Little John answered : "Fear not, master ; we will surely be there in time enough." Then they rode on, and reached York early on the last day of the appointed time.

The Abbot and Prior of St. Mary's

In the meantime the abbot of St. Mary's was counting that Sir Richard's lands were safely his ; he had no pity for the poor unlucky knight, but rather exulted in the legal cruelty which he could inflict. Very joyfully he called aloud, early that morn : "A twelvemonth ago to-day we lent four hundred pounds to a needy knight, Sir Richard of the Lea, and unless he comes by noon to-day to repay the money he will lose all his land and be disinherited, and our abbey will be the richer by a fat estate, worth four hundred pounds a year. Our Lady grant that he keep not his day." "Shame on you ! " cried the prior. "This poor knight may be ill, or beyond the sea ; he may be in hunger and cold as well as poverty, and it will be a foul wrong if you declare his land forfeit."

"This is the set day," replied the abbot, "and he is not here." "You dare not escheat his estates yet," replied the prior stubbornly. "It is too early in the day ; until noon the lands are still Sir Richard's, and

no man shall take them ere the clock strikes. Shame
on your conscience and your greed, to do a good knight
such foul wrong ! I would willingly pay a hundred
pounds myself to prevent it."

"Beshrew your meddlesome temper !" cried the
abbot. "You are always crossing me ! But I have
with me the Lord Chief Justice, and he will declare my
legal right." Just at that moment the high cellarer
of the abbey entered to congratulate the abbot on Sir
Richard's absence. "He is dead or ill, and we shall
have the spending of four hundred pounds a year,"
quoth he.

Sir Richard Returns

On his arrival Sir Richard had quietly gone round to
his old tenants in York, and had a goodly company of
them ready to ride with him, but he was minded to test
the charity and true religion of the abbot, and bade his
followers assume pilgrims' robes. Thus attired, the
company rode to the abbey gate, where the porter recognised Sir Richard, and the news of his coming, carried
to the abbot and justice, caused them great grief ; but
the prior rejoiced, hoping that a cruel injustice would
be prevented. As they dismounted the porter loudly
called grooms to lead the horses into the stable and
have them relieved of their burdens, but Sir Richard
would not allow it, and left Little John to watch over
them at the abbey portal.

The Abbot and Sir Richard

Then Sir Richard came humbly into the hall, where
a great banquet was in progress, and knelt down in
courteous salutation to the abbot and his guests ; but
the prelate, who had made up his mind what conduct
to adopt, greeted him coldly, and many men did not

return his salutation at all. Sir Richard spoke aloud : "Rejoice, Sir Abbot, for I am come to keep my day." "That is well," replied the monk, "but hast thou brought the money?" "No money have I, not one penny," continued Sir Richard sadly. "Pledge me in good red wine, Sir Justice," cried the abbot callously ; "the land is mine. And what dost thou here, Sir Richard, a broken man, with no money to pay thy debt?" "I am come to beg you to grant me a longer time for repayment." "Not one minute past the appointed hour," said the exultant prelate. "Thou hast broken pledge, and thy land is forfeit."

Sir Richard Implores the Justice

Still kneeling, Sir Richard turned to the justice and said : "Good Sir Justice, be my friend and plead for me." "No," he replied, "I hold to the law, and can give thee no help." "Gentle abbot, have pity on me, and let me have my land again, and I will be the humble servant of your monastery till I have repaid in full your four hundred pounds." Then the cruel prelate swore a terrible oath that never should the knight have his land again, and no one in the hall would speak for him, kneeling there poor, friendless, and alone ; so at last he began to threaten violence. "Unless I have my land again," quoth he, "some of you here shall dearly abide it. Now may I see the poor man has no friends, for none will stand by me in my need."

The Justice Suggests a Compromise

The hint of violence made the abbot furiously angry, and, secure in his position and the support of the justice, he shouted loudly : "Out, thou false knight! Out of my hall!" Then at last Sir Richard rose to his feet in just wrath. "Thou liest, Sir Abbot; foully thou liest! I was never a false knight. In joust and tourney I have adventured as far and as boldly as any man alive. There is no true courtesy in thee, abbot, to suffer a knight to kneel so long." The quarrel now seemed so serious that the justice intervened, saying to the angry prelate, "What will you give me if I persuade him to sign a legal deed of release ? Without it you will never hold this land in peace." "You shall have a hundred pounds for yourself," said the abbot, and the justice nodded in token of assent.

Sir Richard Pays the Money

Now Sir Richard thought it was time to drop the mask, for noon was nigh, and he would not risk his land again. Accordingly he cried : "Nay, but not so easily shall ye have my lands. Even if you were to pay a thousand pounds more you should not hold my father's estate. Have here your money back again"; and, calling for Little John, he bade him bring into the hall his coffer with the bags inside. Then he counted out on the table four hundred good golden pounds, and said sternly : "Abbot, here is your money again. Had you but been courteous to me I would have rewarded you well ; now take your money, give me a quittance, and I will take my lands once more. Ye are all witnesses that I have kept my day and have paid in full." Thereupon Sir Richard strode haughtily out of the hall, and rode home gladly to his recovered lands in Uterysdale, where he and his family ever prayed for Robin Hood. The abbot of St. Mary's was bitterly enraged, for he had lost the fair lands of Sir Richard of the Lea and had received a bare four hundred pounds again. As for Little John, he went back to the forest and told his master the whole story, to Robin Hood's great satisfaction,

327

for he enjoyed the chance of thwarting the schemes of a wealthy and usurious prelate.

Sir Richard Sets Out to Repay the Loan

When a year had passed all but a few days, Sir Richard of the Lea said to his wife : "Lady, I must shortly go to Barnesdale to repay Robin Hood the loan which saved my lands, and would fain take him some small gift in addition ; what do you advise ? " " Sir Richard, I would take a hundred bows of Spanish yew and a hundred sheaves of arrows, peacock-feathered, or grey-goose-feathered ; methinks that will be to Robin a most acceptable gift."

Sir Richard followed his wife's advice, and on the morning of the appointed day set out to keep his tryst at the outlaws' oak in Barnesdale, with the money duly counted, and the bows and arrows for his present to the outlaw chief.

The Wrestling

As he rode, however, at the head of his troop he passed through a village where there was a wrestling contest, which he stayed to watch. He soon saw that the victorious wrestler, who was a stranger to the village, would be defrauded of his well-earned prize, which consisted of a white bull, a noble charger gaily caparisoned, a gold ring, a pipe of wine, and a pair of embroidered gloves. This seemed so wrong to Sir Richard that he stayed to defend the right, for love of Robin Hood and of justice, and kept the wrestling ring in awe with his well-appointed troop of men, so that the stranger was allowed to claim his prize and carry it off. Sir Richard, anxious not to arouse the hostility of the villagers, bought the pipe of wine from the winner, and, setting it abroach, allowed all who would to drink ;

and so, in a tumult of cheers and blessings, he rode
away to keep his tryst. By this time, however, it was
nearly three in the afternoon, and he should have been
there at twelve. He comforted himself with the thought
that Robin would forgive the delay, for the sake of its
cause, and so rode on comfortably enough at the head
of his gallant company.

Robin's Impatience

In the meantime Robin had waited patiently at the
trysting tree till noon, but when the hour passed
and Sir Richard had not appeared he began to grow
impatient. "Master, let us dine," said Little John.
"I cannot; I fear Our Lady is angered with me,
for she has not sent me my money," returned the
leader; but his follower replied: "The money is not
due till sunset, master, and Our Lady is true, and so is
Sir Richard; have no fear." "Do you three walk up
through the willow plantation to Watling Street, as
you did last year, and bring me a guest," said Robin
Hood. "He may be a messenger, a minstrel, a poor
man, but he will come in God's name."

The Monks Approach

Again the three yeomen, Little John, Will Scarlet,
and Much the miller's son, took bow in hand and set
out for Watling Street; but this time they had not long
to wait, for they at once saw a little procession approaching. Two black monks rode at the head; then followed
seven sumpter-mules and a train of fifty-two men, so
that the clerics rode in almost royal state. "Seest
thou yon monks?" said Little John. "I will pledge
my soul that they have brought our pay." "But they
are fifty-four, and we are but three," said Scarlet.
"Unless we bring them to dinner we dare not face

our master," cried Little John. "Look well to your bows, your strings and arrows, and have stout hearts and steady hands. I will take the foremost monk, for life or death."

The Capture of the Black Monk

The three outlaws stepped out into the road from the shelter of the wood; they bent their bows and held their arrows on the string, and Little John cried aloud: "Stay, churlish monk, or thou goest to thy death, and it will be on thine own head! Evil on thee for keeping our master fasting so long." "Who is your master?" asked the bewildered monk; and Little John replied: "Robin Hood." The monk tossed his head. "He is a foul thief," cried he, "and will come to a bad end. I have heard no good of him all my days." So speaking, he tried to ride forward and trample down the three yeomen; but Little John cried: "Thou liest, churlish monk, and thou shalt rue the lie. He is a good yeoman of this forest, and has bidden thee to dine with him this day"; and Much, drawing his bow, shot the monk to the heart, so that he fell to the ground dead. The other black monk was taken, but all his followers fled, except a little page, and a groom who tended the sumpter-mules; and thus, with Little John's help and guidance, the panic-stricken cleric and his train of baggage were brought to Robin under the trysting tree.

The Outlaws' Feast

Robin Hood doffed his cap and greeted his guest with all courtesy, but the monk would not reply, and Little John's account of their meeting made it evident that he was a churlish and unwilling guest. However, he was obliged to celebrate the three usual Masses, was

330

"Much shot the monk to the heart"

"Her pleading won relief for them"

THE MONK IS SEARCHED

given water for his ablutions before the banquet, and then when the whole fellowship was assembled he was set in the place of honour at the feast, and reverently served by Robin himself. "Be of good cheer, Sir Monk," said Robin. "Where is your abbey when you are at home, and who is your patron saint?" "I am of St. Mary's Abbey, in York, and, simple though I be, I am the high cellarer."

The High Cellarer and the Suretyship

"For Our Lady's sake," said Robin, "we will give this monk the best of cheer. Drink to me, Sir Monk; the wine is good. But I fear Our Lady is wroth with me, for she has not sent me my money." "Fear not, master," returned Little John; "this monk is her cellarer, and no doubt she has made him her messenger and he carries our money with him." "That is likely," replied Robin. "Sir Monk, Our Lady was surety for a little loan between a good knight and me, and to-day the money was to be repaid. If you have brought it, pay it to me now, and I will thank you heartily." The monk was quite amazed, and cried aloud: "I have never heard of such a suretyship"; and as he spoke he looked so anxiously at his sumpter-mules that Robin guessed there was gold in their pack-saddles.

The Monk is Searched

Accordingly the leader feigned sudden anger. "Sir Monk, how dare you defame our dear Lady? She is always true and faithful, and as you say you are her servant, no doubt she has made you her messenger to bring my money. Tell me truly how much you have in your coffers, and I will thank you for coming so punctually." The monk replied: "Sir, I

331

TB-14

have only twenty marks in my bags"; to which Robin answered : "If that be all, and you have told the truth, I will not touch one penny ; rather will I lend you some if you need it ; but if I find more, I will leave none, Sir Monk, for a religious man should have no silver to spend in luxury." Now the monk looked very greatly alarmed, but he dared make no protest, as Little John began to search his bags and coffers.

Success of the Search

When Little John opened the first coffer he emptied its contents, as before, into his cloak, and counted eight hundred pounds, with which he went to Robin Hood, saying, "Master, the monk has told the truth ; here are twenty marks of his own, and eight hundred pounds which Our Lady has sent you in return for your loan." When Robin heard that he cried to the miserable monk : "Did I not say so, monk ? Is not Our Lady the best surety a man could have ? Has she not repaid me twice ? Go back to your abbey and say that if ever St. Mary's monks need a friend they shall find one in Robin Hood."

The Monk Departs

"Where were you journeying ?" asked the outlaw leader. "To settle accounts with the bailiffs of our manors," replied the cellarer ; but he was in truth journeying to London, to obtain powers from the king against Sir Richard of the Lea. Robin thought for a moment, and then said : "Ah, then we must search your other coffer," and in spite of the cellarer's indignant protests he was deprived of all the money that second coffer contained. Then he was allowed to depart, vowing bitterly that a dinner in Blythe or Doncaster would have cost him much less dear.

332

Sir Richard Arrives

Late that afternoon Sir Richard of the Lea and his little company arrived at the trysting tree, and full courteously the knight greeted his deliverer and apologised for his delay. Robin asked of his welfare, and the knight told of his protection of the poor wrestler, for which Robin thanked him warmly. When he would fain have repaid the loan the generous outlaw refused to accept the money, though he took with hearty thanks the bows and arrows. In answer to the knight's inquiries, Robin said that he had been paid the money twice over before he came ; and he told, to his debtor's great amusement, the story of the high cellarer and his eight hundred pounds, and concluded: " Our Lady owed me no more than four hundred pounds, and she now gives you, by me, the other four hundred. Take them, with her blessing, and if ever you need more come to Robin Hood."

So Sir Richard returned to Uterysdale, and long continued to use his power to protect the bold outlaws, and Robin Hood dwelt securely in the greenwood, doing good to the poor and worthy, but acting as a thorn in the sides of all oppressors and tyrants.

CHAPTER XVI : HEREWARD THE WAKE

Introduction

IN dealing with hero-legends and myths we are sometimes confronted with the curious fact that a hero
whose name and date can be ascertained with exac-
titude has yet in his story mythological elements which
seem to belong to all the ages. This anomaly arises
chiefly from the fact that the imagination of a people is a
myth-making thing, and that the more truly popular the
hero the more likely he is to become the centre of a
whole cycle of myths, which are in different ages
attached to the heroes of different periods. The folk-
lore of primitive races is a great storehouse whence a
people can choose tales and heroic deeds to glorify its
own national hero, careless that the same tales and deeds
have done duty for other peoples and other heroes.
Hence it happens that Hereward the Saxon, a patriot
hero as real and actual as Wellington or Nelson, whose
deeds were recorded in prose and verse within forty
years of his death, was even then surrounded by a cloud
of romance and mystery, which hid in vagueness his
family, his marriage, and even his death.

The Saxon Patriot

Hereward was, naturally, the darling hero of the
Saxons, and for the patriotism of his splendid defence
of Ely they forgave his final surrender to William the
Norman ; then they attributed to him all the virtues
supposed to be inherent in the free-born, and all the
glorious valour on which the English prided themselves ; and, lastly, they surrounded his death with a
halo of desperate fighting, and made his last conflict as
wonderful as that of Roland at Roncesvalles. If Roland
is the ideal of Norman feudal chivalry, Hereward is

equally the ideal of Anglo-Saxon sturdy manliness and knighthood, and it seems fitting that the Saxon ideal in the individual should go down before the representatives, however unworthy, of a higher ideal.

Leofric of Mercia

When the weak but saintly King Edward the Confessor nominally ruled all England the land was divided into four great earldoms, of which Mercia and Kent were held by two powerful rivals. Leofric of Mercia and Godwin of Kent were jealous not only for themselves, but for their families, of each other's power and wealth, and the sons of Leofric and of Godwin were ever at strife, though the two earls were now old and prudent men, whose wars were fought with words and craft, not with swords. The wives of the two great earls were as different as their lords. The Lady Gytha, Godwin's wife, of the royal Danish race, was fierce and haughty, a fit helpmeet for the ambitious earl who was to undermine the strength of England by his efforts to win kingly power for his children. But the Lady Godiva, Leofric's beloved wife, was a gentle, pious, loving woman, who had already won an almost saintly reputation for sympathy and pity by her sacrifice to save her husband's oppressed citizens at Coventry, where her pleading won relief for them from the harsh earl on the pitiless condition of her never-forgotten ride. Happily her gentle self-suppression awoke a nobler spirit in her husband, and enabled him to play a worthier part in England's history. She was in entire sympathy with the religious aspirations of Edward the Confessor, and would gladly have seen one of her sons become a monk, perhaps to win spiritual power and a saintly reputation like those of the great Dunstan.

335

Hereward's Youth

For this holy vocation she fixed on her second son, Hereward, a wild, wayward lad, with long golden curls, eyes of different colours, one grey, one blue, great breadth and strength of limb, and a wild and ungovernable temper which made him difficult of control. This reckless lad the Lady Godiva vainly tried to educate for the monkish life, but he utterly refused to adopt her scheme, would not master any but the barest rudiments of learning, and spent his time in wrestling, boxing, fighting and all manly exercises. Despairing of making him an ecclesiastic, his mother set herself to inspire him with a noble ideal of knighthood, but his wildness and recklessness increased with his years, and often his mother had to stand between the riotous lad and his father's deserved anger.

His Strength and Leadership

When he reached the age of sixteen or seventeen he became the terror of the Fen Country, for at his father's Hall of Bourne he gathered a band of youths as wild and reckless as himself, who accepted him for their leader, and obeyed him implicitly, however outrageous were his commands. The wise Earl Leofric, who was much at court with the saintly king, understood little of the nature of his second son, and looked upon his wild deeds as evidence of a cruel and lawless mind, a menace to the peace of England, while they were in reality but the tokens of a restless energy for which the comparatively peaceable life of England at that time was all too dull and tame.

Leofric and Hereward

Frequent were the disputes between father and son,

and sadly did Lady Godiva forebode an evil ending to the clash of warring natures whenever Hereward and his father met ; yet she could do nothing to avert disaster, for though her entreaties would soften the lad into penitence for some mad prank or reckless outrage, one hint of cold blame from his father would suffice to make him hardened and impenitent ; and so things drifted from bad to worse. In all Hereward's lawless deeds, however, there was no meanness or crafty malice. He hated monks and played many a rough trick upon them, but took his punishment, when it came, with equable cheerfulness ; he robbed merchants with a high hand, but made reparation liberally, counting himself well satisfied with the fun of a fight or the skill of a clever trick ; his band of youths met and fought other bands, but they bore no malice when the strife was over. In one point only was Hereward less than true to his own nobility of character—he was jealous of admitting that any man was his superior in strength or comeliness, and his vanity was well supported by his extraordinary might and beauty.

Hereward at Court

The deeds which brought Earl Leofric's wrath upon his son in a terrible fashion were not matters of wanton wickedness, but of lawless personal violence. Called to attend his father to the Confessor's court, the youth, who had little respect for one so unwarlike as "the miracle-monger," uttered his contempt for saintly king, Norman prelate, and studious monks too loudly, and thereby shocked the weakly devout Edward, who thought piety the whole duty of man. But his wildness touched the king more nearly still ; for in his sturdy patriotism he hated the Norman favourites and courtiers who surrounded the Confessor, and again and again his

337

marvellous strength was shown in the personal injuries
he inflicted on the Normans in mere boyish brawls,
until at last his father could endure the disgrace no
longer.

Hereward's Exile

Begging an audience of the king, Leofric formally
asked for a writ of outlawry against his own son. The
Confessor, surprised, but not displeased, felt some com-
punction as he saw the father's affection overborne by
the judge's severity. Earl Godwin, Leofric's greatest
rival, was present in the council, and his pleading for
the noble lad, whose faults were only those of youth, was
sufficient to make Leofric more urgent in his petition.
The curse of family feud, which afterwards laid England
prostrate at the foot of the Conqueror, was already felt,
and felt so strongly that Hereward resented Godwin's
intercession more than his father's sternness.

Hereward's Farewell

"What!" he cried, "shall a son of Leofric, the noblest
man in England, accept intercession from Godwin or
any of his family? No. I may be unworthy of my
wise father and my saintly mother, but I am not yet sunk
so low as to ask a favour from a Godwin. Father, I
thank you. For years I have fretted against the peace
of the land, and thus have incurred your displeasure;
but in exile I may range abroad and win my fortune at
the sword's point." "Win thy fortune, foolish boy!"
said his father. "And whither wilt thou fare?" "Where-
ever fate and my fortune lead me," he replied recklessly.
"Perhaps to join Harald Hardrada at Constantinople,
and become one of the Emperor's Varangian Guard;
perhaps to follow old Beowa out into the West, at the
end of some day of glorious battle; perhaps to fight
338

giants and dragons and all kinds of monsters. All these things I may do, but never shall Mercia see me again till England calls me home. Farewell, father ; farewell, Earl Godwin ; farewell, reverend king. I go. And pray ye that ye may never need my arm, for it may hap that ye will call me and I will not come." Then Hereward rode away, followed into exile by one man only, Martin Lightfoot, who left the father's service for that of his outlawed son. It was when attending the king's court on this occasion that Hereward first saw and felt the charm of a lovely little Saxon maiden named Alftruda, a ward of the pious king.

Hereward in Northumbria

Though the king's writ of outlawry might run in Mercia, it did not carry more than nominal weight in Northumbria, where Earl Siward ruled almost as an independent lord. Thither Hereward determined to go, for there dwelt his own godfather, Gilbert of Ghent, and his castle was known as a good training school for young aspirants for knighthood. Sailing from Dover, Hereward landed at Whitby, and made his way to Gilbert's castle, where he was well received, since the cunning Fleming knew that an outlawry could be reversed at any time, and Leofric's son might yet come to rule England. Accordingly Hereward was enrolled in the number of young men, mainly Normans or Flemings, who were seeking to perfect themselves in chivalry before taking knighthood. He soon showed himself a brave warrior, an unequalled wrestler, and a wary fighter, and soon no one cared to meddle with the young Mercian, who outdid them all in manly sports. The envy of the young Normans was held in check by Gilbert, and by a wholesome dread of Hereward's

339

strong arm ; until, in Gilbert's absence, an incident occurred which placed the young exile on a pinnacle so far above them that only by his death could they hope to rid themselves of their feeling of inferiority.

The Fairy Bear

Gilbert kept in his castle court an immense white Polar bear, dreaded by all for its enormous strength, and called the Fairy Bear. It was even believed that the huge beast had some kinship to old Earl Siward, who bore a bear upon his crest, and was reputed to have had something of bear-like ferocity in his youth. This white bear was so much dreaded that he was kept chained up in a strong cage. One morning as Hereward was returning with Martin from his morning ride he heard shouts and shrieks from the castle yard, and, reaching the great gate, entered lightly and closed it behind him rapidly, for there outside the shattered cage, with broken chain dangling, stood the Fairy Bear, glaring savagely round the courtyard. But one human figure was in sight, that of a girl of about twelve years of age.

Hereward Slays the Bear

There were sounds of men's voices and women's shrieks from within the castle, but the doors were fast barred, while the maid, in her terror, beat on the portal with her palms, and begged them, for the love of God, to let her in. The cowards refused, and in the meantime the great bear, irritated by the dangling chain, made a rush towards the child. Hereward dashed forward, shouting to distract the bear, and just managed to stop his charge at the girl. The savage animal turned on the new-comer, who needed all his agility to escape the monster's terrible

Alftruda

Hereward and the Princess

onset.   Seizing his battle-axe, the youth swung it around his head and split the skull of the furious beast, which fell dead.   It was a blow so mighty that even Hereward himself was surprised at its deadly effect, and approached cautiously to examine his victim.   In the meantime the little girl, who proved to be no other than the king's ward, Alftruda, had watched with fascinated eyes first the approach of the monster, and then, as she crouched in terror, its sudden slaughter; and now she summoned up courage to run to Hereward, who had always been kind to the pretty child, and to fling herself into his arms.   "Kind Hereward," she whispered, "you have saved me and killed the bear. I love you for it, and I must give you a kiss, for my dame says so do all ladies that choose good knights to be their champions.   Will you be mine?"   As she spoke she kissed Hereward again and again.

Hereward's Trick on the Knights

"Where have they all gone, little one?" asked the young noble; and Alftruda replied: "We were all out here in the courtyard watching the young men at their exercises, when we heard a crash and a roar, and the cage burst open, and we saw the dreadful Fairy Bear. They all ran, the ladies and knights, but I was the last, and they were so frightened that they shut themselves in and left me outside; and when I beat at the door and prayed them to let me in they would not, and I thought the bear would eat me, till you came."

"The cowards!" cried Hereward.   "And they think themselves worthy of knighthood when they will save their own lives and leave a child in danger!   They must be taught a lesson.   Martin, come hither and aid me."   When Martin came, the two, with infinite trouble, raised the carcase of the monstrous beast, and placed

341

it just where the bower door, opening, would show it at once. Then Hereward bade Alftruda call to the knights in the bower that all was safe and they could come out, for the bear would not hurt them. He and Martin, listening, heard with great glee the bitter debate within the bower as to who should risk his life to open the door, the many excuses given for refusal, the mischievous fun in Alftruda's voice as she begged some one to open to her, and, best of all, the cry of horror with which the knight who had ventured to draw the bolt shut the door again on seeing the Fairy Bear waiting to enter. Hereward even carried his trick so far as to thrust the bear heavily against the bower door, making all the people within shriek and implore the protection of the saints. Finally, when he was tired of the jest, he convinced the valiant knights that they might emerge safely from their retirement, and showed how he, a stripling of seventeen, had slain the monster at one blow. From that time Hereward was the darling of the whole castle, petted, praised, beloved by all its inmates, except his jealous rivals.

Hereward Leaves Northumbria

The foreign knights grew so jealous of the Saxon youth, and so restive under his shafts of sarcastic ridicule, that they planned several times to kill him, and once or twice nearly succeeded. This insecurity, and a feeling that perhaps Earl Siward had some kinship with the Fairy Bear, and would wish to avenge his death, made Hereward decide to quit Gilbert's castle. The spirit of adventure was strong upon him, the sea seemed to call him ; now that he had been acknowledged superior to the other noble youths in Gilbert's household, the castle no longer afforded a field for his ambition. Accordingly he took a sad leave of Alftruda, an affectionate one of Sir Gilbert, who wished to knight him for his brave deed, and a mocking one of his angry and unsuccessful foes.

Hereward in Cornwall

Entering into a merchant-ship, he sailed for Cornwall, and there was taken to the court of King Alef, a petty British chief, who, on true patriarchal lines, disposed of his children as he would, and had betrothed his fair daughter to a terrible Pictish giant, breaking off, in order to do it, her troth-plight with Prince Sigtryg of Waterford, son of a Danish king in Ireland. Hereward was ever chivalrous, and little Alftruda had made him feel pitiful to all maidens. Seeing speedily how the princess loathed her new betrothed, a hideous, misshapen wretch, nearly eight feet high, he determined to slay him. With great deliberation he picked a quarrel with the giant, and killed him the next day in fair fight ; but King Alef was driven by the threats of the vengeful Pictish tribe to throw Hereward and his man Martin into prison, promising trial and punishment on the morrow.

Hereward Released from Prison

To the young Saxon's surprise, the released princess appeared to be as grieved and as revengeful as any follower of the Pictish giant, and she not only advocated prison and death the next day, but herself superintended the tying of the thongs that bound the two strangers. When they were left to their lonely confinement Hereward began to blame the princess for hypocrisy, and to protest the impossibility of a man's ever knowing what a woman wants. " Who would have thought," he cried, "that that beautiful maiden loved a giant so hideous as this Pict ? Had I known, I would never have fought

343

him, but her eyes said to me, 'Kill him,' and I have done so ; this is how she rewards me ! " " No," replied Martin, " this is how " ; and he cut Hereward's bonds, laughing silently to himself. " Master, you were so indignant with the lady that you could not make allowances for her. I knew that she must pretend to grieve, for her father's sake, and when she came to test our bonds I was sure of it, for as she fingered a knot she slipped a knife into my hands, and bade me use it. Now we are free from our bonds, and must try to escape from our prison."

The Princess Visits the Captives

In vain, however, the master and man ranged round the room in which they were confined ; it was a tiny chapel, with walls and doors of great thickness, and violently as Hereward exerted himself, he could make no impression on either walls or door, and, sitting sullenly down on the altar steps, he asked Martin what good was freedom from bonds in a secure prison. " Much, every way," replied the servant ; " at least we die with free hands ; and I, for my part, am content to trust that the princess has some good plan, if we will only be ready." While he was speaking they heard footsteps just outside the door, and the sound of a key being inserted into the lock. Hereward beckoned silently to Martin, and the two stood ready, one at each side of the door, to make a dash for freedom, and Martin was prepared to slay any who should hinder. To their great surprise, the princess entered, accompanied by an old priest bearing a lantern, which he set down on the altar step, and then the princess turned to Hereward, crying, "Pardon me, my deliverer ! " The Saxon was still aggrieved and bewildered, and replied : "Do you now say 'deliverer' ? This afternoon it was 'murderer, villain, cut-throat.' How shall I know which is your real mind ?" The princess almost laughed as she said : "How stupid men are ! What could I do but pretend to hate you, since otherwise the Picts would have slain you then and us all afterwards, but I claimed you as my victims, and you have been given to me. How else could I have come here to-night ? Now tell me, if I set you free will you swear to carry a message for me ?"

Sigtryg Ranaldsson of Waterford

"Whither shall I go, lady, and what shall I say ?" asked Hereward. "Take this ring, my ring of betrothal, and go to Prince Sigtryg, son of King Ranald of Waterford. Say to him that I am beset on every side, and beg him to come and claim me as his bride ; otherwise I fear I may be forced to marry some man of my father's choosing, as I was being driven to wed the Pictish giant. From him you have rescued me, and I thank you ; but if my betrothed delays his coming it may be too late, for there are other hateful suitors who would make my father bestow my hand upon one of them. Beg him to come with all speed." "Lady, I will go now," said Hereward, "if you will set me free from this vault."

Hereward Binds the Princess

"Go quickly, and safely," said the princess ; "but ere you go you have one duty to fulfil : you must bind me hand and foot, and fling me, with this old priest, on the ground." "Never," said Hereward, "will I bind a woman ; it were foul disgrace to me for ever." But Martin only laughed, and the maiden said again : "How stupid men are ! I must pretend to have been overpowered by you, or I shall be accused of having freed you, but I will say that I came hither to question

345

you, and you and your man set on me and the priest, bound us, took the key, and so escaped. So shall you be free, and I shall have no blame, and my father no danger ; and may Heaven forgive the lie."

Hereward reluctantly agreed, and, with Martin's help, bound the two hand and foot and laid them before the altar ; then, kissing the maiden's hand, and swearing loyalty and truth, he turned to depart. But the princess had one question to ask. "Who are you, noble stranger, so gallant and strong ? I would fain know for whom to pray." "I am Hereward Leofricsson, and my father is the Earl of Mercia." "Are you that Hereward who slew the Fairy Bear ? Little wonder is it that you have slain my monster and set me free." Then master and man left the chapel, after carefully turning the key in the lock. Making their way to the shore, they succeeded in getting a ship to carry them to Ireland, and in course of time reached Waterford..

Prince Sigtryg

The Danish kingdom of Waterford was ruled by King Ranald, whose only son, Sigtryg, was about Hereward's age, and was as noble-looking a youth as the Saxon hero. The king was at a feast, and Hereward, entering the hall with the captain of the vessel, sat down at one of the lower tables ; but he was not one of those who can pass unnoticed. The prince saw him, distinguished at once his noble bearing, and asked him to come to the king's own table. He gladly obeyed, and as he drank to the prince and their goblets touched together he contrived to drop the ring from the Cornish princess into Sigtryg's cup. The prince saw and recognised it as he drained his cup, and, watching his opportunity, left the hall, and was soon followed by his guest.

346

RETURN TO CORNWALL

Hereward and Sigtryg

Outside in the darkness Sigtryg turned hurriedly to Hereward, saying, " You bring me a message from my betrothed ? " " Yes, if you are that Prince Sigtryg to whom the Princess of Cornwall was affianced." " Was affianced ! What do you mean ? She is still my lady and my love." " Yet you leave her there unaided, while her father gives her in marriage to a hideous giant of a Pict, breaking her betrothal, and driving the hapless maiden to despair. What kind of love is yours ? " Hereward said nothing yet about his own slaying of the giant, because he wished to test Prince Sigtryg's sincerity, and he was satisfied, for the prince burst out : " Would to God that I had gone to her before ! but my father needed my help against foreign invaders and native rebels. I will go immediately and save my lady or die with her ! " " No need of that, for I killed that giant," said Hereward coolly, and Sigtryg embraced him in joy and they swore blood-brotherhood together. Then he asked : " What message do you bring me, and what means her ring ? " The other replied by repeating the Cornish maiden's words, and urging him to start at once if he would save his betrothed from some other hateful marriage.

Return to Cornwall

The prince went at once to his father, told him the whole story, and obtained a ship and men to journey to Cornwall and rescue the princess ; then, with Hereward by his side, he set sail, and soon landed in Cornwall, hoping to obtain his bride peaceably. To his grief he learnt that the princess had just been betrothed to a wild Cornish leader, Haco, and the wedding feast was to be held that very day. Sigtryg was greatly enraged, and sent a troop of forty Danes to King Alef demanding the fulfilment of the troth-plight between himsel, and his daughter, and threatening vengeance if it were broken. To this threat the king returned no answer, and no Dane came back to tell of their reception.

Hereward in the Enemy's Hall

Sigtryg would have waited till morning, trusting in the honour of the king, but Hereward disguised himself as a minstrel and obtained admission to the bridal feast, where he soon won applause by his beautiful singing. The bridegroom, Haco, in a rapture offered him any boon he liked to ask, but he demanded only a cup of wine from the hands of the bride. When she brought it to him he flung into the empty cup the betrothal ring, the token she had sent to Sigtryg, and said : " I thank thee, lady, and would reward thee for thy gentleness to a wandering minstrel ; I give back the cup, richer than before by the kind thoughts o. which it bears the token." The princess looked at him, gazed into the goblet, and saw her ring ; then, looking again, she recognised her deliverer and knew that rescue was at hand.

Haco's Plan

While men feasted Hereward listened and talked, and found out that the forty Danes were prisoners, to be released on the morrow when Haco was sure of his bride, but released useless and miserable, since they would be turned adrift blinded. Haco was taking his lovely bride back to his own land, and Hereward saw that any rescue, to be successful, must be attempted on the march. Yet he knew not the way the bridal company would go, and he lay down to sleep in the

348

Hereward and Sigtryg

hall, hoping that he might hear something more. When all men slept a dark shape came gliding through the hall and touched Hereward on the shoulder ; he slept lightly, and awoke at once to recognise the old nurse of the princess. "Come to her now," the old woman whispered, and Hereward went, though he knew not that the princess was still true to her lover. In her bower, which she was soon to leave, Haco's sorrowful bride awaited the messenger.

Rescue for Haco's Bride

Sadly she smiled on the young Saxon as she said : "I knew your face again in spite of the disguise, but you come too late. Bear my farewell to Sigtryg, and say that my father's will, not mine, makes me false to my troth-plight." "Have you not been told, lady, that he is here?" asked Hereward. "Here?" the princess cried. "I have not heard. He loves me still and has not forsaken me?" "No, lady, he is too true a lover for falsehood. He sent forty Danes yesterday to demand you of your father and threaten his wrath if he refused." "And I knew not of it," said the princess softly ; "yet I had heard that Haco had taken some prisoners, whom he means to blind." "Those are our messengers, and your future subjects," said Hereward. "Help me to save them and you. Do you know Haco's plans?" "Only this, that he will march to-morrow along the river, and where the ravine is darkest and forms the boundary between his kingdom and my father's the prisoners are to be blinded and released." "Is it far hence?" "Three miles to the eastward of this hall," she replied. "We will be there. Have no fear, lady, whatever you may see, but be bold and look for your lover in the fight." So saying, Hereward kissed the hand of the princess, and passed out of the hall unperceived by any one.

The Ambush

Returning to Sigtryg, the young Saxon told all that he had learnt, and the Danes planned an ambush in the ravine where Haco had decided to blind and set free his captives. All was in readiness, and side by side Hereward and Sigtryg were watching the pathway from their covert, when the sound of horses' hoofs heard on the rocks reduced them to silence. The bridal procession came in strange array : first the Danish prisoners, bound each between two Cornishmen, then Haco and his unhappy bride, and last a great throng of Cornishmen. Hereward had taken command, that Sigtryg might look to the safety of his lady, and his plan was simplicity itself. The Danes were to wait till their comrades, with their guards, had passed through the ravine ; then while the leader engaged Haco, and Sigtryg looked to the safety of the princess, the Danes would release the prisoners and slay every Cornishman, and the two parties of Danes, uniting their forces, would restore order to the land and destroy the followers of Haco.

Success

The whole was carried out exactly as Hereward had planned. The Cornishmen, with Danish captives, passed first without attack ; next came Haco, riding grim and ferocious beside his silent bride, he exulting in his success, she looking eagerly for any signs of rescue. As they passed Hereward sprang from his shelter, crying, "Upon them, Danes, and set your brethren free !" and himself struck down Haco and smote off his head. There was a short struggle, but soon the

350

rescued Danes were able to aid their deliverers, and the Cornish guards were all slain ; the men of King Alef, never very zealous for the cause of Haco, fled, and the Danes were left masters of the field. Sigtryg had in the meantime seen to the safety of the princess, and now placing her between himself and Hereward, he escorted her to the ship, which soon brought them to Waterford and a happy bridal. The Prince and Princess of Waterford always recognised in Hereward their deliverer and best friend, and in their gratitude wished him to dwell with them always ; but he knew " how hard a thing it is to look into happiness through another man's eyes," and would not stay. His roving and daring temper drove him to deeds of arms in other lands, where he won a renown second to none, but he always felt glad in his own heart, even in later days, when unfaithfulness to a woman was the one great sin of his life, that his first feats of arms had been wrought to rescue two maidens from their hapless fate, and that he was rightly known as Hereward the Saxon, the Champion of Women.

GLOSSARY AND INDEX

In the following Index no attempt is made to indicate the exact pronunciation of foreign names; but in the case of those from the Anglo-Saxon a rough approximation is given, as being often essential to the reading of the metrical versions. In these indications the letters have their ordinary English values; ĕ indicates the very light, obscure sound heard in the indefinite article in such a phrase as "with a rush."

A

ABLOEC. See Anlaf

ACHILLES. His sulks, 184; Cuchulain, "the Irish," 184

ADEON. Son of Eudav; grandson of Caradoc, 49

AGE. See Golden Age

AILILL. King of Connaught, husband of Queen Meave; to decide claims to title of Chief Champion, 189; seeks aid of Fairy People of the Hills, 193

AILMAR. King of Westernesse, 290; welcomes and adopts Childe Horn, 291; Princess Rymenhild, daughter of, 292; dubs Horn knight, 297; hears of Horn's first exploit, 299; Fikenhild betrays Horn and Rymenhild to, 300; Horn returns to, 304; reluctantly gives his daughter to Horn, 308; Horn leaves Rymenhild to his care, 308, 309

AIX-LA-CHAPELLE. Wondrous springs of, 125; Charlemagne at, 155

ALEF. King of Cornwall; Hereward at court of, 343; casts Hereward into prison, 343; his daughter releases Hereward, 344, 345; Sigtryg sends forty Danes to, 348

ALFTRUDA. Ward of Edward the Confessor, 339; Hereward's first meeting with, 339; rescues from Fairy Bear, 340, 341; Hereward takes farewell of, 342

ALICE OF CLOUDESLEE. Wife of William of Cloudeslee, 227; outlaw husband visits, 227, 228; rescued from burning house, 232; thanks Adam Bell and Clym for delivering her husband, 240; appointed chief woman of bedchamber to the royal children, 246

ALL-FATHER. Praised for Beowulf's victory over Grendel, 18

ALTO-BIS-CA'R. Song of (a forgery), 120

ANGLESEY. Same as Mona, 47

ANGLO-SAXON NOBILITY. Hereward the ideal of, 334, 335

ANGLO-SAXON TIMES. Legends regarding Constantine during, 42

ÆNGUS THE EVER-YOUNG. Irish people and wrath of, 158

ANLAF. Same as Olaf, or Sihtricson; known to Welsh as Abloec or Habloc; romantic stories concerning, 73

ANSEIS, DUKE OF. Mortally wounded, 143

ARABIA. Physicians from, with remedies for Constantine's leprosy, 65

ARMAGH. Capital of Ulster; Cuchulain and Emer dwell at, 186; King Conor and heroes return to, 190; heroes return to, 195

ARNOLDIN, SIR. Cousin of Athulf; helps to save Rymenhild, 312; King Ailmar nominates as his heir, 313

ARTHUR, KING. Uncle of Sir Gawayne, 265; Christmas kept at Carlisle by, 266; Guenever, queen of, 266; uncle of Sir Gareth and Sir Mordred, 266; damsel requests a boon of, 267; his journey to Tarn Wathelan, and fight with giant, 269; humiliated by the giant and released on certain conditions, 270 ; his search for the answer to the giant's question, 270–272 ; learns it from the loathly lady, 272 ; the ransom paid to giant, 273 ; the loathly lady demands a young and handsome knight for husband for helping, 274 ; Sir Gawayne offers to pay ransom for, 275 ; summons court to hunt in greenwood near Tarn Wathelan, 276 ; rebukes Sir Kay, 277 ; his joy over his nephew's wedding with the supposed loathly lady, 284, 285

ARTHURIAN LEGEND. Preserved by mediæval Wales, 265

ARVON. Fertile land of, searched by ambassadors of Maxen Wledig, 47–49

ASBRAND. Brother of Biargey, 113 ; helps Howard against Thorbiorn, 115

ASCHERE (ask-herĕ). One of King Hrothgar's thanes, carried off by Grendel's mother, 21

ATHELBRUS. King Ailmar's steward, to train Childe Horn to be a knight, 291, 292 ; induces Athulf to personate Horn, 293 ; sends Horn to Princess Rymenhild, 294 ; land of King Modi committed to care of, 313

ATHELSTAN. King of England ; kinship of Anlaf with, 73

ATHELWOLD. King of England, father of Goldborough, 80 ; his death and burial, 81

ATHULF. Horn's favourite companion, 287 ; personates Horn before Rymenhild, 293 ; writes to Horn on behalf of Rymenhild, 303 ; plans with Horn the rescue of Rymenhild, 308 ; his father found at Suddene, 309, 310 ; weds Reynild, 313

AUDE THE FAIR. Sister of Oliver, betrothed bride of Roland, 155 ; Charlemagne promises his son Louis to, 155 ; dies of grief for Roland's loss, 155

AUGUSTUS. Constantine's elevation to rank of, 64

AWE, LOCH. Black Colin, Knight of, 249, 250 ; Black Colin dwells at, with wife, 250 ; Lady of, 251 ; Black Colin far away from, 254 ; Black Colin's return to, 258

B

BABYLON, EMIR OF. Marsile's vassal; defeated by Charlemagne, 154

BALTIC SEA. Forefathers who dwelt on shores of, 1

BANIER, SIR. A Knight of the Round Table, 266

BARNESDALE. Forest in South Yorkshire, once dwelling-place of Robin Hood, 314, 315 ; Sir Richard of the Lea sets out for, to repay loan, 328

BARTON, SIR ANDREW. Scottish hero, 248

BASQUES. Attack Charlemagne, 119

BATHSTEAD. Place on shores of Icefirth near where Thorbiorn lived, 97–118

BEAN-STAN. Father of Breca, 12

BEDIVERE, SIR. A Knight of the Round Table, 266

BELI. Son of Manogan ; Britain conquered by Maxen Wledig from, 48

BELL, ADAM. Outlaw leader in forest of Englewood, 226 ; declared powerless to deliver William of Cloudeslee, 233 ; rescues William from death, 237, 238 ; visit to London to see the king, 241 ; the king pardons, 243

BEO'WA. Stories of, crystallised in stories of Beowulf, 1

BEO'WULF. 1. The poem of, 1. 2. Thane of Hygelac, King of Geats, 1 ; son of Ecgtheow, 6 ; nephew of King Hygelac, 6 ; grandson of Hrethel, 6 ; brought up at Geatish court, 6 ; famous swimming match with Breca, 6; his mighty hand-grip, 6; sails for Denmark to attack Grendel, 6; challenged by Warden of Denmark, 6; declares his mission to Hrothgar, 10; disparaged by Hunferth, 12; honoured by Queen Wealhtheow, 14, 20; struggles with Grendel, 16; mortally wounds Grendel, 17; vows to slay mother of Grendel, 23; does so, 26; carries off sword-hilt and Grendel's head, 26; sails to Geatland, 29; welcomed by King Hygelac and Queen Hygd, 29, 30; chief champion of Hygelac, 30; refuses the throne in favour of Heardred, and becomes guardian of, 31; again chosen King of Geatland, 31; encounters with fire-dragon, 31–39; recites slaying of Frankish warrior, Daghrefn, 35; forsaken by Geats in his encounter with the fire-dragon, 36; slays the dragon, 37; his death and funeral, 39–41

BERILD. Son of King Thurston, 301; slain by the Saracens, 302

BERNARD BROWN. Danish magistrate; protects Havelok and Goldborough, 88–89

BER-NA'R-DO DEL CA'R-PIO. Hero in Spanish legend who defeats Roland, 121

BERTRAM. Earl's cook who befriended Havelok, 82–83; marries one of Grim's daughters and becomes Earl of Cornwall, 94

BIARGEY. Wife of Howard the Halt, 97; urges Howard to claim wergild for Olaf, 106, 107, 108; Howard returns to, 111; visits her brothers, Valbrand, Thorbrand, and Asbrand, 112, 113; hails Thorbiorn while out fishing, 112; urges Howard to seek vengeance, 113, 114

BIRKABEYN. Rule of, as king over Denmark, 74; Swanborow and Elfleda, daughters of, and Havelok, son of, 7; commits Havelok to care of Jarl Godard, 75; death and funeral of, 75; Jarl Ubbe, an old friend of, 87

BLACK COLIN OF LOCH AWE, 249; son of Sir Nigel Campbell, 249; Patterson, name of fosterparents, 250; messenger tells of new crusade, 250; decides to go on crusade, 251; his wife's grief, 251; touches at Edinburgh and ships at Leith, *en route* to Holy Land, 253; his desire to see Holy Land and Holy Sepulchre, 253; reaches Rome, 253; sees Pope, 253; regards Pope as Vicar of Christ, 253; journeys to Rhodes, 253; takes service with Knights of St. John, 253; a pilgrim at Jerusalem, 253; letter in name of, forged by Baron MacCorquodale, 255; falsely reported wounded by Saracens, 255; hears news of wife's impending second marriage, 257; returns home, 258; welcomed by fostermother, 259; disguised as a beggar, hands token to his wife, 262; recognised and welcomed by his wife, 262

BLACK DOUGLAS. Scottish hero, 248

BLACK MONK, THE. Captured by Robin Hood's followers, 330; high cellarer in Abbey of St. Mary, 331; Robin Hood confiscates his gold as repayment of loan to Sir Richard of the Lea, 331, 332; departs from greenwood, 332

BLACK SAINGLAIN. One of Cuchulain's magic steeds, 191

BLANCANDRIN. Vassal of King Marsile, 123; overtaken by Ganelon, 130; Ganelon and, plot Roland's destruction, 131

BLAYE. Bodies of Roland, Oliver, and Turpin buried in cathedral of, 155

BLUBMIRE. Dwelling-place of Howard the Halt, 97

BOG OF ALLEN. Cathleen's messenger declared to be sick in, 177

BORS, SIR. A Knight of the Round Table, 266

BOURNE, HALL OF. Home of Leofric, Earl of Mercia, 336

BRAND. Trusted serving-man of Thorbiorn, 97, 102

BRECA. Famous swimming champion, beaten by Beowulf, 6; son of Beanstan, 12

BRICRIU OF THE BITTER TONGUE. Compared with Thersites, 186; invites King Conor and Red Branch heroes to a feast, 186; stirs up strife among heroes of Ulster, 187, 188; flatters the wives of the heroes, 189, 190

BRIGIT. 1. Of the Holy Fire; wrath of, and Irish people, 158. 2. Cathleen's old servant, 173

BRISEIS. Achilles and his sulks concerning, 184

BRITAIN. Legend of "The Dream of Maxen Wledig" shows importance of Constantine to, 42; ambassadors of Maxen Wledig carried to, 47; conquered by Maxen Wledig from Beli, son of Manogan, 48; given by Maxen Wledig to Eudav, 49; Elene summoned from, is baptized, and seeks the sacred Cross, 54–62; Constantine sent to, 63; Constantine proclaimed emperor of, 63

BRITONS, EARLY, Greeks of Homer, and Irish Celts, racial affinity between, 184

BRITTANY. Roland, prefect of marches of, 120

BRUCE, ROBERT. Scottish hero, 248; Sir Nigel Campbell, adherent of, 249

C

CAERLLEON. See Caernarvon, 49

CAERMARTHEN. See Caernarvon, 49

CAERNARVON. Castle in land of Arvon in which Princess Helena dwelt, 48; given with castles Caerlleon and Caermarthen to Princess Helena as dowry, 49

CAIN. Grendel, offspring of, 4

CALEDONIANS. Defeated by Constantius, 63

CALIDORE, SIR. Mediæval Wales had a knight of courtesy equal to, 265

CALVARY. The hill of, 58, 59, 61

CAMPBELL, SIR NIGEL. Leader in Scottish Independence, 249; father of Black Colin, 249; his death, 259; clansmen of, accompany Black Colin to Holy Land, 252

CARADOC. Father of Eudav; grandfather of Princess Helena, and of Princes Kynon and Adeon, 49

CARLISLE. Outlaw band near town of, in Englewood Forest, 226; reference to sheriff of, 227; William of Cloudeslee goes to, 227; sheriff informed of William's presence at, 229; outlaws Adam Bell and Clym go to, 234; the outlaws escape from, 239; King Arthur keeps Christmas at, 266; Sir Gawayne and loathly lady wedded at, 280

CATHBAD. Druid; Cuchulain's tutor, 185

CATHLEEN. Irish countess; legend concerning, 156; antiquity of the legend, 156; the story, 156–183; her grief because of her people's famine, 161; prays to Virgin Mary, 163; Fergus, steward of, 163; value of her wealth, 164; commands Fergus to provide food for sufferers from famine, 165; her goodness extolled by the demons, 169; hears of demon traders, 172; tries to check traffic in souls, 174; visits demons, 176; Oona, foster-mother to, 178; revisits demons, 179; sells her soul, 179, 180; her death, 182

CATHOLIC CHURCH. Pope, head of, 119

CELION. Constantine to send to, for Bishop Sylvester, 71

CELTIC LITERATURE. Spirit of mysticism in all, 156

CELTS. Gospel preached to, by St. Patrick, 157 ; Irish, early Britons, and Greeks of Homer, racial affinity between, 184

CHAMPION. 1. Of Erin: compared with Achilles, 184 ; Cuchulain the, his fame at age of seventeen, 185 ; Bricriu urges Laegaire to claim title of, 187 ; title to go to warrior who obtains Champion's Bit, 187 ; tests to decide claims to title of, 193, 194, 196–203 ; Uath the Stranger challenges the heroes to a test to decide claims to title, 199–203. 2. Of Women: Hereward known as, 351

CHAMPION OF IRELAND. See Champion of Erin.

CHAMPION'S BIT, THE, 187, 188 ; claimed by chariot-drivers of Laegaire, Conall, and Cuchulain, 188, 189 ; awarded by Queen Meave to Laegaire, 195 ; heroes severally claim, 195, 196 ; tests to decide claims to, 196–203

CHANSON DE ROLAND. Roland and, 121 ; late version of Anglo-Norman poem, 122 ; Thorold, author of, 122

CHARLEMAGNE. World - famed equivalent, 119 ; head of Roman Empire, 119 ; Roland, nephew of, 119 ; expedition into Spain, 119 ; receives an embassage from Marsile, 124 ; calls his Twelve Peers to council, 125 ; sends Ganelon to Saragossa, 128–130 ; receives through Ganelon the keys of Saragossa, 134 ; his evil dream, 134, 137 ; hears Roland's horn, 145, 146 ; hastens to the rescue, 146 ; avenges death of Roland and the Peers, 153, 154 ; his return to Aix, 155 ; his son, Louis, promised to Aude the Fair, 155

CHARLES THE GREAT. King of the Franks, world-famed as Charlemagne, 119. See Charlemagne

CHILDE HORN. See Horn

CHOSEN PEOPLE. The Jews the, 56

CHRIST. The Cross the sign of, 53 ; the Resurrection of, preached to Constantine, 53 ; Constantine's desire to find the sacred Cross, 54 ; inhabitants of Suddene who believe on, threatened with death, 287

CHRISTENDOM. Enriched by treasures of the True Cross and Holy Nails, 62

CHRISTIAN-S. Preach the way of life to Constantine, 53 ; the Lord of, 57 ; faith, in Iceland, 96, 97 ; law, to be driven out of Suddene by law of Mahomet, 287

CHURCH OF ROME. Constantine's generosity to, 42

CHURCHMEN. Beaten and battered by Gamelyn, 217

CINDERELLA. Root idea of, similar to " Gamelyn," 204

CLYM OF THE CLEUGH. Outlaw leader in forest of Englewood, 226 ; declared powerless to deliver William of Cloudeslee, 233 ; his stratagem to save William of Cloudeslee, 234 ; rescues William from death, 238 ; visits London to see the king, 241 ; the king pardons, 243

COLIN, BLACK. See Black Colin, 249

COMALA. Hero in Gaelic Highland poems, 248

CONALL CEARNACH. Cuchulain's cousin, a Red Branch chief, 187 ; urged to claim title of Chief Champion, 187 ; awarded Champion's Portion, 195 ; claim tested by Curoi, 196–203 ; disgraced by Uath, 201

CONFESSIO AMANTIS. Early English poem, by " the moral Gower," 42 ; story told in, of Constantine's true charity, 64

CONNAUGHT. Ailill, King of, 189 ; heroes sent to Cruachan in, 190

CONOR. King of Ulster, 185 ; Cuchulain, nephew of, 185 ; Dech-

tire, sister of, 185 ; invited
with the heroes of Red Branch
to a feast by Bricriu, 186; received with court at Dundrum
by Bricriu, 188

CONQUEROR, WILLIAM THE. Cause
of England being laid at feet
of, 338

CONSTANTINE III. King of Scotland ; marriage of Anlaf with
daughter of, 73

CONSTANTINE THE GREAT. Emperor of Rome ; renown in
mediæval England, 42 ; Cynewulf's poem, "Elene," written
on the subject of his conversion,
42 ; his vision of the Holy
Cross, 42, 50, 51 ; generosity to
Church of Rome and Bishop
Sylvester, 42 ; legends concerning, 42 ; the only British-born
Roman emperor, 49 ; his
greatness provokes a confederation to overthrow him by Huns,
Goths, Franks, and Hugas, 50 ;
conquers Huns by Cross standard, 52 ; Christians preach
the way of life to, 53 ; is baptized into the Christian faith,
53 ; his desire to find the sacred
Cross, 54 ; sends for Elene, 54 ;
ordains "Holy Cross Day," 62 ;
eldest son of Constantius, 63 ;
sent to Britain, 63 ; proclaimed
emperor, 63 ; granted title of
"Cæsar," 64 ; marriage with
Fausta, 64 ; elevation to rank
of Augustus, 64 ; Emperor of
Rome, 64 ; attacked by leprosy, 64 ; the remedies suggested, 65–72 ; his noble resolve, 68 ; his vision, 69–70 ;
his healing, 71–72

CONSTANTIUS. Emperor Maxentius hero of the Welsh saga instead of, 42 ; father of Constantine the Great, 63 ; proclaimed
Emperor of Britain, 63

CORNISH PRINCESS, THE. Daughter
o King Alef, affianced to Prince
Sigtryg, 343, 344, 345, 346;
Haco betrothed to, 347, 348,
receives token from Hereward ;

348 ; reveals Haco's plans to
Hereward, 349 ; rescued from
Haco, 350 ; guards, all slain,
351 : wedded by Sigtryg, 351

CORNWALL. Godrich, Earl of,
80 ; Bertram made Earl of, 94 ;
Hereward sails for, 343 ; Alef,
King of, 343 ; Sigtryg and
Hereward sail for, 347

COVENTRY. Lady Godiva's ride
through, 335

CRESCENT. Cross exalted above
the, 253

CROSS. The Holy, Constantine's
vision of, 42, 50, 51 ; Romans
conquer Huns by, 52 ; the
people awed by the standard of
the, 53 ; Constantine's desire
to find the sacred, 54 ; Elene's
quest after, 54–62 ; secret
place of, revealed by Judas, 61 ;
"Holy Cross Day" ordained,
62

CRUACHAN. Conor sends heroes
to Ailill at, 190 ; Good People's
Hill at, 193 ; heroes bid farewell to court at, 195

CRUSADES. Reference to, 249 ;
Black Colin receives tidings of
one about to be set on foot,
250 ; Black Colin decides to go
on, 251 ; story of Horn typical
of romance of the, 286

CUCHULAIN. Reference to Connla
and, 95 ; Irish hero, 156 ; often
called "the Irish Achilles,"
184 ; nephew of King Conor and
son of Dechtire, 185 ; god Lugh,
reputed father of, 185 ; champion
in Ulster and all Ireland, 185 ;
bride sought for, 186 ; wooes
and weds Emer, daughter of
Forgall the Wily, 186 ; Conall
Cearnach, cousin of, 187 ; urged
to claim title of Chief Champion, 188 ; Grey of Macha and
Black Sainglain, magic steeds
of, 191 ; awarded golden cup
and Champion's Portion, 195 ;
claim tested by Curoi, 196–203 ;
answers Uath's tests, 202 ; acclaimed Champion of Heroes of
all Ireland, 203

GLOSSARY AND INDEX

CUROI OF MUNSTER. Failing a judgment from Ailill, to be asked to decide claims to title of Chief Champion, 190; heroes go to, to hear his judgment, 196; puts heroes to certain tests in order to decide claims, 196-203; assumes form of giant under name of Uath, the Stranger, 199-203

CURTIUS. Reference to, 156

CUTHBERT. Name under which Childe Horn serves King Thurston in Ireland, 301, 302

CYNEWULF (ki'nĕ-wulf). Early English religious poet; "Elene," his poem on the subject of conversion of Constantine the Great, 42

CYRIACUS. Baptismal name of Judas, 61; Bishop of Jerusalem, 61

D

DAGDA. Irish people and wrath of, 158

DA'G-HREFN. Frankish warrior who slays Hygelac; killed by Beowulf's deadly hand-grip, 35

DANES. Corpse of Scyld sorrowfully placed in vessel by, 2; feasting of, in Heorot, 4; slain in Heorot by Grendel, 4; desert Heorot, 5; welcome Geats and Beowulf, 10; rejoice over Beowulf's victory, 18-29; friendship with Geats, 30; Gospel preached to, 157; Prince Sigtryg sends forty to King Alaf, 348; plan ambush for Haco, 350; rescue Cornish princess, 350, 351

DANISH. 1. Occupation of England and its influence on language, &c., 73. 2. Invasions, hero-legends which have come down from times of, 286

DANUBE. Huns overwhelmed in, 52

DECHTIRE. Sister of King Conor, 185

DECIUS. Reference to, 156

DEMONS. Appear in Erin to buy souls, 168; visited by Cathleen, 176; revisited by her, 179; Cathleen sells her soul to, to ransom her people, 179; cheated of Cathleen's soul, 182

DENMARK. Under sway of Scyld Scefing, 2; Scyld Scefing mysteriously comes to, as babe, 2; Beowulf sails to deliver King of, from Grendel, 6; Warden of, challenges Beowulf, 6; King Birkabeyn's rule over, 74; Godard made regent of, on behalf of Havelok, 75; Havelok sails from, with Grim, 80; Havelok's dream concerning, 86; Havelok's return to, and recognition as King of, 87-92

DIARMUIT. Irish hero, 156

DIOCLETIAN. Emperor; Constantine evades jealousy of, 63

DODDERER. Horse offered as wergild by Thorbiorn to Howard, 107

DOVER. Princess Goldborough imprisoned in castle of, 81; Hereward sails from, to Whitby, 339

DUBLIN. Demons arrive at village near, 168

DUNDRUM. Bricriu receives King Conor and court at, 188

DUNSTAN. Monk; his saintly reputation, 335

DURENDALA. Roland's famous sword, 136; Roland tries in vain to break, 152

E

ECGTHEOW (eg'theow). Father of Beowulf, 10; shielded by Hrothgar against Wilfings, 11

EDINBURGH. Black Colin at, en route to Holy Land, 253

EDWARD. 1. The First: reference to war between England and Scotland during reign of, 249; 2. The Second: reference, ibid., 249. 3. The Confessor: division of England under, 335; Hereward at court of, 337, 338;

banishes Hereward, 338, 339; Alftruda, ward of, 339

EGYPT. Constantine's valour in wars in, 64 ; philosophers from, with remedies for Constantine's leprosy, 65

ELECTRA. Reference to Orestes and, 95

ELENA. Same as Elene and Helena, 63

"ELENE" (elā'nĕ). Cynewulf's poem of, on the subject of Constantine's conversion, 42 ; summoned from Britain by Constantine, is baptized, and seeks the sacred Cross, 54–62. Same as Helena (Elena), 63

ELFLEDA THE FAIR. Daughter of King Birkabeyn, 74 ; slain by Godard, 76

ELY. Hereward's defence of, 334

EMER. Daughter of Forgall the Wily; wooed and wedded by Cuchulain, 186 ; flattered by Bricriu, 189 ; flattered by Queen Meave, 195 ; adjudged by Uath to have first place among all the women of Ulster, 203

ENGELIER THE GASCON. Mortally wounded, 143

ENGLAND. Mediæval, and Constantine the Great, 42 ; influence on language by Danish occupation, 73 ; Athelstan, King of, 73 ; Athelwold, King of, 80 ; Grim sails from Denmark to, 80 ; arrives at, in Humber (Grimsby), 81 ; Havelok's dream concerning, 86 ; Fergus journeys to, 165 ; the outlaw of mediæval, 225 ; King of, pardons outlaws, William of Cloudeslee, &c., 243 ; war between Scotland and, 249 ; government of, during twelfth, thirteenth, and fourteenth centuries, 314 ; division of, under Edward the Confessor, 335 ; cause of being laid at Conqueror's feet, 338

ENGLEWOOD. Outlaws in forest of, under Adam Bell, William of Cloudeslee, and Clym of the

Cleugh, 226 ; outlaw band broken up, 247

ERCOL. Ailill's foster-father ; heroes sent to, 194

ERIN. See Ireland, 157 ; demons appear in, 168 ; Champion of, compared with Achilles, 184 ; land of, searched for bride for Cuchulain, 186

EUDAV. Son of Caradoc, father of Princess Helena, 49 ; Kynon and Adeon, sons of, 49

EUROPE. Ruled from City of Seven Hills (Rome) by Emperor Maxen Wledig, 43 ; Constantine granted rule over Western, 64 ; relation between Greek and Irish literature among literatures of, 184

EVIL ONE. Tales relating dealings with, reference to, 157 ; demons buy souls for, 168–182

EXCALIBUR. King Arthur's sword, 269

F

FAIRY BEAR, THE. A white Polar bear owned by Gilbert of Ghent, 340 ; reputed kinship of, to Earl Siward, 340, 342 ; slain by Hereward, 341 ; Hereward's trick on Norman knights with, 341, 342

FAIRY PEOPLE OF THE HILLS. King Ailill seeks aid of, 193

FAITH. Bishop Sylvester preaches the Christian, to Constantine, 71 ; Charlemagne fights for, 119 ; Marsile to embrace the Christian, 131 ; the true, English knowledge of, 165 ; Irish sufferers tempted to revolt from, 167

FALL, THE, OF MAN, 71

FAUST. Legends, trend of, 157

FAUSTA. Daughter of Emperor Maximian and wife of Constantine, 64

FEDELM. Wife of Laegaire, 189

FEN COUNTRY. Hereward, the terror of the, 336

GLOSSARY AND INDEX

FENIANS. Champions of the, identical with Highland Gaelic heroes, 248

FERGUS THE WHITE. Cathleen's steward, 163; foster-brother to Cathleen's grandfather, 164; declares value of Cathleen's wealth, 164; sends servant to buy food at Ulster, 165; journeys to England, 165; returns with help, 182

FIKENHILD. Horn's companion next in favour to Athulf, 287; spies on Horn and Rymenhild, 299, 300; demands Rymenhild in marriage, 311; slain by Horn, 313

FINGAL. Hero in Gaelic Highland poems, 248; Scotch embodiment of Finn, 248

FINN. Fingal Scotch embodiment, 248

FINN OF THE FRISIANS. Victory of Danes over, chanted in Heorot, 19

FINNSBURG. Fight in, sung of in Heorot, 19

FITELA. Son of Sigmund; glory of, chanted by Danish bard, 18

FLEMINGS. Or Normans; Hereward enrolled among, to qualify for knighthood, 339; Hereward's trick on, with Fairy Bear, 341, 342

FOREFATHERS. Feelings of our, embodied in "Beowulf," 1

FORGALL THE WILY. Cuchulain wooes Emer, daughter of, 186

FRANCE. Victories of Charlemagne for, 119; Charlemagne sets out for, 134

FRANKISH. 1. Warrior, Daghrefn, slays Hygelac, and is slain by Beowulf, 35. 2. Army marches towards Pyrenees, 134; arrives too late to rescue Roland, 146

FRANKS. Charles the Great (Charlemagne), King of, 119; Saracen host encamps near, 134; and Moors meet in battle, 140; defeat the Saracens, 141; attacked by second Saracen

army, 142; defeat the heathens once more, 143; attacked by third Saracen army, 144

FRENCH LITERATURE, developing "Roland Saga," 121

FRIAR TUCK. See Tuck

G

GALERIUS. Constantine evades hatred of, 63; grants Constantine title of "Cæsar," 63

GAMELYN. Tale of, a variant of fairy-tale "Wicked Elder Brothers," 204; ultimate source, through Lodge's "Euphues' Golden Legacy," of *As You Like It*, 204; literary ancestor of "Robin Hood," 204; Sir John of the Marshes, father of, 205; left in charge of eldest brother, John, 206; resists him, 207, 208; victorious at wrestling match, 210, 211; overcomes his brother's servants, 212; allows himself to be chained, 213; released by Adam Spencer, 214, 215; batters the Churchmen, 217; puts his brother John in chains, 217; puts sheriff's men to flight, 218; goes to the greenwood, 219; joins the outlaws, 220; proclaimed a wolf's-head, 220; arrested, 221; Otho offers himself as surety, 221; fails to appear at court, 222, 223; releases Otho, 223; sits on judge's seat and condemns Sir John, 224; made chief forester by King Edward, 224; made Otho's heir, 224

GANELON. Romance version of Danilo or Nanilo, 121; compared with Judas, 121; one of Charlemagne's Twelve Peers, 125; his hostility to Roland, 126; plots with Blancandrin the destruction of Roland, 131; delivers to Marsile the message of Charlemagne, 131, 132; swears on sacred relics the treacherous death of Roland,

134 ; delivers keys of Saragossa to Charlemagne, 134 ; deceives Charlemagne concerning sound of Roland's horn, 145, 146 ; arrested for treason, 146 ; his death as a traitor, 155 ; his name a byword in France for treachery, 155

GARETH, SIR. One of King Arthur's nephews, 266

GASCONS. Attack Charlemagne, 119

GAUTIER, COUNT. Roland's vassal, 136

GAWAYNE, SIR. King Arthur's nephew, the true Knight of Courtesy, 265 ; learns of King Arthur's adventure with the giant, 274 ; learns the price to be paid for the loathly lady's secret, 275 ; offers to pay it by marrying the loathly lady, 275 ; betroths the loathly lady, 279, 280 ; weds the loathly lady, 280 ; his choice frees the loathly lady from magic spells, 281, 283 ; the beauty of his bride, 281–285

GEATISH COURT. Beowulf brought up at, 6

GEATLAND. Same as Götaland ; news of Grendel's ravages reaches, 6 ; Beowulf sails to, 29 ; welcomed to shores of, 29, 30

GEATS. Hygelac, King of, 1 ; Götaland, realm of, 5 ; arrival with Beowulf at Danish shores, 7 ; friendship with Danes, 30 ; forsake Beowulf in his encounter with the fire-dragon, 36 ; their sorrow over Beowulf's death, 40–41

GERIER. Peer of Charlemagne ; mortally wounded, 143

GERIN. Peer of Charlemagne ; mortally wounded, 143

GERMANY. Forefathers who dwelt in North, 1 ; Hygelac seeks conquest of his neighbours on mainland of, 5

GHENT. See Gilbert

GILBERT OF GHENT. Hereward's godfather. 339 ; Hereward received by, 339 ; his Fairy Bear, slain by Hereward, 340, 341 ; Hereward quits his castle, 342 ; Hereward takes farewell of, 343

GLENURCHY. Glen belonging to MacGregors, given to Sir Niger Campbell, 249 ; Black Colin inherits, 250 ; Lady of, grieves over her husband's departure on crusade, 251 ; Baron Mac-Corquodale's land borders, 256 ; Black Colin's return to, 258 ; new castle built with rents of, 264

GOD. The Unknown, reverenced by Constantine, 51 ; the people awed by the token of the Unknown, 53 ; worship of the True, 157 ; famine cools love for, 167

GODARD, JARL. Counsellor and friend of King Birkabeyn, 75 ; Havelok committed to care of, 75 ; regency over Denmark, 75 ; his cruelty, 76–78 ; his treachery disclosed and punished by death, 91–92

GODHILD. Queen of Suddene, King Murry's consort, the mother of Horn, 286 ; hears of husband's death and flees, 288

GODIVA, LADY. Wife of Leofric, Earl of Mercia, 335 ; her famous ride through Coventry, 335 ; Hereward, second son of, 336

GODRICH. Earl of Cornwall, regent for Princess Goldborough, 80 ; his rule, 81 ; imprisons Princess Goldborough out of jealousy, 81 ; attends sports at Lincoln, 83 ; hears of Havelok's skill and strength, 83 ; enforces a marriage between Havelok and Goldborough, 84 ; captured, tried as a traitor, and burnt at the stake, 93–94

GODWIN. Earl of Kent, 335 ; Lady Gytha, wife of, 335 ; intercedes on behalf of Hereward, 338 ; Hereward bids farewell to, 339

GOLDBOROUGH. English princess, daughter of King Athelwold; orphaned, 80; Earl Godrich regent for, 80; imprisoned in Dover Castle, 81; forced to wed Havelok, 84; learns in a dream of Havelok's royal birth, 86; crowned Queen of England, 94

GOLDEN AGE. Forefathers cherished lifetime of ancestors as, 1

GÖTALAND. Realm of Geats, in south of Sweden, 5. See Geatland, 7

GOTHS. Form a confederation with the Huns, Franks, and Hugas to overthrow Constantine, 50

GOWER, "THE MORAL." Early English poet; his poem "Confessio Amantis" and Constantine's conversion, 42; story told in "Confessio Amantis" of Constantine's true charity, 64

GREECE. Philosophers from, with remedies for Constantine's leprosy, 65

GREEK-S. Elene touches at land of, 56; literature, relation of, to Irish literature, 184; of Homer, early Britons, and Irish Celts, racial affinity between, 184

GRENDEL. A loathsome fen-monster, 3; enmity aroused by the feasting at Heorot, 4; slays and devours Danes in Heorot, 4; master of Heorot, 5; Beowulf determines to attack, 6; struggles with Beowulf in Heorot, 16; worsted by Beowulf, 17; mother of, avenges his death, 21

GREY OF MACHA. Cuchulain's best-beloved horse, 191

GRIM. Legendary hero whose loyalty secured privileges to Grimsby, 74; Godard's thrall, 77; ordered to drown Havelok, 77; saves and maintains Havelok, 79–82; sails from Denmark to England, 80; sends Havelok to Lincoln, 82; his death, 85; his three sons,

Robert the Red, William Wendut, and Hugh the Raven, 87

GRIMSBY. The town of Grim, 74; Havelok at fish-market of, 82; battle near, between Havelok and Godrich, 93

GUDRUN. Reference to Siegfried and, 95

GUENEVER, QUEEN. Wife of King Arthur, 266; dreads magic arts during husband's absence, 274; learns of King Arthur's adventure with the giant, 274; welcomes the loathly lady at court, 280

GUEST, THE WISE. Sister of, marries Thorbiorn, 103; Howard seeks at the Thing, 108, 109, 110; his judgment against Thorbiorn, 110, 111; removes his sister from Thorbiorn, 111; gives judgment at Thing against Howard, 118

GYTHA, LADY. Wife of Godwin, Earl of Kent, 335

H

HABLOC. Welsh name for Havelok, 73

HACO. Cornish leader; betrothed to the Cornish princess, 347; Cornish princess reveals plans of, to Hereward, 349; ambush planned for, 350; slain by Hereward, 350

HAROLD. Son of King Thurston, 301; slain by the Saracens, 302

HART, THE. See Heorot, 3

HASTINGS. Battle of, and "Song of Roland," 122

HATHCYN. Son of King Hrethel, brought up with Beowulf; slays his brother, Herebeald, 34; slain himself by Swedes, 35

HAUTECLAIRE. Oliver's sword, 141

HAVELOK THE DANE. Legend of, 73; Anlaf, equivalent, 73; hero of the strong arm, in mediæval England, 74; son of King Birkabeyn of Denmark, 74; committed to care of Jarl Godard,

75 ; imprisoned by Godard, 76–77 ; saved and maintained by Grim, 78–82 ; brought by Grim to England, 80 ; his feats of strength, 82–84 ; Goldborough forced to wed, 84–85 ; Grim's three sons accompany to Denmark, 87 ; aided by Jarl Ubbe, 88–93 ; Ubbe recognises as heir to throne of Denmark, and renders homage to, 90–91 ; acknowledged King of Denmark, 92 ; and of England, 94

HEALFDENE (ha'lf-dānĕ). Father of King Hrothgar, 9

HEARDRED (ha'rd-red). Son of Hygelac and Hygd ; succeeds his father, 31 ; his death, 31

HECTOR. Reference to death of, 95

HELENA. British princess ; marriage with Constantine glorified in " Mabinogion," 42 ; hailed as Empress of Rome, 48, 49 ; receives three castles as dowry, Caernarvon, Caerlleon, and Caermarthen, 49 ; mother of Constantine the Great, 63

HELL. The purchase of souls for, 170–183 ; Cathleen sells her soul to, 179

HENGEST. Deeds of, chanted in Heorot, 19

HEOROT (hyo'r-ŏt). Hall built by Hrothgar, 3 ; same as " The Hart," 3 ; enmity of Grendel to, 4 ; feasting of Danes in, 4 ; Danes slaughtered in, by Grendel, 4 ; deserted by Danes, 5 ; Grendel master of, 5 ; Geats proceed to, 9 ; feast in, to welcome Beowulf, 12 ; Grendel and Beowulf struggle in, 16 ; Grendel's mother enters and carries off Aschere, 21

HEREBEALD (he'rĕ-bald). Son of King Hrethel, brought up with Beowulf, 34

HEREWARD. One of the famous outlaws, 225 ; the Saxon, personality real, yet surrounded by cloud of romance, 334 ; the ideal of Anglo-Saxon chivalry,

as Roland of Norman, 334 ; second son of Leofric and Godiva, 336 ; terror of Fen Country, 336 ; at court, and his conduct there, 337 ; banished as an outlaw, 338, 339 ; his farewell, 338, 339 ; his first meeting with Alftruda, 339 ; goes to his godfather, Gilbert of Ghent, 339 ; enrolled among Flemings to qualify for knighthood, 339 ; his encounter with the Fairy Bear, 340, 341 ; rescues Alftruda, 341 ; his trick on the Norman knights, 341, 342 ; leaves Northumbria, 342 ; takes farewell of Alftruda, 342 ; takes farewell of Gilbert of Ghent, 343 ; sails for Cornwall, 343 ; at court of King Alef, 343 ; kills the Pictish giant, 343 ; imprisoned by King Alef, 343 ; released by King Alef's daughter, 344, 345 ; sails for Ireland, 346 ; sails for Cornwall with Prince Sigtryg, 347 ; obtains admission to Haco's bridal feast, 348 ; learns Haco's plans, 349 ; slays Haco and helps to rescue Cornish princess, 350, 351 ; known as Hereward the Saxon, the Champion of Women, 351

HEROD. Constantine declared more cruel than, 67

HET-WARE, THE. Expedition against, 31, 34

HIGHLANDS. Gaelic, old ballads, heroes in, 248 ; ballads, merely versions of Irish Gaelic herolegends, 248 ; Irish Gaelic herolegends carried from Erin to, 248

HILDEBURH, QUEEN. Deeds of, chanted in Heorot, 19

HNÆF (nǎf). Deeds of, chanted in Heorot, 19

HOLY CROSS. Constantine's vision of, 42, 50, 51 ; his desire to find, 54 ; Elene's quest after, 54–62 ; Judas confesses to knowledge of sacred truth of, 57 ; Judas refuses to reveal place of, at first, but is pre-vailed upon by starvation, 58, 59 ; the " Day " of, ordained, 62

HOLY INNOCENTS. Constantine declared more cruel than Herod, who killed the, 67

HOLY LAND. Black Colin receives tidings of fresh crusade in, 250 ; sets out for, 252 ; Black Colin's desire to see, 253

HOLY NAILS. Obtained by Elene, 61 ; given to Constantine, 62

HOLY ROOD. King Arthur vows by, 268 ; giant forces him to swear by, 270

HOLY SEPULCHRE. Black Colin's desire to see, 253

HOLY TREE. See Holy Cross

HOMER. Greeks of, early Britons, and Irish Celts, racial affinity between, 184

HOOD, ROBIN. See Robin Hood

HORN. His story originally a story of Viking raids, 286 ; son of King Murry and Queen God-hild, 286, 308 ; Athulf, and next Fikenhild, his favourite companions, 287 ; captured by Saracens, 288 ; cast adrift upon the sea, 288, 289 ; lands on shore of Westernesse, 289 ; questioned by King of Wester-nesse, 290 ; adopted by King Ailmar, 291 ; Athelbrus trains as a knight, 291, 292 ; loved by Princess Rymenhild, 292 ; Athulf personates before Princess Rymenhild, 293 ; welcomed in Rymenhild's bower, and hears her declaration of love, 294, 295 ; dubbed knight, 297 ; his first exploit, 298 ; spied on by Fikenhild, 299, 300 ; banished by King Ailmar, 300 ; sails for Ireland, 301 ; serves King Thurston under name of Cuthbert, 301 ; slays the giant emir, 301, 302 ; King Thurston offers his kingdom and daughter to, 302 ; receives letter from Rymenhild, 304 ; reveals his identity to King Thurston and implores his help, 304 ; returns

to Westernesse, accompanied by Irish knights, 304 ; in disguise, visits Rymenhild's wedding feast, 305 ; his stratagem to test Rymenhild's love, 306, 307 ; the fictitious death of, 307 ; reveals his identity to Rymenhild, 307 ; arranges with Athulf to deliver Rymen-hild, 308 ; weds Rymenhild, 308 ; reconquers Suddene, 310 ; finds his mother, 310, 311 ; crowned King of Suddene, 311 ; warned in dream of Rymen-hild's danger, 311 ; his return to Westernesse, 311, 312 ; slays Fikenhild, 313 ; dwells at Sud-dene with Rymenhild, 313

HOWARD THE HALT. Popular Icelandic saga, 96 ; famous Viking, 97 ; Biargey, wife of, 97 ; Olaf, son of, 97 ; upbraids Olaf, 100 ; removes from Bath-stead, 103 ; mourns Olaf's death, 106 ; claims wergild for Olaf, 106–111 ; sheltered by Steinthor, 108, 109 ; urged by Biargey to seek vengeance, 106, 107, 113 ; seeks help of Val-brand, 114 ; slays Thorbiorn, 116 ; sheltered by Steinthor, 117 ; judgment of Thing against, 118 ; his nephews exiled, 118

HRETHEL (rethel). Father of Hygelac and grandfather of Beowulf, 6 ; Beowulf and the king's sons, Herebeald, Hath-cyn, and Hygelac, 34 ; Beowulf recites his death, 35

HRETHRIC (re'th-ric). Son of Hrothgar ; succeeds his father, 31

HROTHGAR (roth'gär). Great-grandson of Scyld, 2 ; builds the hall Heorot, or "The Hart," 3 ; grief of, over Grendel's fierce ravages, 4 ; champions offer aid to, 5 ; Geats conducted to, 8 ; son of Healfdene, 9 ; Wealh-theow, wife of, 14 ; rejoices over Beowulf's victory, 18–29 ; Aschere, thane of, carried off by Grendel's mother, 21 ; grief of, over loss of Aschere, 22 ; succeeded by his son Hrethric, 31

HRUNTING (runting). Hunferth's sword, lent Beowulf for the purpose of attacking Grendel's mother, 23–25

HUGAS. See Huns, 50

HUGH THE RAVEN. Youngest son of Grim ; accompanies Havelok to Denmark, 87

HUMBER. Grim arrives in, 81

HUNFERTH. Hrothgar's orator, jealous of Beowulf, 12 ; lends Beowulf his sword, Hrunting, 23, 24

HUNS. Form a confederation with the Goths, Franks, and Hugas to overthrow Constantine, 50 ; Romans conquer by Cross standard, 52

HYGD. Wife of King Hygelac ; hails Beowulf's return to Geatland, 29, 30 ; offers crown to Beowulf, 31

HYGELAC (hĕ'gĕ-lac). King of Geats, 1 ; son of King Hrethel, 5, 34 ; brother-in-law of Ecgtheow, 6 ; uncle of Beowulf, 6 ; hails Beowulf's return to Geatland, 29, 30 ; Beowulf chief champion of, 30 ; slain in expedition against the Hetware, 31 ; succeeded by his son, Heardred, 31 ; brought up with brothers, Herebald and Hathcyn, and Beowulf, 34

I

ICEFIRTH. Thorbiorn in, 97

ICELAND. Christian faith in, 96, 97

ICELANDIC. 1. Saga, " Howard the Halt," 96. 2. Ghosts, reference to, 96

INNIS EOALAN. The Lady of Loch Awe builds a castle on ruins of White House on, 257

INNOCENTS, HOLY. Constantine declared more cruel than Herod, who killed the, 67

IRELAND. Characteristics common to people of, 156 ; known in olden Europe as " Isle of Saints," 157 ; Gospel preached to people of, 157 ; High King of, convinced of truth of Trinity, 157 ; strife in, 158 ; famine in, 159–183 ; famine tempts people to revolt from the True Faith, 167 ; demons arrive in, 168 ; Cuchulain without fear among the champions of, 185 ; Horn at, 301–304 ; Horn touches at, on way to Suddene, 313 ; Sigtryg, son of a Danish king, in, 343 ; Hereward sails for, 346

IRISH. Relation of literature, to Greek literature, 184 ; Celts, early Britons, and Greeks of Homer, one stock, 184 ; heroes, and legends concerning, 248

ISLE OF SAINTS. See Ireland, 157

ITALY. Claims Roland in guise of Orlando, Orlando Furioso, Orlando Innamorato, 121

J

JERUSALEM. The place where Christ suffered, 54 ; Elene's quest in, to find the sacred Cross, 54–62 ; Constantine and Elene build a glorious church in, 61 ; Cyriacus (Judas) Bishop of, 61 ; messenger to Black Colin familiar with all holy places in, 250 ; Black Colin as a pilgrim at, 253

JESUS CHRIST. The Cross the sign of, 53 ; the Resurrection and Ascension of, preached to Constantine, 53

JEWS. Elene's quest to land of, to find sacred Cross, 55–58 ; the Chosen People, 56 ; summoned, but dismissed in peace, by Elene, 58

JOHN. 1. Son of Sir John of the Marshes, 205 ; Gamelyn left in charge of, 206 ; Gamelyn resists, 207, 208 ; his great feast, 216 ; put in chains by Gamelyn, 217 ; proclaims Gamelyn a wolf's-head, 220 ; his death by hanging, 224. 2. Little. See Little John

JOSEPH and his brethren, "Gamelyn" a version of story of, 204

JUDÆA. See Jerusalem

JUDAS. Grandson of Zacchæus ; confesses to knowledge of secret truth of Holy Tree, 57 ; refuses at first to disclose the secret place of the Holy Cross, but is prevailed upon by starvation, 58, 59 ; baptismal name Cyriacus, 61 ; Ganelon compared with, 121

JUDGMENT, DAY OF, 71

JULIUS CÆSAR and early Britons, 184

K

KAY, SIR. Steward of King Arthur's household, 266 ; jeers at loathly lady, 277

KENT. Earldom of, held by Godwin, 335

KERRY. Champions drive to, 196

KILCHURN CASTLE. New castle built with rents of Glenurchy, 264

KNIGHT OF COURTESY. The true, is Sir Gawayne, King Arthur's nephew, 265

KNIGHT OF LOCH AWE. Equivalent, Black Colin Campbell, 249

KYNON. Son of Eudav, grandson of Caradoc, 49

L

LADY OF GLENURCHY. Grief of, 251 ; the gold ring token, 252 ; wooed by Baron MacCorquodale, 254–257 ; receives forged letter, 255 ; her stratagem to delay her marriage, 256 ; builds a castle on ruins of White House on Innis Eoalan, 256, 257 ; recognises and welcomes her husband, 262

LADY OF LOCH AWE. Same as Lady of Glenurchy, 251

LAE-GAI'RE. Bricriu urged to

claim title of, 187 ; Fedelm, wife of, 189 ; awarded Champion's Portion by Queen Meave, 195 ; claim tested by Curoi, 196–203 ; disgraced by Uath, 201

LANCELOT, SIR. A Knight of the Round Table, 266

LEA, SIR RICHARD OF THE. Stranger guest of Robin Hood's, 323

LEITH. Black Colin takes ship at, for Holy Land, 253

LENDABAIR. Conall's wife, 189

LEOFRIC. Earl of Mercia, 335 ; Lady Godiva, wife of, 335, Hereward, second son of, 336 ; Hall of Bourne, home of, 336 ; his wrath kindled against Hereward, 337 ; asks for writ of outlawry against Hereward, 338 ; Hereward bids farewell to, 339

LEOFRICSSON, HEREWARD. See Hereward

LEVE (lāvĕ). Wife of Grim the fisherman, 78

LIGHTFOOT, MARTIN. Hereward's follower who accompanied him into exile, 339 ; assists Hereward in his trick on Norman knights, 341, 342 ; cast into prison by King Alef, 343 ; released by King Alef's daughter, 344, 345

LINCOLN. Grim carries fish to, 81 ; Havelok goes to, 82 ; Havelok becomes porter, 82 ; Havelok's fame in, 83 ; Godrich summons his army to, against Havelok, 93 ; Godrich's trial and death at, 94

LITTLE JOHN. One of Robin Hood's followers, 315 ; searches the stranger knight's coffer, 319; counts out four hundred pounds to stranger guest, 322, 323 ; acts as squire to Sir Richard of the Lea, 323–327

LOATHLY LADY, THE, and King Arthur, 271–274 ; demands of King Arthur a young and handsome knight for husband, as price of her help, 274; Sir Gawayne offers to wed, 275; Sir Kay jeers at, 277; her betrothal to Sir Gawayne, 279; her marriage with Sir Gawayne, 280; set free from magic spells, 281–285

LOCH AWE. See Awe, Loch

LONDON. Visit to, of William of Cloudeslee and fellow outlaws, 241

LOUIS. Charlemagne's son, Count of the Marshes, promised to Aude the Fair, 155

LUGH OF THE LONG HAND. Great god, reputed father of Cuchulain, 185

M

MABINOGION. A series of Welsh legends; glorifies marriage of British princess Helena and Constantine, 42

MACCORQUODALE, BARON. Wooes the Lady of Loch Awe, 254–257; his stratagem of a forged letter, 255; hears of Black Colin's return, 263

MACGREGORS. Expelled from Glenurchy, 249

MAHOMET. Saracens declare determination to win land of Suddene according to law of, 287; faith of, thrown off by Saracens for the true faith, 310

MAIRI. Old widow in whose house the demon traders lived, 173

MARSILE. King of Moors; defies Charlemagne, 122; idols of, 122; Blancandrin's advice to, 123; sends an embassage to Charlemagne, 124; offers to become a Christian, 124–126; Ganelon sent to, with Charlemagne's terms, 130; Ganelon's reception by, 131, 132; takes counsel with leaders, 132; swears on the book of Law of Mahomet the treacherous death of Roland, 134; pursues the Frankish army, 137; Roland

slays only son of, 147; mortally wounded, he returns to Saragossa, 147; his death, 154

MARTIN. See Lightfoot

MASSES. Of the Father, of the Holy Spirit, of Our Lady, heard daily by Robin Hood, 315

MAXEN WLEDIG. "The Dream of," preserved in the "Mabinogion," 42–49; Emperor of Rome, 43; expedition down the Tiber, 43; his vision near Rome, 43; his vision declared, 44–47; ambassadors sent out to find the maiden of his dream, 47, 48; journeys himself to land of Arvon, 48, 49; conquers Britain from Beli, son of Manogan, 48; weds Helena, daughter of Eudav, 49; Constantine, son of, the only British-born Emperor of Rome, 49

MAXENTIUS. Emperor; hero of Welsh saga "Mabinogion," 42

MAXIMIAN. The Emperor; father of Fausta, who became Constantine's wife, 64

MEAD. Dwelling-place of Guest the Wise, 103

MEAVE. Queen of Connaught, wife of King Ailill; to decide claims to title of Chief Champion, 189; pronounces judgment, 195

MERCIA. Earldom of, held by Leofric, 335

MODI. King of Reynes; wooes Rymenhild, 303; slain by Horn, 308; land of, committed to care of Sir Athelbrus, 313

MONA. Sacred isle of; same as Anglesey; ambassadors of Maxen Wledig view, 47

"MONTJOIE! MONTJOIE!" Battle-cry of Franks, under Roland, 140, 142, 148

MOORS. Rulers of, and Charlemagne, 119; and Franks meet in battle, 140

MORDRED, SIR. One of King Arthur's nephews, 266

MOST HIGH. Grendel outcast from mercy of, 4

MUCH. One of Robin Hood's followers, 315; assists to count out gold for stranger guest, 323

MURRY. King of Suddene, 286; Queen Godhild consort of, 286; Horn, son of, 286; attacked and slain by Saracens, 287, 288

N

NAESI. Irish hero, 156

NAILS, THE HOLY. Obtained by Elene, 61; given to Constantine, 62

NAIMES, DUKE. One of Charlemagne's Twelve Peers, 126, 136, 137; urges Charlemagne to hasten to rescue of Roland, 146

NORMAN ENGLAND. Royal authority in, how asserted, 314

NORMANS. Or Flemings; Hereward enrolled among, to qualify for knighthood, 339; Hereward's trick on, with Fairy Bear, 341, 342

NORSE influence in connection with story of "King Horn," 286

NORSEMEN. Firm hold of bloodfeud on imagination of, 96

NORTH COUNTRY. Equivalent, Ulster, 165

NORTH SEA. Forefathers who dwelt on shores of, 1; ambassadors of Maxen Wledig reach, 47

NORTHUMBRIA. Inheritance of Anlaf, 73; writ of outlawry against Hereward only of nominal weight in, 339; Earl Siward ruler in, 339; Hereward leaves, 342

NOTTINGHAMSHIRE. The Sheriff of, and Robin Hood, 315

O

ODIN. The raven, the bird of, 115

OISIN. Scotch embodiment of Ossian, 248

OLAF. 1. Same as Anlaf, &c., 73. 2. Son of famous Viking, Howard the Halt, 97; finds Thorbiorn's lost sheep, 98–100;

kills a wizard, 101; second fight with the wizard's ghost, 102; wooes Sigrid, 99, 103; meets Thorbiorn, 103–106; his death, 106; Howard claims wergild for, 106–111; wergild awarded for, 118.

OLIFANT. Roland's horn, 138; blown by Roland, 145, 146; Roland's dying blast on, 149

OLIVER. One of Charlemagne's Twelve Peers, 125, 136; descries the Saracens and proclaims Ganelon's treason, 138; appeals to Roland to blow his horn, 138; Hauteclaire, sword of, 141; objects to Roland blowing his horn, 144; mortally wounded by Marsile's uncle, 148; under misapprehension, strikes Roland with Hauteclaire, 148; his death, 148, 149; avenged by Charlemagne, 153, 154

OONA. Cathleen's foster-mother, 178; her vision, 182

ORCHY. River, running through Glenurchy, 249

ORESTES. Reference to Electra and, 95

ORLANDO, ETC. Italy claims Roland in guise of, 121

OSSIAN. Hero in Gaelic Highland poems, 248; Scotch embodiment of Oisin, 248

OTHO. Son of Sir John of the Marshes, 205; becomes surety for Gamelyn, 221; arrested owing to failure of Gamelyn to appear at court, 223; released by Gamelyn, 223; sits on judge's seat with Gamelyn and condemns Sir John, 224; appointed sheriff by King Edward I., 224; makes Gamelyn his heir, 224

OUR LADY. Robin Hood accepts her surety for four hundred pounds lent to stranger guest, 322; the Black Monk and the suretyship, 331–333

OUTLAWS. Famous: Hereward, Robin Hood, William of Cloudeslee, 226 ; pardoned by king, 243 ; rules of, in case of Robin Hood, 316 ; their feast, 317, 318, 330

P

PAMPELUNA. Taken by Charlemagne, 119
PARADISE. Cathleen's soul in, 182
PATTERSON. Name of foster-parents of Black Colin, 250
PEERS. Of France, 125, 136 ; the champions of the Moors challenge the Twelve, of France, 137 ; of Charlemagne, triumph over Marsile's twelve champions, 141 ; their death, 143–153 ; avenged by Charlemagne, 153, 154
PENELOPE. Lady of Loch Awe turns to guile, as did, 256
PEOPLE OF THE HILLS. Cuchulain's friends among, 198, 199
PERSIA. Constantine's valour in wars in, 64 ; physicians from, with remedies for Constantine's leprosy, 65
PETER AND PAUL. The Apostles ; appear in a vision to Constantine, 70, 71
PICTISH GIANT. King Alef's daughter betrothed to, 343 ; slain by Hereward, 343
PLANTAGENETS. England under, 314
POPE. Head of Holy Catholic Church, 119 ; proclaims Holy War at Rome, 251 ; sees Black Colin, 253 ; regarded by Black Colin as Vicar of Christ on earth, 253
PRIAM. Reference to lament of, 95
PYRENEES. Charlemagne's march through passes of, 119 ; Frankish army marches toward, 134

R

RANALD. King of Waterford, 345, 346 ; Prince Sigtryg, son

of, 345 ; Hereward at feast of, 346, 347
RANALDSSON, SIGTRYG. See Sigtryg
RED BRANCH. Heroes of, invited to feast by Bricriu, 186 ; heroes return to, 199 ; Uath, the Stranger, comes to, 199 ; heroes of, and Uath, the Stranger, 199–203 ; champions of, identical with Highland Gaelic heroes, 248
REYNES. Modi, King of, 303 ; wooes Rymenhild, 303, 304
REYNILD. Daughter of King Thurston ; offered to Horn, 302 ; weds Sir Athulf, 313
RHINE. Black Colin's journey up, 253
RHODES. Black Colin journeys to, 253 ; supposed news from, by man of Black Colin's band, 255
RICHARD, SIR, OF THE LEA, Robin Hood's stranger-guest, 317–324 ; Robin Hood's loan to, 322–324 ; his land in Uterysdale, 323 ; redeems his land from Abbot of St. Mary's, 324–327 ; sets out to repay loan, 328 ; defends the right at a wrestling contest, 328 ; arrives before Robin Hood to repay loan, but is exempt, 333 ; returns to Uterysdale, 333 ; his power used to protect the outlaws, 333
ROBERT THE RED. Eldest son of Grim ; accompanies Havelok to Denmark, 87
ROBIN HOOD. Romantic sympathy with, 225 ; one of the famous outlaws, 226 ; the original, 314 ; forest of Barnesdale at one time his dwelling-place, 314, 315 ; Sherwood Forest, headquarters of, 315 ; Little John, Will Scarlet, and Much, his three most loyal followers, 315 ; three Masses heard by, 315 ; sends his followers to Watling Street, 316 ; his outlaw rules, 316 ; stranger guest brought to, 317 ; lends stranger guest

four hundred pounds, 322 ; sends his followers again to Watling Street, 329 ; his followers capture and bring to greenwood, as guest, the Black Monk, 330 ; appropriates gold of the Black Monk as payment of loan to Sir Richard of the Lea, 331, 332 ; exempts Sir Richard from repayment of four hundred pounds, 333 ; dwells securely in the greenwood under Sir Richard's protection, 333

ROLAND. Charlemagne's nephew ; fame of, in romance, 119 ; historical basis of legend of, 120 ; in Spanish legend, 121 ; " Saga " in French literature, 121 ; " Chanson de Roland " and, 121 ; one of the Twelve Peers, 125 ; destruction plotted by Blancandrin and Ganelon, 131, 134 ; plants his banner on topmost summit of Pyrenees, 134 ; appointed to command rearguard, 135 ; appealed to by Oliver to blow his horn, 138 ; his army defeats Saracens, 141 ; defeats second Saracen army, 143 ; attacked by third Saracen army, 144 ; willing to blow horn, but Oliver objects, 144 ; blows Olifant, 145, 146 ; Charlemagne hastens to rescue of, but arrives too late, 146 ; slays only son of Marsile, 147 ; smitten by Oliver in mistake, 148 ; set upon by four hundred Saracens, 150 ; realising death near, he tries to destroy sword Durendala, 152 ; his death, 153 ; avenged by Charlemagne, 153, 154

ROMAN EMPIRE. Charlemagne head of, 119

ROMANS. Conquer Huns by the Cross standard, 52

ROME. Church of, Constantine's generosity to, 42 ; Maxen Wledig seeks rest near, 43, 46 ; Princess Helena hailed Empress of, 48, 49 ; Constantine calls a council

of all wisest men in, 53 ; Black Colin's messenger just home from, 251 ; Holy War proclaimed by Pope at, 251 ; Black Colin reaches, 253 ; Black Colin's supposed letter from, 255

RONCESVALLES. Roland's glory from, 119 ; celebrated in " Song of Altobiscar," 120 ; Spain claims part of honour of, 120 ; the battle of, 140–153

RONCEVAUX. Same as Roncesvalles, 122

ROUND TABLE. Knights of, 266

RYMENHILD. Princess, daughter of King Ailmar ; loves Horn, 292 ; Athulf personates Horn before, 293 ; welcomes Horn in her bower and declares her love, 294 ; wishes Horn good success as knight, 298 ; gives token to Horn, 298 ; spied on by Fikenhild, 299, 300 ; wooed by King Modi, 303 ; writes to Horn through Athulf, 303 ; Horn at wedding-feast of, 305 ; Horn's stratagem to test her love, 306, 307 ; her knight and lover, Horn, restored, 307 ; wedded to Horn, 308 ; left to her father's care, 309 ; demanded in marriage by traitor, Fikenhild, 311 ; delivered by Horn, 313 ; dwells at Suddene as queen, 313

S

SAMSON. Peer of Charlemagne ; mortally wounded, 143

SARACEN-S. Host, encamps near Franks, 134 ; pursue the Frankish army, 137 ; chiefs vow to slay Roland, 137 ; defeat of, by Roland's army, 141 ; second army attacks Roland, 142 ; defeated once more, 143 ; third army attacks Roland, 144 ; their rule in the Holy Land, 251 ; Horn's hatred of, typical of romance of Crusades, 286 ; attack and slay King Murry,

287, 288 ; Horn's victory over, 298 ; Suddene purged of, by Horn, 310

SARAGOSSA. Charlemagne repulsed at, 119 ; decided to send Ganelon to, as ambassador, 128 ; Charlemagne's threat to take, 132 ; Charlemagne receives through Ganelon the keys of, 134 ; captured by Charlemagne, 154

" SARN HELEN." Roman roads in Wales connecting Helena's three castles known as, 49

SAXON ENGLAND. The maintenance of justice in, 314

SAXON-S. Hereward the, 334 ; the darling hero of the, 334 ; Anglo-, chivalry, Hereward the ideal of, 334, 335 ; Hereward the, known as the Champion of Women, 351

SCARLET, WILL. Cousin to and one of Robin Hood's followers, 315

SCOTLAND. Hero-myths of, 248 ; national heroes of Lowland, actual, not mythical, 248 ; war between England and, 249

SCOTTISH INDEPENDENCE. Sir Nigel Campbell one of leaders in cause of, 249

SCYLD SCEFING (skild ske'f-ing). Founder of Scyldings dynasty, 2 ; coming to and passing from Denmark, 2 ; Hrothgar, great-grandson of, 2

SEVEN HILLS. Rome, the City of, 43 ; Maxen Wledig, emperor, rules Europe from, 43

SHERWOOD, FOREST OF. Headquarters of Robin Hood, 315

SIEGFRIED. Gudrun and, in " Nibelungenlied," 95

SIGMUND. Father of Fitela ; glory of, chanted by Danish bard, 18

SIGRID. Thorbiorn's housekeeper, 97 ; loved by Olaf, 99 ; quits Thorbiorn's service, 103 ; disappearance of, 106

SIGT-RYG RANALDSSON. Prince of Waterford : his troth-plight with King Alef's daughter, 343 ; son of King Ranald, 345 ; Hereward's missio nto, 345–347 ; sails for Cornwall to rescue his love, 347 ; sends forty Danes to demand fulfilment of troth-plight, 348 ; Sigtryg and Danes plan ambush for Haco, 350 ; rescues, and marries, Cornish princess, 350, 351

SI'HT-RIC-SON. Same as Anlaf, Abloec, &c., 73

SIR JOHN OF THE MARSHES. Noble gentleman who lived in Lincolnshire, in reign of Edward I., 204, 205 ; father of John, Otho, and Gamelyn, 205 ; his death, 206

SI-WARD, EARL. Ruler in Northumbria, 339 ; reputed kinship to Fairy Bear, 340, 342

SNOWDON. Mountainous land of, reached by ambassadors of Maxen Wledig, 47

SOCACH. Black Colin's foster-parents' dwelling-place, 250

SOULS. The traffic in, during Irish famine, 170–183 ; Cathleen tries to check traffic in, 174

SPAIN. Charlemagne's expedition into, 119 ; begins to quit, 134 ; returns to, to rescue Roland, 146

SPANISH LEGEND. Bernardo del Carpio and Roland in, 121

SPENCER. 1. Adam, steward in household of Sir John, releases Gamelyn, 214, 215. 2. Edmund, reference to his Red Cross Knight, 265

STEINTHOR OF ERE. Great chieftain who shelters Howard, 108, 109, 117 ; speaks on Howard's behalf at the Thing, 118

ST. JOHN, KNIGHTS OF. Black Colin takes service with, 253 ; Grand Master of, 253

ST. MARY. Abbey of, in York, lands of stranger knight in pledge to Abbot of, 321 ; land redeemed by Sir Richard of the Lea, 324–327 ; the Black Monk high cellarer in Abbey of, 331

Sᴛ. Pᴀᴛʀɪᴄᴋ. Preached Gospel to people of Ireland, 157

Sᴜᴅᴅᴇɴᴇ. King Murry and Queen Godhild, and son Horn, the royal family of, 286 ; Horn sails for, to wrest from Saracens, 309 ; Athulf's father found at, 309, 310 ; Horn reconquers, 310 ; a Christian realm once more, 311 ; Horn crowned king of, 311

Sᴡᴀɴʙᴏʀᴏᴡ. Daughter of King Birkabeyn, 74 ; slain by Godard 76

Sᴡᴇᴅᴇɴ. Götaland, realm of Geats in south of, 5

Sᴡᴇᴅᴇs. Slay Hathcyn, son of King Hrethel, 35

Sᴡɪᴛᴢᴇʀʟᴀɴᴅ. Black Colin and Highland clansmen pass through, 253

Sʏʟᴠᴇsᴛᴇʀ. Bishop of Rome ; and Constantine, 42 ; Constantine told in a vision to send for, 70 ; preaches the Christian faith to Constantine, 71

T

Tᴀɪʟʟᴇғᴇʀ. " Song of Roland " and, 122

Tᴀʀᴀ. Black stone of, 157

Tᴀʀɴ Wᴀᴛʜᴇʟᴀɴ. Giant in castle near, ill-treats maiden, 267 ; King Arthur's journey to, and fight with giant who lived in Castle of, 269, 270 ; King Arthur summons court to hunt near, 276 ; the churlish knight of, set free from magic spells, 284

Tᴇᴜᴛᴏɴɪᴄ Nᴏʀᴛʜ. Beowulf famous throughout, 5

Tʜᴇʀsɪᴛᴇs. Compared with Bricriu of the Bitter Tongue, 186

Tʜɪɴɢ. Howard at the, 107, 108, 117, 118

Tʜᴏʀ-ʙɪᴏʀɴ. Mighty chief on shores of Icefirth, 97 ; Vakr, nephew of, 97 ; Olaf and sheep of, 98–100 ; whale unjustly adjudged to, 102 ; marries sister of Guest, 103 ; Sigrid leaves, 103 ;

meets Olaf, 103–106 ; War-flame, magic sword of, 104-106 thrusts Olaf with Warflame 106 ; Howard claims wergild from, 106–111 ; Guest's judgment against, 110, 111 ; hailed by Biargey while out fishing, 112 ; slain by Howard, 112

Tʜᴏʀ-ʙʀᴀɴᴅ. Brother of Biargey, 113 ; helps Howard against Thorbiorn, 115

Tʜᴏʀ-ᴅɪs. Mother of Vakr ; sends second son to assist in fight against Olaf, 105

Tʜᴏʀ-ᴋᴇʟ. Lawman and arbitrator of Icefirth, 97 ; his false decree concerning a whale, 102

Tʜᴏʀ-ᴏʟᴅ. Same as Turoldus ; author of " Song of Roland," 122

Tʜᴜʀsᴛᴏɴ. King of Ireland ; served by Horn, 301 ; Harold and Berild, sons of, 302 ; offers kingdom and his daughter Reynild to Horn, 302 ; Horn discloses his identity to, 304

Tɪʙᴇʀ. Hunting expedition down, by Maxen Wledig, 43

Tɪʀ-ɴᴀɴ-ᴏɢ. The land of never-dying youth, 163

Tʀᴇᴇ, Tʜᴇ Hᴏʟʏ. See Holy Cross

Tʀɪɴɪᴛʏ. Truth of, demonstrated by shamrock-leaf, 157

Tʀᴏᴊᴀɴ Wᴀʀ. An ancient story, yet well known, 58

Tᴜᴄᴋ, Fʀɪᴀʀ. Masses sung by, for Robin Hood, 318

Tᴜʀᴘɪɴ. Archbishop of Charlemagne, one of Twelve Peers, 125, 136 ; blesses the knights, 139, 140 ; mediates between Roland and Oliver, 145 ; mortally wounded, 149 ; his death, 150, 151

U

Uᴀᴛʜ, ᴛʜᴇ Sᴛʀᴀɴɢᴇʀ. Giant who tests champions, 199–203 ; adjudges Cuchulain Champion of Heroes of all Ireland, 203

Uʙʙᴇ (ub-bĕ). Danish jarl, friend of King Birkabeyn ; befriends

Havelok and Goldborough, 87–93 ; appointed Regent of Denmark for Havelok, 94

ULSTER. Fergus commanded to buy food at, 165 ; Conor, King of, 185 ; Cuchulain peer among champions of, 185 ; Armagh, capital of, 186 ; Red Branch heroes, royal bodyguard of, 186 ; Bricriu stirs up strife among champions of, 187, 188

UNKNOWN GOD. Constantine's acceptance and reverence of the, 51 ; the people awed by token of, 53

UTERYSDALE. Land of Sir Richard of the Lea in, 323 ; Sir Richard redeems the land, 324– 327 ; Sir Richard returns to, 333

V

VAKR. Thorbiorn's nephew, 97 ; mocks Olaf, 100 ; jeers at Brand the Strong, 102, 103 ; accompanies Thorbiorn to meet Olaf, 103–106 ; Thordis, mother of, 105 ; his miserable end, 116

VALBRAND. Brother of Biargey, 112, 113 ; visited by Howard, 114

VALTIERRA. Charlemagne retires to, on way to France, 134

VEILLANTIF. Roland's steed, 136 ; slain by Saracens, 150

VICAR OF CHRIST on earth, Black Colin regards Pope as, 253

VIKINGS. Gospel preached to, 157

VIRGIN MARY. Cult of, 121 ; Cathleen invokes, 163 ; Cathleen's people invoke, 181

W

WALES. Old Roman roads in, that connected Helena's three castles still known as "Sarn Helen," 49 ; legend of Havelok the Dane thought to have originated in, 73 ; mediæval, Arthurian legend preserved by, 265

WALLACE, SIR WILLIAM. Scottish hero, 248 ; schoolfellow and comrade of Sir Nigel Campbell, 249

WARDEN. Of the coast of Denmark, welcomes Beowulf, 6 ; conducts Geats to Heorot, 8 ; Wulfgar, one of Hrothgar's nobles, greets Beowulf, 9 ; of Geatland, welcomes Beowulf's return, 29

WARFLAME. Magic sword, owned by Thorbiorn, and by which he himself is slain by Howard, 115, 116

WASHERS OF THE FORD. Wrath of, and Irish people, 158

WATERFORD. Prince Sigtryg of, his troth-plight with daughter of King Alef, 343 ; Ranald, King of, 345 ; Hereward reaches, 346 ; Prince and Princess of, Hereward the best friend of, 351

WATLING STREET. Robin Hood sends his followers to, 316 ; a year later sends followers once more to, 329

WEALHTHEOW (wal - thyow), QUEEN. Wife of Hrothgar ; honours Beowulf, 14, 20

WELSH. 1. Legends, "Mabinogion" and "The Dream of Maxen Wledig," 42 ; Celtic features in, 185. 2. Saga, hero of, Emperor Maxentius, 42

WEOHSTAN (wyo-stan). Father of Wiglaf, who supported Beowulf in his fight with the firedragon, 36

WEST. Constantine a favourite of Roman soldiery of the, 63 ; Roman soldiery of the, proclaim Constantine emperor, 63 ; the fictitious wanderings of Horn in realms of, 307

WESTERN ISLES. Irish Gaelic hero-legends carried to, from Erin, 248

WESTERNESSE. Childe Horn lands on shore of, 289 ; Ailmar, King of, questions Horn, 290 ; Horn returns to, accompanied by Irish knights, 304 ; recital of the fictitious plans of Horn

GLOSSARY AND INDEX

to reach, within seven years, 307

WHITBY. Hereward lands at, 339

WIG-LAF. Son of Weohstan; supports Beowulf in his fight with the fire-dragon, 36–41

WILF-INGS. Hrothgar shields Ecgtheow from, 11

WILLIAM OF CLOUDESLEE. One of the famous outlaws of England, 226

WILLIAM TELL. William of Cloudeslee the, of England, 226; Alice, wife of, 227; goes to Carlisle, 227; sheriff informed of his presence, 229; attacked by sheriff and his men, 231; capture of, 332; sheriff sentences to be hanged, 232; news of his sentence conveyed to the greenwood, 233; Clym's stratagem to save, 234; rescued from death, 237, 238; visits London to see king, 241; the king pardons, 243; shoots apple from son's head, 245, 246; receives royal favours from king and queen, 246

WILLIAM WENDUT. Second son of Grim; accompanies Havelok to Denmark, 87

WINCHESTER. Godrich takes Goldborough from, to Dover, 81

WLEDIG. See Maxen Wledig

WOMEN, CHAMPION OF. Hereward known as, 351

WYRD (weird). Goddess of Fate, 13, 34

Y

YORK. Archbishop of, unites in marriage Havelok and Goldborough, 85; Abbot of St. Mary's Abbey, in, 321

YORKSHIRE. Barnesdale, forest in, once dwelling-place of Robin Hood, 314, 315

YULETIDE. King Arthur's knights keep, 267

Z

ZACCHÆUS. Grandfather of Judas, 57